Two week loan

Please return on or before the last
date stamped below.
Charges are made for late return.

Subnational Democracy in the European Union

Subnational Democracy in the European Union

Challenges and Opportunities

by

John Loughlin

With the collaboration of

Eliseo Aja
Udo Bullmann
Frank Hendriks
Anders Lidström
Daniel-L. Seiler

OXFORD

UNIVERSITY PRESS

OXFORD
UNIVERSITY PRESS

Great Clarendon Street, Oxford OX2 6DP

Oxford University Press is a department of the University of Oxford.
If furthers the University's objective of excellence in research, scholarship,
and education by publishing worldwide in

Oxford New York

Athens Auckland Bangkok Bogotá Buenos Aires Calcutta
Cape Town Chennai Dar es Salaam Delhi Florence Hong Kong Istanbul
Karachi Kuala Lumpur Madrid Melbourne Mexico City Mumbai
Nairobi Paris São Paulo Shanghai Singapore Taipei Tokyo Toronto Warsaw

and associated companies in Berlin Ibadan

Oxford is a registered trade mark of Oxford University Press
in the UK and certain other countries

Published in the United States
by Oxford University Press Inc., New York

© John Loughlin 2001

British Library Cataloguing in Publication Data

Data available

Library of Congress Cataloging in Publication Data

Loughlin, John.
Subnational democracy in the European union : challenges and opportunities / by John
Loughlin with the collaboration of Eliseo Aja . . . [et al.].
p. cm.
Includes bibliographical references and index.
1. Local government—European Union countries. 2. Decentralization in
government—European Union countries. 3. Regionalism—European Union countries.
4. Democracy—European Union countries. I. Aja, Eliseo. II. Title.
JS3000 .L68 2001   320.8′094—dc21   00-045300

ISBN 0-19-829679-7

1 3 5 7 9 10 8 6 4 2

Typeset by Best-set Typesetter Ltd., Hong Kong
Printed in Great Britain by T.J. International Ltd., Padstow, Cornwall

ACKNOWLEDGEMENTS

A number of people made this work possible. First of all, Christian Gsodam, the Committee of the Regions administrator responsible for guiding the study, provided many of the ideas that went into its design but also patiently assisted the team as one deadline after another was passed. The members of the Expert Study Group worked diligently and always responded positively and constructively to criticisms, even when this sometimes meant a complete rewrite of their chapters. Some (not all) of the national delegations were extremely helpful and provided criticisms based on their experience and perspective as practitioners and provided much useful and up-to-date information that was not always available to us as academics (although two of our members also became politicians—Anders Lidström as a local councillor and Udo Bullmann as a Member of the European Parliament).

I would like to thank Dominic Byatt of Oxford University Press for his enthusiasm and encouragement from the very beginning. Michael Keating of the European University Institute, Florence and Patrick Le Galès of the Institut d'Etudes Politiques, Paris read the entire manuscript and provided many useful positive criticisms. I would also like to thank Richard Balme, Sciences Po, Paris and Albert Mabileau, Institut d'Etudes Politiques, Bordeaux, joint converors of the 'Politique et local' group of the French Political Studies Association, for organizing a study day on the Committee of the Regions report in March 2000. Alain Delcamp, a senior administrator of the French Senate, commented critically on the text. This event was extremely useful just as I was putting the finishing touches to the revised manuscript during a period as Visiting Professor at Sciences Po, Paris and the Institut d'Etudes Politiques, Bordeaux. Other academic colleagues commented on individual chapters and these are acknowledged at the beginning of each chapter. Finally, my research assistant, Maite Puigdevall Serralvo was excellent in collecting much information and in efficiently organizing much of the project.

J. L.

Cardiff
October, 2000

CONTENTS

NOTES ON CONTRIBUTORS

ELISEO AJA is Professor of Law and Political Science at the University of Barcelona and is a member of the Institute of Autonomy Studies, Barcelona. He edits the Informe de las Comunidades Autónomas, published by this Institute.

UDO BULLMANN is Jean Monnet Professor of European Studies at the University of Giessen, Germany. He is the author of numerous chapters and articles on European regions and federalism. In July 1999, he was elected to the European Parliament as a member of the German Social Democratic Party.

FRANK HENDRIKS is Associate Professor in Public Administration at Tilburg University in the Netherlands. His fields of research include urban politics, comparative politics, and political culture. He is the author of *Public Policy and Political Institutions: The Role of Culture in Traffic Policy.*

ANDERS LIDSTRÖM is an Associate Professor at the Department of Political Science, Umeå University, Sweden. His research interests are local government, education policy and comparative public administration. Among recent publications are *Local Government Systems in Europe.* Stockholm: Publica, 1996; 'The Comparative Study of Local Government Systems—a Research Agenda', *Journal of Comparative Policy Analysis*, 1: 1998; and 'Local School Choice Policies in Sweden', *Scandinavian Political Studies*, 22: 1999.

JOHN LOUGHLIN is Professor of European Politics at Cardiff University, Wales and Visiting Professor at the Institute of Political Science (Sciences Po) Paris. He has published several books and many articles on regionalism and federalism and is managing editor of *Regional and Federal Studies.*

DANIEL-L. SEILER is Professor of Political Science at the Institute of Political Science, University of Bordeaux. He is author of numerous works on political parties, especially at the Regional level.

LIST OF TABLES

LIST OF FIGURES

1

Introduction: The Transformation of the Democratic State in Western Europe

John Loughlin

1. The Concept of Democracy and its Institutional Expression in Europe

1.1 Our Common European Heritage

'Democracy' is a European invention and concept with its roots in the political systems of the ancient Greek city-states. It has a variety of meanings, the most important of which for modern states are direct or participatory democracy[1] and representative or liberal democracy (Held 1987). In its modern connotation it owes much to the philosophies of the eighteenth-century Enlightenment with their exalted role of the individual (Mendras 1997), but also to the doctrine of the separation of powers in thinkers such as Montesquieu. This latter doctrine found its fullest institutional expression in the new United States of America and formed the basis of the American Constitution, drafted in 1787, with the separation of the different arms of representative and executive government and the judiciary. Rousseau[2] was also important for the development of the modern concept of democracy in his championing of the individual against the absolute power of the Church and the State and in his concept of the *general will*. The ideas of the Enlightenment were taken over and transformed into the doctrine of the Rights of Man

---

[1] Although sometimes treated as synonyms these two forms of democracy are not identical. Or rather, participatory democracy is always direct, while direct democracy, such as referendums, may not be participatory.

[2] The influence of Rousseau is ambiguous and his ideas may be used to justify participatory democracy when applied to small-scale societies such as his native Geneva but become problematic when applied to large countries such as France. This did not stop the French Jacobins from using his thought in their formulation of the 'one and indivisible Republic'.

and the Citizen at the French Revolution that forms the basis of modern liberal democracy.

This is not to suggest that the concept of democracy is today one on which a consensus exists. On the contrary, the very diverse philosophical heritage underlying the term has led to a number of ambiguities and it is a very contested concept. First of all there have been various political ideologies, such as Fascism and Nazism, but also some older forms of regionalism, which despised and fought against democracy, especially its liberal version. Such political movements systematically opposed and, once in power, dismantled free elections, political parties and representative assemblies, and institutions of the liberal democratic state. Marx and Engels welcomed liberal democracy as a progression from feudalism but thought it would be surpassed by the arrival of socialism and communism. Soviet socialism, despite the appellation of 'peoples' democracies', opposed any kind of democracy in practice, preferring one-party rule behind a façade of 'democratic' constitutions and constitutional guarantees of civil liberties. With the collapse of the Soviet system in the late 1980s we know today the emptiness at the heart of these systems and their alienation from their peoples.

Even among those who accept, both theoretically and in practice, the principles of the modern democratic state and even where these principles are embodied in the institutions and practices of actual states, there remain ambiguities. At the heart of these ambiguities is the tension between an individualist conception of democracy and one that is more communitarian in its orientation, that is, whether democracy is in essence the free expression of the rights of individuals, who vote but also choose how they wish to live, or whether it is an expression of the existence of 'communities', defined in different ways, of which the individual is part and which may, in certain respects, supersede his or her individual interests. Another way of phrasing this is to ask whether in democratic practice emphasis should be given to 'individual' autonomy or to 'communitarian' autonomy (Lapidoth 1997). This tension is at the heart of the epistemological, methodological, and normative debates[3] within contemporary social sciences (Frazer 1996; Macintyre 1984) and underlies the difficulties of finding the appropriate institutional expression of democracy in practice.

[3] Epistemologically, the debate concerns the manner in which our minds grasp reality, either analytically or synthetically, or at least which of these two aspects is dominant. Methodologically, the debate is between 'methodological individualism', which usually takes the form of rational choice approaches, and approaches that are more structuralist, culturalist or institutionalist (whatever the differences among the latter group). Normatively, in terms of public policy, the question is whether democratic practice can be based on the notion that the individual citizen is a member of a collectivity or whether he/she should be seen as a consumerist, rational individual making choices with regard to the use of public services. If the latter model is adopted, 'public' services are increasingly redefined in a more 'privatized' fashion.

Liberal democracy developed in close connection with the emergence of the nation-state as the basic form of political organization in the nineteenth and twentieth centuries, although it is also possible to conceive of nation-states that are not democratic. All of our modern democratic institutions—executives accountable to representative assemblies; political parties elected to these assemblies in free elections; Weberian-type public administration systems;[4] and the various 'freedoms'—of speech, of assembly, of the press, of movement and so on—emanate from the modern nation-state. The nation-state, however, is also beset with ambiguities and has been contested almost throughout its entire existence. Indeed, the fate of the nation-state—its continuing existence and/or its transformation—is the main question for contemporary political and social sciences (Le Galès 1999). If the modern nation-state is, indeed, being significantly transformed, then this has profound consequences for the exercise of democracy. Some authors have taken up this question of the challenge to democracy as a result of the pressures on the nation-state from 'above'—globalization and Europeanization—and have argued for the development of a 'cosmopolitan' democracy (Held 1993; Cerny 1999; Beck 2000). There has also been a debate on the 'democratic deficit' within the European Union where an increasing number of decisions are taken by the EU institutions without these being held accountable to the peoples of Europe (see below).

What have not been examined systematically are the consequences of this transformation, from the point of view of democratic practice, for the *sub-national* level. One of the primary aims of this book is to remedy this lack by raising the question of subnational democracy. The democratic nature of subnational systems of government is not as self-evident as it appears at first sight. In fact, if, as is argued here, modern democracy developed basically in conjunction with the nation-state, then the theory and practice of subnational government becomes highly problematic. For example, it might be asked whether the legitimacy of subnational government emanates from national government or whether it has a basis of legitimacy in its own right. Historically, nation-states developed mainly at the expense of the autonomy of other forms of territorial organization—towns, cities, communes, provinces, regions, etc.—which have been in existence for much longer periods of time than nation-states. A striking example is Scotland which was an independent national monarchy before being joined to England in the Act of Union of 1707. Today, there is an interesting question with regard to the basis of legitimacy of the restored Scottish Parliament. Does this derive from the Scottish

---

[4] Of course, Weberian-type adminstrations may occur in non-democratic states, such as nineteenth-century Prussia. However, the 'rational' basis of this kind of public administration served admirably as the underpinning of the executive branch of liberal democratic government.

people, expressed in the referendum of 1997, or does it derive from the Scottish Act of the Westminster Parliament by which the Scottish Parliament was established? In Spain, many Basques question the legitimacy of the Spanish Constitution which defines Spain as the 'one and indivisible nation' and includes the Basque Country as one of the 'regions and nationalities' (the constitution does not specify which Spanish territories and which are nationalities but the Basque Country is usually understood to be one of the 'nationalities'). In France, there is a conflict with regard to Corsica in which most Corsicans would define themselves as a 'people' which would be the basis of legitimacy of a Corsican Assembly, while the French Constitutional Court ruled this out as infringing the constitution which only recognizes one 'people' in France—'*le peuple français*'. Examples of this kind could be multiplied. There are several ways, ranging from permissive federalism or decentralization to simple repression, in which states have dealt with this and these are outlined in this book.

There has been little systematic theoretical work on the question of regional and local democracy in European states. Most theoretical work on local democracy, or urban politics, seems to have originated in the United States, and migrated to the United Kingdom, to be applied in a piecemeal fashion to other European countries. This is, however, highly problematic and unsatisfactory as the political histories, institutions and conditions of European states are quite different from those of North America.[5] At root the problem here is one of a lack of awareness of the importance of state traditions and, in particular, of the differences that exist between the Anglo-American state tradition and the state traditions of continental Europe (see Table 1.1).[6] Another way of expressing this is to say that in North America, or at least in the United

---

[5] This statement might be qualified in two ways. First, the UK and Ireland do share a number of features of a general Anglo-Saxon state tradition as argued in this chapter. Second, Canada, despite its proximity to the US, which remains a strong influence on it, has many features more similar to European traditions, for example, its stronger, albeit declining, welfare state tradition. Within the Canadian federation, Quebec is even more strikingly similar to European countries.

[6] A good example of this may be found in the book edited by D. Judge, G. Stoker and H. Wolman (1995). What emerges from this book is, in fact, the theoretical confusion that characterizes this debate probably as a result of the excessive influence of the rather sterile American theoretical debates between public choice theorists and neo-institutionalists. It is clear in this collection that the authors are struggling to find an appropriate conceptual framework within which to debate the meaning and evolution of democratic practice at the subnational level. What is missing is, in fact, an appreciation of the nature and role of the state and of the influence of distinct state traditions. The chapters by Goldsmith (1995) and Wolman (1995) do begin to address this question while that by Keating (1995) is a trenchant critique of the lack of 'politics' and, implicitly, of the state in public choice theorizing. A more recent edited work by King and Stoker (1996) suffers from the same defects even if this work concentrates more fully on the UK rather than on the US. Again it is Goldsmith (1996) who draws attention to the European dimension.

TABLE 1.1 State traditions in the European Union

Feature	Tradition			
	Anglo-Saxon	Germanic	French	Scandinavian
Is there a legal basis for the state?	No	Yes	Yes	Yes
State–society relations	Pluralistic	Organicist	Antagonistic	Organicist
Form of political organization	Union state/ Limited federalist	Integral/ Organic federalist	Jacobin, 'one and indivisible'	Decentralized unitary
Basis of policy style	Incrementalist, 'muddling through'	Legal corporatist	Legal technocratic	Consensual
Form of decentralization	'State power' (US), devolution/local government (UK)	Cooperative federalism	Regionalized unitary state	Strong local autonomy
Dominant approach to discipline of public administration	Political science/ Sociology	Public law	Public law	Public law (Sweden), organization theory (Norway)
Countries	UK, US, Canada (not Quebec), Ireland	Germany, Austria, Netherlands, Spain (post 1978), Belgium (post 1988)	France, Italy, Spain (pre 1978), Portugal, Quebec, Greece, Belgium (pre 1988)	Sweden, Norway, Denmark, Finland

Source: Loughlin and Peters (1997).

States, the dominant social science paradigm has been pluralism or a society-centred approach to understanding politics. In this approach, the state and the specific nature of governmental insitutions tended to become lost and the debate became about the distribution and exercise of power among different groups, with governments and public institutions being treated simply as groups among the others. The rational and public choice schools have reinforced this tendency. Thus, the state has been almost absent from this debate and in recent years some authors have tried to 'bring it back in' or to reassess the importance of institutions. These debates and approaches are important for the development of democratic theory as they raise the question of whether there exists a 'public space' that is more than just an arena for the exercise of individual choices and whether governmental institutions differ significantly from other kinds of individual or collective actors. Undoubtedly, these theories and the research which they underpin have produced significant results. To some extent, they have been successfully transposed into a British context through the work of authors such as Rod Rhodes and Jeremy Richardson. They have even had some success in France through the Organization School approach of Michel Crozier, François Dupuy, and Jean-Claude Thoenig who have analysed French public administration from this kind of perspective (Crozier 1963; Dupuy and Thoenig 1985). Nevertheless, the American approach seriously underestimates the importance of the State (with a capital 'S') in European countries which is quite different from that in North America and even Britain. This is why it is so important to refer to the different state traditions in western Europe which each have quite distinct ways of understanding both central–local relations and the philosophical foundations of democracy itself. It is not possible simply to transpose the North American debates on 'urban politics' as a way of clarifying and analysing theoretically the nature of regional and local democracy in a European context. On the contrary, while paying attention and sometimes drawing on the debates among our transatlantic colleagues, we need to build a specifically European social science approach to tackle these issues.

This book seeks to contribute to remedying these defects by adopting both explicitly European and subnational perspectives. It analyses both the particular configuration of central–local relations and of subnational democracy in each member state of the union but also outlines the consequences for democratic practice of the changes involved in the shifting system of governance related to the transformation of the nation-state mentioned above. It argues that the emergence of a new kind of governance has direct consequences for the regional and local levels which are becoming increasingly important alongside and implicated within the national and supranational levels. In fact, they may be even more important as the locus of the exercise of power shifts away from national governments both upwards to European and other transnational types of organization but also downwards to regions and local authorities. Democracy is also about citizens holding decision-makers accountable for their activities and this is becoming increasingly difficult given this shift in power. The supranational dimension has largely escaped conrol of any kind but this makes it all the more imperative to strengthen the other levels.

In this present context of shifting forms of governance the argument for stronger subnational democracy is rather different from John Stuart Mill's conception of local government as a kind of training ground for the exercise of national citizenship. In effect, what is being argued is that national governments no longer hold the same monopoly on democratic governance that they once did and that it has become necessary to invent new forms of democratic participation and practice at different levels and in different contexts (Beck 2000). The regional and the local will become the privileged loci of a certain kind of democratic practice and new institutional forms will be necessary to give this expression. The old nation-state system, however, will not simply disappear but must somehow be integrated into the newly emerging one.

These general trends all take place within a variety of state, regional, and local traditions that make the analysis extremely complex. This book seeks to lay out and put some order into this complexity and make it susceptible to analysis. There is not an infinite variety of state, regional and local traditions and cultures nor is there an infinite number of kinds of state. This introductory chapter, then, has three principal aims. First, it examines the hypothesis that the nation-state is central to liberal democratic governance and that this has been undergoing significant change in the recent past. Second, it outlines what might be called the *pesanteurs*, the continuities of philosophical conceptions and state traditions of democratic practice, in each state at both national and subnational levels. Third, it examines the impact on democratic practice of the various influences that today affect all states as well as factors emanating from within states themselves.

1.2 The Nation-State

1.2.1 Historical Background

'Nations' have been around for a long period of time—European nations such as France, England, Scotland, and Sweden emerged in the eleventh and twelfth centuries—and 'states' have existed for even longer—one needs only think of the states of the ancient empires such as existed in China, Egypt, and

India. Their combination into the 'nation-state' couple is much more recent and can probably be dated from the French Revolution.[7] According to the concept of the nation-state, the 'nation' is identical with 'the people', who, in contradistinction to the theory of the divine right of kings, are the fount of sovereignty and state legitimacy.[8] The nation-state concept also had a normative dimension, which was that nations *ought* to have 'states' (whereas, previously, a single state might encompass several nations, as previously in the Austro-Hungarian Empire or even today in the United Kingdom) and that states and nations *ought* to be coterminous. In the French case, it was thought that the state also existed to create the nation and, during the Third Republic, universal education controlled by the central government was seen as one way of doing this.

The doctrine of the Rights of Man led to the concept of *citizenship*: individuals had the right of participating in running the affairs of the nation, provided they met certain criteria of aptitude (e.g., the possession of property). These criteria were gradually extended throughout the nineteenth and twentieth centuries, so that now every adult, regardless of gender, ethnic background, or religion, is regarded as a citizen (although there are still some restrictions such as nationality, mental capacity, or a criminal record). The implication was that citizens would eventually come to share a common culture and language and abandon whatever specific cultural features they might have possessed. The French experience represents an extreme application of this doctrine and practice varied considerably across different European states but it remains that the general tendency of the nineteenth and twentieth centuries has been towards the cultural and linguistic homogenization of nation-states, with just a few exceptions such as Switzerland and Finland. The United Kingdom remains something of an exception in this regard as it has tended to speak of British subjects rather

---

[7] The American Revolution was primarily aimed at breaking with England rather than creating a new political nation—in effect, the thirteen colonies continued to regard themselves as distinct 'nations' while the federation was not a new 'nation'. This concept of federalism is evident in the writings of Jefferson while Madison sought to create a new American nation. If we think in terms of the French Revolution, Jefferson was a Girondin while Madison was a Jacobin. In the United States, there has always been a tension between the two traditions, although the Jeffersonian tradition has probably been the stronger. In France, too, there were several political traditions at the time of the Revolution from the advocates of direct democracy among the followers of Babeuf, through the federalism of the Girondins, to the Jacobinism of Robespierre. These traditions never completely died out but it is the Jacobin tradition that has been strongest.

[8] In effect, under the absolute monarchy, it was the monarch who was thought to embody the 'nation', membership of which was restricted to certain categories of person who constituted only a small minority of the people living in France. This 'embodiment' was transferred to the 'people' at the time of the Revolution although, again, the notion of 'people' was a restrictive one.

than citizens and was more tolerant than France of linguistic or cultural differences.[9]

This French understanding of nationhood has sometimes been called the voluntaristic concept (one chooses one's nationality) or nation as *demos*. It was graphically expressed by Renan who said, in his *Qu'est-ce une nation?*, that the French nation is '*un plebiscite quotidien du peuple français*' ('a daily plebiscite of the French people'). The 'Germanic' concept of 'nation' was rather different and was based on the notion of sharing a common linguistic culture (even if this was divided into many mutually incomprehensible dialects)—the *Kultuurnation* or nation as *ethnos*. At the time of the Revolution, France already had a fairly high degree of political centralization (albeit with a great deal of administrative diversity) because of the centralizing activities of the French monarchs. On the other hand, it was culturally and linguistically quite diverse.[10] The case of 'Germany' was quite different. Here, there was to some extent a common linguistic culture, but politically a great variety of territorial arrangements (from such large and powerful empires as the Austro-Hungarian Empire and kingdoms such as Prussia and Bavaria to city states such as Bremen or Hamburg). Nationalism in Germany and later in Italy, which was quite similar in this respect, meant the attempt to build a unified political state on the basis of this alleged common culture. The two notions of nation as *demos* and nation as *ethnos* are closely related, and the one tends to shade into the other—thus in France, membership of the French nation eventually came to mean that an individual was expected to assimilate into French culture and language. In Germany, cultural nationhood finally had to find an expression in a democratic system or nation as demos—which can be said to have consolidated only in the second half of the twentieth century. In all countries and nationalist movements there is a tension between these two aspects of nationhood and this is one of the reasons for the difficulties many contemporary states and nationalist movements have in defining the meanings of nationality and citizenship (Alter 1994).[11] The United Kingdom differed from both the French and German experiences in that it retained the pre-modern arrangement of a multinational state albeit with a modernizing system of public administration. This meant a great deal of ambiguity over the concepts of 'nation' and 'state' in this country.

[9] This statement needs to be qualified by recalling the attempts that were made to penalize the speaking of Irish, Welsh, or Scots Gaelic right up to the twentieth century.

[10] It has been estimated that, at the Revolution, the majority of people living in France spoke a language other than French, a situation which lasted until the end of the nineteenth century.

[11] The French, German, and British governments have all, in recent years, reformulated their laws regarding citizenship and nationality while the EU's concept of citizenship has further complicated the issue.

The coupling of 'nation' with 'state' led to the development of *nationalism* as an ideology, and this gave rise to a series of political movements throughout the nineteenth century. Nations such as Ireland and Greece sought independence from the empires in which they found themselves. As remarked above, attempts were made by territories sharing a similar culture or language to form single states as in the case of Poland which was divided among three empires. Nationalism has been a powerful but ambiguous political force. It was sometimes linked to imperialism, Fascism, and Nazism, but, as argued above, it also laid the foundations of our modern political systems and was also closely linked to the creation of liberal democracy. The nation-state became one of the most successful forms of political organization in the developed world by the early part of the twentieth century. Woodrow Wilson confirmed this at the Treaty of Versailles with the proclamation of the principle of the self-determination of peoples.[12] After the Second World War the nation-state system was also adopted by the former colonies that achieved independence from the imperialist powers. More recently, it is the system adopted by the nations of the former Soviet bloc. It might be remarked, therefore, that the nation-state represents one of the most successful political systems ever seen in human history, if by success we mean the willingness of others to imitate it (Alter 1994).

1.2.2 Democracy, Capitalism, and the Nation-State

Historians point to the link between the emergence of the nation-state, capitalism, and the development of the institutions of liberal democracy in the nineteenth century (Hobsbawn 1992). Ulrich Beck (2000) has called this 'the first modernity'. This refers to the link between the creation of 'national' markets, through the breaking down of internal barriers to trade, and the freedom to exercise trade and commerce. It also meant the creation of political institutions in which the industrial bourgeoisie could exercise power.

European states democratized at different times and did not all adopt the system at the same time and in the same manner. Some European states such as Spain and Portugal became democratic as late as the 1970s, and the transition to democracy was consolidated only in the 1980s.[13] Although there is

---

[12] It seems that Wilson approached the question of self-determination in a not totally principled fashion, changing his attitude depending on the circumstances. Thus it was acceptable in the Trianon Treaty, which broke up the Austro-Hungarian Empire, but he was less adamant at Versailles where he tried to keep the British happy, undoubtedly because the latter feared the application of the principle in their own Empire.

[13] The UK and the Scandinavian countries passed directly to liberal democracy, without major revolutionary upheavals or reversals. Most other states—France, Germany, Italy, Spain to name just a few of the large states—alternated between democratic and non-democratic forms of regime before finally settling down in the democratic family. Finland has also progressed smoothly to liberal democracy, although it did experience a civil war in the 1920s.

no country in which democracy functions perfectly and many scholars today speak of a crisis of our democratic systems, nevertheless, we might remark that today it is basically entrenched in all of the member states of the European Union as well as many other states. It is still fragile in several of the countries of the former Soviet Union, although the experience here is quite mixed with some states more solidly democratic than others.

1.3 Variations across Europe: State Traditions and State Forms

Another important feature of western European democracy is the variety of ways in which it is understood and expressed in different countries. The chapters of this book outline the main features of the origins and evolution of the concept of democracy in each state in the European Union. This variety of understandings of a common term should be regarded as part of the rich fabric of the political history of Europe. There is not, however, an infinite variety of institutional expressions and, even at the level of the state, one can speak of a limited number of 'state traditions', or 'families' of states. Castles (1998) and Esping-Anderson (1988) have employed the notion of 'families' of countries in their studies of welfare states. Page and Goldsmith (1987) distinguish between northern and southern European states in their study of central–local relations and Page (1991) and Goldsmith (1996) distinguish between 'political localism' characteristic of southern European countries and 'legal localism' found in northern European countries. In a system characterized by legal localism, there is a high degree of administrative regulation from above, while where there is political localism, informal relationships—such as clientelism or more formal settings such as the French *cumul des mandats*— become important. Page and Goldsmith developed their typology in reaction to that developed by Hesse and Sharpe (1991) who distinguished between three types of state: an Anglo group (United Kingdom, Ireland, and North America); a Franco group (France, Italy, Spain, Belgium, Portugal and, to some extent, Greece); and a northern and middle European group (Scandinavian countries, the Netherlands, and Germany).

The Page/Goldsmith typology, while useful in drawing attention to the different legal or political bases of local government in Europe, is probably too 'broad brush' to be capable of analysing with any degree of finesse the variety of situations. In this sense it is a regression compared to the Hesse/Sharpe analysis even if this too needs to be further refined. This introductory chapter follows the lead of Dyson (1980) who, like Hesse and Sharpe, distinguishes three 'state traditions' in Europe, the Anglo-Saxon, the Germanic, the Napoleonic, but adds a fourth, the Scandinavian (Loughlin and Peters 1997). Dyson's approach was basically an exploration of the philosophical traditions underlying different state forms while Loughlin and Peters attempt to give this a more focused empirical application and to situate different aspects of state and political features within these underlying traditions and cultures (Table 1.1).

Each of these state traditions conceives of the state in a particular manner, and this has given rise to distinct political and administrative cultures, forms of state organization, and kinds of state-society relationships. However, it must be remembered that, within each of these 'families', there exist distinct *national* traditions as well. In southern Europe, for example, although there is a common heritage deriving from the Napoleonic state and what is sometimes claimed to be a common Mediterranean culture (Loughlin 1994), there are important differences among the different countries from the point of view of their historical development, their political and administrative cultures, and their understanding of democracy itself. The same remarks might be made of the other 'families' mentioned in Table 1.1. Nevertheless, this table is helpful as a starting point and as a means of comparison across the different states. It also illustrates the rich diversity of institutional forms and of policy styles that exist within West Europe.[14] There are key differences in both the *understanding* and *practice* of democracy depending on each state tradition. The place of subnational government also varies considerably across the different traditions as well as in other ways. Different state traditions express subnational political systems in different ways. The two extremes are the Napoleonic tradition, expressed most fully in France, which allows little variation across its national territory and the Anglo-Saxon tradition which tolerates wide variations, as in the United Kingdom.

There are also a limited number of distinct state forms such as federal and unitary states (Loughlin 1996a). However, these two basic forms need to be further differentiated. There exist different types of federations, such as 'dual federalism', where the different levels of the federation operate independently of each other, as in Belgium or the United States, and 'cooperative federalism', where the levels operate in close conjunction with each other, as in Germany (Hix 1998). However, 'unitary' states are also differentiated. First, the United Kingdom has been described as a 'union' rather than a unitary state given that its formation occurred through a series of Acts of Union, with Wales, Scotland, and Ireland, respectively (Urwin 1982). Among the rest, there is a variety of central–local relationships giving rise to distinct models of unitary state: centralized unitary, decentralized unitary, regionalized unitary (Bullmann 1996; Loughlin 1996b, 1998). There thus emerges a complex picture of the variety of the expression of democracy at the national and subnational levels within the member states of the European Union, as illustrated

---

[14] Although we note too the analysis of Richardson *et al.* (1982) who sought to explore whether there was an emerging common policy style across western states.

in Table 1.2. All of these state forms, operating within state traditions, would claim to be 'nation-states' but, clearly, this general concept has been interpreted in a variety of ways.

The importance of state traditions for the understanding and expression of democracy lies in the ways in which the institutions of liberal democracy and the practices of policy-making have developed. Thus, although it is outside the scope of this introductory chapter to do so, we need to revisit in this light the various typologies of electoral and party systems that have been developed in past decades such as Lijphart's distinction between majoritarian and consociational forms of democracy.

These are the historical parameters within which European states evolve and change. However, we need also to keep in mind that all of our states are evolving and changing, albeit at different rates. There is a certain convergence towards common patterns—policy styles, for example—while there are also divergences. Some of these convergences and divergences will be treated in the conclusion to this book.

1.5 Regional and Local Democracy

All European Union member states have democratic political systems at levels below the national. However, as already pointed out, there is also a great variety in the arrangements between the national and the subnational, ranging from federations to unitary states. There are several different ways of electing political parties, and the role and functions of parties in political systems display a great variety, but also a capacity for evolution and change (Broughton and Donovan 1999). There is a variety of methods used for electing political leaders, from presidents and prime ministers to the mayors of communes.

In some cases, the regional and local political systems replicate the national, in others it is different. In the United Kingdom, for example, there will be, as a result of the current reforms, three different electoral systems in operation—the 'first-past-the-post' or plurality system at the national level, the single transferable vote (STV) system of proportional representation in Northern Ireland, and the 'additional-member' system that will operate for the Scottish Parliament and the Welsh National Assembly alongside the 'first-past-the-post' system. In federal and regionalized states, such as Germany, Belgium, Italy, and Spain, there may be different party systems at the subnational level with the existence of regionally based parties, such as the Bavarian *Christlich Sozial Union* (CSU, Christian Social Union), the Catalan *Convergencia i Unío* (CíU, Convergence and Union), and the Basque *Partido Nacionalista Vasco* (PNV, Basque Nationalist Party). Such regionally based parties may also play a role at the national level. In the United Kingdom, there has always been a

TABLE 1.2 Central–local relations in European Union member states

Type of state	State	Political region[a]	Administrative/planning regions[b]	Right of regions to participate in national policy-making	Right of regions to conclude foreign treaties[c]	Political/legislative control over subregional authorities
Federal	Austria	Länder (10)		Yes	Yes (but limited)	Yes (not absolute)
	Belgium	Communities[d] (3) Regions (3)		Yes	Yes (but limited) Yes (but limited)	No Yes (not absolute)
	Germany	Länder (16)		Yes	Yes (but limited)	Yes (not absolute)
Regionalized unitary	Italy[e]	Regioni[g] (20)		Consultative	No	Yes
	France	Régions[h] (21)		Consultative	No	No
	Spain	Comunidades autonomas (17)		No	No	Yes
	United Kingdom[f]	Scottish Parliament Welsh National Assembly Northern Ireland Assembly	English standard regions	No with regard to English regions Still unclear with regard to Scotland, Wales, NI	Not at present, but may evolve	Yes in Scotland and NI No in Wales (so far)
Decentralized unitary	Denmark	Faroe Islands	Groups of Amter	No	No	No
	Finland	Åaland Islands	Counties have a regional planning function	No	No (but has a seat in the Nordic Council)	Yes
	Netherlands	Rijnmond region[i]	Landsdelen	Consultative	No	No
	Sweden		Regional administrative bodies	No	No	No
Centralized unitary	Greece		Development regions (13)	No	No	No
	Ireland		Regional authorities (8)	No	No	No
	Luxembourg					
	Portugal	Island regions[j]	Potential planning regions	No	No	No

a This refers to regions and nations (as in Scotland, Wales, Catalonia, the Basque Country, and Galicia) with a directly elected assembly to which a regional executive is accountable.

b This refers to regions without a directly elected assembly, which exist primarily for administrative/planning purposes.

c There is a sharp distinction between the federal and non-federal states in this regard; however, the majority of non-federal states may engage in international activities with the approval of, and under the control of, the national governments.

d The Flemish linguistic community and the Flanders economic region have decided to form one body; the French-speaking community and the Walloon region remain separate.

e Italy is currently undergoing a process of political reform that involves the transformation of the old state into a new kind of state with some federal features. However, although the position of the regions will be strengthened, this will not be a federal state such as Germany or Belgium.

f The UK was, until the referendums in Scotland and Wales in September 1997, a highly centralized 'Union' state. However, the positive outcome of the referendums means that there will be a Scottish Parliament and a Welsh National Assembly by 1999. A referendum in 1998 on a Greater London Authority with an elected mayor was also successful, and this is seen as a precursor to possible regional assemblies in England. The successful outcome of the Northern Ireland peace process means there will be a Northern Ireland Assembly as well as other new institutions linking together the different nations and peoples of the islands.

g In Italy there are 17 'ordinary' regions and 5 regions with a special statute because of their linguistic or geographical peculiarities: Sicily, Sardinia, Trentino-Alto Adige (South Tyrol, large German-speaking population), Val d'Aosta, and Friuli-Venezia Giulia.

h There are 21 regions in mainland France. However, to this one must add Corsica and the overseas departments and territories (the DOM and TOM). Since 1991 Corsica has a special statute and is officially a *Collectivité territoriale* rather than a region. The TOM too have special statutes, and one of them, New Caledonia, has recently (May 1998) been permitted to accede to independence within a period of 20 years.

i In 1991 it was decided to set up a new metropolitan region with an elected government in the Rotterdam area to replace the *Gemeente* of Rotterdam and the Province of South Holland. However, this was rejected by a referendum held in Rotterdam as was a similar scheme for the greater Amsterdam region.

j Portugal, while making provision in its constitution for regionalization, has so far only granted autonomy to the island groups of the Azores and Madeira. The mainland remains highly centralized.

different party system in Northern Ireland, where, until recently, the British parties did not organize (in recent years, the Conservative Party has permitted a Northern Irish branch). With devolution, the tendency to develop regionalized political cultures and party systems in Scotland and Wales will intensify as the dividing cleavages will vary from nation to nation or region to region. In Scotland, for example, the 'national question' is generally regarded as 'settled' in the sense that most of those living within Scotland regard their society as constituting a 'nation' distinct from the other nations and regions of the United Kingdom. The political cleavage of the future is likely to concern the political expression and relationship of the Scottish nation to the rest: the current status quo, independence within Europe, or a federal United Kingdom. In Wales there is no sense of 'settled nationhood' and the cleavage (among many others) is much more one between those who supported devolution and those who oppose it. This cleavage exists within the Welsh Labour Party as well as in the wider society. In Northern Ireland, the cleavage is different again: even if the Good Friday settlement seems to have ended the war for the time being, there is still a bitter dispute between unionists and nationalists as to the interpretation of the Agreement.

Similar regionalization and differentiation of political systems is taking place across Europe: Catalan and Basque politics are as different from each other as they both differ from Madrid; Bretons and Corsicans are as different from each other as are Bretons and Parisians, and so on. This is reinforced by the development of regional or subnational branches of national parties that take on different characteristics from the party at the national level as, for example, with the Catalan and Basque sections of the Spanish Socialist Party or the Scottish Conservatives who are now more in favour of devolution than their English counterparts. There are of course wide variations in this regard. In some cases, such as those just mentioned, the regional system may develop in an autonomous manner. In others, the regional and local are completely dominated by the national parties who control local politics from the centre. This is largely the case in Ireland and France and, even in the decentralized United Kingdom, the central organs of the Labour Party have difficulty in letting go of control over the parties in the periphery.

A final point to be made with regard to changing local patterns of governance is that there is in western and central Europe a tradition of local self-government and autonomy that predates the emergence of the nation-state. One thinks, for example, of the cities of the Hanseatic League or the Italian city-states such as Florence and Venice. Although these communes were not democratic in the modern sense, as they were often ruled by local oligarchies, nevertheless, the tradition of communalism may be regarded as a forerunner of local democracy. Without accepting the thesis of a neo-medievalism (because of the very 'modern' or 'post-modern' nature of these developments) it is clear that one of the consequences of the changing nature of the nation-state and the loosening of central–local bonds is that this tradition is reasserting itself today.

1.6 The European Union

A further complication has entered the equation with the creation and development of the European Community/Union. The background to this was the devastation of the Second World War, but also the experience of the collapse of democracy in Germany and Italy and the threat to liberal democracy from the Soviet Union. One of the primary reasons for the setting up of the European Community, therefore, was to protect democracy in the states where it had existed and to strengthen it in those countries that had experienced dictatorship. Indeed, one of the conditions of entry into the EU today is that candidate states should possess the characteristics of liberal democracy outlined above. Many commentators agree that the EU has been successful in achieving most of these aims. All of its member states are successful functioning democracies, even if they all contain imperfections of various kinds. Countries such as Spain, Portugal, and Greece, which became members not long after having experienced non-democratic systems, found that membership helped them to consolidate their democratic systems.

It is ironic that, despite these successes, the EU has itself failed to develop into a fully democratic system. One of the major criticisms levelled against it is its serious 'democratic deficit'. Despite efforts to fill this deficit, such as strengthening the role of the European Parliament and the creation of the Committee of the Regions, the European system still lacks the democratic legitimacy characteristic of the nation-states which comprise its members. One of the reasons for this deficit is that liberal democracy, as has been pointed out above, has grown up along with the nation-state form of political organization whether this is federal or one of the kinds of unitary state. However, it is unlikely that the EU will develop into such a nation-state or even into a federation such as Germany or Austria (Hix 1998). One of the problems with filling the EU's democratic deficit is that this is measured against the democratic system of nation-states, that is, liberal representative democracy. But if the EU is not, nor will it become, a nation-state, then such a comparison is inappropriate. Rather, new mechanisms of democratic accountability need to be found that are appropriate to the kind of decision-making system into which the EU has evolved. The challenge is, therefore, both to strengthen the democratic institutions that do exist within the member states and to create new mechanisms whereby democratic control might be strengthened at the European level.[15]

---

[15] The British government has suggested that a new body representing the national parliaments might be created to oversee the activities of the Commission.

It is true that the European Parliament, as a directly elected body, has been able to fill the democratic deficit to some extent and, through the co-decision procedure, does participate in the decision-making processes of the Council of Ministers. Nevertheless, it still lacks the legislative powers of control and accountability characteristic of national parliaments.[16] Furthermore, it is unable to table initiatives or drafts for legislation such as directives. It can only ask the Commission to present such proposals. The creation of the Committee of the Regions in 1994 also goes some way toward filling the democratic deficit by allowing, for the first time, the representation of regional and local authorities at the European level of decision-making (Loughlin 1996a). However, while this is an important breakthrough, and the Committee of the Regions has managed to establish a niche for itself in the decision-making architecture of Europe, it still has no more than consultative powers and its Opinions *may* be ignored.[17]

Despite these cautionary comments, two points should be made. First, the democratic gains of the EU outweigh any democratic losses given the general success of the democratic systems of the member states. Furthermore, the EU has been an important factor in bringing about social and economic development, the *sine qua non* of democratic practice, in many European countries and regions.[18] The second point is that, especially since the 1980s, the EU has developed into a policy-making system in its own right and that the decisions made by the EU institutions have an important and direct impact on the member states (Cram 1997). Those who are opposed to further European integration have experienced this as a threat and as a burden. However, it can be seen more positively as the opportunity for European decision-makers to develop closer relationships both at the national and at the subnational levels. Government ministers meet regularly in the European Council and the Council of Ministers. Elected politicians work together in the European

---

[16] This is true even if there has been a significant decline in the powers of national parliaments such as the French Assemblée Nationale, which remains extremely weak under the constitution of the Fifth Republic, or even the Westminster Parliament, allegedly the exemplar of parliamentary democracy, which has increasingly become dominated by the cabinet and executive, thanks to the two-party majoritarian system. The European Parliament compares rather poorly with these. But it may be that one should not be comparing it with national parliaments since it is the parliament, not of a nation-state but of a quite different kind of political system.

[17] In practice, there seems to be a close working relationship between the Committee of the Regions and DG XVI (now renamed as DG Regio); the latter is responsible for Regional Policy and ensures that most of the Committee of the Region's Opinions are taken into account. The Committee of the Regions has also developed a positive relationship with the European Parliament.

[18] It is also true that European regions are still divided into 'leaders' and 'laggards' and that, in the latter, EU Regional Funds have not brought about the transformation that was hoped for.

Parliament. The Committee of the Regions brings together regional and local politicians from all of the member states. Undoubtedly, these forums are the *loci* of intense experiences of learning and exchange and are the means by which different democratic experiences and examples of best practice can be shared across Europe. Nevertheless, these developments have still not solved the problem of democratic practice at the European level and more thought needs to be given to this problem in terms of institutional design.

2. The Practice of Regional and Local Democracy

It is citizens who 'practise' democracy through electing leaders but also seeking to influence decision-making and the running the affairs of their communities or localities in a variety of other ways. Although theorists such as Schumpeter looked askance at *participatory* democracy, in the contemporary period (at least since the 1960s), the practice of democracy has been closely related to the existence of an *informed* and *involved* citizenry,[19] and, therefore, the attitude of ordinary citizens toward their subnational levels of government is extremely important. This book attempts to present, where data were available,[20] exactly what ordinary citizens feel about their governments at this level. Related to attitudes is practical involvement. To what extent do citizens get involved in subnational government? This may express itself in a number of ways: electoral turnout, standing for election, contacting the council, maintaining an awareness of council decisions and activities.[21] In some countries, voting is compulsory and, therefore, not a true indicator of commitment to democratic practice at this level.

Democracy is rarely practised in a manner that is completely faithful to the liberal-democratic schema outlined above, whereby elected representatives legislate and their decisions are translated into policies and executed by local administrators. Some authors, in the American pluralistic tradition of social science, have gone as far as to speak of 'post-parliamentary democracy' arguing that democracy might occur through the competition of elites or of

---

[19] In the Schumpeterian model, the role of 'citizens' was to elect their political leaders and decision-makers and, in the event of the latter failing to live up to their expectations, 'to cast the rascals out' (Held 1987). 'Participation' interfered with the good running of government.

[20] In some countries, such as the UK, there was a great deal of information on this topic. In others, such as Greece and Portugal, there were scarcely any available data. The *Eurobarometer* was only partially helpful.

[21] Again, in some countries the data on these questions were rich, while in others they barely existed.

policy networks. The neo-corporatist literature of the 1980s also pointed to a shift away from formal parliamentary decision-making to a system involving concertation between governments, employers' associations, and trade unions. Here, the American and British debate between elitists and pluralists is useful to some extent in pointing to the dimension of power relations in political systems: is power widely diffused, as pluralists would argue, or is it concentrated in the hands of a few, as elitists maintain? With regard to the subnational level, the neo-corporatist analysts claimed to find a tendency towards 'meso-corporatism' (Cawson 1985). Although these debates occurred in the context of the period of the welfare state, either in expansion (pluralists vs elitists) or in decline (neo-corporatists), and this kind of state has significantly changed under the pressure of neo-liberalism, nevertheless they are useful in pointing to the more hidden mechanisms of the distribution and exercise of power and decision-making and in relativizing the role of elected assemblies. The problem is to transpose these analytical categories into political systems in continental Europe where the state and the administrative systems have a quite different role to that found in the Anglo-Saxon tradition.

The distinction currently found in the literature between 'government' and 'governance' may be useful here as it points to these wider dimensions of the way in which power is exercised (Kohler-Koch 1996; Rhodes 1997; Le Galès 1999). 'Governance' refers to the phenomenon that decisions are often taken within policy networks and communities, including non-elected participants, who constitute a 'system' that is wider than the institutional structures of 'government'. Outside of these policy networks and communities, pressure groups of various kinds often attempt to have an influence on these decisions. Whether this is 'post-parliamentary democracy' or 'non-democracy' is what the current debate needs to clarify but certainly this form of decision-making radically affects the nature of democratic practice. The distinction is also useful for characterizing the nature of the EU as a political system. This is clearly not a 'government' in the sense that national governments are in the nation-state system. However, it is equally clearly a system of decision-making and governing, that is, a system of 'governance' with distinct patterns of institutions, actors, and processes. One of the limitations of the concept of 'multi-level governance' popularized in recent years through the works of Gary Marks (1992) and Liesbet Hooghe (1996) is that it seems to be more about multilevel govern*ment* rather than multilevel govern*ance*.

What has emerged, therefore, in recent years, is a complex set of overlapping and nested systems of governance involving European, national, regional and local actors, groups, and networks. These have profound implications for the practice of liberal representative democracy and government. It is methodologically difficult to identify the existence and ascertain the effects of such policy networks and pressure groups on democratic practice and it is important not to set up 'government' against 'governance' as if the latter was somehow displacing the former. On the contrary, one of the features of contemporary government is that it coexists and is intermingled with governance. This presents a challenge to the traditional concepts of liberal democracy: representation, legitimacy, and effectiveness. The question thus becomes how a wider system of governance will affect the democratic features of traditional government. It could be argued, for example, that the influence of these more or less hidden networks and pressure groups damages these three features of democratic government and should be reduced. On the other hand, it could be argued that it is impossible to avoid this type of decision-making system and it is more necessary to democratize them. A third approach might be to try to combine both traditional liberal democratic approaches with forms of representation and involvement that recognizes more explicitly the role of groups and give them a clearer institutional form. Whatever the response, it is not always easy even to recognize the existence and influence of these more or less hidden groups and it is even more difficult to design institutional systems that might reconcile to two aspects of governing in ways that are compatible with democracy. This book at least attempts to point out their existence and some of the problems that have arisen by their coexistence.

3. Challenges and Opportunities to Regional and Local Democracy

So far we have outlined the more static aspects of democratic government: the historical traditions that provide the context within which change occurs. It is essential, however, to recognize that these systems are under continual pressure and change continuously. Change may be the result of a gradual and incremental adjustment to various stimuli from within and without states. Or it may be the result of explicit and deliberate reform programmes such as French decentralization in the 1980s, British neo-liberal reforms by Margaret Thatcher in the 1980s and 1990s, or the current devolution reforms of Tony Blair. Whatever the case, our governmental systems never simply stand still.

Our argument here is that national, regional, and local democratic systems have, in recent years, faced a number of challenges. Some of these challenges are common to all states while others are specific to particular states. Sometimes a general challenge may take a particular configuration in an individual state. Among the most important of the challenges common to all states are the following.

Globalization

This rather nebulous and contested term has been the subject of a vigorous debate among social scientists. Basically, there are those, mainly on the left but also some traditional nationalists, who argue that the concept of 'globalization' refers to nothing that is new but is used as a way of disciplining, demoralizing, and undermining political and social movements that might in some way threaten capitalist development (Hirst 1997). This is because these movements grew up in the context of the nation-state and attempted to influence decision-making at that (key) level. If globalization undermines the nation-state, then the activities of these groups are also reduced to insignificance. According to this approach, 'globalization' refers to little more than global trade flows and has existed at least since the end of the nineteenth century. Furthermore, they argue, national governments still retain a great deal of control over decision-making in many areas. They point out too that most multinational corporations—the alleged purveyors of globalization—are, in fact, nationally based companies who happen to have a global outreach and national governments can influence and affect their activities if they so choose. The counter-argument to this, probably accepted by most social scientists, is that globalization refers today to a specifically new set of developments that have changed the nature of our societies, political systems, and international relations (for a good summary of the arguments see Beck 2000). We may like or dislike the phenonemon from both right and left points of view but it is here to stay. This is the position taken in this chapter. On the other hand, it seems equally clear that there is not a single world market but rather a world dominated by three large economic 'blocs': the United States, Japan, and western Europe. Nevertheless, in practical terms, for the majority of the world's nations, the hegemony of these three blocs and their increasing interdependence and the power of international financial markets means that there is a *de facto* world economic system. This discussion is extremely relevant to the question of democratic government and practice as it raises the question as to the fate of the nation-state faced with globalization, and the fate of the nation-state is central to the fate of democracy. It is essential, therefore, to clarify what is happening at this level.

Part of the confusion surrounding this debate is that globalization refers to several different kinds of phenomenon: economic, financial, cultural, political, and social processes. The relationships among these different facets of the problem is not always very clear. It is also true that some aspects of globalization have indeed been around for a very long time—in some cases we might even refer to the Renaissance as the starting point, in others to early financial capitalism, to the spread of industrial capitalism in the nineteenth century, and so on. What seems to be new today is their combination into a powerful set of forces that have become increasingly mutually reinforcing and domi-

nant over other forms and processes of political, economic, and social organization. Underlying them all has been the successful transformation of capitalism itself following the crisis in the 1970s of the Keynesian welfare state
model of economic management and the subsequent development of
neo-liberal models of free trade, the end of protectionism, and the rapid
spread of new technologies, communications, and productive systems
around the world. All of these developments have radically changed the
context within which national governments operate. In all cases, the latter
are now constrained by parameters that did not exist before. However,
this does not necessarily mean they are weaker—simply that national governing elites must now develop new political strategies often in partnership
with their counterparts in other states and sometimes with subnational elites
as even large or medium-sized states such as Germany and the United States,
have proved incapable of responding effectively by themselves to these
processes.

Globalization also affects subnational levels of government and administration. Some authors give a positive spin to this and link globalization to
the emergence of a new model of economic development that stresses the
importance of the regional and the local and the return of 'territory' (a
good summary of this work is found in Le Galès 1999). This linking of
the global and the regional/local is sometimes referred to as 'glocalization',
in which the key *loci* of economic development are specific regions or
localities such as Silicon Valley in the United States or the Dutch *Randstadt*.
'Regions' here do not necessarily, and usually do not, correspond to political
or administrative regions. On the other hand, globalization has led to
greater competition among regions and cities even within the same state,
while many national governments, influenced by neo-liberal approaches
to public policy, have cut down or abolished regional aid programmes
that might have helped subnational levels of government cope with the
changes. What seems to have happened is that the stronger regions, such as
the 'Four Motors' group of Baden-Würtemberg, Catalonia, Lombardy,
and Rhône-Alpes have become even stronger while weaker regions such as
those in southern Italy and Spain, Greece, or parts of Great Britain
have become weaker. On the other hand, some previously peripheral
regions and countries such as Ireland and Portugal and parts of Spain have
managed to use the new developments to achieve economic performances that
are quite spectacular.[22] What is clear is that the old conceptualization of
centres and peripheries, dear to authors such as Rokkan and Urwin, no longer
hold and that the very concepts of space and territory need to be radically
reformulated.

---

[22] Ireland is the most spectacular of all and is sometimes referred to as the 'Celtic Tiger'
by analogy with the Asian 'tigers'—see Chapter 3.

These developments are central to the attempt to grasp the challenges facing regions and localities as they respond to globalization. First, globalization seems to have encouraged approaches to public action that are more sympathetic to competition and markets than to solidarity and equalization among territories. National governments have cut back aid programmes to regions in difficulty while regions see themselves in competition with each other. Second, regional development is sometimes viewed in purely economic or financial terms rather than in a wider sense as social, political, and cultural development. This has favoured the influence of economic or business elites rather than other sections of the community (this is really what is meant by 'governance'). Third, the concepts of 'citizenship' and 'democracy' have become defined in different ways emphasizing the elements of public choice and consumerism. Fourth, as economic processes seem to dominate over the political and as economic regions and localities no longer correspond to political and administrative structures, the latter have increasingly more difficulty in providing democratic control over the former. Finally, globalization has exacerbated tendencies toward societal fragmentation and social exclusion. This both harms the communitarian basis of democratic politics and creates extra burdens on subnational authorities which have to deal with the consequences. The ineffectiveness of regional and local governments, and the withdrawal of citizens' consent, are both harmful to democratic legitimacy of subnational governance.

Europeanization and the 'New' Regionalism

The relaunch of Europe in the 1980s, with the 1992 Single European Market project, is often interpreted as a response by national governments and business elites to the perceived threat of a global economy dominated by the United States and Japan. However, it was also the result of intense lobbying by governmental actors and other elites who wished to see the strengthening of the federal elements of an integrated Europe (Pinder 1995; Loughlin 1996b). Concurrent with these processes of integration and federalization has been the re-emergence of the notion of a 'Europe of the Regions' in the 1990s.[23] What is important here is not the rather sterile debate as to whether there is a 'Europe of the Regions' or not, but the fact that the intensifying of European integration through the 1987 Single European Act and the revision of the EC treaties at Maastricht and Amsterdam has created a new administrative and legal environment for local and regional

---

[23] This notion originally referred to a federal Europe in which the constituent units would be not the nation-states, but the regions (at least those that possessed a strong identity such as Corsica, Brittany, Flanders, Wales, Scotland, etc.). Clearly, such a federal Europe is highly unlikely today, as nation-states will remain the key levels of government within the EU. Nevertheless, the term is valuable as an indicator of the importance of regions in the new Europe.

authorities, to which they have been obliged to adapt. This new environment is neither the arrival of a European nation-state nor a European federation but what might be described as a European system of governance that has both state-like and federal-type characteristics (Richardson 1996). This creates both challenges and also new opportunities for regional and local authorities.

In this new context, regionalism has found a second wind and some authors have spoken of a 'new' regionalism (Keating and Loughlin 1997; Keating 1998). There is, of course, an 'old' regionalism, which was both a political idea or ideology and a set of political movements, the origins of which are to be found in the nineteenth century. Many of the early regionalists were opposed to the modern nation-state and even to the forms of liberal democracy because of what they regarded as its levelling tendencies and breaking up of natural communities. In recent years, and certainly since the 1960s, there developed another more 'progressive' form of regionalism, which may be conceived as a 'modernizing' project (Keating 1998). This kind of 'new' regionalism received a stimulus from the increased level of integration of the EU and the challenges and opportunities opened up by the Single European Market and Economic and Monetary Union. These have been in part responsible for the strengthening of regional and structural action policy and the reinforcement of the principles of subsidiarity and partnership.

It would be going too far, nevertheless, to say that we are witnessing the emergence of a 'Europe of the Regions'. There are great difficulties with the notion of a Europe of the Regions. First, there are many ways of defining what is a region (Loughlin 1996a): a Europe of *which* regions? Second, national governments show no signs of disappearing but are, on the contrary, still the most powerful actors in the new system of European governance. Third, their representation at the European level, through the Committee of the Regions or via DG XVI of the European Commission or the European Parliament, still remains quite weak and marginal. Nevertheless, despite these limitations, regions and other local authorities have found a new place in the new Europe: we can speak of a 'Europe *with* the Regions', in the sense that subnational authorities have today a greater salience in policy-making terms and a new-found freedom to operate on a broader European scale than was hitherto the case (Hooghe and Marks 1996). This is quite different from the previous situation when most subnational authorities were more or less completely restrained by their national governments as to the kinds of activities they might engage in and which were firmly limited to within the boundaries of the nation-state. Now, subnational authorities have discovered a new freedom to develop links both with the EU institutions themselves and also with their counterparts in the rest of Europe and beyond, through associations such as the Assembly of European Regions, the Conference of Peripheral Maritime Regions, and many others. This new situation of regions and local authorities in Europe was formally recognized by the Treaty on European Union (Maastricht), which set up the Committee of the Regions in 1994. The Committee of the Regions, despite its limited constitutional powers (it is purely advisory) is nevertheless establishing an important niche for itself in the institutional architecture of the EU to represent the interests of regions and local authorities. This is likely to grow in the future (Loughlin 1996a; Loughlin and Seiler 1999). The Committee of the Regions is also an important factor for the strengthening of democracy in the EU, as it has the potential to bring the processes of European decision-making closer to the ordinary citizens.

Governance in Flux

The consequences of these developments are that the role, nature, and functions of different levels of government—national, regional, and local—are in a state of flux. Some already strong nations and regions are likely to become even stronger, while the weaker may suffer further deprivation. Nevertheless, the new situation may also be an opportunity for regions and local authorities to formulate new models of regional and local development based more on a judicious use of resources that are both endogenous—including regional and local cultures and lifestyles—and exogenous—for example, European structural funds.

Societal Changes

Western societies are undergoing continual and rapid change with a radical upheaval in terms of attitudes, values, and lifestyles (Mendras 1997; Loughlin 1998). There has been a growth of individualism. This is an ambiguous phenomenon. On the one hand, it might mean a decline in willingness to participate in traditional forms of collective action such as political parties, churches, and trade unions. However, it might also mean a search to find new forms of participation and a desire to replace some of the more traditional institutions. The development of car ownership and cheaper foreign travel have led to much greater levels of mobility and new residential patterns in cities and the countryside. New forms of entertainment, through television, video, and the internet, are also centred on the possibility of individual choice and have encouraged people to stay at home. It has been claimed that there has been a decline in the sense of, and commitment to, community in many western societies although, of course, it is notoriously difficult to operationalize the concept of 'community' in this context since new ways of defining 'community' might be evolving. Related to this is the problematic concept of 'social capital', developed by Robert Putnam originally in his analysis of Italian regions

(Putnam, Leonardi, and Nanetti 1993) but subsequently applied to the United States.[24]

These societal changes, especially the trend toward individualism, have important consequences for democratic practice and may to some extent explain the apathy and withdrawal from politics that has been evident in recent years, some of which are reported in this book. They also represent a challenge to traditional politics, which developed in a much more stable and communitarian society. The concept of 'community' is hotly contested on both sides of the Atlantic. In the United States, the political scientist Amitai Etzioni has launched a 'communitarian' movement which claims to offer an alternative to the excessive individualism of some contemporary approaches as represented, for example, by the American Civil Liberties Union. It seems that Etzioni has been of some influence in the reformulation of the UK New Labour's policies and the word 'community' may be found in various parts of the current devolution programme—including renewing local democracy. This conflict has a political or ideological edge. Some authors, however (e.g., Frazer 1996) are uneasy and believe that the emphasis on local 'community' might in fact be retrogressive in terms of civil liberties as these communities might be morally and politically conservative and, therefore, might be unwilling to tolerate what these authors would regard as the gains of the new individualism, for example in the area of sexual behaviour or orientation.[25]

However, 'individualism' may also be an opportunity as the masses of the population (at least in western Europe and other parts of the developed world) are today better educated and healthier than was the case in previous generations and therefore more capable of making instantaneous political judgements than previously. They are also much better informed than were their forebears—news is now available almost instantaneously from every part of

---

[24] The concept of 'social capital' is problematic because of the difficulties of defining and operationalizing the term. The work of Putnam and his disciples, Leonardi and Nanetti, has been severely criticized for its simplistic and superficial reading of Italian history. This does not mean that the concept is without usefulness as it has spawned a certain amount of interesting research which seeks to analyse the significance of the societal dimension in processes of governing and institutional development.

[25] A striking example of this kind of ideological and moral conflict occurred recently in Scotland when the Scottish Labour Government, supported by the British Labour Government at Westminster, proposed removing Clause 28 of the 1988 Education Act which forbids 'homosexual propaganda' in schools. Civil liberties and homosexual rights groups had been bitterly opposed to this clause on the grounds that it discriminated against homosexuals. The problem was that a large majority of the Scottish population, according to opinion polls, were strongly opposed to dropping the clause even though a majority of parliamentarians in the Scottish Parliament were in favour of dropping it. Given the 'traditional' position of most Scots on this issue, which course would have been more 'democratic'?

the world. The challenge for policy-makers and citizens is to translate these positive features into new forms of commitment and institutional design. Many of the regional and local authorities surveyed in this book are experimenting with different methods of bringing citizens more into the political system at this level.

Technological Developments

The period since the Second World War has seen enormous technological changes in telecommunications, transport, and forms of economic production. This process of change seems to accelerate exponentially as new developments feed into each other at an extraordinary rate. The societal changes noted in the previous paragraph are to some extent the result of these changes, which seem to have removed many of the limitations of space and time in human existence as well as enhancing the capacity of choice of the individual. It is also true that governments at all levels—European, national, regional, and local—have great difficulty in controlling and mastering these changes and seem to be continually trying to catch up with them. In other words, the locus of power in important areas has shifted from the political domain to the manufacturers of new technologies and new lifestyles (one can think of the 'manufacture' of lifestyles by advertisers, television and film producers, popular magazines, etc.).

The question is, of course, whether governments *ought* to try to control or at least influence these processes of change in the name of the (or *a*) common good as some of the changes might be considered harmful. If the answer is yes, then greater thought needs to be given to the level at which control can take place. The principle of subsidiarity may be useful as a guide to which level of government (or governance) is appropriate to which kind of activity and decision-making.[26] The regional and local are the appropriate levels for dealing with specific kinds of problem while the national and supranational are appropriate for other kinds. The problem is to apply effectively the principle and to draw up criteria which help us to decide which level is appropriate or not. At least one element in these criteria is the democratic involvement of those living in a region or locality. This is particularly the case with regard to problems such as the environment, urban policy, spatial planning, or

---

[26] We need to remember, however, the difficulties of defining and operationalizing 'subsidiarity'. In a speech to the European Parliament, the President of the European Commission, Romano Prodi, distinguished between a Germanic, or legalistic, understanding of the concept and one that was based on 'governance'. Although Germans and others objected that the practice in Germany was much more complicated than Prodi had suggested, his point provides a useful starting point for a discussion.

tourism. The answer to this problem may lie in devising new forms of institutional design more appropriate to a system of governance than a system of government. It may be that the latter, based on hierarchy, routine, and slow responses, needs to be complemented by a system that is more flexible, horizontal, and open and that can respond to the ever increasing challenges of a turbulent environment.

Besides these general challenges faced by all regional and local authorities (and indeed by national governments and Europe as well), there exist a certain number of challenges that are particular to each member state. In some cases, this may be conflictual central–local relations that have hampered the development of regional and local democracy. In others, there has been the problem of a low level of institutional capacity at the regional or local level. This is caused either by the existence of too many small councils that lack the resources and expertise to respond to the problems of modern government or by a general lack of institutional capacity in the public-administration tradition of that state in general. For example, in some states not all local authorities have been able to manage and use the quite considerable funds that have arrived from the European Union for purposes of regional and local development. These have lain unused and development has not occurred. The country chapters of this study present some of these problems in much greater detail.

4. The Origins and Plan of This Book

This book originated with an invitation from the Committee of the Regions to this author to prepare a report on the state of democracy at the subnational level in all fifteen member states of the European Union. The Committee of the Regions felt that they had probably reached the limits of their own constitutional position in the institutional architecture of the Union (they still had basically the same status as the Economic and Social Committee and their more radical demands were not accepted in the Amsterdam Treaty).[27] Jacques Delors, in his address to the inaugural meeting of the Committee when he was President of the European Commission, had remarked that one of the

[27] They had sought to become a fully fledged 'institution', that is on the same level constitutionally as the European Parliament and the Commission, and also to have the function of guardian of the principle of subsidiarity. The latter would have permitted them to bring breaches of the principle by member states or the other EU institutions before the European Court of Justice. These proposals proved to be too much for the member state negotiators or for the other EU institutions at Amsterdam and were not accepted.

primary aims of the new body was to help fill the democratic deficit of the EU by bringing decision-making closer to the peoples of Europe. The regional and local authorities represented in the Committee could do this because they were the levels of government closest to the people. The Committee reasoned that it would be as 'democratic' and 'legitimate' as were its own members. It could therefore strengthen its own position on the European scene by strengthening the democratic features of these members. That meant, however, taking an inventory of the 'state of democratic health' of these members.

What seemed to be a good idea at the time turned out to be much difficult to achieve than was first suspected. A team of five experts, chaired by John Loughlin, was set up to carry out this inventory for all fifteen member states. This meant that each expert would be responsible for reporting on more than one country. John Loughlin was responsible for the overall coordination of the project but also covered several countries: France (Daniel-L. Seiler provided some input on this chapter), Greece, Ireland, Italy, Portugal, and the United Kingdom. Eliseo Aja (University of Barcelona) wrote on Spain. Frank Hendriks (Tilburg University) covered the Benelux countries. Udo Bullmann (University of Giessen and now Member of the European Parliament) reported on Germany and Austria. Anders Lidström (Umeå University) was responsible for the three Scandinavian countries: Denmark, Finland, and Sweden. To some extent this division was made on the basis of linguistic and cultural competences. However, it roughly followed the schema of state traditions mentioned earlier in this introduction. Each author worked within a specified framework—that outlined in this introduction—covering basically similar areas. Thus, there is a strongly comparative dimension to the study. The organization of the chapters into state traditions should be seen simply as a convenient set of analytical starting points and the inclusion of a country in a particular tradition could be debated. For example, both the Netherlands and Finland could be seen as Napeolonic states. However, more important than the superficial structures is the content these are given in terms of administrative and policy styles and cultures. The Netherlands is thus more 'Germanic' than 'Napoleonic' despite its superficial similarity to the latter.

This was a vast and ambitious undertaking but the team was able to work with and have regular meetings with a small group of Committee of the Regions politicians and administrators, although the Committee provided little financial resources. Each country draft was discussed and criticized by the national delegations to the Committee (mainly administrators who service their countries' delegations). The entire exercise thus became a political and diplomatic tightrope as the team attempted to balance criticism based on their independence and scientific expertise with sensitivity to the reputations and self-understanding of the individual countries. A first version of the study was published by the Committee of the Regions and the Office of Official Publications of the European Communities in 1999 (Loughlin *et al.* 1999). That version was aimed at practitioners and is mainly descriptive. The Committee, however, gave permission for a more comprehensive academic version to be published and this has resulted in this book. The earlier work has been completely revised and updated and a stronger analytical and theoretical dimension has been added. Thus, it is hoped that the present work will be a valuable contribution to the literature not just on regional and local government but to understanding a key dimension of the functioning of the European Union which has been much neglected. It raises the question of the complexity of the concept 'democracy' and lays out the many ways in which this is understood in a European context. The book should be seen as laying out a framework for future research in this area rather than a definitive statement about the question of regional and local democracy.

References

ALTER, P. (1994). *Nationalism*, 2nd edn. London: Edward Arnold.

BECK, U. (2000). *What is Globalization?* Cambridge: Polity Press.

BROUGHTON, D. and DONOVAN, M. (eds) (1999). *Changing Party Systems in Western Europe*. London: Pinter.

BULLMANN, U. (1996). 'The Politics of the Third Level'. *Regional and Federal Studies*, 6/2: 3–19.

CASTLES, F. (1998). *Comparative Public Policy: Patterns of Post-war Transformation*. Cheltenham: Edward Elgar.

CAWSON, A. (1985). *Organised Interests and the State: studies in Meso-corporatism*. London: Sage.

CERNY, P. (1999). 'Globalization and the Erosion of Democracy'. *European Journal of Political Research*, 36/1: 1–26.

CRAM, L. (1997). *Policy-making in the European Union: Conceptual Lenses and the Integration Process*. London: Routledge.

CROZIER, M. (1963). *Le phénomène bureaucratique: essai sur les tendances bureaucratiques des systèmes d'organisation modernes et sur leurs relations en France avec le système social et culturel*. Paris: Seuil.

DUPUY, F. and THOENIG, J.-C. (1985). *L'administration en miettes*. Paris: Presses Universitaires de France.

DYSON, K. (1980). *The State Tradition in Western Europe: A Study of an Idea and Institution*. Oxford: Martin Robertson.

ESPING-ANDERSON, G. (1988). *The Three Political Economies of the Welfare State* (EUI working paper). Florence: European University Institute.

FRAZER, E. (1996). 'The Value of Locality', in King and Stoker (eds), op. cit., 89–110.

GOLDSMITH, M. (1995). 'Autonomy and City Limits', in Judge *et al.* (eds), op. cit., 228–52.

GOLDSMITH, M. (1996). 'Normative Theories of Local Government: a European Comparison', in King and Stoker (eds), op. cit., 174–92.

HELD, D. (1987). *Models of Democracy*. Cambridge: Polity Press.

——(1993). 'Democracy: From City-states to a Cosmopolitain Order', in D. Held (ed.), *Prospects for Democracy*. Cambridge: Polity Press.

HIRST, P. (1997). *From Statism to Pluralism: Democracy, Civil society and Global Politics*. London: UCL Press.

HIX, S. (1998). 'Elections, Parties and Institutional Design: a Comparative Perspective on European Union Democracy'. *West European Politics*, 21/3: 19–52.

HOBSBAWN, E. (1992). *Nations and Nationalism since 1780: Programme, Myth, Reality*, 2nd edn. Cambridge: Cambridge University Press.

HOOGHE, L. (ed.) (1996). *Cohesion Policy, the European Community and Subnational Government*. Oxford: Oxford University Press.

——and MARKS, G. (1996). ' "Europe *with* the Regions". Channels of Interest Representation in the European Union', *Publius*, 26/1: 73–91.

JUDGE, D., STOKER, G., and H. WOLMAN (eds) (1995). *Theories of Urban Politics*. London: Sage.

KEATING, M. (1995). 'Size, Efficiency and Democracy: Consolidation, Fragmentation and Public Choice', in Judge *et al.* (eds), op. cit., 117–34.

——(1998). *The New Regionalism in Western Europe: Territorial Restructuring and Political Change*. Cheltenham: Edward Elgar.

——and LOUGHLIN, J. (eds) (1997). *The Political Economy of Regionalism*. London: Frank Cass.

KING, D. and STOKER, G. (eds) (1996). *Rethinking Local Democracy*. Basingstoke: Macmillan.

KOHLER-KOCH, B. (1996). 'The Strength of Weakness: The Transformation of Governance in the EU', in S. Gustavsson and L. Lewin (eds), *The Future of the Nation-State: Essays in Cultural Pluralism and Political Integration*. London: Routledge.

LAPIDOTH, R. (1997). *Autonomy: Flexible Solutions to Ethnic Conflicts*. Washington, DC: University of Washington Press.

LE GALÈS, P. (1999). 'Crise de Gouvernance et Globalisation'. *Revue internationale de Politique comparée*, no. 4.

LOUGHLIN, J. (ed.) (1994). *Southern Europe Studies Guide*. London: Bowker-Saur.

——(1996a). 'Representing Regions in Europe: The Committee of the Regions'. *Regional and Federal Studies*, 6/2: 147–65.

——(1996b). ' "Europe of the Regions" and the Federalization of Europe', *Publius*, 26/4.

——(1998). 'Autonomy is Strength', in R. Wilson (ed.), *Hard Choices: Policy Autonomy and Priority Setting in Public Expenditure*. Belfast: Democratic. Dialogue/Eastern Health and Social Services Board/Northern Ireland Economic Council.

——and PETERS, B. G. (1997). 'State Traditions, Administrative Reform and Regionalization', in M. Keating and J. Loughlin (eds), *The Political Economy of Regionalism*. London: Frank Cass.

——and SEILER, D. (1999). 'Le Comité des Régions et la supranationalité en Europe'. *Etudes Internationales*, Dec. 1999.

——*et al.* (1999). *Regional and Local Democracy in the European Union.* Committee of the Regions/Office of Official Publication of the European Union: Luxembourg.

MACINTYRE, A. (1984). *After Virtue: A Study in Moral Theory,* 2nd edn. Indiana: University of Notre Dame.

MARKS, G. (1992), 'Structural Policy and 1992', in Alberta Sbragia (ed.) (1992). *Europolitics: Institutions and Policy-making in the 'New' European Community.* Washington, DC: Brookings Institution.

MENDRAS, H. (1997). *L'Europe des Européens.* Paris: Gallimard.

PAGE, E. (1991). *Localism and Centralism in Europe.* Oxford: Oxford University Press.

——and GOLDSMITH, M. (eds) (1987). *Central and Local Government Relations.* London: Sage.

PINDER, J. (1995). *European Community: the Building of a Union,* 2nd edn. Oxford: Oxford University Press.

PUTNAM, R., LEONARDI, R., and NANETTI, R. (1993). *Making Democracy Work: Civic Traditions in Modern Italy.* Princeton: Princeton University Press.

RHODES, R. A. W. (1997). *Understanding Governance: Policy Networks, Governance, Reflexivity and Accountability.* Buckingham: Open University Press.

RICHARDSON, J. (ed.) (1996). *European Union: Power and Policy-making.* London: Routledge.

——*et al.* (ed.) (1982). *Policy Styles in Western Europe.* London: Allen & Unwin.

SCHARPF, F. Article on comparing the EU with German federalism.

URWIN, D. (1982). 'Territorial Structures and Political Developments in the United Kingdom', in S. Rokkan and D. Urwin (eds), *The Politics of Territorial Identity.* London: Sage.

WOLMAN, H. (1995). 'Local Government Institutions and Democratic Governance', in Judge *et al.* (eds), op. cit., 135–59.

Part 1

THE ANGLO-SAXON TRADITION

2

The United Kingdom: From Hypercentralization to Devolution

John Loughlin

1. History and Concept of Democracy

1.1 Historical Background

The United Kingdom (UK) is a liberal democratic state where democracy is exercised in the context of the doctrine of the sovereignty of parliament. Neither the democratic features of the UK nor even the doctrine of parliamentary sovereignty are codified in a written constitution, but are rather the accumulation of unwritten 'conventions' as well as written rules—laws passed by parliament and case-laws made by judges—that have developed over long periods of time. The concept of democracy in the UK has similarly developed over time and in a piecemeal manner during a period of about two hundred years. It is based on the liberal concept of the primacy of the individual, conceived as someone in possession of a bundle of 'rights', in particular the right to conduct commerce, that could be exercised provided that they did not interfere with the rights of others. At first, it was restricted to gentlemen of means and property, thus excluding the lower classes and women. This 'economic' right was also the basis of other rights: the right to freedom of speech, the right to a free press; the right to vote and stand in elections, the right to representation in parliament.

In the British tradition, there is no 'state' which is the equivalent of the French *état* or the German *Staat*, understood as an overarching entity standing above and separate from civil society. Indeed, in the democratic tradition peculiar to Britain and countries that it influenced, such as the United States and Canada, it was felt that 'government' ought to be restricted to very general functions that would ensure the unhindered activity of commerce: protecting the security of the realm and maintaining internal order. This was the famous 'night-watchman' state of nineteenth-century liberalism.

Democracy, then, could be seen in the Anglo-Saxon tradition of political theory as the exercise by individuals of their rights to engage in activities such as trade and commerce unhindered by government. With the development of the welfare state, however, the 'state' intervened increasingly in all aspects of society, including economic affairs and social matters from the 'womb to the tomb'.

1.2 Democracy at the Subnational Levels

The United Kingdom has been described as a 'union' rather than a 'unitary' state. This refers to the way it developed historically. First, England became a unified monarchy. Then, from the thirteenth century to the Acts of Union of the sixteenth century, it absorbed Wales into its political and administrative system while (unenthusiastically) tolerating the survival of a distinct Welsh language and culture. It was not until the 1960s that Wales gained some administrative devolution with the setting up of the Welsh Office and the appointment of a Secretary of State for Wales with a seat in the cabinet. Scotland was a separate state until the Act of Union of 1707. In effect, the Act of Union abolished both the English and Scottish Parliaments and created a new Parliament of Great Britain. Already in 1603 the two monarchies had been united. Scotland was allowed to retain some features of its 'civil society'—its (Roman) legal system, its educational system, its established church (Calvinist rather than Anglican). At the end of the nineteenth century (in 1885), the Scottish Office was established, headed by a Secretary for Scotland with a seat in the British cabinet who, in 1926, became the Secretary of State for Scotland.

The Scottish and Welsh Offices had responsibility for a wide range of services (although not the same services in each country) and represented a form of administrative devolution. However, one of the problems that arose in the pre-devolution period (i.e., before 1997) was that the Secretaries of State for Scotland and Wales were Conservative ministers while the majority of people in these countries were opposed to the Conservative Party and its policies. Furthermore, especially in Wales, many services were delivered by non-elected bodies known popularly as 'quangos' (quasi non-elected government organizations), which were heavily criticized. There was a kind of devolved government in both Scotland and Wales, but one which was not directly accountable to their people. There was thus a democratic deficit in these countries.

Ireland's links to the UK are different again. An Irish Parliament (but with members drawn exclusively from the Protestant minority on the island) sat in Dublin until 1800 when it was abolished following the 1798 rebellion. From the 1801 Act of Union, Ireland was governed from Dublin Castle and Irish MPs sat in Westminster. Throughout the nineteenth and early twentieth centuries, nationalist and unionist movements clashed and political violence was widespread. The island was partitioned in 1920, with six counties of the Northern province of Ulster (which contains nine counties) remaining in the UK, and the remaining twenty-six gaining partial independence as the Irish Free State (later becoming a Republic). Northern Ireland had its own parliament and a Northern Ireland Civil Service (NICS) modelled on Westminster lines. There was a convention that Northern Irish affairs could not be discussed in the UK Parliament even though the Northern Ireland Parliament was dominated by the Protestant Ulster Unionist Party and condoned widespread discrimination against the Catholic minority between 1920 and the 1970s. Civil rights protests and the outbreak of the 'Troubles' in the late 1960s led to the Northern Ireland Parliament being 'prorogued' (but, in effect, abolished) in 1972 . The NICS remained with a Secretary of State at its head who is a member of the UK Cabinet.

Democracy never really functioned in Northern Ireland except in a purely formal sense. The basic political cleavages centred on the 'constitutional question'—whether Northern Ireland should remain within the UK or be joined to the Republic of Ireland. Today, the governments of the UK and the Irish Republic have accepted that Northern Ireland is different and, in conjunction with most of the main protagonists to the conflict, have devised a solution—the Good Friday Agreement—which recognizes this difference.

British constitutional development has thus taken a variety of forms, in each of which politics has a particular complexion. Local government has followed a similar pattern throughout the UK, although both Scotland and Northern Ireland have had different systems from those of England and Wales. Local government reached the peak of its influence as a democratic institution at the end of the nineteenth century and the beginning of the twentieth century. From about the 1930s until the present day its power has declined.

2. The Institutional Expression of Democracy

2.1 The National Level

Parliament consists of the Crown, the House of Commons, and the House of Lords. However, only the House of Commons is truly democratic with its 635 elected Members of Parliament. The Crown is a hereditary monarchy, while the House of Lords consists of unelected hereditary and 'life' peers (current reforms have reduced the number of hereditary peers although it is not as yet known how the new House will be constituted). MPs are elected on a constituency basis using the first-past-the-post (FPTP) or 'plurality' system. Advocates of the plurality system of voting argue that it tends to eliminate the smaller parties and the political extremes and thus leads to relatively stable government with two large parties alternating in power. However, its critics point out that it seriously distorts the representation of political groups in the country.[1]

2.2 The Local Level

Local government in the United Kingdom is regarded as a form of *government* and not simply a level of *local administration* although it has tended to become the latter in recent years. Councillors are democratically elected to represent the interests of their constituents. Unlike countries such as Sweden, it has no general competencies but may perform only what is permitted by Parliament which defines the 'powers beyond which' (*'ultra vires'*) it cannot go. In Great Britain (England, Scotland, and Wales) local government is, nevertheless, still responsible for a large number of services including education, personal social services, community care, fire, highways, housing, and town planning, as well as a range of environmental services. In Northern Ireland, because of the political conflict there, local authorities are responsible for only a limited number of functions, such as refuse collection and street cleansing. Local authorities in the UK levy a local tax, but receive the bulk of their funding as block grants from central government. An important feature of the local-government system in Britain is the committee system. Basically, policies are overseen by elected councillors who sit on committees dealing with a specific policy area.

Local-government and European elections in Great Britain have used the same plurality system of voting as is used in Westminster elections, although a form of PR is now proposed for European elections. Northern Ireland, because of its deeply fragmented character, mentioned above, uses the proportional representation (PR) system known as the single transferable vote (STV) for its local and European elections.

The powers and functions of UK local government have been steadily eroded over the past fifty years. The welfare state, set up after the Second World

---

[1] A Committee set up by the government and headed by Lord Jenkins reported in October 1998, recommending that a proportional representation system be adopted in Great Britain, although the Blair government has reacted coolly to this recommendation.

War, meant a greater degree of centralization in policy-making with local government sometimes being reduced to the role of administering centrally decided policies. Centralization accelerated following the Conservative victory in 1979. There was a great deal of antagonism toward local government on the part of the Conservatives, who regarded it as wasteful and inefficient. This led to a number of important reforms to improve services (Committee of the Regions 1996: 218):

- *'Agentization'*: This refers to the transfer of functions including some educational responsibilities and transport and urban development in some areas to agencies of central government.
- The notion of local authorities as *'enabling'* authorities, rather than providing services directly, through: *privatization* of some services; *limitations* on the proportion of services that can be provided 'in-house', the rest being farmed out to private sector providers; and *compulsory competitive tendering* (CCT). This reduced the discretion of local authorities over service delivery.
- *Reduced autonomy over total spending.* Since 1984, central government has been able to 'cap' the overall expenditure level of local authorities.

We might add to this list the abolition of the Welsh counties and the Scottish regions and their replacement by 'unitary authorities', which had the effect of fragmenting local government.

Underlying these Conservative reforms was a particular conception of democracy, different from the traditional notion of representative democracy. This new approach is based on 'neo-liberalism' which considers the individual to be a 'rational' actor freely choosing what is best for him or her. In this perspective, governmental institutions, whether at the central or local levels, hinder the individual's exercise of free choice. In fact, according to this theory, bureaucrats tend to inflate their own bureaucracies and services in inefficient and wasteful ways (Niskanen 1971). Neo-liberal politicians considered local government to be among the worst offenders in this regard and sought to curb its activities. The result, ironically, was the strengthening of central government and the creation of new bureaucracies, which Mrs Thatcher allegedly wished to diminish.

2.3 The Role of Political Parties

Political parties originally developed in the United Kingdom at the national level, while at local level there was a strong tradition of independents. Today, however, party politics is a central feature of UK local government (Wilson and Game 1994: 245) although non-partisanship (i.e., independent councillors) has survived. By 1997 the Labour Party was the predominant

TABLE 2.1   Political party control and membership of councils, June 1997

	Conservatives	Labour	Liberal Democrats	Independents/ others	Nationalists	NOC
Members						
Scotland	82	615	126	235	186	—
Wales	42	725	78	312	115	—
London	518	1,047	321	31	0	—
Mets	197	1,875	357	52	0	—
Counties	881	746	495	81	0	—
Districts	2,306	4,263	2,829	1,362	0	—
Unitaries	423	1,372	550	80	0	—
Total	4,449	10,643	4,756	2,153	301	—
Councils						
Scotland	0	20	0	6	3	3
Wales	0	14	0	4	1	3
London	4	17	3	0	0	8
Mets	0	32	0	0	0	4
Counties	9	8	2	0	0	15
Districts	9	85	39	13	0	93
Unitaries	8	29	6	1	0	8
Total	23	205	50	24	4	134

Source: Rallings and Thrasher, *Local Government Chronicle*, 13 June 1997.

party in British local government (excluding Northern Ireland), followed by the Liberal Democrats who had overtaken the Conservatives as the second largest party at this level (Table 2.1). However, the Conservatives did show some recovery in the 1998 elections. In Northern Ireland the local authorities have fewer powers, but, nevertheless, have been important arenas for playing out the political conflict and have been the arena of the initial electoral successes of Sinn Féin. All the political parties there have used the councils in the absence, until recently, of Northern Ireland political institutions.

Parties, therefore, play an important role in both British and Northern Irish local government. They could be seen as affecting local democracy in two ways. First, increasing partisanship might be seen as lessening the *local* element of democracy as the party competition at the local level may be seen as the translation of national issues to the local level. The same might be said of European elections, which are often simply referendums on the state of play of national politics. However, the presence of parties at the local level does allow local preferences to be expressed in a way that can then be translated into local public policies. Often, local authorities may attempt, within the bounds of the *ultra vires* principle, to develop initiatives appropriate to the

local community even if this is different from the policies being pursued at
the national level.

3. The Practice of Subnational Democracy

3.1 The Roles of Councillors and Officials

We can distinguish between (*i*) those elected to, or appointed to work officially for, local government, and (*ii*) those who are not elected but who seek
to influence in some way the outcome of local-authority policies (Wilson and
Game 1994). Elected councillors represent a greater number of constituents
in the United Kingdom than in other European countries (1:2,200 as against
1:110 in France and 1:420 in Germany). Backbench councillors are important as they sit on the various local-government committees, help to make
policy decisions, and give the overall policy direction. Among those *appointed*
to local government we may distinguish between local-government officers
who are responsible for the operational management of the policies decided
by the elected councillors, and local-government employees who are
responsible for the delivery of the vast array of services still provided by local
authorities.

The policy-making system of local authorities is remarkably similar all over
the UK. According to the theory of liberal democracy, elected councillors
decide on policy, which is then implemented by an army of faithful bureaucrats. In reality, similarly to what happens at the level of national government,
'policy' is the outcome of a process involving elected councillors and principally the leader or mayor and his or her executive and the most senior administrators of the council. Probably the most accurate model to describe this is
elitism, which sees power as concentrated in the hands of a few, rather than
pluralism. It is also true that efforts are being made in many British local
authorities to reduce its elitist character and to broaden the decision-making
power base.

Finally, to add to the complexity of the UK system of local government,
mention must be made of both the representation of local government at the
national level through different local-authority associations and the diversity
that exists at the 'regional' level, that is, in Scotland, Wales, and Northern
Ireland. In 1996 three local authority associations merged to form the Local
Government Association (LGA), representing the majority of the local authorities in England and Wales. Wales is represented in this association, but also
has its own representative body: the Welsh Local Government Association
(WLGA). Scotland set up a single association for all Scottish local authorities

in 1975: the Convention of Scottish Local Authorities (COSLA), which is still in existence.

3.2 Pressure Groups in Local Government

Stoker (1991) has distinguished four types of group:

- *producer or economic groups*—Trades Councils or Chambers of Commerce;
- *community groups*—with distinct social support bases, for example amenity groups, tenants' associations, women's groups, and groups representing ethnic minorities;
- *cause groups*—promoting a particular set of ideas and beliefs rather than their immediate material interests (e.g., the Campaign for Nuclear Disarmament);
- *voluntary sector groups*—set up to meet a need of the community on a non-commercial, non-statutory basis, and receiving substantial financial support from local authorities.

Not all of these groups are equally important or influential, depending on the political complexion of the local authority. In authorities where the left-wing of the Labour Party is in power, as in some London boroughs, there is more sympathy to the cause groups than in more traditional Labour- or Conservative-controlled authorities.

3.3 Critiques of Local Democracy

In recent years many political and academic observers have noted a crisis in local government in the United Kingdom (Pratchett and Wilson 1997). The Congress of Local and Regional Authorities of Europe (CLRAE), a body of the Council of Europe, passed a resolution in June 1997 that included the UK among a number of countries with serious deficiencies in the practice of local democracy (the others were Croatia, Bulgaria, Latvia, Moldova, Ukraine). The congress identified as problems:

- that the concentration of many local authorities into a single level and the dismantling of others, in conjunction with the creation of quasi non-governmental organizations ('quangos') to replace local authorities in supplying a number of services to the public, have considerably reduced the powers of local authorities;
- the limits imposed by central government on local-authority expenditure and the diminishing revenue available for local authorities;
- the difficulties concerning the signature and ratification of the European Charter of Local Self-Government (Committee of Regions Resolution 58

[1997] on the Situation of Local Democracy in Member Countries, para. 17).[2]

In July 1992 the Local Government Commission for England (LGCE) was established. Part of its remit was to examine issues such as the identity and interests of local communities with regard to local democracy and also the question of the number of councillors needed to ensure they effectively carried out their representative role (Burton and Duncan 1996). The LGCE recommended that the ratio of councillors to residents should be around 1 in 4,000, although many councillors thought that this was still too high (ibid.).

In November 1993 the Commission for Local Democracy (CLD) with members from the three major parties, local officials, and academics was launched to examine how local democracy could be improved (Pratchett and Wilson 1997). The brief of the commission was to enquire into all forms of democratic activity at subnational level and not just elected local government. In June 1995 they produced their final report, *Taking Charge: The Rebirth of Local Democracy*. The CLD concentrated on three areas of concern: the internal organization of local government, the relationship between localities and the centre, and the nature of citizenship at the local level (Burton and Pratchett 1996). Among their most noteworthy recommendations were: a *reduction* in the ratio of councillors to residents, the introduction of the post of *elected mayor*; and the primacy of democracy over efficiency at the local level. They also made some recommendations for practical measures to bring about these changes: all local authorities should prepare an annual 'democracy plan'; there should be a programme for educating the public, and the use of *deliberative polling* (this refers to a polling method developed in the United States that encourages respondents to reflect on what ought to happen given a range of options rather than simply saying what they think now). The Audit Commission of the UK government, in a report published in February 1997, echoing the Widdicombe Report of 1986, criticized local-government councillors for being too remote from citizens and for spending too much time (around 50 per cent) in committees rather than in contact with their electors (around 30 per cent).

The Labour Party too, while in opposition, examined the question of local democracy and issued a policy discussion document with the title *Renewing Democracy: Rebuilding Communities*. This document is important as it provides the background to reforms proposed by the new Labour Government after it came to power in May 1997 (discussed below). Among the proposals advocated in this policy document were: the introduction of 'local performance programmes' to allow citizens to evaluate the performance of their

[2] However, the situation is now changing, and the Labour Government has both signed and ratified the European Charter of Local Self-Government.

council, citizens' juries, community forums, advisory panels, public hearings, and opinion polls. The document encourages councils to experiment with ways of encouraging citizens to become councillors, but it also tries to encourage the participation of wider groups of citizens in the decision-making process—two forms of representation that are not always easy to reconcile (Burton and Duncan 1996).

3.4 Citizens' Attitudes to Local Government

There has been a considerable amount of research on citizens' attitudes carried out in recent years both by government commissions (e.g., the Widdicombe Committee) and by the local authorities. Local government is generally viewed more favourably than other levels of government. The 1995 State of the Nation, conducted by the Joseph Rowntree Reform Trust, found the following: 49 per cent were satisfied and 21 per cent dissatisfied with their council, 18 per cent were satisfied and 33 per cent dissatisfied with the European Union, 34 per cent were satisfied and 31 per cent dissatisfied with Parliament, 28 per cent were satisfied and 25 per cent dissatisfied with the House of Lords (quoted in Page 1996). In a MORI poll commissioned by the Local Government Association, twice as many of those polled were happier with local government than with central government. Sixty per cent said they would like their council to have more freedom to set the council tax at the level needed to provide more services (*Local Government Chronicle*, 27 March 1997).

Nevertheless, the general picture that emerges from these surveys is of a large gap between the average citizen and his or her local authority, seen as primarily a provider of services. Few citizens wished to become more involved in council activities themselves. A MORI survey for the Local Government Commission for England, found that 58 per cent were interested in what the council does, but were happy to let them get on with the job (Page 1996). Two per cent were completely uninterested and unworried about whether they did their job, and 17 per cent were not interested in what the council does so long as they get on with it. But just 19 per cent wanted to have a say in what the council does and the services it provides. With regard to contact with the council only 6 per cent had attended a council meeting in the previous three years; around four in ten had contacted their district council; and only one in five their county council in the previous year. The results of the survey, illustrated in Table 2.2, showed that the primary concerns for the majority of people were the quality of services (64 per cent) and responding to local people's wishes (58 per cent), although the cost of services was also an issue for a substantial minority (44 per cent). Only minorities indicated a concern for several issues deemed important for local democracy by most commentators: accountability (33 per cent), ease of contacting the council (20

TABLE 2.2   A sample of the MORI survey results on local government structure
(percentages), 1995

'Which three of these, if any do you think should be most important in deciding the local government structure in your area?'	Total	Age 15–34	Age 35–54	Age 55+
Quality of services	64	67	64	59
Responding to local people's wishes	58	57	63	54
Cost of services	44	45	42	44
Accountability	36	23	41	45
Ease of contacting the council	20	21	19	19
Sense of local community	18	19	20	15
Access to local councillors	18	15	17	16
Level of information about the council	16	15	17	16
Size of population covered	10	12	11	6
Historical or traditional boundaries	6	6	6	7

Source: Page (1996).

TABLE 2.3   A sample of the MORI survey results on knowledge of local council
functions (percentages), 1995

'How much, if anything, do you feel you know about your local council?'	Total	Age 18–24	Age 25–34	Age 35–54	Age 55+
Great deal	5	3	3	6	5
Fair amount	27	17	20	31	32
Just a little	42	39	45	43	41
Hardly anything at all	24	41	30	19	20
Never heard of	—	—	1	—	—
Don't know	1	1	1	1	2

Source: Page (1996).

per cent), a sense of local community (18 per cent), access to local councillors (18 per cent), level of information about the council (16 per cent), size of population covered (10 per cent), historical or traditional boundaries (6 per cent). These results are important as several recent initiatives in Britain to strengthen local democracy are attempts to strengthen these aspects of local government. There is also a great deal of ignorance about what the council does or who the councillors are: less than one in ten could name any of their local councillors. Table 2.3 illustrates the degree of ignorance, particularly among younger age groups: 66 per cent of the total sample knew 'just a little' or 'hardly anything at all'; among 18- to 24-year-olds this was 80 per cent and among 25- to 34-year-olds 75 per cent.

Given this level of apathy and ignorance with regard to local government in Britain, it comes as no surprise that electoral turnout is also extremely low, in fact it is the lowest of all the member states of the EU. In the 1996 local elections only 30.5 per cent of registered voters in the metropolitan boroughs and 37.1 per cent in the districts went to the polls (Rallings and Thrasher 1996).

4. Challenges and Opportunities for Subnational Democracy

Local government in the United Kingdom has faced two sets of challenges. First, there has been the challenge from increasing Europeanization. Second, there was the challenge from a hostile central government and the increasing centralization of power in Westminster (although the strained relations between the centre and the local have now considerably eased since the new Labour Government has come to power).

4.1 The European Challenge

Local authorities have responded to the European challenge in a number of ways. There is little doubt that the incentive to obtain funds from European sources has been very strong (Loughlin and Mathias 1996). This has sparked a mobilization of local authorities in England, Scotland, and Wales. Many British local authorities have been members, sometimes very active members, of European groupings such as the Assembly of European Regions. Mobilization has also led to the creation of regional offices in Brussels. These activities have been important not so much because British local authorities have obtained large sums of money from 'Brussels', but because they have been a learning process whereby local politicians have adopted new and wider political perspectives. This is also true of the Committee of the Regions, despite this body's limitations (Loughlin 1996; Loughlin and Seiler 1999).

Finally, the European dimension has been important for providing a context for the constitutional restructuring at present occurring in the United Kingdom and Ireland. The 1985 Anglo-Irish Agreement, the 1997 devolution programme, and the 1998 Good Friday Agreement were possible, at least in part, because of 'Europe'.

4.2 Central–Local Relations

During the 1980s and 1990s, councils tried to cope with the financial constraints imposed by hostile Tory governments, although the tension has lessened since the election of the Labour Government, which has promised to develop a new and more positive relationship, the financial constraints remain.

4.3 Strengthening Local Democracy

Many councils have been aware of the 'democratic deficit' at the local level and of the apathy and ignorance of the local resident population. Reformers suggested two general approaches to solving this problem. The first was to reorganize the structures of local government in order to allow elected representatives to operate more effectively. The second was to attempt to involve local citizens either through increasing their knowledge of, and interest in, the affairs of the council or by involving them directly in decision-making. These two approaches were not always compatible since the first was based on strengthening the notion of *representative democracy* exercised by councillors on behalf of residents, while the second involved an approach based more on *participatory democracy*. Some argued that the two functions were not necessarily incompatible, but could reinforce each other.

4.3.1 Structural Reorganization

The following reforms were suggested as means of improving representative democracy:

- elected mayors (Commission for Local Democracy, see *Local Government Chronicle*, 1 May 1996);
- cabinet systems of local government (Jones and Stewart 1996);
- central executives as in Scandinavia (ibid.);
- improved committee systems (Widdicombe), for example, the abolition of the old committee structure and the setting up of a small number of *strategic committees* and several *neighbourhood committees* as carried out by the Royal Borough of Kingston-upon-Thames (Tilley 1996);
- local decentralization.

Previous legislation made it impossible to implement the more radical of these reforms, such as elected mayors and some forms of committee reorganization (Jones and Stewart 1996) but this will now be possible under current reforms.

4.3.2 Improving Participation by the Public

Given these legislative constraints, many councils opted for this approach. A survey of democratic innovations by local authorities in England carried out by the University of Portsmouth and Portsmouth City Council revealed some of the methods adopted by the 65 per cent of the local authorities who responded (Sweeting and Cope 1997):

- local-authority-wide surveys (used by 52 per cent of respondents);
- customer panels (29 per cent);
- consultative forums (54 per cent);
- citizens' juries (5 per cent);
- computer terminals providing public information (19 per cent);
- Internet homepage (18 per cent);
- electronic democracy (5 per cent);
- quango registers (28 per cent).

It is clear that only surveys and consultative forums are the most used, although these are used by just over half of the respondents. Citizens' juries, a method of community consultation imported from the United States, are used by only four local authorities (Lewisham Borough Council and Hertfordshire, Cambridge, and Nottingham County Councils), while referendums are extremely rare. However, it seems that the use of computer-based innovations is growing and will become more widespread as the new technology is adopted by councils. Nevertheless, the overall picture is not encouraging. The authors of the study point to a 'perceived tension between representative and participative forms of local democracy' (Sweeting and Cope 1997: 7). Elected councillors often feel that community involvement undermines their representative role. Furthermore, there are a number of problems associated with each of the methods: surveys, for example, tend to provide simply a 'snapshot' of residents' attitudes frozen at a moment in time; citizens' juries involve a great deal of time and effort and might involve no more than particular interest groups rather than the wider population; similar comments can also be made about customer panels and consultative fora. Nevertheless, it is argued that local authorities will fill their democratic deficit only by inaugurating such reforms alongside structural innovations (Stewart and Stoker 1995).

4.4 Subnational Government and the New Labour Government (May 1997)

The British Labour Party fought the 1997 General Election on the basis of a manifesto committed to a radical overhaul of the British constitutional system to make government more open, democratic, and accountable. The new government tackled the reforms with vigour, determined to implement them in the early phase of government while it had a huge majority in the House of Commons and a great deal of goodwill in the population at large.[3] Every

---

[3] This is similar to the approach adopted by the French Socialists when they came to power in 1981 and launched the decentralization reforms in the following year by an avalanche of legislation (see Chapter 8 and Loughlin and Mazey 1995).

aspect of the constitutional system was to be reformed. The bulk of these reforms have now been carried out with others still in the pipeline.

4.4.1 Scotland

The most important measure, was the setting up of a Scottish Parliament of 129 members, 73 elected by the first-past-the-post (FPTP) system, and 56 additional members (seven from each of the eight European Parliament constituencies elected by a form of proportional representation). The party that wins the most seats in the parliament can form the Executive, led by a First Minister, who will nominate the other ministers. The Scottish Parliament has powers of primary and secondary legislation over a wide range of devolved matters—those formerly exercised by the Scottish Office—and several more.[4] An important development here is that the legislation to set up the parliament defined what will be reserved for Westminster[5] rather than what will be devolved to Scotland, an interesting modification of the *ultra vires* rule. The parliament also has some financial discretion consisting in the ability to vary the rate of income tax of those living in Scotland by plus or minus 3 per cent, although it is unlikely that it will decide to lower this. The Scottish Parliament will have legislative and financial control over Scottish local authorities (a development that is causing some anxiety among members of COSLA). Taken together, the proposals for Scotland could be interpreted as *a step toward the federalization of the United Kingdom*, following the resounding majorities of yes-votes to the two questions in the referendum on 11 September 1997.[6] The first elections to the Parliament were held and resulted in a close race between the Labour Party and the Scottish Nationalist Party. Labour won a majority of votes but not enough to form a majority government. As a result, it has formed a coalition with the Liberal Democrats with the SNP as the official opposition. The elections also permitted the Conservatives to win some seats and thus have a political voice in Scotland absent since the 1997 General Election. Opinion polls seem to indicate the emergence of a specifically Scottish political system and culture, albeit one that is still within a British context where issues of control by, or autonomy from, Westminster are still paramount and are still evolving.

[4] These include: health; education and training; local government; housing; social work; economic development; transport; the law and home affairs; the environment, including the natural and built heritage; agriculture, fisheries, and forestry; sport; and the arts.

[5] These matters include: the constitution of the United Kingdom; UK foreign policy, including relations with Europe; UK defence and national security; the stability of the UK's fiscal, economic, and monetary system; common markets for UK goods and services; employment legislation; social security; and most aspects of transport safety and regulation.

[6] The results were: 74.3% in favour of setting up a Scottish Parliament, 63.5% in favour of the parliament having tax-varying powers (of 3%), with a turnout of 60.4%.

4.4.2 Wales

In Wales, the yes-vote in the referendum succeeded, but only just and with a very low turnout.[7] The proposals for Wales were very different from those for Scotland. Wales will have a National Assembly (rather than a parliament) with only secondary legislative powers (the same as local government) and no taxation powers. Nevertheless, despite these differences, there is the possibility that the Welsh reforms may transform the nature of governance in Wales. Almost all the powers exercised by the Secretary of State for Wales[8] are transferred to the assembly and those powers remaining at Westminster are basically the same as in the Scottish case.[9] Furthermore, as the Welsh Bill passed through the UK Parliament, some of the original plans of the White Paper were modified. As a result, the assembly will have a First Secretary, in effect a First Minister, who will have the power to appoint a cabinet rather than an executive consisting of the chairpersons of the assembly committees as had been originally planned. This strengthens the political and constitutional status of the new body.

There are several reasons for the diluted nature of the Welsh proposals. First, public opinion in Wales was more divided than in Scotland with regard to devolution, as an analysis of the referendum results shows. The Welsh Labour Party was more divided than its Scottish counterpart, with some 'Old Labour' stalwarts opposed to devolution. In Scotland, the situation was quite different with all the major parties (except the Conservatives) and many other bodies such as the Protestant and Catholic Churches in favour. A second reason may be that in Scotland there was a much stronger sense of Scottish citizenship and 'civil society' than in Wales because of its very different history. The differences between the approaches to the two countries might be summed up by saying that the Scottish proposals seem to be based on giving Scotland the institutional trappings appropriate to nationhood, while the Welsh proposals are more based on the idea that Wales should become a dynamic European region. The Welsh National Assembly is, nevertheless, an important step toward the democratization of government in Wales and in the institutional expression of Wales as a distinct political, cultural, social, and economic entity. The Secretary of State for Wales in welcoming the Government of Wales Bill in November 1997 said that neither Westminster nor

---

[7] The results were: 50.3% in favour of a Welsh Assembly, 49.7% against, with a turnout of 50.1%.

[8] These are: economic development; agriculture, forestry, fisheries, and food; industry and training; education; local government; health and personal social services; housing; environment; planning; transport and roads; arts, culture, and the Welsh language; the built heritage; sport and recreation.

[9] They include foreign affairs, defence, taxation, macro-economic policy, policy on fiscal and common markets, social security, and broadcasting.

local government would provide the model for the new assembly, but best practices from around the world.

The assembly has sixty members elected by the same electoral system as Scotland: forty members elected by FPTP from the Westminster constituencies, and twenty additional members elected under the additional-member system from the European constituencies in Wales. It is hoped that this will allow the assembly to function effectively, but at the same time give representation both to minority parties and to geographical areas. The assembly will be bilingual, with English and Welsh having equal status. The different regions of Wales will have their own committees of which one must be for North Wales. This is important as the North is separated from the South by high mountains, and there were fears that the assembly would be dominated by the dynamic region around Cardiff, which is already the political and economic, if not the geographical, centre of Wales. The powers exercised by the National Assembly may be increased in the future but it will not be possible for the assembly to gain primary legislation or tax-varying powers as in Scotland without another referendum.

The assembly will not have direct control over Welsh local government but proposes to work with the Welsh Local Government Association (WLGA) through a Partnership Council. The government will decide the size of the budget available to the assembly, but the assembly will decide how much will go to the Welsh local authorities and how this is split between individual councils. It is hoped that this will be done on the basis of consensus and through the Partnership Council, with representatives from local government and the assembly.

It must be said that the assembly has got off to a bad start. First, there were undignified wrangles within the Labour Party as to who should lead the party. Second, there was an equally undignified wrangle concerning the location of the new institution—Cardiff or another Welsh city, or if Cardiff, where in the city. Third, the first elections to the assembly were disappointing in the level of public interest they provoked and in the low turnout. The assembly has, on the whole, functioned rather poorly since its inception and has a lot of work to do to catch up with the status of the Scottish Parliament or even the Northern Ireland Assembly.

4.4.3 London

Since the abolition of the Greater London Council in 1986, London has been the only major city in the world without its own government. Instead, it has been governed by thirty-two borough councils and the City of London (which basically covers the financial district). Most commentators agree that it has suffered as a result of this lacuna as it has been unable to develop an integrated development plan for the entire area. The new Labour Government called attention to these problems and claimed, in a Green Paper, that there was an important 'democratic deficit' in London (DETR 1997). In the referendum held in London on 7 May 1998—in which 72 per cent of those voting said yes, against 28 per cent who said no (but with a very low 30 per cent turnout)—a Greater London Authority (GLA) would be established, led by a directly elected and salaried mayor[10] with an assembly of twenty-five members. The mayor would have a permanent support staff. The GLA, that is, the mayor and the assembly, would be meant to give a democratic voice to the thirty-two boroughs and the City of London and provide the lead in creating a 'Sustainable City'. It would develop strategies and be responsible for a number of key areas.[11]

The first elections for the post of mayor and the authority were held on 4 May 2000 using two election systems: a two-round system for the mayoral election, and a mixture of FPTP and list system for the authority. It cannot be said that they were an auspicious start for the new institutions as the government became embroiled in a row with Ken Livingstone, the former far-left leader of the old Greater London Council and currently Labour Member of Parliament. Prime Minister Blair, seeing in Livingstone a key figure of the old extreme left which had made the Labour Party unelectable for almost twenty years, was totally opposed to his candidacy and instead the party adopted Frank Dobson, Minister for Health as its official candidate. With a very low turnout of below 30 per cent, Livingstone gained 41 per cent of first preference votes in the first round and stomped easily to victory beating the Conservative candidate Steven Norris in the second round with 57.93 per cent. In the election to the GLA, out of the total of twenty-five seats, Labour won nine, the Conservatives nine, the Liberal Democrats four, and the Greens three.

The government sees this as a precursor to the setting up of regional government in the rest of England and the more general introduction of elected mayors at least in the large cities. Elected mayors are seen as a way of answering some of the criticisms levelled at local government in Britain, namely as an antidote to the committee system. Furthermore, it is argued that the low turnout in local elections undermines the democratic legitimacy of councillors, including the leaders and executive. The current government believes that dynamic mayors, directly elected by their people, will have stronger democratic legitimacy than the old-style leadership and will be able to design and put into effect overall strategies and policies.

[10] The government sees five key roles for the mayor: proposing the budget, devising strategies and action plans, promoting action to implement London-wide strategies, being a voice for London, and making appointments to executive bodies under the GLA's control.
[11] These areas are: land-use planning; transport; economic development and regeneration; environment protection; culture, media, and leisure; police; fire services; pan-London bodies.

4.4.4 Northern Ireland

On Good Friday 1998 almost all of the feuding parties in Northern Ireland as well as the British and Irish governments signed an agreement, which devised new institutions to transform the relationships within Northern Ireland, between the Republic of Ireland and Northern Ireland, and between the island of Ireland and the island of Great Britain (known as the 'three strands'). There will be a new Northern Ireland Assembly, elected by proportional representation (single transferable vote) with a power-sharing executive to ensure the participation of the two communities in the government of Northern Ireland. There will be a North–South ministerial council consisting of ministers from the Northern Ireland Assembly and of the government of the Republic. Ministers of specific policy sectors will meet their counterparts periodically to 'develop consultation, co-operation, and action within the island of Ireland—including through implementation on an all-island and cross-border basis—on matters of mutual interest within the competence of the administrations, North and South'. There will be a British–Irish Council, with representatives of the parliaments and assemblies of the UK, Ireland, Scotland, Wales, and Northern Ireland, as well as the Isle of Man and the Channel Islands. This council will try to develop mutually beneficial policies, but its decisions will not be binding on any of the constituent members. Finally, there will be a new British–Irish intergovernmental conference, which will replace the machinery set up by the 1985 Anglo-Irish Agreement.

The Good Friday Agreement was endorsed by referendums in both Northern Ireland and the Republic of Ireland (the first time that the population of the entire island has voted together since 1918). The result in the South was 94 per cent in favour but with a rather low turnout of 56 per cent. In the North the result was more decisive: 71.12 per cent in favour with a turnout of 81.1 per cent. Elections to the new Assembly were held on 25 May 1998 and returned a majority of pro-Agreement candidates. What was remarkable was that, according to the d'Hondt system of election, Sinn Fein would have two seats in the executive alongside the Unionist Parties and the moderate nationalist Social and Democratic Labour Party. After eighteen months of wrangling over the decommissioning of IRA weapons, the executive was finally formed at the end of 1999, suspended again, and finally came into operation in 2000, which meant that the other institutions could also begin to function. A new era truly seems to have begun for that troubled region.

4.4.5 Regional Chambers and Regional Development Agencies in England

Mr John Prescott, deputy leader of the Labour Party and Minister for the Environment, Transport and the Regions (DETR), has made it clear that the new government would like to see regional governments in England. However, the question of regional government in England is less clear-cut than in Scotland

and Wales. The latter are nations with strong identities and borders that have been defined for centuries and where there are strong movements in favour of devolution. In England, there is little tradition of regionalism, and, while there do exist regional identities in places such as Cornwall, Yorkshire, or Sunderland, there are no clear geographical boundaries separating one region from another. Administrative regions do exist for planning purposes or for the delivery of services such as health, but these rarely coincide with each other; and it is not too exaggerated to say that they originated as lines drawn on a map by statisticians in London. Nevertheless, in recent years there has been a certain regional mobilization in England with groups being established such as the North-West Regional Association. In some regions of England these have been well developed, while in others they barely exist.

For all these reasons, the British Government has adopted a gradualist approach and hopes that the existence of a Scottish Parliament, a Welsh Assembly, and a Greater London Authority will act as a stimulant to set up regional government in England. The first step will be to set up regional development agencies whose operations will be overseen by regional chambers of which some have already come into existence. The latter will consist of elected councillors nominated from the local authorities. Thus, the proposals do introduce an element of electoral legitimacy even if this is indirect.

4.4.6 Reform of Local Government in the UK as a Whole

The new Labour Government wishes to reverse the decades of conflict in central–local relations and to rebuild local democracy. It has announced that its approach will no longer be based on antagonism, but on *partnership*. The Local Government Association welcomed this announcement and was the first organization contacted by John Prescott after taking up his post as Minister of the Environment, Transport and the Regions, which has responsibility for local government. In a speech to the LGA in July 1997, Prescott affirmed the partnership approach and announced that his aim was to achieve social justice for all: 'For too long central and local government have been at loggerheads. There has been a war where there should be constructive co-operation . . . I invite you . . . to join us in a new partnership for the good of the people we are elected to serve' (DETR Press Release, 21 July 1997). To translate these worthy comments into practice, the Government and the LGA set up a Central Local Partnership Meeting, which will work together on twenty key areas including: central–local relations, democracy, best value (see below), personal social services, education, and economic development.

The Labour Government also announced in its election manifesto a number of measures to strengthen both the effectiveness (and not simply the efficiency and economy) and the democratic credentials of local government (*Local Government Chronicle*, 11 April 1997). In July 1998 the government issued a White Paper entitled *Modern Local Government: In Touch with the*

People (DETR 1998). This White Paper accepts many of the critiques made throughout this chapter and gives detailed information with regard to the reforms necessary to enhance local democracy. The following are the most significant points:

- there will be new political structures: the committee system will be over-hauled and there will be new models for the political management of councils;
- the role of mayors will change and councils will be able to choose from three models: an executive mayor with a cabinet directly elected by the people, a leader appointed by the council and a cabinet either appointed by the leader or by the council, a directly elected mayor with a council manager—the basic logic here is to distinguish between the executive role of the mayor and the backbench role of the councillors;
- there will be more frequent elections and councils will have the power to hold local referendums;
- there will be guidance to maximize voter registration, turnout, and experiments to make it easier to vote: electronic voting, increased postal voting, mobile polling stations, voting on different days;
- attempts will be made to improve local financial accountability and there will be an end to council tax capping, although the government will retain a reserve power to control excessive council tax increases;
- compulsory competitive tendering (CCT) will be replaced by best value tendering;
- there will be 'beacon councils' who will be examples ('lights') for particular services or for the council as a whole—these councils will obtain increased scope to act for the benefit of the local community.

4.4.7 Elected Mayors

The rationale behind this has already been outlined above under the section on London. Basically, it is thought that a directly elected mayor will have a democratic legitimacy coming from his direct election by the people in the area. The experience in London will be used as a pilot before the scheme is introduced to the rest of the country.

4.4.8 Compulsory Competitive Tendering and Best Value[12]

Compulsory competitive tendering (CCT) was severely criticized as being a means primarily of *efficiency* (i.e., cutting costs) rather than of *effectiveness*

---

[12] 'Best value' is based on twelve principles: (1) Councils will owe a duty of best value to local people, as taxpayers and service customers. (2) Best value is about effectiveness and quality and not just economy and efficiency. (3) Best value would apply to a wider range of services than CCT. (4) There is no presumption of the superiority of either

(i.e., improving the delivery of services). It was assumed that the private sector could deliver such services better than the public sector simply because it was private. At least this seemed to be the philosophy emanating from the highest reaches of central government, especially when Mrs Thatcher was prime minister. These assumptions were largely based on ideological presuppositions rather than on empirical verification. As a result, a tender often went to the lowest bidder even if the latter was not the one offering the highest quality service. The practice across local authorities varied with some services being improved through CCT while others declined. The new Labour Government announced the abolition of CCT (or its continued suspension in Scotland and Wales), but did not propose going back to the previous system where all services were provided exclusively by local government. What they sought was a new system that would combine some of the advantages of CCT, *with competition remaining at the heart of the system*, with a search for the maintenance of *quality* of service delivery. This they call 'best value'. In other words, services may be tendered out, but those who win the tender will do so on the basis of offering the best value for money and not simply the lowest cost. In June 1997 Hillary Armstrong, Minister for Local Government, announced the blueprint for the implementation of best value. CCT would end by April 1998 and a number of pilot schemes would operate before the scheme was made universal. The government would oversee progress in consultation with the Local Government Association.

5. *Conclusions*

For many years, Britain has suffered from an increasing democratic deficit, especially at the regional and local levels. After peaking in the 1930s, local government entered into a long but sure decline in its prestige, power, and influence. There were also serious democratic deficits, each different, in the territories of Scotland, Wales, and Northern Ireland. In Scotland and Wales, Tory rule led to serious disaffection on the part of many people and the growth of nationalism in both countries. The situation in Northern Ireland was a

privatization or direct delivery. What matters is what works best. (5) Competition will remain as a tool of management but is not in itself a demonstration of best value. (6) Central government will set the framework for service provision. (7) Local targets will have regard for national target. (8) Both national and local targets will be decided on the basis of performance information. (9) This will be confirmed by auditors. (10) Auditors will report publicly on whether best value has been achieved and will help to achieve this. (11) The Department of the Environment may intervene, on the advice of the Audit Commission, to tackle councils that fail. (12) This intervention should be appropriate to the nature of the failure.

disgrace for a democratic country like Britain and can only be described as a nightmare for the people living there. Fortunately, after eighteen years of Tory rule, a new reforming government took over the reins of power and decided to tackle this vast array of problems with its devolution programme. Taken together, the proposals of this programme are a radical reform of subnational government in the United Kingdom. There can be little doubt that, if they are carried through, and everything indicates that they will, that both regional and local democracy will be vastly improved in the UK. First, democracy will exist for the first time at the regional level once the Scottish Parliament, the Welsh Assembly, and the English regions are set up. The new institutions set up under the Good Friday Agreement also signify new relationships among the nations and regions of the British Isles, as well as contributing to a peaceful resolution of the conflict in Northern Ireland. This will end the anomalous position of the UK as the only large state in the European Union without a regional tier of government. Second, the reforms proposed for local government will increase the link between the councils and their electors (through the elected mayors) while the quality of services will increase.

References

BURTON, P. and DUNCAN, S. (1996). 'Democracy and Accountability in Public Bodies: New Agendas in British Governance'. *Policy and Politics*, 24/1: 5–16.

COMMITTEE OF THE REGIONS (1996). *Regional and Local Government in the European Union: Luxembourg*. Brussels: CoR.

DETR (Department of the Environment, Transport and the Regions) (1997). *New Leadership for London. The Government's Proposal for a Greater London Authority. A Consultation Paper*. Cmnd. 3724. London: HMSO.

JONES, G. and STEWART, J. (1996). 'More Room for Innovation'. *Local Government Chronicle*, 12 July, 8.

LOUGHLIN, J. (1996). 'Representing Regions in Europe: the Committee of the Regions'. *Regional and Federal Studies*, 6/2: 147–65.

——and MATHIAS, J. (1996). 'Mobilisations et co-opération au Royaume-Uni', in R. Balme (ed.), *Les Politiques du Néo-Régionalisme*. Paris: Economica.

——and MAZEY, S. (1995). *The End of the French Unitary State: Ten Years of Regionalization in France (1982–1992)*. London: Frank Cass.

——and SEILER, D. (1999). 'Le Comité des Régions et la supranationalité en Europe', *Etudes Internationales*, Dec.

NISKANEN, W. (1971). *Bureaucracy and Representative Government*. Chicago: Aldine/Atherton.

PAGE, B. (1996). 'Serving the Public Interest'. *Local Government Chronicle*, 25 Oct., 12–13.

PRATCHETT, L. and WILSON, D. (1997). 'The Rebirth of Local Democracy?' *Local Government Studies*, 23/1: 16–27.

RALLINGS, C. and THRASHER, M. (1996). 'Stemming the Flood of Electoral Decline'. *Local Government Chronicle*, 11 Oct., 16–17.

STEWART, J. and STOKER, G. (eds) (1995). *Local Government in the 1990s.* Basingstoke: Macmillan.

STOKER, G. (1991). *The Politics of Local Government*, 2nd edn. Basingstoke: Macmillan.

SWEETING, D. and COPE, S. (1997). 'Modernising Local Democracy: Democratic Innovations in Local Government'. *Local Government Policy Making*, 23/5: 3–8.

TILLEY, J. (1996). 'New Life in the Local Forum'. *Local Government Chronicle*, 5 July.

WIDDICOMBE, D. (1986). *The Conduct of Local Authority Business. Report of the Committee of Inquiry into the Conduct of Local Authority Business.* Cmnd. 9797. London: HMSO.

WILSON, D. and GAME, C. (1994). *Local Government in the United Kingdom.* Basingstoke: Macmillan.

3

Ireland: From Colonized Nation to 'Celtic Tiger'

John Loughlin

1. History and Concept of Democracy

1.1 Historical Background

The entire island of Ireland, consisting of thirty-two counties, used to form part of the United Kingdom of Great Britain and Ireland, and constituted one of its four nations. In 1921, after a long campaign for Home Rule in the nineteenth century and a War of Independence between 1916 and 1920, the island was partitioned. Six of the nine northern counties of Ulster became Northern Ireland and remained within the United Kingdom. The other twenty-six became independent as the Irish Free State within the British Commonwealth. In 1949 the Free State declared itself a Republic and left the Commonwealth. It is this history of being part of the United Kingdom and then separating from it to form an independent state that has shaped the institutions and political culture of modern Ireland.

Although Ireland has developed a distinctive political culture of its own, its political and administrative institutions have their origins in the period before independence. There was an Irish Parliament for the entire island in the eighteenth century, in which the Protestant minority were represented. This was abolished in 1800 after which was passed the Act of Union of 1801, the founding date of the 'first' United Kingdom. Ireland was then administered from Dublin Castle in a quasi-colonial manner. Throughout the nineteenth century, the pattern of democratization was the same as in the rest of the United Kingdom: a series of Victorian legislative acts, culminating in the 1898 Local Government (Ireland) Act, resulted in a two-tier structure of authorities

I would like to thank Brigid Laffan, Susan Baker, and members of the Irish National Delegation to the Committee of the Regions for commenting on this chapter.

elected on a wide franchise. The upper tier consisted of county-level author-ities in the form of county councils and county boroughs (cities). The second tier consisted of rural district councils and, in the smaller towns, non-rating town commissioners. These acts were passed by the British Parliament at Westminster and, until the Local Government Act 1991, formed the legisla-tive basis for Irish local government. Although Ireland, unlike the United Kingdom, has a written constitution, local government follows the British approach and has a statutory (that is based on Acts of Parliament) rather than a constitutional basis (that is based on a written constitution). The same *ultra vires* rule applied to Irish local government as it does to British local govern-ment: the *Oreachtais* (Irish Parliament) defines the areas of competence of local government that did not possess a general competence. This rule was changed by the Local Government Act 1991 (see below), but the political culture of dependence on the centre that it engendered has taken longer to change (Collins and Haslam 1997; Quinn 1998).

A number of features differentiate the history and understanding of democ-racy in Ireland from Great Britain. Unlike Britain, which underwent rapid industrialization in the nineteenth century, most of Ireland (with the excep-tion of the north-east corner around Belfast) remained rural and agricultural. The majority of Irish land-dwellers were small tenant farmers who were penal-ized if they improved their holdings. These farmers lived in great insecurity; and there were several famines in the country, the most serious being in 1845–52 when about one million people died and another million emigrated (Lyons 1971). These events had enormous consequences for the political development of the island and led to an intense conflict about the issue of land ownership and its reform.

Related to this was the problem of religion: the small minority who pos-sessed the bulk of the land were the Protestant Anglo-Irish gentry, while those who possessed little land or none at all were mostly Catholic. Furthermore, Catholics were penalized in a number of ways until the middle of the nine-teenth century. Even though these penalties were lifted by the Emancipation Act of 1832, power still lay in the hands of the Protestant ruling classes sup-ported by the considerable numbers of Protestant tenant farmers in the North of Ireland. In this situation, the Catholic Church and the small Catholic middle class assumed important roles as the leaders of the people. Indeed, the Catholic clergy were largely drawn from this class.

The conflict over land and religion became bound up with another cleav-age: nationality. Most Catholics were nationalists of one kind or another who sought to change Ireland's relationship with Great Britain, either through greater autonomy (Home Rule) within the United Kingdom or through com-plete independence (Republicanism). Although many of the leaders of Irish nationalism were Protestant aristocrats, most Protestants, especially in the North, were Unionists; that is, they opposed any change and wished to remain within the United Kingdom. Although class was not absent from these conflicts, it was not a primary issue and both communities within Ireland tended to form interclass alliances.

Thus, nineteenth-century Ireland experienced intense conflict around three issues: land, religion, and nationality; while in Great Britain the basic political cleavages were much more related to social class. In Ireland, these cleavages led to continual political unrest and violence on a scale much greater than occurred in Great Britain. The conflicts involving the Nationalists, Unionists, and the British led to the partition of the island following the Anglo-Irish Treaty of 1921. This led to a division in nationalist ranks and a Civil War in the South (1921–3) fought between those who supported and those who rejected the treaty settlement. It is this conflict that has dominated, at least until very recently, the politics of Ireland with the two major parties (*Fianna Fáil* and *Fine Gael*) being the inheritors of the opposing sides in the conflict.

1.2 Democracy at the Subnational Levels

What is important is that in the latter half of the nineteenth century, when democratic institutions were being set up, the cleavages concerning land, religion, and nationality became fixed, as it were, and continued to dominate the political life of the island and to condition the nature of democracy itself throughout the twentieth century. They have done so in a number of ways. First, most Irish Catholics became alienated from the political system and distrusted the central government, whether in London or in Dublin. Irish Members of Parliament, the majority of them Nationalists, did sit in the Westminster Parliament, but felt impotent to influence affairs in Ireland. With the democratization of local government in the 1890s, the latter became a base from which to build either nationalism (in the Catholic parts of Ireland) or unionism (in the Protestant parts). The second important effect was the high degree of centralization in Ireland. Because of the quasi-colonial nature of Ireland's relationship with Britain and the continual unrest throughout the island, Dublin Castle, the centre of Irish administration, became the centre of a system of control over the entire island. This was reinforced by the political violence that accompanied the foundation of the new state when the government in power felt it had to impose a system of strict control over the country. Finally, the rural character of much of Ireland encouraged a system of patronage or clientelism especially at local government level. In fact, it could be argued that this system was necessary given the weakness of Irish democracy at the level of Dublin and the distance of these rural communities from Westminster. It was also necessary given the chronic insecurity, whether caused by economic reasons or by political violence, that was endemic in the countryside.

2. The Institutional Expression of Democracy

2.1 The National Level

Ireland is a parliamentary democracy that follows the Westminster pattern, although, unlike the United Kingdom, it has a written constitution. Elections take place to the Dáil (Lower House of Parliament) at least once every five years. There are other elections: the president is elected every seven years, elections to the European Parliament are held every five years, and there are referendums on amendments to the constitution. Elections to local authorities are held at the discretion of central government, but never less than five years apart and the interval can be as great as nine.[1] The electoral system is proportional representation by means of a single transferable vote (PR-STV). All resident Irish citizens aged over eighteen are entitled to vote in all of these elections. Britain and Ireland have had a Common Travel Area since the foundation of the Irish state, and British citizens resident in Ireland may vote at Dáil, European, and local elections (as Irish citizens may so vote in Britain). European Union citizens may vote at European and local elections and all residents, regardless of citizenship, may vote at local elections. There are sixty members in the Seanad (Upper House of Parliament). Eleven are nominated directly by the incoming prime minister, six are elected to represent the universities, while the remaining forty-three are elected on a restricted franchise that mainly consists of the 883 county and city councillors in the state.

2.2 The Local Level

The basis of political organization at the local level and important reference points of identity for Irish citizens are the twenty-six counties.

At present, there are twenty-nine county councils (CCs)—twenty-four of the twenty-six counties have one council, Tipperary has two councils, Dublin has three—and five county borough corporations (CBCs) that cover the five largest cities in the state. These thirty-four authorities have the same powers and form the core of the local administrative system (Coyle 1996). There is, however, no uniform system of subcounty administration and different systems exist in different parts of the country: there are five borough corporations, forty-nine urban district councils, and twenty-six boards of town commissioners (see Table 3.1).

[1] This constitutes a serious democratic deficit as local elections may be postponed by central government for purely political reasons.

TABLE 3.1   Subnational government

Type of authority	No. of authorities	Membership
County councils	29	20–48
County borough (city) corporations	5	15–52
Borough corporations	5	12
Urban disctrict councils	49	9–12
Town commissioners	26	9
Total	114	1,627

Source: DoE (1996*b*: app. 1).

2.2.1 Functions and Finances of the CCs and CBCs

Functions that are carried out by local authorities in other European countries, even in a (until recently) highly centralized country like the United Kingdom, such as education, police, and social welfare, are the responsibility of central departments in Ireland, with the exception of some minor contributions by local authorities. In 1980 and 1990, Ireland ranked lowest among the twelve EU countries for the level of local government spending as a percentage of national output (DoE 1996*a*). Local authorities are responsible only for functions that fall into two basic categories: (*i*) planning and development, and (*ii*) environmental management and control (Coyle 1996). These cover: housing and building, road transportation and safety, water supply and sewerage, development incentives and controls, environmental protection, recreation and amenity, and miscellaneous services.

Irish local authorities have a very weak financial base. Almost all capital spending (35 per cent of the total) is funded by state grants and is spent on roads, water and sanitary-services facilities, and much of the housing construction programme. Current expenditure (65 per cent of the total) has traditionally been financed from state grants, local rates, fees, charges, rents, and services provided by the local authorities. The financing of Irish local government has been controversial since the abolition of household rates in 1978, made following a commitment given in a national election campaign. Attempts by local authorities to make good the deficiency by levying charges for household water supply met with resistance and threatened political upsets in the large cities. In 1996 these charges were also abolished, and a new system was set up whereby local motor tax revenues previously directed to the national exchequer would now be made available for local spending. This was boosted in March 1998 with the announcement that a dedicated slice of national revenue (index-linked) in addition to the revenue from motor taxation would be made available for distribution to the local authorities. This promises a buoyant and predictable supply of funds albeit a highly centralized one. The only discretionary local funding sources are rates on commercial premises and a miscellany of charges for services.

2.3 The Role of Political Parties

Despite the limited political and policy-making role of Irish local authorities, the political parties and the electorate take local elections very seriously. There is something of a paradox here in that the tendency of central government to delay local elections never provokes a public outcry, despite the seriousness with which they are taken. Elections are usually held midway through the life of the *Dáil* and are often seen as tests of the popularity of the government. Furthermore, county councillors, although they have a weak democratic base in the councils and despite the truncated nature of their functions, serve as conduits between the locality and the centre.[2] There is also a small number of non-party councillors. Electoral turnout is quite high and stood at 55.7 per cent in the last local elections for the larger authorities (councils and county borough councils) held in 1991 (Donnelly 1992). The highest turnouts were in Leitrim (79.4 per cent) and Roscommon (73 per cent), while the lowest were in the Dublin area—Dublin South (41.4 per cent), Dun Laoighaire (42.1 per cent), Dublin Fingal (48.8 per cent)—in Kildare (48.5 per cent), and Galway Corporation (49 per cent). All the others were above 50 per cent (ibid.). These results are important as they show that, while local elections are taken seriously in the rural parts of Ireland, there is a certain amount of disaffection in the urban areas, especially in Dublin.

The results of the last two elections, held in 1985 and 1991 (Table 3.2), show that local politics reflects party politics at the national level and is dominated by the two large parties, *Fianna Fáil* and *Fine Gael*, but with the former holding a predominant position in terms of the percentage of the vote and the number of seats. The Labour Party is the third party at this level. The two main parties both lost seats and dropped in percentage points, but this is largely explained by the appearance of a new party, the Progressive Democrats, formed in 1985, as a result of a split from *Fianna Fáil*. Local elections were held in June 1999 simultaneously with elections to the European Parliament and a referendum on whether the Irish constitution should recognize the position of local government in the Irish political system. There was a low turnout with a slide to below 50 per cent (compared to 56 per cent in the 1991 elections, although only 44 per cent voted in the 1994 European elections) and a high number of spoiled ballots in the referendum (109,066 out of

---

[2] This is what is meant by 'clientelism' referred to above.

TABLE 3.2   Party votes in local elections (counties and county boroughs), 1985 and 1991

Party	1985			1991			% change	No. of seats changed
	No. of candidates	No. of seats	% of votes	No. of candidates	No. of seats	% of votes		
FF	687	437	45.49	644	357	37.9	−7.59	−80
FG	572	283	29.82	471	270	26.4	−3.43	−13
Lab	227	58	7.7	201	90	10.63	2.92	32
PD	0	0	0	125	37	5.05	5.05	37
WP	81	20	3.19	82	24	3.66	0.48	4
GP	34	0	0.55	60	13	2.36	1.81	13
SF	77	10	0.3	61	7	2.04	−0.96	−3
NP	280	75	10.25	329	85	11.96	1.71	10
Total	1,958	883		1,973	883			

FF, *Fianna Fáil*; FG, *Fine Gael*; Lab, Labour Party; PD, Progressive Democrats; WP, Workers' Party; GP, Green Party; SF, *Sinn Féin*; NP, non party.

Source: Donnelly (1992).

1,024,850 cast were spoiled). However, there was still a higher turnout in rural areas (e.g., 80 per cent in Drumshanbo, County Leitrim) compared to Dublin areas (26 per cent in an inner city constituency). In the local elections only *Fine Gael* and *Sinn Féin* increased their share of the vote compared to the 1991 results, the former by 1.5 points to 27.9 per cent, the latter by 1.5 points to 3.5 per cent. Support dropped for both *Fianna Fáil* (by 0.6 per cent) and the Progressive Democrats (whose vote was halved to 2.7 per cent). The Labour Party and the Greens slightly increased their vote. The referendum, passed by 77.83 per cent of those voting with a turnout of 51.08 per cent, was a significant step toward strengthening local government by giving it constitutional recognition by adding a new article (28A) to the constitution. This article 'recognizes the role of local government in providing a forum for the democratic representation of local communities . . .'. It obliges the government to hold local elections at least every five years, thus removing these from the whim of government ministers who had postponed them each time for the previous twenty years.

2.3.1 Description of Councillors

The largest category of councillors elected in 1991 were farmers (18 per cent) followed by *Teachta Dála* (TDs, Members of Parliament—12 per cent), teachers (10.5 per cent), and business people (7.8 per cent); there were very few workers or employees. Most councillors are male, but a noteworthy feature of the 1991 elections was the increase in the number of women elected: 103

compared to 74 in 1985, a 39 per cent increase (Donnelly 1992). Dublin councils have the largest proportion of women councillors: Dublin South (30.8 per cent), Dublin Fingal (29.2 per cent), and Dun Laoghaire (28.6 per cent) (ibid.).

2.4 The 'Regional' Level: *Údarás na Gaeltachta* and the Shannon Development Authority

There is no level of regional government in Ireland although a regional level of administration has been in existence since 1994 (see below). The Irish-language community in Ireland has its own authority, *Údarás na Gaeltachta*, which exists to promote economic development as well as community, cultural, and language-development activities. This does not cover a single region, but represents the various Irish-language communities dispersed throughout the country.[3] There are thirteen members on the board, seven of whom are directly elected by the electorate of the Gaeltacht, the other six being appointed by the Minister of Arts, Heritage, Gaeltacht, and the Islands. The Shannon Development Authority is an economic development agency in the west of the country that came into existence in relation to the development of Shannon Airport, but with a wide brief to promote sustainable regional development in the entire region.

3. The Practice of Subnational Democracy

3.1 The Role of Policy Networks and Pressure Groups in Local Government

These have tended to be less well-developed in Ireland compared to other European countries, possibly because of the weakness of the powers of Irish local authorities and the clientelistic nature of local politics. Mediation between the centre and the locality usually occurred through personal contacts with politicians who were present in both national and local politics. Furthermore, the community development sector (outlined below), which is seen as a new form of local governance that has developed in Ireland in the past several years, has developed largely outside the traditional system of local government (Sabel 1996).

[3] The Gaeltacht covers parts of counties Donegal, Mayo, Galway, Kerry, Cork, Meath, and Waterford with an Irish-speaking population of 86,000, all of whom also speak English.

3.2 Critiques of Local Democracy in Ireland

Harvey (1997) summarizes the weaknesses of Irish local government as follows:

- restricted ability to raise its own revenue;
- limited powers and functions;
- the small number of councillors per head of population.

This has attracted a great deal of criticism, and government reports have suggested changes, although Ireland, unlike most other western states, has, until recently, resisted change in this regard. As Coyle comments: 'Ireland is almost unique among its European neighbours in not having implemented any major reform of local government in the post-war years' (1996: 282). In 1993, Barrington commented that 'here in the South [of Ireland] we now have by far the most centralised state in Western or Middle Europe. We are fifty per cent more centralised than the European norm, and over three times as centralised as the leading local democracy, Denmark' (Barrington [1991], quoted in Quinn 1998).

3.2.1 The County Manager System

The county and city manager system was introduced into Ireland in 1929 under the influence of city management models in the United States (Collins and Haslam 1997). The manager is a full-time chief executive with a supporting administrative staff. The key to the system is the division of functions into 'reserved' and 'executive'. Reserved functions are the responsibility of the elected councillors and cover important matters of policy and principle: financial affairs, development plans, passing of by-laws. All other functions are 'executive' and automatically come under the authority of the manager. In theory, the elected members have powers to oversee the managers, and the latter have a duty to assist the elected members. It is generally recognized that the managers, as quasi-permanent,[4] professional, and salaried officials, are in a stronger position than the elected councillors, who are unpaid, part-time, and often transient (Coyle 1996). The manager's position is further enhanced by the fact that his/her appointment is the responsibility of the Local Appointments Commission, a national agency. However he/she may only be dismissed by the Minister for the Environment and Local Government. Elected councillors may, after a two-thirds majority vote, only suspend him/her for incompetence or misconduct and must request the Minister for the Environment to remove him/her from office (Coyle and Sinnott 1992: 75). A survey of regional

---

[4] Until 1991 the county managers were appointed on a permanent basis, but after that date they have been appointed to seven-year terms; nevertheless, this contrasts with the transitory nature of the elected councillors.

and local elites from both the private and public sectors, published in 1992, showed that 73 per cent thought that the county managers wielded power in the county, second to, and almost as much as, government ministers (74 per cent), and more than national party leaders (69 per cent) (Coyle and Sinnott 1992: 92). Although county managers have undoubtedly contributed to the effective and efficient running of local-authority affairs, there is little doubt that this has tended to undermine the role of the councillors and, therefore, of the system of representative democracy at the local level.

3.2.2 Elected Councillors and Clientelism

It has been generally recognized by scholars and commentators that political culture in Ireland, especially at the local level, is characterized by a system of patronage (Collins and Haslam 1997). One of the most important roles of politicians is to secure benefits for either individuals or territories. Most politicians hold a dual mandate: 73 per cent of the TDs (Members of Parliament) who were elected at the 1992 General Election were also members of a local authority, and 90 per cent had been a local councillor at some stage in their political careers (Gallagher and Komito, quoted in Coyle 1996: 294). Unlike the French system of *cumul des mandats*, which elevates local concerns to the national level, the Irish system completely subordinates local politics to the national. This system of central–local relations has, therefore, tended to reinforce rather than reduce the political culture of clientelism. With the emasculation of the political power of local authorities, local communities tend to look to their TD to represent their interests. There has, thus, developed a system of 'brokerage' whereby politicians went straight to the top in Dublin. This in turn reinforced the centralized nature of the Irish system.

3.2.3 Irish Local Government and Local Development

Writing for the Community Directors' Forum, a body concerned with local development, Harvey (1997) points out that:

- local authorities have been unwilling or unable to adopt a developmental role, with negative social consequences;
- the powers given to the local authorities to work with local communities through approved local councils, as given in a 1941 act, fell into disuse;
- local government has not addressed social or economic disadvantage in a strategic way;
- relationships with local authorities have frequently been poor.

3.3 Citizens' Attitudes to Local Government in Ireland

According to the 1996 *Eurobarometer* results, Irish people have a strong sense of identity with their town or village (92 per cent) although they have an even stronger attachment to their country (97 per cent) (*Eurobarometer*, 44, 1996). There is also a strong attachment to the county for sporting purposes. However, there are few direct data on citizens' attitudes toward local government, nor the degree to which they participate in local government. Nevertheless, the electoral turnout figures quoted above (section 2.3) indicate that turnout for local elections is much higher in rural Ireland than it is in the area around Dublin. This suggests that people living in rural Ireland are more attached to local government than those living in the Dublin conurbation. These findings are borne out by an unpublished survey carried out for the Devolution Commission by Lansdowne Market Research.[5] This survey also found that active community involvement is at relatively low ebb. Only one-quarter of the respondents expressed an interest in local politics, and about two-thirds had had no contact with the local council in the previous twelve months. A majority rejected the idea of becoming involved in the local community themselves, with one in five stating that nothing would encourage them to participate. A majority said they knew 'just a little' about their own council and most felt the council did not keep them well informed about its services. Most people felt their own opinions had little or no influence on council decisions. Nevertheless, despite these negative findings, the majority were satisfied with the working of democracy in their area and a majority wished to see councils have more powers.

4. Challenges and Opportunities for Subnational Democracy

The major challenge facing Irish local government in the period since independence has been the transformation of the Irish economy and society since the 1980s. Ireland has gone through a number of phases of economic development. As an independent state, it inherited a legacy of economic underdevelopment and backwardness. First, there was a period of economic nationalism and autarchy, which lasted until the late 1950s, characterized by protectionism and attempts at developing native industry as well as farming. However, this failed to bring economic prosperity and was followed by a change of models and a period of free trade between Britain and other countries and Ireland's entry into the European Economic Community in 1973. The emphasis during this period was on the encouragement of foreign direct investment by multinational companies through tax incentives and the provision of infrastructure (Baker 1987). However, this approach also failed to bring about the sought after prosperity and was accompanied by a rural

---

[5] The Department of the Environment has kindly allowed the author access to this report and has given permission to quote the main findings, but not the detailed results.

exodus, the uneven growth of the area around Dublin, and continuing unemployment and emigration. During all of these phases, local government was marginalized or seen simply from a centralist perspective.

4.1 Attempts at Economic Modernization (1958–)

The Irish government, from 1958 onwards, attempted to 'catch up', economically and socially, with other European nations by way of several programmes of economic expansion (Baker 1987). These programmes had implications for the politico-administrative system, including a degree of regionalization (in the sense of a top-down approach to regional planning). The approach adopted in Ireland in the 1960s was based on the Keynesian model of macroeconomic management, indicative planning, and welfare statism. Economic development was based on the 'growth pole' idea, which meant choosing a region or city as a centre of growth in which investment would be concentrated with the expectation that its growth would have spin-off effects on the surrounding area (Loughlin 1996). This implies a certain amount of economic 'decentralization'. However, in the Irish context two points should be noted. First, the process of distribution remained firmly in the hands of central departments such as the Department of Finance or centrally controlled agencies (known in Ireland as 'semi-state' bodies) such as the Industrial Development Agency (IDA). The local population had little say in the decisions that were taken. Second, the 'growth pole' idea was modified with a concern by government ministers to achieve a 'balanced' growth. What this meant in practice was that the old clientelistic system would not be disrupted too much and that different 'clients' (and not just 'growth poles') would receive the benefits of industrialization. Whichever approach was emphasized, it is clear that they did not serve to enhance the quality of local democracy as key decisions affecting the local societies continued to be taken centrally by politicians or bureaucrats in Dublin.

In the 1960s there was a gradual regionalization of Irish planning (in the sense of top-down regional policies designed by the centre) (Laffan 1995). In 1963 the Local Government (Planning and Development) Act was passed. In 1964 the Minister for the Environment designated planning regions. In the same year *An Foras Forbartha* (The National Institute for Physical Planning and Construction Research) was established (and has since been disbanded). Regional development organizations (RDOs) were also established during this period. Another development was the setting up of regional administrative units such as the regional health authorities. In the 1970s and 1980s several reports recommended local government reform (*Local Government Reorganisation* White Paper, 1971; *More Local Government*, Institute of Public Administration, 1971; *Local Government Discussion Document*, 1973; *Local*

Government Reform, 1985; *Towards a New Democracy: Implications of Local Government Reform*, Muintir na Tire, 1985). However, the regionalization of planning and administration did little to change the pre-existing system. On the contrary, the counties remained the key levels of government even in the RDOs, and central government continued to play the predominant role in final decision-making. In the 1980s, with changes in the local taxation system, local government lost much of its financial resource base and became even more dependent on central government block grants. The reports were, for the most part, ignored by central government, and regionalization continued to be largely cosmetic and uncoordinated (Coyle and Sinnott 1992).

4.2 Ireland and the European Community

Ireland's entry, alongside the United Kingdom and Denmark, into the EEC in 1973 did not significantly modify this state of affairs. Indeed, the centrally managed development programmes of the 1960s were to a large extent designed to prepare for Ireland's entry (Baker 1987). Ireland benefited enormously from membership through the Common Agricultural Policy (CAP) as well as through the European Regional Development Fund (ERDF), which began operation in 1975 (to a large extent as a result of the 1973 enlargement). The early 'project'-based approach of the ERDF (whereby the Commission distributed discrete funds to national governments who then used them for individual projects) was ideally suited to the Irish political culture of clientelism. The 1985 and 1988 reforms of the ERDF that upgraded the role of subnational authorities and moved from a project to a programme-based approach did not radically alter the situation. In fact, they enhanced the centralized nature of the Irish system by declaring Ireland to be a single Objective One priority region. It was argued by the Irish government that this was necessary given the smallness of both the territory and the Irish population, which did not justify a further subdivision into regions. In effect, the National Development Plans were drawn up by the Department of Finance with very little input from any level of local government. Arguably, this was economically beneficial in an earlier period when it was necessary for central government to engage in major economic programmes to build the basic infrastructure for further economic growth.

4.3 Regionalization

The highly centralized Irish approach to EU regional policy attracted a great deal of criticism from the European Commission as well as the European Parliament. John Hume, member of the European Parliament for Northern

Ireland and a committed European federalist, drew up a report for the parliament in which he was highly critical of the lack of a regional level of government in Ireland (European Commission and European Parliament 1987). Within Ireland, too, was a growing regionalist lobby. This manifested its displeasure in the Barrington Report (1991), which recommended a number of government reforms including the setting up of eight indirectly elected regional authorities. The government accepted this recommendation and gave effect to it in the Local Government Act (1991). The new regional authorities came into existence on 1 January 1994. These are statutory bodies (i.e., they are established by Acts of Parliament) and are composed entirely of local councillors selected by the local authorities within the region. The main tasks of the regional authorities are to:

- promote the coordination of the provision of public services in the region;
- promote the consultation between local authorities and other organizations in the region, relating service provision;
- promote the coordination of plans and programmes of government in the region;
- promote public authorities' consideration of the implications' of their decisions, activities, and services on the region as a whole;
- review the overall needs and development requirements of the region;
- review and advise on the implementation of EU Structural and Cohesion Funds in the region;
- review the development plans of the local authorities and, where relevant, the development plans of local authorities in adjoining regions;
- prepare a regional report concerning the above every five years.

Some commentators have dismissed the new regional structures as purely cosmetic and have pointed out that the counties still jealously guard their prerogatives. Quinn, however, comments that 'the implementing structures have been more successful and the consultative process for preparation of the second National Development Plan [submitted to obtain Structural Funds] was more extensive and purposeful' (1998: 11). In general, it seems that the European Union has been a factor encouraging a greater input from the local and regional levels in decision-making in Ireland. Some further recognition to the role of the regional authorities was granted in an amendment to the Order establishing the regional authorities (1991) allowing county councillors appointed to the Committee of the Regions to become members of the authorities.[6] In the same amendment it was stated that, in the appointment of members and alternate members of the Committee of the Regions, there should be an appropriate measure of gender and territorial balance.

---

[6] Statutory Instrument 1998, no. 1.

4.4 Changes in the Irish State and Society

Ireland has been undergoing extensive and radical change since the 1980s. It has the fastest growing GDP in the European Union and its economic success shows no signs yet of slowing down. These changes are due to a number of factors: successful implementation of EU regional funds; a young, dynamic, and well-educated population; a heavy investment in education and training; and a successful exploitation of the development of new technologies such as computer software. However, according to an OECD Report, drawn up by Charles Sabel (1996), a major factor in this success has been the development of an approach to policy-making at the national level based on 'partnership'. This approach to economic and social planning involves the government and the 'social partners' (business and trade unions).

However, the benefits of Ireland's undoubted economic success are unevenly distributed and mask the continuing unemployment and high levels of poverty for a significant minority of the population. Much of this poverty is concentrated in rural areas and in some districts of Irish towns and cities, including Dublin. Some authors have claimed that the local authorities have been unable to tackle the problem with great success (Harvey 1997). They also claim that this has led to the growth of successful local development organizations called area-based partnerships (ABPs), which involve a range of actors in planning in a strategic way to tackle some of these problems, as well as by partnerships working on the EU-funded LEADER programme (Sabel 1996; see case studies below). This approach has been encouraged by central government, especially the Office of the *Taoiseach* (prime minister), which has sought to apply the partnership approach, successful at the national level, to the local level (Quinn 1998). The European Commission has also encouraged this approach in the LEADER programme. According to the OECD Report written by Sabel (1996), this approach, which he terms 'democratic experimentalism' has been highly successful and innovative. The approach adopted by the ABPs is very similar to, and to a large extent modelled on, new approaches to economic development adopted by large firms, that is based on horizontal linkages, teamwork, creative use of knowledge, and the continual redesigning of objectives in terms of continual change. This has led to problems with relating it to traditional local government, as it has developed to a large extent outside the structures and institutions of representative democracy. It is also only fair to point out that traditional local governments operate in a regulatory environment. For example, local authorities have to manage or monitor traffic, construction and land use, and industrial discharges to the environment; and thus they are obliged to constrain the activities of some groups in the community. This, of course, contrasts with the relatively unconstrained activities of the partnership groups. It is also true that county development officers facilitate incoming industries to find a path through various regulatory processes. Finally, it remains the case that the partnership groups are non-elected and therefore non-accountable. Our evaluation of the activities of the local authorities compared with those of the partnerships should therefore be nuanced in this way. Furthermore, in the Lansdowne Market Research survey commissioned by the Devolution Commission (see above), very few local residents had heard of these organizations.

Nevertheless, the Irish government has responded very positively to the community development model and in a number of measures proposes to reform local government by integrating the local-development bodies into a wider system of local planning. In 1992, county enterprise boards were established involving representatives from the local authorities and the community development sector. In June 1996 the Department of the Environment, which has responsibility for local government, issued a document, *The Financing of Local Government in Ireland*, which also noted these trends and recommended that community development functions be devolved to local authorities. The Devolution Commission, which had been set up by the government in 1995, made a strong recommendation in its *Interim Report* that decision-making be further decentralized and that there be improved linkages between the community development groups and local government (Devolution Commission 1996). The government responded by affirming that the role of elected members of local authorities be enhanced in setting policy for local services and giving political leadership to socio-economic development at the local level. It also affirmed that local authorities will be encouraged to develop 'a more structured relationship' with the ABPs and the LEADER groups. The government further issued a White Paper, *Better Local Government—A Programme for Change*, in December 1996, which represents current thinking on the question. The White Paper outlines four core principles of better local government:

- serving the customer better;
- developing efficiency;
- proper resources;
- enhancing democracy.

The last point basically affirms the link between local authorities and community development and expresses the desire to strengthen representative democracy by the involvement of local people in devising new approaches to meet community needs. It recommends that this be institutionalized by setting up between two and five strategic policy committees (SPCs) in each local authority, each under a programme manager. SPCs are to be made up of councillors and local interests (for at least a third). One SPC will be the Community and Enterprise Development Group, of which half the membership will be made up of local-development bodies (Harvey 1997). Finally, the White Paper argues for greater integration, simplification, and reorganization, because of the multiplicity of groups operating at the local level. The Minister for the Environment published the Local Government Bill in June 2000 incorporating these changes as well as those resulting from the June 1999 referendum. The Bill also announced the end of the dual national/local mandate and the direct election of the chair of county and city councils for a five-year term.

Undoubtedly, these developments represent the most ambitious and promising programme of reform of local government in Ireland for decades and, if implemented, should enhance the quality of local democracy. However, the integration of the two streams of local government and community development (ABPs and LEADER) may not be easy. Local government is based on a certain type of organization that is hierarchical, bureaucratic, and traditionally rule-based, while the new community development organizations are based on an approach that is horizontal, non-bureaucratic, innovative, and creative (Sabel 1996). One of the fears of the community development protagonists is that the reforms, especially those influenced by the Department of the Environment, will be simply a means by which traditional local government will take control (and emasculate) the creative community development stream (Harvey 1997). On the other hand, many county councillors look askance at the community development groups as unelected and, therefore, lacking in political legitimacy, which the councillors alone possess as a result of their election through the ballot box.

5. Innovative Approaches to Improving Subnational Democracy[7]

5.1 Area-based Partnerships (ABPs)

- formed in 1991 as limited companies subject to the Companies Act (1991);
- typically a board of directors of eighteen members drawn from:
  - statutory agencies (including national government bureaux),
  - social partners (trade unions, farmers, business associations),
  - community sector (groups active in matters such as welfare and tenants' rights or crime-fighting);
- outside the traditional system of representative local government.

[7] The following draws on Sabel (1996).

5.2 The Pilot Area Programme for Integrated Rural Development (IRD)

- covered the years 1988–90;
- organized by the Department of Agriculture to raise income levels in rural areas;
- based on a local coordinator facilitating a core group of (8–10 members) of representatives of voluntary organizations;
- developed the aim of policy learning and coordination among otherwise isolated groups;
- met with some success in the areas covered.

5.3 The EU LEADER Programme

- there is considerable continuity between this and the IRD;
- part of an EU-wide programme that led, in Ireland, to setting up sixteen local-development 'companies' with a budget of Ir£2–3 million each;
- local actors invited to form partnership companies that were legal companies and not just loose groupings (several of the groups had participated in the IRD, some had existed before IRD, and some were created in response to LEADER).

5.4 County Enterprise Boards (CEBs)

- these were created under the mantle of the Ministry of Enterprise and Employment as locally controlled companies;
- but the ministry exercises greater control over them;
- the board must include representatives from local authorities (which is not the case with the ABPs or LEADER groups).

5.5 Operational Programme for Local Urban and Rural Development (1994–9) and County Strategy Groups (CSGs)

- Operational Programme co-funded by the European Commission and the Irish government;
- creation of county strategy groups (CSGs) as instruments of coordination and consisting of chairs of the CEBs, ABPs, LEADER companies, County Tourism Committees, county managers, and, perhaps eventually, elected local councillors;
- appointment of a Minister for Local Development who is also responsible for European Affairs.

6. *Conclusions*

Local government in Ireland has been traditionally very weak with local authorities exercising few functions, with a limited financial base, and a low level of democratic legitimacy of elected councillors. Ireland has been highly centralized and local government subordinated to the central government. Political culture at the local level has also tended to be clientelistic, and local politics was largely a conduit by which national politicians could have a local base and channel funds or resources to their clients. However, the past ten years or so have seen a transformation of Irish society, the economy, the development of a new political culture, and a new self-confidence on the part of Irish people. A new policy-making style, based on the partnership approach, has been highly successful at the national level and is being applied now, with the encouragement of central government, at the local level. There has been a growth of community development organizations, called area-based partnerships, and also of groups involved in the EU LEADER initiative, which have quite successfully applied the partnership approach to local community development. However, these new groups have developed outside the traditional local-authority system and have not involved local councillors very much. The Irish government wishes to change this and to integrate the two streams in such a way as to enhance representative democracy at the local level. It has embodied these aspirations in a legislative programme that promises to effect real local-government reform for the first time in decades.

References

BAKER, S. (1987). 'Dependency, Ideology and the Industrial Policy of Fianna Fail in Ireland, 1958–1972'. PhD thesis, European University Institute.

BARRINGTON REPORT (1991), *Local Government Reorganisation and Reform*. Dublin: The Stationery Office.

COLLINS, N. and HASLAM, R. (1997). 'Trends Towards Decentralization in the Republic of Ireland'. *Regional and Federal Studies*, 7/3: 165–72.

COYLE, C. (1996). 'Local and Regional Administrative Structures and Rural Poverty', in C. Curtin *et al.* (eds), *Poverty in Ireland. A Political Economy Perspective*. Dublin: Oak Tree Press.

——and SINNOTT, R. (1992). 'Regional Elites, Regional "Powerlessness" and European Regional Policy in Ireland'. *Regional Politics and Policy*, 2/1–2: 71–108.

DEVOLUTION COMMISSION (1996). *Interim Report*. Dublin: The Stationery Office.

——(1997). *Second Report*. Dublin: The Stationery Office.

DoE (Department of the Environment) (1996a). *Financing of Local Government in Ireland*. Dublin: The Stationery Office.

DoE (Department of the Environment) (1996*b*). *Better Local Government: A Programme for Change*. Dublin: The Stationery Office.

DONNELLY, S. (1992). *Poll Position: An Analysis of the 1991 Local Elections*. Dublin: Sean Donnelly.

EUROPEAN COMMISSION and EUROPEAN PARLIAMENT (1987). *Hume Report on the Regional Problems of Ireland*. Document B 910/85, 6 April.

HARVEY, B. (1997). *The Shape of Things to Come? The Implications of Local Government Reform*. Dublin: Community Directors' Forum.

LAFFAN, B. (1995). 'Ireland: a Region without Regions—the Odd Man Out?', in L. Hooghe (ed.), *European Integration, Cohesion Policy, and Subnational Mobilisation*. Oxford: Oxford University Press.

LOUGHLIN, J. (1996). 'Ireland: Nationalism, Regionalisation and Regionalism in Ireland', in G. Färber and M. Forsyth (eds), *The Regions: Factors of Integration or Distintegration in Europe?* Baden-Baden: Nomos, 79–90.

LYONS, F. S. L. (1971). *Ireland since the Famine*. London: Weidenfeld & Nicolson.

QUINN, B. (1998). 'The Evolution of Devolution? Ireland in Transition', paper presented at the conference on 'Europe of the Regions: the Issue of Governance in EU Regional Policy', University of Twente, Enschede, February.

SABEL, C. (1996). *Ireland: Local Partnerships and Social Innovation*. Paris: OECD.

Part 2

THE GERMANIC TRADITION

4

Germany: Federalism under Strain

Udo Bullmann

1. History and Concept of Democracy

1.1 Development and Consolidation of the Concept of Democracy

Under the terms of its constitution (*Grundgesetz* or Basic Law), the Federal Republic of Germany is a democratic and social federal state (Art. 20 I). Its constitutional order at federal as well as at the *Länder* (state) level must conform to the principles of a republican, democratic, and social state governed by the rule of law (Art. 28 I). The *Rechtsstaatsprinzip* (or state-of-law principle) reflects the rejection—already established in nineteenth-century German constitutional thinking—of the absolutist administrative state. In its place is a liberal constitutional order that only permits the exercise of democratically legitimized political power, a power itself limited by civil rights such as the right to religious freedom, freedom of expression and assembly, freedom of the press, and freedom of movement. Interpretation of the Basic Law's *Sozialstaatsprinzip* (principle of the 'social state') is not without controversy. Conservative constitutionalists tend to view it as a non-binding declaration, subordinate to the rule-of-law principle, since, in contrast to the former Weimar constitution, there is no guarantee of social rights in the Basic Law. The left, on the other hand, considers the *Sozialstaatsprinzip*, in the absence of more detailed regulations, to mean that public life in general, including its social and economic aspects, should be organized along democratic and socially responsible lines.

Historically, however, German constitutional thinking was not based on the idea of a sovereign people acting to allow society—or rather the changing majorities within society—to take charge of government. Rather, government and society were conceived as two separate spheres between which balances, mutual checks, and ordered legal relations had to be put in place. The idea of strong government as the guarantor of a successfully functioning polity dates from as far back as the early nineteenth century. About that time, the geographical and functional fragmentation of political power among some three hundred kingdoms, principalities, and city-states under the umbrella of the Holy Roman Empire came to its end. Prussia, in the eighteenth century, had already pioneered in establishing a modern territorial administration. Under Prussian influence, and also under the impact of the occupying French armies, the preconditions for modern statehood were created. After Napoleon's defeat, the Vienna Congress of 1815 attempted to restore the old aristocratic order and consolidated the German territories into thirty-eight states. Two dominant powers remained—the multinational Austrian Empire of the Habsburgs in the south, and Prussia in the north. In Germany, no bourgeois revolution was able to shake this nineteenth-century image of an authoritarian state. After the defeat of the democratic movement in 1848/49, the liberal bourgeoisie concentrated on taking control of municipal government, while the principalities, kingdoms, and what was later the Empire were led by the aristocratic military classes. It was not until the 1860s that the emerging social democracy began to call for a universal and equal right to vote. This right was granted to men in 1871 and extended on a general basis to all the *Länder* after the establishment of the Weimar Republic in the wake of the November revolution of 1918. The short democratic period of the Weimar Republic, which began in 1918/19, ended in the debacle of Nazism, after years of decline. Hitler, installed in 1933 as Chancellor, established a regime organized according to the principle of all-powerful leadership ('*Führerprinzip*') in which democratic government at all levels was abolished. While preparing for the Second World War rearmament was stepped up, and the borders were extended at the expense of Austria, Czechoslovakia, and then Poland. In the twelve years of Nazi rule over 20 million people died in the war and more than 6 million were subject to official persecution and planned murder in Germany and the occupied territories. The so-called Third Reich collapsed as a result of its defeat in the Second World War.

The German Federal Republic of today has embraced a political system in which all state authority emanates from the people (principle of people's sovereignty). The 1949 Basic Law provided for a predominantly representative, parliamentary democracy. Under Article 20 II of this law, state authority is 'exercized by the people through elections and [ballots] and by specific legislative, executive and judicial bodies'. The political parties are explicitly recognized in the constitution as helping to express the political will of the people. Members of parliament, however, are not bound by orders and instructions and, as representatives of the people as a whole, should be subject only to their own conscience.

In 1948–9 the Parliamentary Council—the constituent assembly—debated whether or not to incorporate referendums and plebiscites into the Basic Law. In the end, however, it decided not to establish this form of direct democracy for specific issues and to forego the direct election of political leaders. The reason for such scepticism towards the direct expression of sovereignty is often explained in historical terms, given the impact of National Socialist agitation on the masses. In the aftermath of the Second World War and at the beginning of the East–West conflict Western allies as well as influential German politicians seemed also to be in fear of a possible rise of left-wing movements. At federal level, this historical scepticism towards direct democracy has persisted to this day. German unification, for example, was effected not in the way originally conceived in the Basic Law—by plebiscite on the adoption of a new constitution—but by the simple accession to the Federal Republic of the re-established east German *Länder*. Similarly, the European treaties and the Maastricht and Amsterdam amendments were not adopted by plebiscite or advance referendum, but solely on the basis of decisions taken by the representative federal authorities—the *Bundestag* and *Bundesrat*. The *Sozial Demokratische Partei Deutschlands* (SPD) and *Bündnis '90/Die Grünen* (Alliance '90/The Greens) which form the new German government since the election of September 1998 promised in their coalition agreement to introduce more elements of direct democracy (petitions and referendums) at the federal level. More detailed suggestions or bills are still to come.

One of the inalienable pillars of constitutional order in contemporary Germany is the federal structure of government. The principles of a republican, democratic, and social state governed by the rule of law also apply in the *Länder*. Local authorities are guaranteed the right to local self-government. One of the Basic Law's few direct-democracy provisions requires a referendum to confirm any modification of *Länder* boundaries.

From a contemporary viewpoint, government practice in the Federal Republic of Germany is marked by the interaction—sometimes cooperative, sometimes fraught with conflict—of the three political levels (federal, *Länder*, and local authority). The political parties exercise a certain influence on policy-making and are themselves the port of call for demands from strong organized interest groups (particularly business associations and trade unions). Traditionally, grass-roots input takes the form not so much of direct political participation as largely voluntary involvement in societies, associations, and political parties. However, the citizens' action groups and new social movements that have come to the fore since the 1970s have changed this picture, leading to the re-emergence of direct-democracy forms of political participation. A survey taken a few years ago, for example, showed that while just 32 per cent of those Germans questioned said they could envisage joining a political party, 51 per cent said they could imagine taking part in a citizens' action group (Roth 1997).

This indicates that, in Germany as in other western European countries, there is a trend away from fixed commitment to political parties towards spontaneous, less binding involvement in single-issue initiatives. Radical approaches to democracy that occurred during the last decades—such as the ecological movement or the people's movements in East Germany—nonetheless often resulted in new departures and even a broadening of the spectrum of political parties (a case in point being the establishment of *Die Grünen* (The Green Party), known today, following its fusion with sections of former German Democratic Republic (GDR) people's movements, as Alliance '90/The Greens). Since the 1970s, however, Germany's political culture has also drawn on a range of vivid, often internationally active and well-connected, non-governmental organizations.

1.2 Democracy in the Länder and Local Authorities

1.2.1 German Federalism and the Länder

The division of the German territory into *Länder*—and thus the principle of federal government—very much pre-dates the democratic republic. In the nineteenth century, German federalism developed initially as a confederation of sovereign German principalities and free cities. The German Confederation—including Austria—was established in 1815 and lasted until Austria's defeat by Prussia in 1866. Under Prussian hegemony, a North German Confederation was then established (1866–71) before the founding, in 1871, of the German Empire as a *kleindeutsche* confederation including the southern German states, but not Austria. It was not until 1919, with the establishment of the Weimar Republic, that a democratically legitimate German federal state emerged. Compared with the federal set-up in Germany today, however, the Weimar Republic more resembled a unitary state.

In Europe, political modernization was often linked to the emergence of territorial authority and the establishment of nation-states with clearly defined borders, a sense of national awareness among the people, and a viable administration. In Germany, this came about by the precursors of the nation-state, which, retrospectively, we can now see were found at what is today the *Länder* level. As a result, German constitutional theory reflected this by developing very early on a specifically federal view of how tasks should be divided between the various political levels. From the German Confederation of the early nineteenth century to the present day, this has thus presumed specific *Länder* responsibilities unless the constitution explicitly states that competence for a particular matter lies at a higher level (the Confederation, later the Empire, and then the federal state). Thus, even in the 1871 Constitution of the German Empire, we find the structural characteristics of German (administrative) federalism that are still crucial today—administration is a matter for the *Länder*, which have to enforce federal laws in areas for which the federal government is responsible. Conversely, the *Länder* have to be involved in the formation of federal legislation.

Unlike the federal system in the United States, which was already well known and of interest for German observers during the nineteenth century, the German model eschewed a dual political structure with state systems working in parallel. German federalism rather gave preference to a system of interlinked (instead of separated) competences with a specific division of labour and responsibilities between the two levels of government. This solution also reflected the historical development of modern German statehood. The German *Länder* have always had a twofold key role in this 'organicist' settlement: they served internally as a focus of integration for people living there, and externally, as the basis for the establishment or re-establishment of the nation-state (Bullmann, Goldsmith, and Page 1997).

1.2.2 Local Self-government

This is anchored in today's German Basic Law but also has its roots in the early nineteenth century. Civic statutes began to be adopted—first in Prussia (in 1808), then in other German states—to regulate the right of citizens to exercise self-government in matters relating to municipal administration. In Prussia, local councils were established under the three-class voting system. Political rights to local self-government were also designed to preserve the feudal and aristocratic structure of the *Länder* by using internal reform as a means to head off any attempts at revolt, and as a means to improve the economic basis for the levying of government taxes (not least in order to finance the war against the Napoleonic armies).

The bourgeoisie used the local level to develop their freedoms and economic interests and—in contrast to other European nations—more or less came to terms with the pre-democratic structure of the state. Strong city government arose under these conditions but the powers of local government were used in an ambiguous manner. Despite continued friction with the feudal state bureaucracy, the towns evolved into political entities, facilitating economic development and industrialization during the nineteenth century. The local authorities provided the manufacturing infrastructure (e.g., water, gas and electricity supply, and transport), ensured the circulation of goods and capital (banks and credit institutions, customs associations), and made the first moves towards social policy (e.g., health, industrial safety, and housing). On the other hand, the working poor and rising labour movements had been subject to oppression and were denied universal suffrage until 1919 (whereas it was granted to all adult men in the Empire from 1871). The municipal framework had also been the place where the working classes were progressively 'socialized', long before reform policies in the nineteenth century were introduced (Leibfried and Tennstedt 1985).

Thus, in practice, the communes became, from an early date, an important arena of social conflict, before they could serve as a source of modernization and problem-solving for society as a whole. Their expanding activities finally resulted in an extensive range of public policies which were partly taken on by state and central government agencies later on. Against this backdrop, the original concept of limited self-government which aimed ambivalently at containing the activities of the bourgeoisie to the local level, whilst keeping higher political authorities immune to more radical claims for democracy, was undermined. It was unable to stand up to the impact of social change in the long run. Step by step the restrictions to local democracy became politicized and successfully transformed by amendments to voting rights, the spread of the professional classes, and the emergence of political parties.

Today, the constitution guarantees local authorities the right to deal with all local matters affecting the municipality (Art. 28 II Basic Law). They are provided with a general competence to undertake all public affairs for their territories in so far as the rights and duties are not already expressly assigned to or reserved by law for other authorities. It would not, therefore, be permissible for the state to list local-government tasks.

2. The Institutional Expression of Democracy

2.1 The Federation and Interaction of the Various Political and Administrative Levels

The Federal Republic of Germany is a parliamentary democracy; its government is formed by the majority in the *Bundestag*. Since unification, there have been 656 members of parliament (not counting the thirteen *Überhangmandate* in the current parliamentary session 1998–2002; these are seats gained as a result of votes for a specific candidate over and above the seats to which a party is entitled by the number of votes cast for the party in the specific *Land*). Parliament is elected every four years under a system of personalized proportional representation ('*Personalisiertes Verhältnis-wahlrecht*'). Each elector has two votes, the first one for a constituency representative to be elected on a first-past-the-post-system, the second for the party list of his choice. According to this system half of the elected German MPs won their constituencies, and half were additionally recruited from party lists drawn up in the various *Länder*). Parties may only enter the *Bundestag* if they gain at least 5 per cent of the popular vote or three direct constituency seats. The majority in the *Bundestag*—as a rule the product of a coalition—elects the federal chancellor, who puts forward cabinet members for appointment by the federal president. The chancellor is constitutionally by far the strongest political figure who determines the broad lines of government policy.

TABLE 4.1 Central, *Länder*, and local government staff (full- and part-time), 1998

Level of government	No. of staff	%
Federation	515,992	11
Länder (states)	2,361,411	52
Local level	1,649,637	37
Total	4,527,040	100

Source: Statistisches Jahrbuch 1999.

Current legislation focuses on the federation. From the Basic Law, it might be assumed that the *Länder* basically hold the legislative remit, with federal-level responsibility in only a few, well-defined areas ('exclusive legislation', e.g., foreign affairs and defence). In political practice, however, this relationship has been reversed in favour of the federal level. Most domestic policy comes under what is termed 'concurrent legislation'. Here, the right to legislate lies in priority with the federation. Even in areas originally within the remit of the *Länder* (e.g., higher education), the federation has been able to expand its power using a right to adopt 'framework legislation'. The reason for this shift in remit was the constitutional requirement for uniform living conditions, a precept to which the Federal Constitutional Court also gave high priority. On the other hand, the strength of the *Länder's* position lies in its broad involvement in federal legislation. Roughly 60 per cent of federal laws are dependent on endorsement by the *Länder* chamber, the *Bundesrat*.

Overall, Germany's political and administrative system is marked by a highly interwoven division of responsibilities between the various levels. While, by virtue of its pre-eminence in legislative matters, the federation also definitively sets the level of government revenue, the *Länder* and local authorities are responsible for the lion's share of government administration and public expenditure. (See Tables 4.1 and 4.2.)

2.2 The Länder

With a few exceptions (Bavaria and, to some extent, Hesse), the western German, post-war *Länder* are artificial constructions that have no significant history as territorial units. In contrast, the five eastern German *Länder* that were re-established in 1990 almost exactly within their 1946 borders are largely traditional historical and geographical entities. Major differences exist among the sixteen *Länder* in terms of size, population, and economic clout, ranging from the largest, North Rhine-Westphalia, with a population of over

TABLE 4.2   Public expenditure, 1999*

Level of government	DM (million)	%
Federation	522,670	40.2
Länder (states)		37.1
Local level	294,852	22.7
Total	1,298,408	100

* according to budget plans.
Source: *Statistisches Jahrbuch 1999.*

17 million, to the three *Länder* of Berlin, Hamburg, and the smallest, Bremen (population 680,000), which have the status of city-states.

The position of the *Länder* within the federal German political system stems on the one hand from the resources they can muster to orchestrate independent *Länder* policies and, on the other, from their participatory rights at federal level.

The *Länder* exercise their rights of participation in federal policy above all via the *Bundesrat*, whose main remit is the co-determination of federal legislation. The *Länder* representation's remit increases the more the *Länder*'s own interests are involved. Legislation to change the constitution requires a two-thirds majority in the *Bundesrat*. Law affecting *Länder* finances, their administrative sovereignty, areas of joint government responsibility, or a modification of *Länder* boundaries requires an absolute majority. For all other bills, the *Bundesrat* is free to file objections, which may, however, be rejected by a majority in the *Bundestag*. If the *Bundestag* and *Bundesrat* cannot agree on legislation requiring approval, a mediation committee consisting of sixteen members from both houses is convened under the terms of the constitution. The *Bundesrat* itself has the power to initiate bills, which are then transferred to the *Bundestag* for decision.

In contrast to a senate, the members of the *Bundesrat* are not directly elected, but are delegated by the *Länder* governments. They are cabinet members bound by instructions and must cast en bloc the votes of the federal *Land* in question. The distribution of votes among the *Länder* is laid down in the constitution. Table 4.3 shows how the votes are distributed following the changes after unification; the third column gives the current political majorities (Spring 2000).

In the main, the *Länder* have exclusive legislative competence for areas such as cultural policy (particularly schools and education), radio and television, municipal affairs, and police law. In all other fields of domestic policy, the *Länder* must give their own slant to policy frameworks set out at federal level; they do this via complementary co-legislation and by pooling their financial

TABLE 4.3 *Länder* representation in the *Bundesrat*, spring 2000

Land	Votes	Government
Baden-Württemberg	6	CDU + FDP
Bavaria	6	CSU
Berlin	4	CDU + SPD
Brandenburg	4	SPD
Bremen	3	SPD + CDU
Hamburg	3	SPD + Alliance '90/The Greens
Hesse	5	CDU + FDP
Mecklenburg-West Pomerania	3	SPD + PDS
Lower Saxony	6	SPD
North Rhine-Westphalia	6	SPD + Alliance '90/The Greens
Rhineland-Palatinate	4	SPD + FDP
Saarland	3	CDU
Saxony	4	CDU
Saxony-Anhalt	4	SPD + Alliance '90/The Greens
Schleswig-Holstein	4	SPD + Alliance '90/The Greens
Thuringia	4	CDU
Total	69	

CDU, *Christlich-Demokratische Union* (Christian Democratic Union); FDP, *Freie Demokratische Partei* (Free Democratic Party); CSU, *Christlich Soziale Union* (Christian Social Union); SPD, *Sozialdemokratische Partei Deutschlands* (Social Democratic Party of Germany); PDS, *Partei des Demokratischen Sozialismus* (former *Sozialistische Einheitspartei Deutschlands* of the GDR).

and administrative resources. A horizontal financial-equalization scheme exists among the *Länder* themselves, which largely levels out differences in tax revenue.

The *Länder* constitutions that came into force after the Second World War in the American, French, and, indeed, Soviet zones generally contained more elements of direct democracy (popularly initiated legislation and/or various forms of referendums). This was more than the Basic Law or the *Länder* constitutions adopted in the British occupation zone (which covered northern Germany, except Bremen). It has taken until the 1990s to make changes on any large scale to *Länder* and local-authority constitutions strengthening direct methods in all federal *Länder*. (See Table 4.4 which shows the current levels of government.)

2.3 The Local Authorities

Under constitutional law, local authorities are public bodies directly related to *Land* level, and as such are constituent parts of the *Länder*. However, in

TABLE 4.4   Levels of government

Level	No.
Länder (states)	16 (incl. 3 city-states)
Kommunen (local authorities)	
Landkreise (counties)	323
Kreisfreie Städte (non-county urban municipalities)	116
Kreisangehörige Gemeinde (county-constituent municipalities)	14.511

terms of the constitutional understanding of democracy, and in political practice, they may be regarded as an independent third level (or fourth if the European Union is counted) of the political and administrative system.

Local authorities' current remit is very varied. It ranges from the provision of basic economic and social necessities and the building of public infrastructure to comprehensive, local development planning. Its main focus is on social affairs (housing, social and youth welfare, nursery schools, hospitals, senior citizens), education (schools, adult education centres), leisure (promotion of associations, sports facilities, swimming pools), business development and environmental policy (e.g., business parks, technology centres, waste policy). About two-thirds of real public investment goes to local authorities. Local public utilities (e.g., gas, water, electricity, local transport, refuse collection) play a major role here.

Counties have a supralocal remit, which would overstretch the administrative capacity of the mainly smaller county-constituent municipalities. In non-county urban municipalities, both administrative levels coincide. One-third of local authority revenue comes from taxation, one-third from government allocations (particularly from the *Länder*), and the remainder via levies, contributions, and other income. The eastern German municipalities, which have a narrower tax base, are much more dependent on government allowances.

Local authorities are suffering financially as a result of the substantial growth in social welfare costs caused by continued mass unemployment. At the same time, the past few years have seen a decline in local-authority tax revenues, primarily because of government income tax incentives (with a local-authority share of 15 per cent).

Municipal statutes are structured within the framework of the Basic Law under *Land* legislation. Different municipal traditions, not to mention the influence of the Allies, resulted in the establishment of a number of basic variants, although the gaps between these are now narrowing. The differences relate largely to the local statute, in particular how the executive is set up and how it relates to the municipal council. Differences are also found in how the council is elected and in direct rights of grass-roots participation.

Municipal (as well as county) councils were given the strongest position in the British-influenced northern German *Ratsverfassung* (council constitution) adopted in North Rhine-Westphalia and Lower Saxony. Here, the council was given an all-encompassing remit. A full-time local executive, acting for a fixed term of office, was made responsible for administering council policy implementation.

In contrast, the southern German council-mayoral constitutions (Bavaria, Baden-Württemberg) are characterized by the strong position of the directly elected mayor, who also heads the administration and chairs the municipal council and all its committees. Proportional representation is used for council elections, with uninominal elements allowing voters to amend the order of candidates proposed. It is thus permitted to pool votes for candidates on one list (*kumulieren*) or to distribute them among candidates from different lists (*panaschieren*, ticket-splitting). In a lesser form, this variant is also practised in the Rhenish mayoral constitutions (Rhineland-Palatinate, Saarland, and rural municipalities in Schleswig-Holstein), although here mayors used to be traditionally elected by the council, which is itself elected under proportional representation.

Under the *Magistrat* constitution (Hesse, Bremerhaven, and, formally, in towns in Schleswig-Holstein), the council elects not only the full-time mayor but also the *Magistrat* as a collective body to head the administration. The *Magistrat* is made up of full-time *Beigeordnete* (executives) to run the administration and honorary members elected according to the relative strength of the political parties in the council. The municipal council is elected under proportional representation. In Hesse, which used to be a typical *Land* representing the *Magistrat* form, the CDU/FDP coalition used its period in office (1987–91 and since 1999) twice to remodel the constitution towards the southern prototype. Both times the governing majority took over elements which personalized the voting system (direct election of mayors and county chief executives in 1991, *kumulieren* and *panaschieren* after 1999). But unlike the provisions in Baden-Württemberg (from the very beginning) and Bavaria (after recent demands and struggles from the grass-roots) they deliberately refused to strengthen the participatory rights of the electorate at the same time.

In contrast to the northern German council constitution and the *Magistrat* constitution, the southern German variant contained elements of direct democracy from the very outset. These took the form of public petitions and referendums. In the 1990s these arrangements have been transposed, with various modifications (quorums, restrictions on the subject matter), to the other *Länder*. The reforms of the past few years have also resulted in greater conformity between arrangements for the 'top job' in the administration. Municipal statutes in all the *Länder* now provide for direct elections of mayors to head the local administration.

In eastern Germany a democratic local-authority constitution was promulgated as early as 1990 to cover the whole of what was then the German Democratic Republic (GDR). This constitution comprised both traditional elements and various components taken from western models. The five new *Länder* now each have their own local constitutions that correspond more to the basic southern German variant. Here, direct-democracy features have also been introduced, such as various forms of public petition and referendums.

Thus, in the 1990s, all of the *Länder* have taken on board main elements of the direct forms of participation originally found only in southern German local authorities. This is especially true for the spread out of personalized voting schemes. The mayors in all the *Länder* are now directly elected, resulting in lasting changes particularly to northern German local-authority constitutions.

2.4 The Role of the Political Parties

Although the political interrelationships in the German federal state make for a high degree of consensus democracy, political competition is assured in the first instance by the political parties. Parties in opposition at federal level are regularly in power in individual *Länder* and local authorities. As a result, they are also obliged to work together within the federal context. Conversely, the parties also use their power in *Länder* and local-authority governments as an opportunity to develop and promote alternatives to federal policies.

Until well into the 1970s, the German federal party system was marked by the dominance of three political groups: the *Christlich-Demokratische Union/Christlich Soziale Union* (CDU/CSU, Christian Democratic Union/Christian Social Union), the *Sozialdemokratische Partei Deutschlands* (SPD, Social Democratic Party of Germany), and the *Freie Demokratische Partei* (FDP, Free Democratic Party). The ecology movement spawned an additional force at national level—The Greens, known now as Alliance '90/The Greens since their fusion with some sections of the former GDR civil rights movement. Since unification, the *Partei des Demokratischen Sozialismus* (PDS, Party of Democratic Socialism), the successor to the former (communist) GDR state party, has also been represented in the *Bundestag*. On the right-wing fringes, parties such as the *Republikaner* (Republicans), the *Nationaldemokratische Partei Deutschlands* (NDP, National Democratic Party of Germany), or the *Deutsche Volksunion* (DVU, German People's Union) fail to cross the 5 per cent hurdle in national elections. Following unification, the CDU and FDP absorbed their eastern German counterparts of the same name that had formerly been part of the GDR machinery of state as so-called 'block' parties under *Sozialistische Einheitspartei Deutschlands* (SED, Socialist Unity Party of Germany) hegemony. Membership of the five parties represented in the

TABLE 4.5   Party seats in the federal parliament, 1998

	Winners of constituency	Party lists at *Land* level	Total seats	Seats according to PR[*]	'Excess seats'
SPD	212	86	298	285	13
CDU	74	124	198	198	—
CSU	38	9	47	47	—
Alliance '90/ The Greens	—	47	47	47	—
FDP	—	43	43	43	—
PDS	4	32	36	36	—
Total	328	341	669	656	—

[*] PR, proportional representation.
Source: Deutscher Bundestag (1999).

Bundestag is currently as follows: CDU: 657,643; CSU: 179,647; SPD: 817,650; Alliance '90/The Greens: 46,410; FDP: 80,431; and PDS: 105,029 (Wiesendahl 1997; Zeuner 1997).

Since the federal republic was founded, the CDU—and its sister party the CSU, which operates only in Bavaria—have been the driving force in federal politics; with the exception of the SPD/FDP coalition of 1969–82 and the recent development with the coalition of SPD and Alliance '90/The Greens since autumn 1998, the federal chancellor has come from the CDU as the main party of government. Lasting changes to the constitution were adopted during the only CDU/CSU/SPD 'grand coalition' government of 1966–9 (e.g., the 'emergency powers' provision [*Notstandsgesetze*] and the expansion of broad-based business taxation arrangements, incorporating the budget policy of the *Länder* and the local authorities). (Table 4.5.)

As things stood until the last federal election of September 1998, ten of the sixteen *Land* governments were SPD-led, giving the opposition in Bonn at that time a majority in the *Bundesrat*. After Gerhard Schröder was elected chancellor, the SPD and Green coalition lost the following election in Hesse mainly because of struggles about new federal legislation which intended to extend the full status of citizenship to foreign residents. Thus, the new majority in the *Bundestag* lost its majority in the *Bundesrat*. The situation became even worse for the SPD after the retreat of party leader and finance minister Oskar Lafontaine in early 1999. The party lost the Saarland government and had to face dramatic results in Saxony and Thuringia where the SPD was outdistanced not only by the governing CDU but also by the former communist PDS which gained profits from the new coalition's weaknesses. The picture changed again by early 2000 when the recovering CDU was racked with the republic's so far greatest party donation scandal as a result of which former

Chancellor Kohl lost his role as honorary chairman and several CDU leaders, including party group leader and Kohl's succeeding chairman Schäuble, had to resign.

All the parties see *Land* politics, in particular, as an important field of recruitment for federal-level jobs. Although prevailing trends indicate a decline in the importance of party strongholds, geographical and cultural factors continue to influence electoral preferences. The SPD is stronger in Protestant and industrial areas, while the CDU/CSU dominates in rural regions. Even the political work done in local authorities, to a very large extent unpaid, is now crucially influenced by parties represented federally, although, particularly in smaller municipalities, there are still a considerable number of independent electoral groups.

The number of representatives in *Land* parliaments as well as of councillors in municipal assemblies shows that the conservative CDU/CSU is the leading party in German politics (Table 4.6). The SPD follows closely in *Länder* parliaments and keeps up with the Conservatives in cities with more than 100,000 inhabitants. Alliance '90/The Greens is nationwide the third important party in the *Länder* and communes, significantly supressed only by the PDS in eastern Germany.

Current trends show turnouts of about 80 per cent for *Bundestag* elections, although the figure for *Land* and local elections is some 10–15 per cent lower (Table 4.7). Turnout at direct mayoral elections is sometimes less than 30 per cent, and the larger the municipality the lower the turnout. The general trend is downwards at all levels, one reason for which is given as the advancing phenomenon of 'social disintegration' (Niedermayer 1997). Since the beginning of 1996, citizens from other EU states have had the right to vote and stand as candidates in local elections. Attempts by some SPD-led *Länder* to extend local voting rights to foreign inhabitants from non-EU countries have up to now been thwarted by the Federal Constitutional Court.

The 1990s have seen the resurgence of a debate—more or less dormant since the 1970s—on the strengthening of internal party democracy. Against the backdrop of shrinking membership, direct forms of participation by party members have been stepped up but, to some extent, have lagged far behind practices in other European countries. Plebiscitary elements such as possible or occasional members' ballots or member surveys (as the Greens have done since 1980, the SPD on an optional basis since 1993 on specific vacant posts, the CDU on some similar decisions at *Land* level, and the FDP on a planned change to the Basic Law regarding large-scale bugging operations) are not features of everyday political life and, in the era of media-led democracy, also run counter to the prevailing trend towards centralizing decisions on policy-making and the filling of vacant posts.

TABLE 4.6   Party seats in the *Länder* parliaments, spring 2000

Land[a]	CDU/ CSU	SPD	FDP	Alliance '90/ The Greens	PDS	Rep, DVU	Others	Total
BW (1996)	69	39	14	19	—	14	—	155
BA (1998)	123[b]	67	—	14	—	—	—	204
BE (1999)	76	42	—	18	33	—	—	169
BB (1999)	25	37	—	—	22	5[c]	—	89
HB (1999)	42	47	—	10	—	1	—	100
HH (1997)	46	54	—	21	—	—	—	121
HE (1999)	50	46	6	8	—	—	—	110
MWP (1998)	24	27	—	—	20	—	—	71
LS (1998)	62	81	—	12	—	—	—	155
NRW (1995)	89	108	—	24	—	—	—	221
RP (1996)	41	43	10	7	—	—	—	101
SAA (1999)	26	25	—	—	—	—	—	51
SAX (1999)	76	14	—	—	30	—	—	120
SAX-A (1998)	28	47	—	—	25	16[c]	—	116
SH (2000)	33	41	7	5	—	—	3[d]	89
TH (1999)	49	18	—	—	21	—	—	88
Total	859	736	37	138	151	36	3[d]	1960

[a] BW, Baden-Württemberg; BA, Bavaria; BE, Berlin; BB, Brandenburg; HB, Bremen; HH, Hamburg; HE, Hesse; MWP, Mecklenburg-West Pomerania; LS, Lower Saxony; NRW, North Rhine-Westphalia; RP, Rhineland-Palatinate; SAA, Saarland; SAX, Saxony; SAX-A, Saxony-Anhalt; SH, Schleswig-Holstein; TH, Thuringia.
[b] Seats of CSU.
[c] Seats of the DVU.
[d] Seats of the South Schleswig Voters List (*Südschleswiger Wählerverband*), a list of the Danish minority in Schleswig-Holstein.

Source: Deutscher Bundestag (2000).

TABLE 4.7   Councillors in German municipalities with more than 10,000 inhabitants, 1997

No. in municipality	Councillors		Parties and electoral groups						
	Total numbers								
	No. councillors	Female councillors	CDU/ CSU	SPD	FDP	Alliance '90/ The Greens	PDS	Independent	Indepent Green
>1,000,000	407	159	164	140	2	59	34	1	1
500,000–1,000,000	712	243	256	314	11	102	1	16	—
200,000–500,000	1,715	537	636	653	28	191	108	35	16
100,000–200,000	2,339	719	865	900	65	227	80	117	20
>100,000	5,173	1,658	1,921	2,007	106	579	223	169	37
50,000–100,000	5,128	1,353	1,971	1,981	113	415	149	328	53
20,000–50,000	17,627	4,064	7,104	6,278	492	1,138	535	1,497	291
10,000–20,000	23,837	4,911	9,597	8,093	637	1,241	468	3,174	331
Total	51,765	11,986	20,593	18,359	1,348	3,373	1,393	5,168	712

Source: Deutscher Stäatetag (1998).

3. Regional and Local Democracy in Practice

3.1 The Role of Policy Networks

A feature of local and regional democracy is the presence of 'networks' of players involved; this is a vertical and horizontal phenomenon pervading the entire political and administrative system.

For example, the regular meetings between specific ministries (e.g., the conference of culture ministers who are responsible for education policy) have developed into an important working interface between the federation and the *Länder* at which the preliminary work is done on far-reaching decisions and coordinated with the views expressed by the *Länder* governments. It generally remains for the *Land* parliaments merely to endorse the findings.

Local interests are represented by three umbrella organizations: the *Deutscher Städtetag* (German Association of Towns) representing larger municipalities; the *Deutscher Städte- und Gemeindebund*—German Federation of (county-constituent) Towns and (smaller) Municipalities); and the *Deutscher Landkreistag* (German Association of Counties).The spokespersons of these organizations are usually local politicians from the two main parties, CDU and SPD, who seek as broad a consensus as possible from a local viewpoint. In doing so, they are prepared to accept occasional disputes with the party at federal level or with their *Land* governments but the position they stand for is, due to consensus-seeking procedures, often emasculated in advance.

Many networks are set up by specialized associations to exert influence on specific policy areas; in social policy, for example, these include agencies active in non-governmental welfare work, with the churches playing an influential role.

3.2 Interest Groups

The aim of organized interest groups is generally to influence the decisions and results of the political and administrative system. In government systems run on federal lines, therefore, there is a multitier system of associations exerting an influence at federal, *Land*, and local level. The associations focus their organizational energies on the level of government most suited to the interests they represent. Thus, the major industrial associations are active mainly at federal level, where business and labour relations are largely regulated. In the education sector, associations (e.g., parent groups) operate mainly at *Land* level since the *Länder* are responsible for cultural policy. The lobby activities of sectoral associations and large groups of companies reflect the economic profile of the *Länder*, which, for their part, seek to carve out an image for themselves as a good location for industry, be it cars, information and communication technology, or the media.

At local level too, there is a wide range of organized interest groups, particularly in economic, employment, and social policy. Local industry is represented by chambers of industry and commerce (as mandatory-membership agencies under public law), which also play a crucial role in vocational training. Other important players at local level include trade unions, citizens' action groups, self-help groups, and charitable associations, which are mainly involved in the provision of social infrastructure. For local industry, it is particularly important that Germany has a wide network of decentralized public or cooperatively run banks and savings banks that, apart from offering the lion's share of private banking services, generally also grant loans to small and medium-sized businesses.

In contrast to, say, Austria, associations in Germany are more pluralist, and, while they are also generally committed to prevailing political currents, affiliation is not as clear-cut as in Germany's southern neighbour. The *Länder* and local authorities have institutional powers that are strong enough to play a dominant role in the various network structures. The extent to which they use these powers at the decentralized level to moderate and direct by laying down substantive, result-driven specifications is often more a question of style on the part of the players and groups in government than of political hue.

3.3 Critiques of Regional and Local Democracy in Germany

Both the political and academic domains now largely agree to see benefits in decentralized or regionalized government. German conservatism as represented by the CDU/CSU had traditionally closer links with the Roman Catholic Church and laid stress on the subsidiarity principle (*Subsidiaritätsprinzip*), which finds its origins in Catholic doctrines that give preference to smaller societal entities, especially to the family (*Katholische Soziallehre*, see for example the encyclical *Quadragesimo Anno* of Pope Pius XI). The CDU/CSU has therefore usually taken a more federal than centralist tack. Historically, social democracy and trade unions looked more to the nation-state, but the past few decades—the result of experience of government and of crisis management—have seen a shift to a pro-federal approach. The citizens' action groups and new social movements of the 1970s—culminating in the establishment of the Green Party—sought grass-roots democracy and thus, from the very outset, a stronger local level.

Academic critics object that German federalism is a 'crypto-unitarist state' in which the *Länder* no longer enjoy adequate scope to modulate their policies (Abromeit 1992). Following unification, the establishment of five relatively small *Länder* in eastern Germany has sometimes been considered to have weakened federal structures, given the dependence of these *Länder* on redistribution from central government. On the other hand, however, this view is countered by the impact—both real and symbolic—of the existence of the new *Länder* in integrating the people living in eastern Germany.

Criticism also continues to be directed at the fact that the unification process did not result in more sustained backing for elements of direct democracy; a demand also voiced by popular movements in eastern Germany at the time of the constitutional debate ('round table' democracy, see Nassmacher 1997). Initiatives of the red and green federal government are still expected. That said, some commentators have been positive in their assessment, citing the emergence of channels of direct democracy in the *Länder* and local authorities in the 1990s (Jung 1998).

As things stand, the main complaint of the *Länder* and local authorities themselves is their shortage of funding; the result, they say, of misguided tax policy at federal level. On the other hand, their spending patterns expose them to criticism particularly from the liberal economic wing, with calls for them to trim their administration and privatize services. Criticism expressed by local and regional authorities is recently directed also against the new federal SPD/Alliance '90/The Greens coalition which dedicated itself to rigid cost-cutting policies since the former minister of finance and SPD party leader Oskar Lafontaine resigned from office. Some of the SPD *Land* politicians claim with regard to social issues for better balanced budget policies and especially demand to reintroduce a wealth tax (entitled to the *Länder*) which was abolished under Chancellor Kohl after the Constitutional Court condemned the former regulation for being partly unconstitutional in the mid 1990s.

3.4 Citizens' Attitudes

Surveys carried out in selected areas of both western and eastern Germany in the mid 1990s show that, generally, ordinary people have a considerable interest in local politics. Seventy per cent of those questioned in eastern Germany said they were interested in local politics (compared with 68 per cent interested in politics in general). In western Germany, 64 per cent expressed an interest in local politics and 71 per cent in politics in general.

Sixty-five per cent of western Germans said they were basically satisfied with democracy in Germany; only 38 per cent of eastern Germans could say the same. Figures for the local level are less divergent, with 51 per cent of those questioned in western Germany saying they were happy with the services of local politics, compared with 47 per cent in the east. Substantial differences emerge in the assessment of individual local authorities; the satisfaction rate in eastern Germany ranges from a high of 75 per cent to a low of 27 per cent.

In western Germany this ranges between 75 per cent and 26 per cent. Breaking down these figures into assessments of specific players at the local level, municipal administrations come off best (with an average satisfaction level of almost 75 per cent in western Germany and over 66 per cent in the east). People are also positively disposed towards senior local officials and local councils, well ahead of the local parties (46 per cent satisfaction rate in eastern Germany and 52.6 per cent in the west), although the widest range of assessment is found here (between 27.3 per cent and 64.1 per cent in the east and between 35 per cent and almost 75 per cent in western Germany) (Cusack and Wessels 1996).

The figures in this study demonstrate the continued differences in political culture between western and eastern Germany and also clearly show that people's attitudes to local democracy performance and the players involved can vary substantially from one case to the next. Only cautious generalizations may be drawn, however, given the size of the sample and the differing local conditions on the ground.

Both ordinary citizens and local politicians regard the economic situation as the main concern. Ordinary people who have been surveyed, however, attach primary importance to unemployment, while politicians consider local finance as the foremost issue. Leading German local politicians see in their remit substantially more—and more sustained—problems than their international counterparts. This is often put down to specific 'disappointment factors'; while, in the east, many hopes have remained unfulfilled, local leaders in the west, following many relatively trouble-free decades, are still unused to the scale of the difficulties to be tackled (Cusack and Wessels 1996).

4. *Democracy in the* Länder *and Local Authorities: Opportunities and Challenges*

New demands facing the *Länder* and local authorities stem from an enormous expanding need for action in a broad range of old and new policy fields—a process that began to take hold from the 1970s onwards. The reconstruction of the *Länder* and local authorities in eastern Germany in the early 1990s is a further factor of change, again raising questions about a just equalization of burdens within society and between the various levels of the federal structure. Europeanization is a major challenge for both the *Länder* and the local authorities. A fourth field is the new role of subnational entities as the idea of government changes, particularly in respect of the capacity of political steering and need for collaboration of different actors in modern Western societies. Fifth, in political practice, the question remains of whether the decentralized levels can make for more democracy by moving from a partly undermined 'consensual' democratic system to one grounded in participation, or whether, conversely, developments are afoot that tend to emasculate democracy.

4.1 New Remits at the Decentralized Level

Since the 1970s, new remits have increasingly been assigned to regional and local players, making it even more difficult to determine which of the different political levels is responsible for which specific issue. Three characteristic trends have emerged in particular:

- The previously little-analysed, 'material' side of infrastructure and production has been targeted as a matter for politics. This includes, for example, energy supply, waste management, or transport policy—areas that have been increasingly exposed to ecologically inspired criticism of traditional growth technologies and large-scale technical remedies. A need arose for new, 'alternative' lines of technology (resource-saving 'closed-loop' recycling schemes, decentralized energy supply, expansion of local public transport), requiring locally coordinated, tailor-made responses. Against this background, a new kind of expertise emerged, which was taken on board in particular by reform-minded local authorities. There were changes of direction and 'administrative expansions' in the new policy areas; initially, the *Länder* and local authorities set up new expert panels, later followed by fresh administrative departments.
- At the same time, emphasis was put on the societal aspect of decentralized politics. One example of this was the response—initially at local level in particular—to the women's movement. Feminist initiatives, which were in part transposed into the party spectrum, were initially a catalyst for a dedicated, decentralized gender-equality policy; as matters progressed, gender issues became an element in broad areas of traditional local policy, such as urban planning and transport. At first, this took the practical form of the establishment of women's equality boards; these were followed by specific units promoting women's issues, culminating in women's agencies and ministries for women.
- Traditionally, the local authorities and regions have been responsible for vocational schools, local economic structures, local business development, and social assistance; only since the 1980s, however, has this evolved into a more closely integrated network of local economic and employment policy. The initial reason for this was mass unemployment—with figures now partly far in excess of 10 per cent—and the fact that, with local authorities responsible for social welfare payouts, long-term unemployment represents

a substantial and rising cost factor. This situation led—first in the west, but since unification particularly also in the east—to the establishment of employment agencies whose remit covers occupational training, the reintegration of the long-term unemployed, and sometimes also encouraging new departures from products and production processes in the region. There is now a broad-based spectrum of business- and employment-development departments in local authorities and in the *Länder*, which sometimes, however, embrace very divergent schools of thought. As a result, the individual programmes differ substantially.

4.2 The Need for Reorganization in the Federal Policy Mix

One of the main problems facing the *Länder* and local authorities is the narrowing of financial margins of manoeuvre, particularly in the 1990s. As a result of massive transfers of funds from west to east (around DM170 billion per year) and the highly redistributive *Länder* financial equalization arrangements, few options remain open to even the more economically strong western *Länder*. Another reason for this development, however, is the national-revenue policy, which forewent tax increases during unification, and instead offered lavish write-off schemes for higher incomes, thereby generating fresh tax waivers. Thus, in what are normally the richest local authorities situated around prosperous conurbations, local politicians are (aptly) wont to note that the 'champagne tax' currently brings in more revenues than income tax. Net-paying *Länder* (Baden-Württemberg, Bavaria, and Hesse) partly succeeded in instituting proceedings before the Federal Constitutional Court against the *Länder* financial equalization arrangements with the aim of achieving a wider spread. At federal level, a proposed tax reform has been blocked for years because of different objectives on the parts of the former Kohl government and the at that time SPD-led *Länder* majority in the *Bundesrat*. Struggles under the new political settlement after 1998 still continue. In various *Länder* the local authorities are pressing for constitutional guarantees that the assignment of new remits will also be directly linked to financial transfers. In addition, the ongoing general debate on a new alignment of public policies in Germany, also fostered by conflicts within the parties in government, will affect the interlinked system of *Politikverflechtung* as well as the capacity of action under the command of regional and local authorities.

Differences in *Länder* size and economic clout regularly fuel discussions about a reorganization of *Land* boundaries. As early as 1973 the federal government set up a commission (*Ernst* commission), which suggested a reduction in the number of western German *Länder* from eleven to five or six. The reorganization plans primarily affected northern Germany (with the proposed merger of Schleswig-Holstein and Lower Saxony with the city-states of

Hamburg and Bremen) and midwestern Germany (one variation being the unification of Hesse, Rhineland-Palatinate, and Saarland). A reform of this kind would have created *Länder* of more or less the same size and economic weight. It would have required the agreement of the *Bundesrat* and endorsement by referendum. Such reform concepts, however, including those put forward during the process of German unification, failed from the very outset because of the inertia of the *Länder*. Institutional self-interest on the part of all *Land* bodies that would otherwise become superfluous and the now more marked awareness of specific *Land* identities have prevented any changes to date.

As the occupying powers after the Second World War were quite arbitrary in their demarcation of the *Länder* boundaries, the Basic Law, as originally framed, assumed that a revision of *Länder* boundaries would be needed. In fact, this happened only once, with the establishment of Baden-Württemberg in 1952. Moves to unite Brandenburg with the capital, Berlin, in the wake of unification failed. Although the requisite two-thirds majority in favour was forthcoming in both parliaments, more than 62 per cent of Brandenburg's eligible voters rejected the fusion in 1996 (Laufer and Münch 1997).

4.3 Europeanization of Subnational Government

Since the process of European integration accelerated in the mid 1980s, regions and municipalities became increasingly aware of the new challenges. Local authorities were traditionally involved in bilateral twinning activities but were far from a systematic policy approach towards Europe. The *Länder* had been concentrating on cross-border collaboration with neighbouring regions. What is known as 'Arge Alp', 'SaarLorLux' or 'Euregios' alongside the Dutch- and Belgium-German border partly traces back to the 1960s and arose from the need to solve concrete problems (traffic, tourism, labour market, and ecological questions) in cross-border cooperation. These activities were intensified in the 1980s and 1990s. Currently a 'trial-and-error process of regional self-definition' can be witnessed (Sturm 1994: 11) as a result of which historically interlinked territories transcend national boundaries. In numerous projects the collaboration goes beyond pragmatic single-issue purposes and instead tends to create 'policy communities' with an increasing range of action and a growing sense of shared regional identity.

Apart from the practice of cross-border cooperation, most of the *Länder* meanwhile set up inter-regional partnerships with one or more not necessarily contiguous regions of other European Union member states. The dominant motives here are common economic, political, or cultural interests. Actors in these comparatively new types of transnational collaboration often adopt a 'Europeanized' policy approach: the idea prevails of being ready for a new form of regional 'foreign policy' which looks out for suitable partners in order to exchange experiences with 'best practices' and European institutions but also to address mutual demands to Brussels as well as to the central states. In addition, several EU initiatives and structural funds' programmes meanwhile require the set-up of inter-regional or inter-local partnerships and thus boosted the respective subnational activities. In this field the stronger west German *Länder* like North Rhine-Westphalia, Bavaria and Baden-Württemberg pioneered, the latter with its well-known 'four motors of Europe' initiative (an association with Catalonia, Lombardy, and Rhône-Alpes). In the meantime this pattern was also adopted by the medium-sized and smaller *Länder* as for example Hesse (in its partnership with the Emilia Romagna and Aquitaine, see Eissel *et al.* 1999). Transnational European activities are, however, by no means reserved to *Länder* politicians. Recent examples of innovative local authorities show that transnational networks successfully claim for EU funds and are able to provide ordinary people and even underprivileged groups with empirical knowledge and worthwhile European experiences (e.g., programmes such as in the county of Kassel where pro-active civil servants organize vocational training schemes for younger unemployed on a county-partnership basis, Lecke 1997; Bennewitz and Bullmann 1999).

The major boost to subnational European activities, however, was caused by the ongoing integration process itself. Especially since the Single European Act, the *Länder* felt the threat of losing out in competence once the central state proceeded to transfer national sovereignty to Europe. Thus, the German *Länder* took an active stance in organizing multilateral fora as 'political voices' of the European regions (Weyand 1997). Together with Belgium and Spanish regions, they were the driving force in establishing regional demands in the Maastricht Treaty: the insertion of the principle of subsidiarity, the setting up of the Committee of the Regions, even if it has only advisory competences, and the access of subcentral government to the Council of Ministers. Only the right of appeal to the European Court of Justice, which they also lobbied for, was completely rejected.

When it came to the transformation of the Maastricht Treaty into national legislation it was again the *Länder* which gained from succesful domestic bargaining. Since an amendment to the Basic Law (requiring a two-thirds majority in the *Bundestag* as well as in the *Bundesrat*) was needed to ratify the Treaty the *Länder* could press for a new constitutional regulation which demands a *Bundesrat* consent for any further transfer of sovereign rights to the EU. Moreover, in its EU policy, the federal government must accommodate the views of the *Länder* in the same way as it has to take account of their position in the current federation-*Länder* relationship. Where essentially the exclusive legislation of the *Länder* is affected, German representation in the Council of Ministers is transferred to a member of a *Land* government (Art. 23 of the Basic Law). The German *Länder* and local authorities have twenty-four members in the Committee of the Regions. Twenty-one of these members are from the *Länder*, mainly delegated ministers or, in some cases, also members of the *Land* parliaments. The local-authority associations, which make up the federal association of local-authority boards, decide on the three remaining seats. All the German *Länder* as well as many local authorities have their own contact offices in Brussels.

As observers note, the *Länder* meanwhile think in relative terms about the concept of a 'Europe of the Regions' they had pushed for prior to the Maastricht conference. They seem now to concentrate more on the channels of domestic policy and trying to improve the usage of their powers under Article 23 of the Basic Law (Jeffery 1997). Furthermore, the *Länder* take a more critical stance towards EU regional and internal market policies which prospectively will not offer the same benefits but insist on prohibitive regulations of regional subsidies. Above all, Bavaria is harshest in its criticism of 'EU-centralism' and demands a release from Brussels' obligations. SPD-led *Länder* remain more moderate. But all German *Länder* and local authorities, irrespective of their differing political hue, share a common interest in protecting their corridor of public services (e.g., municipal transport, departments of energy supply, public and saving banks) from European deregulation policies and pushed for a respective amendment in the Amsterdam Treaty. The German 'organicist' settlement, which incorporates the local and regional state to a large extent as a responsible actor and service provider in the economic and social sphere, is challenged by a radical neo-liberal approach to which the EU's competition policy dedicated itself in recent years. The EU administration claims that a distinct separation of public service production and profit-seeking economic activities is necessary, whereas German public sector representatives suspect the European Commission of siding with their private business competitors (like major banks keen to take over lucrative private banking services).

4.4 Changes in the Concept of Government

The ever more complex range of tasks, coupled with the increasing number of players involved, have changed both the form and the character of decentralized government. The *Länder* and local authorities more and more find themselves as initiators and mediators, bringing a whole range of players within society into their problem-solving strategies. Increasingly, this is accompanied by a reorganization of public administration activities.

4.4.1 Administrative Reform

Within their national context German local authorities lead the way in terms of new departures in public administration, leaving the *Länder* and federal authorities trailing behind. Overall and against the backdrop of international developments, however, the German government is among the late developers in this field, since attempts at modernization were, in the main, not made until the 1990s (Naschold 1997).

At the local level, the focus is on internal administrative modernization, particularly in financial management. Local authorities' preference for business-led rationalization is a response to recommendations from the *Kommunale Gemeinschaftsstelle für Verwaltungsvereinfachung* (the Joint Office for Administrative Simplification, sponsored by local authorities) whose reports play a very valuable role in promoting uniform, local administrative organization. On the other hand, efforts towards greater democracy that touch on the relationship between politics and the local council or that advocate more grass-roots involvement have not moved forward (Bogumil and Kissler 1997).

4.4.2 Meso- and Micro-corporatism

Because of their expanded tasks in the fields of economic and social reorganization, the *Länder* and the local authorities have had to strive much harder to bring in organized interests in a fresh way.

In the *Länder* the 1980s and 1990s saw the emergence of sometimes prototypical development policies along 'social-democratic' or 'neo-conservative'[1] lines, which differed in the extent to which they brought in not only the academic and business world, but also trade unions and critically minded action groups. The extended 'social-democratic' variant replaced business-related strategies with regional-specific approaches. In North Rhine-Westphalia, for example, a support scheme was developed initially for the Ruhr region, bringing together a wide spectrum of players via a system of regional conferences. In practice, however, differences between the various *Länder* concepts are now narrowing (Heinze and Schmid 1994).

German local policy has a long tradition of working together with associations and organizations. In local-level social policy, cooperation with private charitable associations is well established. This has been joined by corporate arrangements, particularly for business development and labour-market support. Alternative agencies and new social initiatives are also often involved

---

[1] In the German discussion, the expression 'neo-conservative' (*neo-konservativ*) is sometimes used in distinction from the term 'neo-liberal' in the Anglo-Saxon sense of the word. Whereas the latter describes a Thatcherite political attitude of deregulation, *neo-konservativ* stands for a political strategy in which a strong state intervenes actively to modernize its industrial base but excludes trade unions and alternative experts from the dialogue about the intended means and goals. For example, the German CDU *Land* politicians Lothar Späth (former prime minister of Baden-Württemberg and today one of the most influential managers in east German industries) or Kurt Biedenkopf (prime minister of Saxony) were regarded as typical exponents of neo-conservative thinking in contrast to Thatcherite liberals dominating in the FDP and parts of the CDU/CSU (Saage 1985).

in the local, collective decision-making mechanism, thereby ensuring that, in many cases, local users can exert a more effective influence (Heinze and Voelzkow 1999).

4.5 Renewal of Direct Democracy

In contrast to the federal level, the 1990s have seen a marked expansion of direct forms of democratic participation in the *Länder* and local authorities. It is still unclear, however, how far this really represents a qualitative step towards more democracy.

Between 1992 and 1994, in the wake of German unification, proposals were mooted both in the joint constitutional commission and in *Bundestag* consultations to insert referendums and petitions for referendums into the Basic Law. These were rejected by the governing CDU/CSU/FDP majority as a matter of principle. Therefore, new federal legislation was not forthcoming although the opposition called for this issue to be put back on the agenda. It still remains to be seen what kind of policy the new government coalition of SPD and Alliance '90/The Greens will adopt.

Instead, the 1990s have seen a steady expansion of elements of direct democracy in the *Länder* and local authorities. This development was backed up by the experience of the people's movements in the former GDR and the then widespread practice of 'round-table' participation. The action groups of the democracy movement were largely responsible for these 'round tables' and also played a major practical role in shaping political renewal. They receded into the background, however, as the administration in the newly created *Länder* and local authorities was reorganized along western lines.

Since the foundation of the Federal Republic, a number of *Länder* have made provision for petitioning for and holding referendums. In Schleswig-Holstein, changes were made in the constitution to allow such options in the wake of an affair involving the then *Land* Prime Minister Uwe Barschel.[2] The new *Länder* took a similar constitutional path and other western *Länder* followed suit, so that, today, each *Land* has a system of representation that incorporates plebiscitary elements. In political practice, however, direct democracy is less important at *Land* level than in the local authorities. This is due, on the one hand, to quorum levels required and, on the other, to the narrowness of

---

[2] The CDU politician Uwe Barschel was prime minister of Schleswig-Holstein from 1982 to 1987. According to official police documents, in 1997 he committed suicide in a Swiss hotel, a version which has been strongly disputed by his family. In one of the most sensational affairs of the old FRG, an investigating committee of the Schleswig-Holstein *Landtag* found him responsible for an ex-officio smear campaign against his competitor and successor as prime minister, the later federal SPD chief Björn Engholm. The affair caused serious claims for more public control of the power exerted by politicians.

what legislative power remains and to 'excluded' concerns such as, in North Rhine-Westphalia, financial matters, levy-related legislation, and pay scale arrangements. The foremost referendum in Germany's recent history was held in Bavaria in 1995, when a very large majority voted in favour of establishing more plebiscites at local level. Since 1990, elements of direct democracy (particularly public petitions and referendums) have taken their lead from Baden-Württemberg and become established practice across Germany.

5. Innovative Approaches to Improving Regional and Local Democracy

In practical terms, ordinary citizens have different ways of taking part in local policy-making. These include either representative or direct forms of participation, allowing varying degrees of democratic influence (Roth 1997).

In local council elections, the originally specifically southern German practices of '*kumulieren*' (i.e., accumulation of votes on one candidate) and ticket-splitting ('*panaschieren*', i.e., distribution of votes to candidates from different lists) have also been adopted by other *Länder*. That said, about half of the *Länder* still retain a rigid party list. Experience from southern Germany shows that about 50 per cent of voters use this option. The small number of invalid votes proves that voters evidently do not feel overstretched by the system. Occasionally, this voting system has also been used in efforts to influence the composition of the local council (in Munich, for example, to increase the percentage of women represented). This electoral procedure also makes more of candidates' professional image, how politically well-known they are, or of their economic or social position in the community concerned.

In each *Land*, direct election has strengthened the position of the mayor as head of the administration, at the expense of party influence. Most commentators see this as a democratic plus, tempered in some cases by an extremely low turnout. As a result, the image of candidates is also changing, with a tendency towards populist stage management. The plus in terms of wider grass-roots participation is thus debatable given the stronger, executive-style leadership in local politics.

For some time now, most local statutes have made provision for other, somewhat unspectacular forms of grass-roots participation to expand the representative system.

- Citizens' experts in a certain field may take part and sometimes vote in committees of the local assembly. This helps to boost expert knowledge as the basis for decision-making, but does little to change the fact that the work of

local councillors and party groups might sometimes be out of touch with reality.
- Advisory councils, for example for foreigners who lack the full rights of citizenship including the right to vote, help in supporting the work of local and regional assemblies and their respective executives. Low turnout shows, however, that the foreigners concerned see such councils as the second-best option.
- The territorial reorganizations of the 1970s already saw the establishment of directly elected representative bodies in many municipalities. Their remit is, however, very limited.
- Citizens' and neighbourhood assemblies exist at the local level of all *Länder*, although no binding decisions are taken here. In practice, they allow the administration to state its own case, but also make for more transparency and more appropriate responses.
- Since the 1970s, a whole range of building, planning, and environmental legislation has required grass-roots involvement. Many of these provisions came under pressure in the debate on the acceleration of public approval procedures.
- Citizens and residents may also make application to force the local council to tackle or take a decision on a particular issue within a specified time limit. This tool is now widespread and requires a low quorum.

One central plank of direct democracy that—taking the lead from Baden-Württemberg—has been incorporated into all local statutes since 1990 is public petition and different types of referendums. These options give ordinary citizens the right to raise important local matters in the form of a public petition and then to have the final say in the form of a plebiscite. In most *Länder*, the referendum initiated by citizens is complemented by a council plebiscite which the local representative body can get under way with its qualified majority. Because of, among other things, high quora, these are exceptions in the practice of local democracy and can complement only in part the representative system, however. In Baden-Württemberg, where this system originated, 127 public petitions were raised between 1975 and 1991. In the resulting fifty-nine instances of referendums, thirty-one were successful, mostly relating to building projects and road plans (Roth 1997: 431).

Bavaria, where local public petitions and plebiscites were introduced as result of an overwhelming succesful petition for a referendum campaign at the *Land* level in 1995, has the most extensive regulations. Against the hardened opposition of the conservative *Land* government and the mainly CSU-influenced local-authority associations, a citizens' action group calling itself *Mehr Demokratie in Bayern e.V.* (More Democracy in Bavaria) scored the most spectacular success in the recent history of popular legislation in Germany. The main reason why the draft was rejected by the *Land* parliament and the governing CSU was the lack of a quorum rule for the conclusive referendum provision. The plan was that a simple majority of those voting would be enough for a valid decision. The *Land* parliament, therefore, put forward an alternative bill requiring a 25 per cent quorum. However, this was rejected by plebiscite by 38.7–57.8 per cent in favour of a quorum-free regulation (Jung 1996).

It now appears that the current arrangement with low quora for public petitions (between 3 and 10 per cent depending on the size of the local authority) and referendums without a quorum has resulted in a strong upswing in new grass-roots commitment. In Bavaria, the first five months with the new rule in place saw 170 public petitions brought forward (a figure that Baden-Württemberg, where the scheme originated, took thirty-five years to reach). After two years, Bavaria had had 390 public petitions and 256 instances of citizens' decision-making, thereby exceeding the number of known cases in all the other *Länder* that had instituted this reform (Jung 1996). This must, of course, also be seen as a sign of previously blocked reforms in the local authorities concerned.

In practice, however, the outcome of the various decisions demonstrates that the new direct-democratic forms of participation may well lead to inconsistencies. It is also worth noting that initial opponents of the current arrangement are the very ones now seeking its wider application. New plebiscitary options are thus being also brought into play in the old conflict between parties and political groupings (Roth 1997; Jung 1998).

There is also a whole range of other systematic forms of participation based on informal negotiating arrangements and procedural forms of management (Gessenharter 1996).

One of the tasks of the 'round table' during the period of transformation in eastern Germany was to re-establish the public participation needed to articulate interests and pursue negotiations. While this new form of popular participation was quickly swamped by western-style institutional arrangements, 'round tables' also, in some cases, made the transition from east to west in matters such as poverty and extreme right-wing violence, which seemed unmanageable to western local authorities.

In environmental conflicts in particular (landfill sites, waste management, Berlin and Frankfurt airports), mediation procedures have become a popular instrument of negotiation and arbitration.

More open forms of participation better designed to pre-empt conflicts include popular for what Robert Jung has termed 'futures workshops'. These are often brought to bear as an instrument of knowledge and information transfer among regional players to prepare joint projects such as the planning of green-belt schemes in cities.

Multistage dialogue as propagated by Gessenharter involves three mutually related stages (look, appraise, act). It starts with random qualitative interviews in the regions concerned. The relevant groups then consider the issues at hand and put forward possible solutions. The final stage is the formation of a 'planning cell' in which a randomly selected group of citizens work out proposed solutions ('popular examination'). This method was used to good effect, for example, in Buxtehude, Lower Saxony, following outbursts of xenophobic violence. It helped to ensure that appropriate action was taken and also improved social harmony in this small town.

The various participatory schemes have different specific advantages, but also blind spots (Eissel 1997). Paucity of public funds also means they are less widespread and not used by policy-makers in as systematic a way as might be hoped. Longer-term, systematic participatory projects such as Local Agenda 21 could prove the catalyst for further development.

6. *Conclusions*

The challenges and opportunities of decentralized policy in Germany may be summarized as follows.

A great deal has been achieved at the decentralized level, not least in the transformation of eastern Germany. The political and administrative renewal along western lines is largely complete, making for uniform structures of administration across Germany today. The almost complete adoption of western patterns of organization has, however, also meant that positive approaches in terms of direct, participatory democracy that had emerged during the transition years have again quickly fallen into oblivion. The western idea of democracy prevailed in political life. That said, elements of direct democracy did find their way into the newly drafted *Länder* and local-authority constitutions. For the people living in eastern Germany, however, the experience of everyday life is somewhat different. In many places in eastern Germany the persistence of extremely high unemployment—with an average of over 15 per cent—is threatening to turn into political apathy or protest voting (as for example witnessed at the April 1998 election to the Saxony-Anhalt *Land* parliament in which the extreme right-wing *Deutsche Volksunion* (DVU, German People's Union) gained over 13 per cent of the vote). Nonetheless, it is evident especially in eastern Germany that local and regional decision-makers are most likely to enjoy political standing.

The new beginning in eastern Germany was not seen in the west as an opportunity for a critical reappraisal of its own organizational structures and democratic practices. As it is, the multilevel political system of German federalism tends to be marked by inertia and is slower to react to new stimuli than centralized forms of government. Its strengths lie in the fact that it balances out disparities; makes it possible, by exploiting the pattern of rivalry among the federal *Länder*, to test out best practices in a multifaceted, if cautious way. On the other hand, however, current arrangements mean that urgent nationwide reforms, such as reform of the finance system and the action needed to loosen red tape or to tap into grass-roots potential for innovation, are more likely to risk delay.

It remains to be seen how people in the *Länder* and local authorities deal with the new possibilities for direct democracy. In southern Germany, in particular, there is palpable acceptance of, and interest in, new forms of democratic expression, without, however, thereby seriously altering the established mechanisms of raising public opinion on politics in terms of parties and administration. Equally unclear is the impact of the direct, presidential-style election of those holding top positions in local government; a practice that has now spread across Germany. The new opportunity for direct elections has, in larger towns and cities especially, been accompanied by an alarming decline in turnout. It is also debatable whether direct elections and the formation of local parliaments on the basis of a more personalized election process—thereby weakening the position of political parties—really makes for enhanced public influence on decision-making. Such a development might also be a sign of an increasingly symbolic way of tackling now overly complex issues, replacing debate on political alternatives by differing elements of style.

Over the past few decades, nonetheless, decentralized levels of government in the Federal Republic have launched sustainable reforms. Lasting success on the basis of innovations in subnational politics was mainly the result of: (*i*) clearly defined strategic concepts mostly fostered by party political rivalry, (*ii*) pressure from citizens' initiatives and new social movements, and (*iii*) impetus from committed experts. The emergence of reform-minded networks from among these three groups of players allowed the *Länder* and local authorities to do much in searching for innovative solutions to social problems. The *Länder* and local authorities developed new fields of action, particularly where multidimensional difficulties necessitated tailor-made answers designed to achieve a number of objectives simultaneously. Over the past fifteen years, for example, new forms of economic and employment policy have been tried out at decentralized level; environmentally sound approaches to energy and waste policy have also been promoted. Successful *Länder* and local authorities are increasingly taking on the role of concept developers and initiators, monitoring the activities of a range of companies and groups and institutions within society.

Compared with territorial units in other European countries, the clear strength of the German *Länder* and local authorities is their dominant position in the decentralized political network. Although in Germany, too, some public services are being privatized and outsourced as newly created agencies, this does not always, or necessarily, involve a loss of public control or influence. On the contrary, more flexible forms of organization can help create machinery more able to respond to complex difficulties.

The German local authorities and regions are well placed to tackle the tasks ahead in an expanded multilevel political system with their existing institutional framework. However, the critical challenges they face in a Europe that is growing ever closer together are still to come. In their current, strained relationship of competition and cooperation, Europe's regions must increasingly work at cross-border, interinstitutional learning. This will require further trials with effective forms of participation in internal affairs if the potential for innovation is to be tapped fully and productively. A prerequisite is the firm establishment both within society and in the economy of a culture of democratic participation.

References

ABROMEIT, H. (1992). *Der verkappte Einheitsstaat*. Opladen: Leske & Budrich.

BENNEWITZ, H. and BULLMANN, U. (1999). 'Die Europäisierung der kommunalen Sozialpolitik', in B. Dietz, D. Eissel, and D. Naumann (eds), *Handbuch für Kommunale Sozialpolitik*. Opladen: Leske & Budrich.

BULLMANN, U., GOLDSMITH, M., and PAGE, E. C. (1997). 'Regieren unter dem Zentralstaat: Regionen, Kommunen und eine sich verändernde Machtbalance in Europa', in U. Bullmann and R. G. Heinze (eds), *Regionale Modernisierungspolitik. Nationale und internationale Perspektiven*. Opladen: Leske & Budrich.

BOGUMIL, J. and KISSLER, L. (1997). 'Modernisierung der Kommunalverwaltungen auf dem Prüfstand der Praxis', in H. Heinelt (ed.), *Modernisierung der Kommunalpolitik*. Opladen: Leske & Budrich.

CUSACK, T. R. and WESSELS, B. (1996). *Problemreich und konfliktgeladen. Lokale Demokratie in Deutschland fünf Jahre nach der Vereinigung*. Berlin: Wissenschaftszentrum Berlin für Sozialforschung.

DEUTSCHER BUNDESTAG (1998, 1999, 2000). Internet website 〉*http://www.bundestag.de*〈.

DEUTSCHER STÄDTETAG (1998). *Statistisches Jahrbuch Deutscher Gemeinden 1998*. Köln and Berlin.

EISSEL, D. (1997). 'Bürgerbeteiligung und strategische Netzwerke in der lokalen Umweltpolitik', in K. Lange (ed.), *Gesamtverantwortung statt Verantwortungsparzellierung im Umweltrecht*. Baden-Baden: Nomos.

——GRASSE, A., PAESCHKE, B., and SÄNGER, R. (1999). *Interregionale Zusammenarbeit in Europa. Die Partnerschaft von Hesen, Emilia-Romagna und Aquitaine*. Opladen: Leske & Budrich.

GESSENHARTER, W. (1996). 'Warum neue Beteiligungsmodelle auf kommunaler Ebene?' *Aus Politik und Zeitgeschichte*, 50/96.

HEINZE, R. G. and SCHMID, J. (1994). 'Mesokorporatistische Strategien im Vergleich: Industrieller Strukturwandel und Kontingenz politischer Steuerung in drei

Bundesländern', in W. Streeck (ed.), *Staat und Verbände*. Opladen: Westdeutscher Verlag.

——and VOELZKOW, H. (1999). 'Verbände und "Neokorporatismus"', in H. Wollmann and R. Roth (eds), *Kommunalpolitik Politisches Handeln in den Gemeinden*, 2nd edn. Opladen: Leske & Budrich.

JEFFERY, C. (1997). 'Farewell the Third Level? The German Länder and the European Policy Process', in C. Jeffery (ed.), *The Regional Dimension of the European Union. Towards a Third Level in Europe?* London: Frank Cass.

JUNG, O. (1996). 'Volksentscheide in der Bundesrepublik. Eine aktuelle Übersicht'. *Blätter für deutsche und internationale Politik*, 41: 567–76.

——(1998). 'Keine Erneuerung der Demokratie "von unten"? Kritische Stellungnahme zu Hiltrud Nassmachers Beitrag in Heft 3/97 der Zparl'. *Zeitschrift für Parlamentsfragen*, 29/1: 190–6.

LAUFER, H. and MÜNCH, U. (1997). *Das föderative System der Bundesrepublik Deutschland*. Bonn: Bundeszentrale für politische Bildung.

LECKE, D. (1997). Mehr als nur ein Händedruck—Die Regionalkooperationen des Kreises Kassel, in *Regionalreport*. Hofgeismar: Verein für Regionalentwicklung im Landkreis Kassel.

LEIBFRIED, S. and TENNSTEDT, F. (eds) (1985). *Politik der Armut und die Spaltung des Sozialstaats*. Frankfurt/M: Suhrkamp.

NASCHOLD, F. (1997). 'Binnenmodernisierung, Wettbewerb, Haushaltskonsolidierung. Internationale Erfahrungen zur Verwaltungsreform', in H. Heinelt (ed.), *Modernisierung der Kommunalpolitik*. Opladen: Leske & Budrich.

NASSMACHER, H. (1997). 'Keine Erneuerung der Demokratie "von unten"'. *Zeitschrift für Parlamentsfragen*, 28/3: 445–60.

NIEDERMAYER, O. (1997). 'Das gesamtdeutsche Parteiensystem', in O. W. Gabriel, O. Niedermayer, and R. Stöss (eds), *Parteiendemokratie in Deutschland*. Opladen: Westdeutscher Verlag.

ROTH, R. (1997). 'Die Kommune als Ort der Bürgerbeteiligung', in A. Klein and R. Schmalz-Bruns (eds), *Politische Beteiligung und Bürgerengagement in Deutschland*. Bonn: Bundeszentrale für politische Bildung.

SAAGE, R. (1985). 'Technik und Gesellschaft im Neokonservatismus', in *Gewerkschaftliche Monatshefte*, 9: 71–6.

STURM, R. (1994). 'Economic Regionalism in a Federal State. Germany and the Challenge of the Single European Market'. Europäisches Zentrum für Föderalismus Forschung. *Occasional Papers*, no. 1. Tübingen: EZFF.

WIESENDAHL, E. (1997). 'Noch Zukunft für die Mitgliederparteien? Erstarrung und Revitalisierung innerparteilicher Partizipation', in A. Klein and R. Schmalz-Bruns (eds), *Politische Beteiligung und Bürgerengagement in Deutschland*. Bonn: Bundeszentrale für politische Bildung.

WEYAND, S. (1997). 'Inter-Regional Associations and the European Integration Process', in Ch. Jeffery (ed.), *The Regional Dimension of the European Union. Towards a Third Level in Europe?* London: Frank Cass.

ZEUNER, B. (1997). 'Innerparteiliche Demokratie', in U. Andersen and W. Woyke (eds), *Handwörterbuch des politischen Systems der Bundesrepublic Deutschland*, 3rd edn. Opladen: Leske & Budrich.

5

Austria: The End of Proportional Government?

Udo Bullmann

1. History and Concept of Democracy

1.1 Historical Background

Austria is a federal republic with a population of some 8 million people; it comprises nine independent *Länder* (federal states): Burgenland, *Kärnten* (Carinthia), *Niederösterreich* (Lower Austria), *Oberösterreich* (Upper Austria), Salzburg, *Steiermark* (Styria), *Tirol* (Tyrol), Vorarlberg, and *Wien* (Vienna). The Austrian constitution is founded on a number of other fundamental principles: federalism, democracy, republicanism, and the rule of law. Any new legal provision which has a bearing on any of these priniciples could be implemented only by means of an amendment to the constitution and ratified by referendum.

From the point of view of constitutional law, political democracy in Austria came into being with the 'First Republic' (1918–34). In 1934 this was abolished and an authoritarian corporate state was set up, established on a federal basis. The state comprised representatives of the various professions rather than a parliament. Between 1938 and 1945 Austria became part of the Third Reich, following its annexation by the Nazis. Austria regained its independence in 1945, but did not achieve full sovereignty until 1955.

The present 'Second Republic', set up after the Second World War, did not introduce a new constitution, but was founded basically on the constitution of 1920 and its 1929 amendments, which were subsequently further amended on a number of occasions. This reflected a compromise between the socialist and conservative camps that have to this day a decisive influence on Austrian political life. As the representatives of these parties were unable to reach agreement on a common body of constitutional laws, the constitution of the 1920s was a continuation of laws dating from the period of the monarchy, as defined in the *Staatsgrundgesetzen* (basic constitutional laws) of 1867. The principles of the social state and the welfare state are thus not set out under basic law provisions, but are based on subsequent political developments, in particular of the post-1945 period.

Austria has a parliamentary system of government with strong presidential overtones, which, at first sight, brings to mind the constitution of the Weimar Republic in Germany or the Fifth Republic in France. Under the Austrian constitution, the federal president is elected directly by the people; the first election was not, however, held until 1951. The president appoints the chancellor and the federal government. In this—as in the president's right to dismiss the federal government—the president is, according to the constitution, not bound to act in accordance with parliamentary majorities. This strong power of the federal president was introduced under the constitutional amendments of 1929; it was once again the result of a compromise under which the governing conservatives (Christian Social Party) sought to introduce a presidential system, whilst the *Sozialdemokratische Partei Österreichs* (Social Democratic Party), which had been in opposition since 1920, favoured a parliamentary democracy. The federal presidents who have been in office since the Second World War have in practice waived this right and have respected the right of the parliamentary majority in the *Nationalrat* (National Assembly) to form a government. The federal chancellor is thus *de facto* the leading political figure.

Political parties, in the current meaning of the term, came into being between 1880 and 1890, reflecting three political families: the conservative-Christian movement, the social-democratic movement, and the German-national movement that stood for the safeguarding of the 'German element' in the multinational state of the Austro-Hungarian Empire. The Social Democrats sought to achieve universal suffrage, which came into being at federal level (at first, however, only for men) in the 1907 elections of the House of Representatives (of the Federal Council). Until 1918 the *Land* parliaments remained essentially bodies representing corporate interests, with representatives being appointed on the basis of the old-style electoral system influenced by the Catholic Church, whereby voters were divided into different classes, each occupying a proportion of the seats.

In contrast to the forceful political debates of the interwar years, which gave rise to militant action in the 1930s and led to two civil wars in 1934, the political scene in Austria during the Second Republic has been marked by political equilibrium and a high level of stability. The two major political movements work closely together, as do the associations linked to these movements. Over the past few decades, employers' organizations and trade unions have developed effective instruments for reducing conflict and resolving opposing interests. Agreement has been reached on the basis of what is called 'social partnership' and 'proportional government'.

The tendency for the system of 'proportional government' to become a fossilized structure is increasingly criticized, particularly by young people, alongside the recent growing interest in the development of democracy and democratic reform. In the wake of this criticism, the realigned *Freiheitliche Partei Österreichs* (FPÖ, Austrian Freedom Party)—a right-wing populist party—has notched up clear successes against the two main parties since the second half of the 1980s. At the same time, citizens are increasingly launching initiatives aimed at reducing the level of concentration of political power. The recent extension of direct elections indicates that Austria is moving towards a more open and dynamic concept of democracy. This goes hand in hand with a gradual shift away from a form of democracy based on agreement towards one based on competition (Pelinka 1997).

Under the federal constitution there are two forms of direct democratic action: petitions for new legislation and referendums. For a petition to be successful, it has to be supported by at least 100,000 signatures (representing some 1.8 per cent of the total electorate) or one-sixth of the electorate in three *Länder*. If such backing is received, the proposed law will then be treated by the National Assembly as if it were a bill submitted by the government. Petitions may be launched once they have the support of: (*i*) at least 10,000 eligible voters whose main residence is in Austria, (*ii*) at least eight members of the National Assembly, or (*iii*) at least four members from each of three *Land* parliaments. Referendums may take place under one of the following three conditions:

- the National Assembly decides, by a majority vote, to cede its legislative powers in this area to the people;
- if at least one-third of the members of the National Assembly or the Federal Council (comprising members of the *Land* parliaments) call for a referendum as part of a projected partial amendment of the constitution (something which has not yet happened in Austria);
- in the case of a 'comprehensive amendment' of the constitution involving one of the fundamental principles underlying the constitution; this has happened only once: Austria's accession to the European Union was supported by 66 per cent of the electorate in a referendum in June 1994.

Austria's accession to the EU, which took effect on 1 January 1995, was also widely supported in each of the individual *Länder* and by all of the major groups in Austrian society.

In 1955, Austria committed itself, 'of its own free will', to permanent neutrality, with a view to regaining its full sovereignty. The background to this undertaking was the desire for the approval of all four occupying powers to the national treaty and to avoid partition, as occurred in Germany. However, the principle of external neutrality is regarded by commentators as a factor in promoting internal political stability in the Second Republic (Winter 1995).

The end of the cold war and the collapse of the Communist system in 1989 presented Austria with completely new prospects as regards security policy. The initial steps taken in this direction include EU membership, observer status in the WEU, and involvement in the NATO *Partnership for Peace* programme.

Recently, Austrian membership of NATO has been firmly supported in public opinion, particularly by the *Österreichische Volkspartei* (ÖVP, Austrian Conservative Party); the larger, governing *Sozialdemokratische Partei Österreichs* (SPÖ, Social Democratic Party) has, however, so far rejected membership on the grounds of Austrian neutrality.

1.2 Democracy at the Subnational Levels

1.2.1 The Länder

From 1918 to 1920, following the collapse of the Austro-Hungarian Empire, Austria passed from being a decentralized unitary state into a federal state. The German-speaking crown states of the former Austro-Hungarian Empire joined together to form the federal state of 'German Austria' (the name officially given to the new republic in the earliest documents).

The existence of the *Länder*, however, does have a much longer pedigree. Unlike most of the artificially formed (west-)German *Länder*, most of the Austrian *Länder* can trace their origins back to the Middle Ages. Carinthia, Styria, and Austria (which later became Lower and Upper Austria), in particular, trace their history as territorial units as far back as the early Middle Ages. Tyrol, Salzburg, and Vorarlberg (the so-called *Vorländer* of the Austro-Hungarian Empire) have existed as geographical entities, forming part of one and the same sovereign territory, since at least the sixteenth century. Only the federal states of Vienna (which has a dual status as a *Land* and a municipality) and Burgenland (comprising areas settled by German-speakers of what was previously Hungary) came into being either during or as a result of the establishment of the First Republic (Brauneder and Lachmayer 1987). The centuries-old history of the *Länder* continues to this day to strengthen their identity and to enable them to make better use of their legal and political powers. Even in the pre-republican period, Austria, as a country in which allegiance to a particular *Land* and multi-ethnicity were emphasized, was characterized by both territorial individuality and politico-cultural diversity. The long history of the Austrian *Länder* represents a significant difference in comparison to present-day Germany, which is the other classical federal state in the EU.

It would, however, be precipitate to conclude, in the light of these factors, that the Austrian *Länder* have a stronger position within the national framework than have the German *Länder*. The history of federalism in both Germany and Austria is marked by a further significant difference that continues to have an impact on the organization of the present-day political system. During the transition to the modern period in the nineteenth century, Germany had no framework of central government. Fundamental efforts to bring about modernization took place primarily in Prussia; in that state, progress was made towards establishing a territorial administration replacing the powers of an absolute prince. The central ruling family in Austria already held a dominant position at an earlier stage. Even in the Middle Ages, under a monarchy, a union was established in Austria, bringing together the various *Länder*. This union had a joint monarch, a central administration, a uniform administrative process, and, to a certain extent, common laws (until 1749). In the period up to 1848—and in particular during the reactionary regime of Metternich in the run-up to the March revolution of 1848—a highly orga-nized, centralized state developed, centred on the capital of Vienna; under this system the *Länder* lost some powers, but continued to exist. In the ensuing period, the conflicts between federalists and centralists played an increasingly decisive role in the political struggles surrounding the monarchy. The period of 'neo-absolutism', which followed an early constitutional transitional phase (1848–51), brought important reforms, such as commercial freedom and the separation of the judiciary from other branches of government. In that same period, however, federal structures were removed and an administrative system based on a united state was established. The *Länder* were reduced to the role of mere administrative districts. It was only in the wake of the Austro-Hungarian settlement, which in 1867 divided the Habsburg Empire into two parts enjoying equal rights (Austria and Hungary), and the introduction of a constitutional system in the same year that the powers of the *Länder* were once again gradually increased, enabling them to become real federal states rather than clusters of local authorities (Brauneder and Lachmayer 1987).

The collapse of the Austro-Hungarian Empire and the establishment of a democratic republic led to the reintroduction of federalism into an Austrian state that by now had developed a tradition of central government. In Germany, on the other hand, the existence of independent *Länder* with their own admin-istrative structures helped Prussia to establish a German Reich, bringing together the core German states. This difference in the history of the political systems of Austria and Germany remains important to the present day.

1.2.2 Local Government

Local self-government, in the current sense of the term, has a long history in Austria. It goes back to the medieval 'free cities' and the revolution of 1848 and gradually gained the upper hand over attempts to restore authoritarian government in the nineteenth century. The present-day Austrian local author-ities/municipalities were set up on the basis of a Provisional Local Govern-ment Act of 1849. However, self-government was not introduced effectively until after the establishment of the constitutional monarchy (1860–1), under which a Local Government Act was adopted in 1862.

   This Act already made provision for basic structures which continue to be a feature of local democracy to the present day. Under the Act, the uniform units of local government, the *Gemeinde*, became self-governing bodies. Cities and local authorities of particular importance were given special statutes (*Statutarstädte*, statutory cities). Such entities obtained additional powers and generally became the leading administrative authorities. A distinction should be drawn between: (*i*) the areas in which local authorities have autonomous powers (i.e., those areas in which, under a blanket provision, they have the right to act); and (*ii*) areas in which local authorities exercise powers delegated by central government and act on its behalf. Local government bodies comprise the *Gemeinderat* (district council, elected by a direct ballot), the *Gemeindevorstand* (district administrative board, consisting of members of several district councils), and the *Bürgermeister* (mayor, the sole person to have decision-making powers). The mayor is responsible for implementing the delegated powers; hence, he is both answerable to and subject to the directions of central government.

   From the final quarter of the nineteenth century onwards, the political importance of local authorities increased considerably as a result of economic development and immigration. In particular, the capital cities of the *Länder* and local authorities, situated in the most important industrial areas and at key intersections of traffic routes, set about establishing effective administrations for various services (gas and electricity supply, sewage, road building, education, etc.). Universal suffrage was not introduced in local authority elections until the democratic republic was set up in 1918. Vienna became a *Land*, in addition to being the state capital, and developed into the most important bastion of 'municipal socialism' of the interwar period. Vienna was particularly well known for its extensive and imaginative schemes for building low-cost housing as part of a more general plan for social reform. This scheme was financed, *inter alia*, by an aggressive tax policy regarding house ownership and the consumption of luxury goods. Workers' militias sprung to the defence of 'Red Vienna' when it faced the abolition of democracy in 1934.

2. The Institutional Expression of Democracy

2.1 The National Level

The Austrian National Assembly and the parliaments of the *Länder* and local authorities are, in principle, all elected through a system of proportional representation. In 1992 the electoral law regarding national elections was amended to include provisions to promote the election of candidates in their own right. The Austrian system does not involve dual voting for directly elected candidates and political parties, which generally favours the smaller political parties. Instead, provision has been made for part of the overall number of MPs to be elected in forty-three, relatively small constituencies. The distortion of the system of proportional representation by these small constituencies is cancelled out at two subsequent stages in the electoral process. Political parties need to obtain 4 per cent of the overall number of votes cast in the national elections before they may be awarded any of the 183 seats in parliament, which is elected for a four-year term (Pelinka 1997).

The Austrian *Bundesregierung* (federal government) is a collegiate body that takes action on the basis of unanimous decisions and is answerable to the *Nationalrat* (National Assembly). The National Assembly is able to pass a vote of no confidence in the federal chancellor or a member of the national government. Successful no confidence motions lead to the dismissal of the minister by the federal government. The federal chancellor has only very general powers and is not able to give instructions to members of the cabinet. The chancellor's political strength derives rather from the fact that he is generally the leader of the political party with the largest number of seats in the assembly.

Ninety per cent of all federal laws originate from government initiatives. In these cases the legislative procedure in the National Assembly is preceded by a prior-appraisal procedure in which a bill proposed by a ministry is discussed by the other federal ministers, the *Land* governments, the associations representing the economic interests of the social partners, and other interest groups particularly concerned with the proposal. It is only after the *Ministerrat* (council of ministers or cabinet) has unanimously endorsed the proposal—if necessary in an amended form—that the National Assembly starts the legislative process. Proposals for legislation made by the National Assembly itself constitute an exception to this rule. Such proposals may be put forward by at least eight MPs, one of the parliamentary committees, or one of the *Land* parliaments; these proposals are not subject to the above-mentioned, extensive, prior-appraisal procedure. In practice, this method is used by the opposition to enhance its political profile or by MPs from the governing party/parties in the case of a lack of time. In the period 1990–4 some 46 per cent of legislation was either passed unanimously or at least with the approval of the three largest parliamentary parties (SPÖ, ÖVP, and FPÖ).

It is also possible to initiate legislation at national level on the basis of popular petitions. This instrument has so far been employed more than twenty times, with varying rates of success; frequently, such initiatives take the form of attempts to introduce legislation by the opposition parties.

Under the national constitution, the state is responsible for:

• tasks for which the federal government has exclusive powers of legislation and implementation (Art. 10);

- tasks for which the *Länder* have responsibility for legislation and implementation (Art. 15);
- tasks for which the federal government has legislative powers, but for which
  the *Länder* have responsibility for implemention (Art. 11);
- and finally, tasks for which the federal government has responsibility for
  framework legislation and the *Länder* have responsibility for implementing
  legislation and application (Art. 12).

The federal government plays the dominant role in the division of overall
powers between the various administrative levels. It has sole legislative and
implementing powers regarding most of the important government tasks. The
powers of government are particularly evident in economic and social legislation. The federal government has sole responsibility for jurisdiction and for
administrative procedures. It has the power to issue framework laws in areas
such as the administration of the *Länder*, hospitals, and parts of the system of
social protection (such as care provisions for mothers, children, and young
people). In these areas, the *Länder* have the power to introduce implementing legislation and to apply the laws.

The dominant position of the federal government is, however, tempered by
a system of 'indirect federal administration': extensive federal responsibilities
regarding the implementation of legislation are carried out by *Land* bodies or
by authorities that are answerable to the *Länder*. As a result of this allocation
of responsibility and in the light of the powers regarding specific fields, there
are many ways of framing a broad range of administrative procedures.

Article 15 of the constitution defines all areas for which competence does
not rest with the federal government as the responsibility of the *Länder*.
However, this does not greatly detract from the real dominance of the federal
government in the legislative field. The *Länder* have exclusive legislative and
implementation powers in fields such as local inspection of safety provisions,
locally organized events, hunting and fishing, sports, and local medical and
rescue services. A number of other fields—such as building matters, spatial
planning, and the protection of nature and the environment—come under
the responsibility of the *Länder* in so far as competence has not been awarded
to the federal government under other provisions.

The federal government has sole responsibility for public finance. Here, too,
the *Länder* and local government bodies are subordinate to the federal government. The division of federal tax revenues between central government
and the *Länder* is determined by federal legislation. A federal law determines
which tax revenues accrue wholly or partly to the central government. The
Länder are entitled to levy taxes, by virtue of *Land* legislation, for the benefit
of themselves and local government bodies only in cases where equivalent
taxes have not already been introduced under federal legislation. The federal
government is entitled to introduce legislation regarding any kind of taxation.

Both the number of and the revenues from taxes deriving from *Land* legislation fall well behind that of federal taxes.

The overall system of public finance has enjoyed stability over many decades; this is mainly due to an effective, internal financial compensation system. Specific federal laws, of limited time duration, are introduced to allocate particular taxes and tax revenues ('primary' financial compensation). A system of 'secondary' compensation consists essentially of intergovernmental financial transfers. Finally, the compensation system is backed up by 'grey' financial compensation arrangements, parts of which are arranged by private companies; these arrangements serve to iron out inequalities between the *Länder*. The adoption of laws governing financial compensation arrangements are preceded by intensive negotiations between the various tiers of administration—though this is not a legal requirement; in the course of these negotiations, account is taken primarily of the past financial requirements of the various levels of administration. These regular negotiations on the allocation of federal tax revenues have enabled the *Länder* to regain some of the influence withheld from them by the constitution (Kostelka and Unkart 1977).

2.2 The Federal *Länder*

From a constitutional-law standpoint, the federal system adopted by Austria is rather weaker than in other countries. This fact is demonstrated by the way in which the parliament representing the various *Länder* at national level (the *Bundesrat*, Federal Assembly) is organized; compared with the equivalent body in Germany, the Austrian Federal Assembly has only limited powers. Its main power consists of the right to issue a temporary veto against draft legislation passed by the National Assembly. Since 1984 the Federal Assembly has been given limited powers to ratify constitutional laws and constitutional provisions set out in federal laws, which would lead to a reduction in the powers of the *Länder* to issue and implement laws. The *Länder* have asked the federal government to increase the powers of the Federal Assembly.

The members of the Federal Assembly are elected by the members of the *Land* parliaments and serve for the duration of their mandate as *Land* MPs. Membership of the Federal Assembly reflects the political balance of power after each election of the *Land* parliaments. Members of the Federal Assembly are not, however, answerable for their decisions to the *Land* parliaments that elected them to the Assembly. The federal president determines the number of members of the Federal Assembly on the basis of the national censuses, the last of which was carried out in 1993. The largest of the *Länder* has twelve seats in the Federal Assembly; the other *Länder* have a smaller number of seats depending on their respective population sizes, but a minimum of three seats. The second largest party in each of the respective *Land* parliaments is entitled to at least one seat in the Federal Assembly. The Federal Assembly currently has sixty-four members, comprising: twenty-six members representing the Austrian Conservative Party (ÖVP), twenty-four members representing the Social Democratic Party (SPÖ), and fourteen members representing the Austrian Freedom Party (FPÖ).

The nine federal *Länder* in Austria are governed on the basis of the parliamentary system. Each *Land* has a directly elected *Landtag* (parliament); in the case of Vienna, the *Land* parliament also acts as a municipal council. Each *Land* parliament elects a head of government (*Landeshauptmann*, first minister of the *Land*) and the other members of the *Land* government (the *Land* ministers). The first minister and the other ministers are politically answerable to the *Land* parliament. The first minister of the *Land* has a prominent position in the *Land* government, because he or she is the external representative of parliament and is responsible for exercising the powers delegated by the federal government (under the system of indirect administration). Under the federal constitution, the first minister of each *Land* is appointed by the federal president and can be called before the constitutional court to defend his or her actions to the federal government. The first minister is authorized to give directions to the other *Land* ministers in cases where *Land* governments exercise powers delegated by the federal government. In most cases the first minister also has ultimate jurisdiction regarding the appointment of staff in all departments. Under the *Land* constitutions of seven of the *Länder* (Vienna and Vorarlberg are excluded), the parties represented in the *Land* parliament are entitled to take part in the government of the *Land* on the basis of their respective number of seats in the *Land* parliament ('proportional government').

Decisions are taken by a majority vote in all of the *Länder* parliaments; this means that, despite the application of the system of 'proportional government', the largest party in each of the *Land* parliaments should be able to carry out its policies. In practice, however, decisions tend to be taken unanimously. Between 80 and 90 per cent of the legislative provisions are adopted unanimously by the *Land* parliaments. This situation can often be attributed to the overall political climate in each of the *Länder*; however, critics do point to the high percentage of 'non-decisions'. The legislative process in the *Land* parliaments is based mainly on the submission of bills by the government, as is the case with the federal government (Marko 1992).

Political competition among the various political parties involved in 'proportional government' takes two forms in parliament: on the one hand, lively debates take place on departmental responsibilities and dividing up the work of the *Land* parliaments; on the other hand, political parties seek to establish a high profile for themselves on controversial issues for which the other parties are responsible ('opposition in respect of particular political fields').

Land parliaments are charged with: (*i*) regional administrative tasks forming part of their own specific responsibilities; and (*ii*) national administrative tasks delegated to the *Länder* by the federal government, which involve the *Länder* acting on behalf of the central government. The administrative role of the *Land* parliaments, therefore, covers almost all areas of administration, but the degree to which the *Land* parliaments are able to shape provisions varies considerably. At the one end of the spectrum, the *Land* parliaments are responsible only for implementing legislation, whilst at the other end of the spectrum, they make planning decisions which will determine the future course of action.

The most important tasks of the *Land* governments include activities relating to the administration of private enterprise (Art. 17 of the constitution); this includes, for example, measures relating to (regional) structural policy, economic policy and labour market policy, spatial planning, cultural policy, transnational cooperation, and the administration of all forms of aid for which the federal government has responsibility. The way in which administrative powers are divided among the various tiers of government in Austria does not affect the position of the *Länder* as private-law bodies. Just like other players, the *Länder* are able to be party to legal transactions, for example by taking a share in undertakings. The federal government and the *Länder*, on the one hand, and the *Länder* amongst themselves, on the other, are entitled to conclude agreements relating to matters that fall within their remit. The *Länder* are entitled to conclude treaties with foreign states, or regions of such states, regarding matters that fall within their remit (Pernthaler and Weber 1992).

The political clout of the *Länder* should, therefore, not be underestimated, despite their relatively weak position under the constitution. Unlike the German *Länder*, which have major powers of co-determination regarding federal legislation, the Austrian *Länder*, for their part, have other resources at their disposal.

By longstanding tradition, people in the *Länder* are able to maintain a separate political and cultural identity, which is often reflected in a solidly 'anti-centralist' attitude. Voters' identification with a particular *Land* is also reflected in the party-political context; six *Länder* (the exceptions being Vienna, Carinthia, and Burgenland) have been governed by the ÖVP without interruption since 1945, whereas at national level the SPÖ has been in power since 1970 (Table 5.1).

The practice of 'proportional government' and the extensive participation of associations in government have ensured political integration over many decades, in particular at *Land* level. This has given the *Land* governments an undisputed, clear mandate to represent the interests of their respective *Länder*, cooperating with the other tiers of government, within the overall administration of Austria. The various interests are balanced

TABLE 5.1 Composition of the governments of the Second Republic, 1945–97

Term of office	Federal chancellor	Form of government
1945	Karl Renner (SPÖ)	Provisional national government
1945–7	Leopord Figl (ÖVP)	All-party government ÖVP/SPÖ/KPÖ
1947–53	Leopord Figl (ÖVP)	Grand coalition ÖVP/SPÖ
1953–61	Julius Raab (ÖVP)	Grand coalition ÖVP/SPÖ
1961–4	Alfons Gorbach (ÖVP)	Grand coalition ÖVP/SPÖ
1964–6	Josef Klaus (ÖVP)	Grand coalition ÖVP/SPÖ
1966–70	Josef Klaus (ÖVP)	One-party government ÖVP
1970–1	Bruno Kreisky (SPÖ)	Minority govenment SPÖ
1971–83	Bruno Kreisky (SPÖ)	One-party government SPÖ
1983–6	Fred Sinowatz (SPÖ)	Small coalition SPÖ/FPÖ
1986–7	Franz Vranitzky (SPÖ)	Small coalition SPÖ/FPÖ
1987–97	Franz Vranitzky (SPÖ)	Grand coalition SPÖ/ÖVP
1997–	Viktor Klima (ÖVP)	SPÖ/ÖVP

SPÖ, *Sozialdemokratische Partei Österreichs* (Social Democratic Party of Austria); ÖVP, *Österreichische Volkspartei* (Austrian People's Party); FPÖ, *Freiheitliche Partei Österreichs* (Freedom Party of Austria); KPÖ, *Kommunistische Partei Österreichs* (Communist Party of Austria).

not only by means of legal provisions, but also, to a very large extent, by way of negotiations.

Under the specifically Austrian form of political administration, the *Länder* do indeed have less direct influence on the policy of the federal government, but these two tiers of administration are more closely linked in the administration of the country. The Austrian system of administration gives the *Länder* and local governments considerable leeway for developing a programme-based strategy for implementing legislation.

2.3 The Local Level

The 2,357 local authorities enjoy autonomy under both the national and the *Land* constitutions. Local authorities have both their own autonomous powers and delegated powers. As part of their autonomous powers, local government bodies implement measures enacted by the federal government and the *Länder* (e.g., the inspection, at local level, of safety, public health, and building provisions or by setting up local government bodies or other bodies to carry out local government tasks). As regards the delegated powers, local authorities set their own criteria. In addition to fulfilling their autonomous roles, local authorities are extensive providers of services: as 'independent economic bodies' or through private enterprise bodies. Such services, some of which are mandatory, include the establishment and running of kindergartens, schools, adult training facilities, sports facilities, public utilities, and waste disposal systems.

Local government funding is to a large extent dependent on the redistribution of funding by the federal government and the *Länder*. Funding stems from a tax system that is partially interlinked. Under this system, local authorities are able to levy their own taxes (e.g., land taxes, alcohol taxes, and local government taxes), whilst at the same time receiving a share of the federal tax revenues. In addition, local authorities receive dedicated payments, charges, and other forms of remuneration. The allocation of taxation rights and the entitlement to receive tax proceeds are determined by virtue of the above-mentioned negotiation procedure involving the *Länder*; the outcome of these negotiations is embodied in a specific federal law.

There are no counties under the Austrian system. Fourteen local authority bodies (mostly representing large cities) have their own statutes under which they take over the role of district authorities.

Local government is essentially organized in accordance with the parliamentary principle. Four *Länder* have already introduced direct elections for the post of mayor, which has increased the personalized and quasi-presidential nature of the political system.

The principle of 'proportional government' is applied to local authorities, as it is in the majority of *Land* governments. Under this principle, political parties are represented on the executive of the local authority in proportion to the number of seats they hold in the local council. Mayors are elected either by a system of direct election or on the basis of a majority decision by the members of the council of the local authority. Coalitions can thus be established which may result in the election of candidates other than representatives of the party holding the highest number of seats.

2.4 The Role of Political Parties

Until the mid 1980s, Austria represented a classic example of a three-party system, which largely reflected the party-political groupings of the late nineteenth century. The two largest parties, the SPÖ and the ÖVP, were the key political players; they were backed up by a third, small party, the FPÖ. Criticism levelled at the highly organized party system, a decline in the political 'camps', and overall changes in the socio-cultural field and in attitudes have clearly changed the Austrian party-political system at the end of the twentieth century. These changes are reflected by a number of events.

- The Greens have become established as the fourth political party. They entered the National Assembly after the 1986 elections and have consolidated their position since (4.8 per cent of the votes in the 1995 elections). Green political parties are also represented in five *Land* parliaments and in

the case of their main bastion, Tyrol (10.7 per cent of the votes in the 1994 elections), they are also represented in the *Land* government.
- Since 1986 the FPÖ has positioned itself largely as a right-wing populist party; as a result it has made substantial gains at the expense of the other two major parties (21.9 per cent of the votes in the federal elections of 1995, as against 9.7 per cent in the 1986 elections).
- The *Liberale Forum* (Liberal Forum) broke away from the FPÖ in protest and is also represented in the National Assembly since 1994 (5.5 per cent of the votes in the 1995 election).

Austria now has a five-party system, which has considerably reduced the power of the two major political groupings, the ÖVP and SPÖ. In 1995 the ÖVP received 28.3 per cent of the votes against 41.3 per cent in 1986. The SPÖ received 38.1 per cent of the votes in the 1995 elections and 43.1 per cent in the 1986 elections. However, these changes have not opened the door to new possibilities for coalitions at the federal government level. Since 1987, as for most of the Second Republic, Austria has been governed by a large coalition.

Although a change in the party-political system would suggest that Austria was moving away from grand coalitions, such coalitions are clearly well entrenched, particularly because of the stance taken by the FPÖ, which is, to a large extent, a xenophobic, right-wing populist party. Therefore, paradoxically, the FPÖ both profits from and perpetuates the outdated nature of the present form of government (Pelinka 1997).

Since the mid 1980s the democratic system based on agreements between parties has increasingly been losing ground in both the *Länder* and local government. This has been caused mainly by the spectacular successes of the FPÖ under the leadership of Jörg Haider (since 1986) in elections of the *Land* parliaments and in the mayoral elections. The FPÖ is now represented in all of the *Land* parliaments in Austria and in seven *Land* governments. It has become the second most important party in the parliaments of both Vienna (27.9 per cent of the votes in the 1996 election) and Carinthia (33.3 per cent of the votes in 1994). Jörg Haider even held the post of first minister of Carinthia for a time. The FPÖ has also been successful in local government elections, including the mayoral elections in the *Land* capitals of Graz, Klagenfurt, and Bregenz.

Despite the decline in political allegiance and the falling numbers of political party members since the beginning of the 1980s, membership of the two main parties in Austria remains extremely high when measured against the equivalent figures for other west European countries. Taken together, the ÖVP and the SPÖ still have a membership of almost one million out of an electorate of some 5.8 million. Membership arrangements of the two parties do, however, differ. The SPÖ is a relatively centralized organization based on individual membership, whilst ÖVP membership generally derives from membership of one of its six affiliated organizations:

- the *Österreichischen Arbeiter- und Angestelltenbund* (ÖAAB, Austrian Workers and Employees Federation);
- the *Österreichischen Bauernbund* (ÖBB, Federation of Austrian Farmers);
- the *Österreichischen Wirtschaftsbund* (ÖWB, Austrian Business Federation);
- the *Österreichischen Frauenbewegung* (Austrian Women's Movement); and
- the *Junge Volkspartei* (Young ÖVP).

The first three affiliated organizations (ÖAAB, ÖBB, and ÖWB) have traditionally claimed set quotas of posts (for example at elections for the National Assembly and the *Land* parliaments). The same applies for the SPÖ, particularly in respect of the party's women's organization and its *Fraktion sozialdemokratischer Gewerkschafter* (FSG, social-democratic trade union wing). The increasing trend towards the preliminary election of candidates within parties in the 1990s (by the ÖVP, the SPÖ, and the Greens) has cast doubt on such traditional claims.

Until 1995 the FPÖ represented a relatively loosely organized political party; it has, however, since then established itself as a 'movement' and has consciously cultivated an 'anti-party' image. In contrast to the ossified grand coalitions, the FPÖ has taken on the title of *Freiheitliche Bewegung-Bündnis Bürger '98* (Freedom Movement-Citizens' Alliance '98). On 1 May 1998 it set up a rival trade union in opposition to the unitary *Österreichischen Gewerkschaftsbund* (ÖGB, Austrian Trade Union Federation). The main aim of the FPÖ's new trade union is to secure 'work for Austrians first'.

3. The Practice of Subnational Democracy

3.1 The Role of Policy Networks

Austria is a highly federalized country. This applies even more to its social structure than to the organization of its political institutions, as laid down in the constitution. Commentators stress that it is at school, at the latest, that Austrian children learn about the characteristics of their region and begin to think of themselves as, for example, Tyrolean, Viennese, Carinthian, etc.

Borders between regions are very important, not only in terms of government, but also in social and economic terms. The boundaries of federal administrative districts, where these exist, broadly conform to these borders. Horizontal policy networks, therefore, arise virtually automatically within individual *Länder*.

The federal influence on political decision making is further strengthened by the strong representation of the *Länder* in the economic *Kammern* (chambers) and in free associations. The two major parties, the ÖVP and the SPÖ, rely, not only at federal level but also at *Land* level, on allied associations and self-governing bodies. The social players at *Land* level thus complement each other and do preparatory work for the political parties (Kostelka and Unkart 1977).

A coordinating body was set up, under an inter-*Land* agreement, to enable the *Länder* to exchange views and coordinate policy. The regular conferences of *Land* first ministers and their experts are prepared here, the main aim being to hammer out a common position *vis-à-vis* the federal government. This body plays a particularly important role in the preparation of the *Finanzausgleich* (financial redistribution) negotiations.

The local authorities come together, across *Land* boundaries, in two organizations at federal level. The *Österreichischer Städtebund* (ÖSB, Association of Austrian Towns) currently comprises 218, mostly larger, towns with a combined population of 4.2 million. The ÖSB negotiates with the federal government and the *Länder*, in particular in the financial redistribution negotiations. It also represents the local authorities in the detailed discussions leading to the adoption of laws and regulations. The *Österreichischer Gemeindebund* (Association of Austrian Municipalities) represents the interests of smaller municipalities and differs little from the ÖSB in its field of activities.

3.2 Interest Groups

Interest groups play an important part in Austria's political system, alongside the political parties. Cooperation between interest groups in the framework of social partnership is the counterpart of party-based parliamentarism.

The institutions of social partnership, built up by the interest groups in collaboration with the political parties since 1945, are (neo-)corporatist vehicles for the regulation of social life. Their main features are:

- a joint commission for wages and prices, set up in 1957, that deals with (voluntary and non-binding) controls on wages and prices;
- a multiplicity of subcommittees and commissions, through which interest groups are involved in policy at *Land* and federal level;
- the involvement of economic interest groups in the preparation of legislation (under the prior-appraisal procedure);
- the involvement in the legally required supervision of the social security institutions.

TABLE 5.2   The main economic associations and their relationship with the political parties

Economic association	Party		
	SPÖ	ÖVP	FPÖ
ÖGB (Austrian Trade Union Federation)	Majority	Minority	Minority
Workers' chambers	Majority	Minority	Minority
Economic chambers	Majority	Majority	Minority
Agricultural chambers	Minority	Majority	Minority

SPÖ, *Sozialdemokratische Partei Österreichs* (Social Democratic Party of Austria); ÖVP, *Österreichische Volkspartei* (Austrian People's Party); FPÖ, *Freiheitliche Partei Österreichs* (Freedom Party of Austria).
Source: Pelinka (1997).

One of the main economic bodies is the *Österreichischer Gewerkschaftsbund* (ÖGB, Austrian Trade Union Federation), an umbrella organization for fourteen trade unions; 50 to 60 per cent of all employed workers are members of the ÖGB (Table 5.2).

The *Verein Österreichischer Industrieller* (VÖI, Association of Austrian Industrialists) represents Austria's main firms. It is also involved in party financing (with funds mainly going to the ÖVP, but also to the FPÖ) and the breakaway *Liberale Partei* (Liberal Party).

Chambers for blue- and white-collar workers as well as economic chambers—split into six sections: trade, commerce, industry, transport, tourism, and banking, loans, and insurance—exist not only at federal level but also in all nine *Länder*. These bodies provide legal advice to their members and also represent their interests in conflicts related to the social partnership. Hence, the umbrella organization of the economic chambers opposes the ÖGB in questions of wage policy. An agricultural chamber with legal status exists to represent farming interests.

The chamber organizations must hold elections. Political groupings close to the political parties select candidates. The ÖGB holds no direct elections, but is guided by the results of the workers' and staff council elections, which are usually also contested by party-political lists. Thus, party-political co-operation and cooperation between the interest groups are closely interrelated; this is typical of Austrian democracy at all political levels.

The Catholic Church, with its very active, autonomous lay organizations, is an important social group. Both Catholic and Protestant denominations (about 80 per cent and 5 per cent of the population, respectively) contribute to social welfare in many areas and as such act as partners for the local authorities.

3.3 Critiques of Local and Regional Democracy in Austria

Until the early 1980s, public opinion was strongly in favour of the Austrian political system, as compared with that of other countries. Austrians had a high degree of confidence in the state and an unusually high regard for the way they were governed. This was true in particular of economic and social policy, with its high level of social guarantees and lasting influence on the economy, not least via an extensive public sector (Ulram 1992).

A particularly high approval rating was traditionally enjoyed by the *Land* governments, by which Austrians felt even better governed than by the federal government. Only in Vienna was public approval of the federal government higher than that of the *Land* government (Kostelka and Unkart 1977). These results also reflect a very low level of conflict in *Land* politics at that time and a strong identification with the region or *Land*. Thus, a poll conducted in the mid 1990s to establish whether Austrians identified most strongly with their municipality, region, or state produced figures of 70 per cent, 61 per cent, and 59 per cent for region, municipality, and state respectively (*Eurobarometer*, no. 1996).

Since the 1980s there is strong evidence to suggest that radical changes in state and society are feeding through more clearly and more rapidly to the local and regional levels. Indicators for this trend are declining party membership and turnout levels at regional and local elections, which, whilst still high by European standards, are perceptibly falling (e.g., only 61 per cent in Graz, Styria, in January 1998).

A criticism levelled at *Land* politics is that the proportional system of government is no longer in step with the increasing polarization of the *Land* assemblies. At the local level too the executive is becoming increasingly personalized. The direct election of mayors, which already occurs in four *Länder* and is being advocated in others, is difficult to reconcile with consensus politics aiming for the broadest possible basis of support for political decisions.

Two conflicting trends manifest themselves earlier at the level of the *Länder* and the local authorities than at federal level. On the one hand, the trend towards greater fluidity in politics has accelerated since the mid 1980s. Party allegiance has declined sharply. Younger voters exhibit little or no party alignment. Willingness to shift support and tactical voting are the result (Ulram 1992). On the other hand, the consensus-based democratic model of the post-war decades has in many respects served its purpose. The unstable democracy of the interwar years became stabilized. Various groups in society organized at the public level. Thus, in comparison with other European countries, the social and economic progress of the post-war decades lasted longer and was more widely shared.

However, to many younger Austrians the inherited participation and welfare structures seem to be relics of a system of patronage that is in many respects outmoded. The participants in local and regional democracy, who have outgrown their party ties, have become more individualistic, but also more mature. The question is whether they will continue to take an interest in the democratic process and what forms of intervention and participation they will favour.

4. *Challenges and Opportunities for Subnational Democracy*

The challenges facing local and regional politics in Austria can be summarized as follows. The tasks assigned to the regional and local levels of government have been expanding since the mid 1970s. Increasingly complex problems require new approaches and responses from the local authorities and regions. These changed demands on subnational politics come at a time when institutional arrangements and ways of balancing interests specific to Austria are becoming increasingly 'Europeanized'. From the point of view of local and regional democracy the question arises whether and how new forms of appropriate participation and democratic legitimization can be identified which will permit the further organic development of the Austrian political system.

4.1 New Tasks and Areas of Activity

Austria's local authorities and regions are also affected by globalization, the increased economic competition at the international level, and they are confronted with the limits on the ability of the state to regulate the various fields of economic and social activity. Although the unemployment rate is between 4 and 5 per cent—after Luxembourg the second lowest national rate in the EU, according to European Commission figures (1998)—deep cuts in social spending have been made with a view to fiscal consolidation, particularly by the central government, during the current legislative period. This shows that the economic and social questions, which in the past were dealt with by consensus, have by no means disappeared. In future, the political institutions at regional and local level will be concerned to an even greater degree with the tasks of job creation, social security, and economic reorganization. These tasks can no longer be addressed by politics that are based exclusively on national growth coalitions. Regions and local authorities are increasingly resorting to the establishment of decentralized networks of operators and new, 'corporatist' working relationships between the parties concerned at the middle and lower levels.

In the past, Austrian policy has been highly interventionist in both the economic and social fields. However, in the wake of radical privatization, the influence of government has declined perceptibly. Agreements based on social partnership are suffering from the reduced scope for redistribution and have so far failed to resolve the problem of mass unemployment.

Moreover, criticism of the traditional economic-growth model was voiced at an early stage. Thus, as early as 1978, when an inquiry was carried out by the *Nationalrat* (National Assembly), a majority of voters came out against the commissioning of Austria's first nuclear power station (at Zwentendorf). Although the social partners had pressed for commissioning and although initially the SPÖ was officially in favour of nuclear power, a referendum put an early end to Austria's nuclear programme. Commentators see this as a key conflict that strengthened the environmental movement in the 1980s and 1990s and led to the foundation of green parties that have now, to a large extent, combined forces. As a result of further local and federal disputes, since 1994 all major projects have been subject to an environmental impact assessment with public participation. Other social movements developed alongside the environmental movement, in particular the women's movement, which, in addition to establishing a feminist counterculture, succeeded in politicizing the gender issue within the established institutional system.

The *Länder* and local authorities have reacted to this politicization by extending their administrative apparatus, by opening themselves up to the discussion of new issues, and by offering new forms of democratic participation. The polarization of the political agenda has heightened competition in the regional assemblies and has increased the pressure on members to perform their duties in a more effective manner (Marko 1992).

4.2 Parliamentary Procedure and Efforts at Reform

The rules for elections to the *Land* assemblies now offer a greater degree of flexibility. Only two *Länder* (Burgenland and Vienna) still retain rigid party lists. All other *Länder* allow selection, deletion, or preferential votes. Only Vorarlberg has open lists to which other names may be added; this freedom of nomination is associated, however, with a system of preferential votes.

Parliamentary practices are criticized when changes in the number of committee members disadvantage the smaller parties or where no proportional requirements exist for supervisory or investigative committees. The interparty negotiations on the filling of posts in firms in which the *Land* has a stake, where proportional rules may also exist, have also been called into question.

Efforts to increase the efficiency of the work of the *Land* assemblies have taken two different directions.

- The pooling of expertise in *Land* committees drawn from the *Land* government, members of the *Land* parliament, and the *Land* administration—modelled on the Burgenland constitution of 1981. A committee of this kind on administrative reform was set up, for example, in Burgenland. In Salzburg, this arrangement was adopted to set up an informal, *Land*, policy working committee. Similar arrangements are provided for in the new Styrian *Land* constitution.
- The search for ways of ending the interlocking structure of political power. In some *Länder* (Upper Austria, Salzburg, Styria, Tyrol), government political office is incompatible with a mandate as member of the *Land* assembly. In Carinthia, heads of 'chambers' are not allowed to be, at the same time, members of the *Land* government. In the early 1990s the Styrian ÖVP began a more comprehensive programme of separating government offices, political roles, and positions of economic power. However, critics of this initiative expect areas of influence to become even less transparent.

One part of the reform efforts is aimed at strengthening the supervisory rights of the *Land* assemblies through an easier use of investigative committees or enquiry commissions. In Salzburg, for instance, three commissions of this kind were set up as soon as enquiries had been established (on transit traffic, the EU, and hospitals) at the end of 1989. Particularly exemplary in this respect is Vorarlberg, which has constitutionally based enquiry commissions, only a third of the members of which must be members of the *Land* assembly; a similar situation exists in Styria.

Since the mid 1970s an amendment to the federal constitution has made it possible for one-third of the members of a *Land* parliament, at the request of the members of a political party represented in the *Land* assembly, to refer *Land* laws to the constitutional court for scrutiny. Styria has broken new ground in linking supervision with direct democracy. Here, an initiative by 2 per cent of the citizens of the *Land* can force referral to the Court of Auditors. The FPÖ and the Green Party have been attempting to present themselves as the parties of supervision by seeking the chair of the *Land* assembly supervisory committees. Some *Länder* (Lower Austria, Salzburg) have their own *Land* Courts of Auditors, which are an additional supervisory body responsible to the *Land* assembly. The establishment of such a body is being discussed in several other *Länder*.

The post of *Volksanwalt* (ombudsman) was established for the prevention of abuses in the late 1970s, based on the Scandinavian model. The *Länder* can choose whether to appoint their own ombudsmen or to assign responsibility to the federal level. Thus, in the course of the 1980s, most of the *Länder* set up environmental ombudsman offices; these play mediating roles between government and citizens (Gottweis 1992).

All these reform measures, some of which are now well established, have not, however, silenced the critics of the organization of democracy at *Land* level. The current discussion continues to concentrate on the abolition of proportionally based government in favour of a clear distinction between opposition and governing coalition. This call was made at *Land* level initially by the FPÖ as part of its campaign against the proportional system. Now, however, the Greens, as well as the two main parties, the SPÖ and the ÖVP, have begun increasingly to discuss changes of the form of government in Tyrol, Salzburg, Upper Austria, and Styria. Steps towards reform of the constitution were initiated, via a referendum, in Tyrol and Salzburg in the spring of 1998.

In Salzburg, 90 per cent of the votes cast were in favour of ending the proportional system in the *Land* government. However, the turnout, at 10 per cent of the electorate, was disappointing for the initiators. Upper Austria has decided to await the results of the 1999 Salzburg election and the formation of the new government before discussing the abolition of the proportional system any further.

In all *Länder* the FPÖ has moved away from its formerly positive attitude to the abolition of the proportional system, and now opposes it—probably in view of the lack of coalition offers from the SPÖ and the ÖVP.

At the local level, the movement for the abolition of the proportional system in the *Land* governments is now complemented by a debate on the extension of direct elections for the post of mayor (e.g., in Vorarlberg and Styria).

5. Innovative Approaches to Improving Subnational Democracy

In recent years, the reappraisal of traditional political methods has led to the strengthening of direct democracy in virtually all of the *Länder*.

5.1 Referendums

Almost all Austrian *Länder* (with the exception of Upper Austria) have enshrined the instrument of referendums in their constitutions, revealing a West–East shift in the preference for this form of citizen participation.

Four *Länder* (Lower Austria, Styria, Tyrol, and Vorarlberg) provide for a 'municipality veto', whereby a given number of local authorities are entitled to call for a referendum, which has to be authorized by the municipal council, to oppose a legal provision adopted by the *Land* parliament. This instrument, above all, provides smaller partners in a proportional government with the opportunity to continue their opposition at municipality level.

Most *Länder* offer the possibility of a 'people's veto' against decisions of a *Land* parliament, while prescribing different levels of participation. Vorarlberg also makes provision for the linking of petitions for new legislation with legally binding referendums.

However, certain limitations have been placed on extensive use of this form of direct democracy. In Tyrol, for example, a petition for new legislation that is subsequently rejected in a referendum cannot be reintroduced for at least five years. In Tyrol and Vienna there must be a turnout of at least 50 per cent of the electorate for a referendum to be valid.

5.2 Petitions for New Legislation

With the exception of Salzburg, all *Land* constitutions provide for petitions for new legislation. Participation thresholds between 2 per cent and 5 per cent have to be attained if petitions are to be placed before *Land* parliaments. In Burgenland, Lower Austria, Styria, and Vorarlberg, petitions are also provided for regarding administrative matters; higher participation thresholds are sometimes required in these cases than for petitions for new legislation.

In general, petitions are more common in the area of legislation, while referendums are more widely used in administrative matters. In Styria and Tyrol, the *Land* government can initiate a referendum on new legislation; while in Styria, Tyrol, and Vorarlberg the *Land* parliament can initiate a referendum on administrative matters. In Styria this is regarded in both areas as a right that may be invoked by one-third of the members of the *Land* parliament (in the case of Salzburg, for administrative matters only). Such measures also enable coalition partners in proportional governments to seek solutions to stalemate situations or to broaden their influence.

5.3 Prior Appraisal of Legislation by the Public

In Burgenland, Styria, and Vorarlberg the public has to be given an opportunity to express its opinion on government proposals. In the case of motions put forward by parliamentary members or parliamentary committees, the public has to be asked to give its views when: (*i*) at least half of the members of the *Land* parliament are present for a debate, and (*ii*) a request for public consultation is supported by a two-thirds majority of the members present.

In some cases, significant exceptions apply to the exercise of these popular rights. Individual *Land* constitutions rule out the use of these rights in particular in respect of electoral procedures, staff issues, financial matters, and administrative decisions regarding particular persons. Instead, individual rights of petition have been expanded into an overall right to information and right of appeal (Art. 20(4) of the 1988 Federal Constitution).

An appraisal of the results of these new possibilities to participate in direct democracy shows that they have had a party-political impact and have given rise to cross-party action. The new instruments will, therefore, continue to be used as a means of strengthening the role of the opposition in the representative system. The success or failure of these measures is increasingly determined by the media. Overall, however, politics at *Land* and local-government level continue to be predominantly determined by the governing triangle, constituted by party leaders, association leaders, and bureaucracy (Marko 1992).

6. Conclusions

The political developments already under way in Austria's *Länder* and local authorities will change the ways in which government and parliamentary work is conducted. It will provide a new and lasting basis for cooperation between political spheres and the leading interest groups in society and will thus considerably change many aspects of Austria's post-war consensus model. These changes will also affect government. There is an inevitable shift from an agreement-based model of administration towards a conflict- and competition-orientated model, which, nonetheless, provides Austria's decentralized levels of government with significant opportunities to establish new political arrangements.

Since the mid 1970s, critical initiatives and new social movements have thus served to widen the agenda of local politics. The commitment and expertise of these new movements have also brought changes in the way administrations are run. The now well-established networks that link these initiatives have provided the necessary infrastructure for the establishment of democratic openness, participation, and accountability.

The Austrian *Länder* and local authorities are administrative bodies that have many resources at their disposal and that traditionally draw on extensive experience from the business world. There is much evidence that the *Länder* and local authorities have been successful in moving away from an inherited, inflexible corporatism towards more open and flexible network structures. Examples, especially in the field of economic and environmental policy, show that local authorities play a leading role in the establishment of new and effective bodies and links between organizations.

One such example is the way in which the City of Vienna has been bringing together, since 1982, the activities of various environmental technology firms within the *Umweltkompetenzzentrum Wien* (Vienna Environmental Expertise Centre). The City of Vienna runs the centre in cooperation with the social partners and two large banks. The aim is to make best-possible use of administrative assistance and advisory services. Since the mid 1980s the centre has in this way been able to attract 561 Austrian and international companies to Vienna and has contributed to the creation of 32,700 new jobs. There are other, similar examples, including the City of Graz and its environmental authority, whose eco-profit scheme reduces energy consumption and waste production in private companies.

Decentralized political bodies also appear to redefine the interfaces between public bodies and private or social groups in other practical areas, such as social policy, housing assistance, and youth and women's policy. By means of a gradual transformation of cooperation based on associations and through greater pluralism in the networks of players, the public sector is becoming sufficiently effective and focused at subnational level to avoid drowning in a sea of overlapping and chaotic, private, quango-type structures.

References

BRAUNEDER, W. and LACHMAYER, F. (eds) (1987). *Österreichische Verfassungsgeschichte*, 4th edn. Wien: Manz.

GOTTWEIS, H. (1992). 'Neue soziale Bewegungen in Österreich', in H. Dachs *et al.* (eds), *Handbuch des Politischen Systems Österreichs*, 2nd edn. Wien: Manz.

KOSTELKA, P. and UNKART, R. (1977). 'Vom Stellenwert des Föderalismus in Österreich', in H. Fischer (ed.), *Das politische System Österreichs*, 2nd edn. Wien: Europaverlag.

MARKO, J. (1992). 'Die Verfassungssysteme der Bundesländer: Institutionen und Verfahren repräsentativer und direkter Demokratie', in H. Dachs *et al.* (eds), *Handbuch des Politischen Systems Österreichs*, 2nd edn. Wien: Europaverlag.

PELINKA, A. (1997). 'Das politische System Österreichs', in W. Ismayr (ed.), *Die politischen Systeme Westeuropas*. Opladen: Leske & Budrich.

PERNTHALER, P. and WEBER, K. (1992). 'Landesregierung', in H. Dachs *et al.* (ed.), *Handbuch des Politischen Systems Österreichs*, 2nd edn. Wien: Manz.

ULRAM, P. A. (1992). 'Politische Kultur der Bevölkerung', in H. Dachs *et al.* (ed.), *Handbuch des Politischen Systems Deutschlands*, 2nd edn. Wien: Manz.

WINTER, B. (1995). 'Haider oder ein neues Reformprojekt. Elemente und Ursprünge der österreichischen Krise'. *Blätter für deutsche und internationale Politik*, 7: 835–44.

6

The Netherlands: Reinventing Tradition in Local and Regional Democracy

Frank Hendriks

1. History and Concept of Democracy

1.1 Historical Background

Towns and municipalities have played a key role in the history of state formation in the Netherlands. Within the wider association of the Holy Roman Empire, towns and municipalities enjoyed more or less autonomous status. Under the Burgundians and Spanish Hapsburgs, there were various attempts at centralization, but they were ultimately unsuccessful. In the years after 1568, towns and municipalities in the northern Netherlands became increasingly independent from Spanish-Hapsburg rule. The Republic of the Seven United Provinces was declared in 1588. This republic, which existed until 1795, was a highly *decentralized federation* with a weak government. Sovereignty lay with the provinces, *de facto* and *de jure*. The provinces in their turn were highly dependent on local administrations, especially the western provinces. The governing culture of the republic was one of improvisation, horizontal consultation between partners who were very dependent upon each other. Both 'priest' (referring to the dominant Calvinist ethos) and 'merchant' (referring to the Dutch spirit of commercialism) were influential in this political culture. Cooperation between the public and private sectors was tried very successfully in the Republic.

During the Batavian French period (1795–1813), Napoleonic features were introduced into the Dutch system of government: the power of the provinces was radically curtailed and the provinces were forced into the straitjacket of a *unitary state after the French model*. Municipalities were the lowest level of the administrative structure, which showed unmistakable hierarchical traits. It was less easy to reform the administrative culture than the administrative

I would like to thank Rodney Wetering and Peter Tops for commenting on this chapter.

structure. Diffusion of power, power-sharing, decentralization, improvisation: even the Napoleonic system could not eliminate these administrative concepts.

Under the kingdom that was built on the foundations of the Batavian-French system, there was little change at first in interadministrative relations. The kingdom was a unitary state with a relatively decentralized administrative culture still, but which structurally had acquired hierarchical features under the influence of the French model. The authorities were able to resist reform for a long time, until in 1848, the year of international revolutions, King William II, rather suddenly, decided to commission the drawing up of a new constitution. The task was entrusted to J. R. Thorbecke, who had been influenced by the German historical school of law and its organic theory of the state. Thorbecke's political and constitutional work of 1848–51 had a crucial impact on Dutch government and on the role and position of its local authorities. During this period, Thorbecke sketched the outlines of the *decentralized unitary state* that still exists today (Van Deth and Vis 1995).

1.2 Subnational Government and the Thorbeckean Constitution

With his Constitution (1848), Provinces Act (1850), and Municipalities Act (1851), Thorbecke provided the structure to which the Dutch system of government more or less still corresponds today. This structure is generally classified as a 'decentralized unitary state'. The unitary nature of this type of state is not based on central government, but on agreement between the three active components of the state (central government, provinces, and local authorities). The tradition of decentralization and power distribution that characterized the old Republic of the Seven United Provinces was preserved in Thorbecke's constitution (Breunese 1982).

In his basic constitutional plan for Dutch government, Thorbecke endeavoured to create an 'association of mutually restricting bodies designed to work freely together'—local and provincial authorities have broad, general powers to deal with matters of local concern. There is no question of pre-defined competences as in the United Kingdom *ultra vires* rule. As long as local and provincial authorities take account of legislation passed by higher authorities, they are free to do and allow anything that they consider necessary and useful.

Thorbecke resisted the view that the independence of local government should be associated with protecting and isolating one authority from the other. His system is typified by the 'freedom in restraint' of higher and lower authorities. Local authorities' freedom lies in their right of initiative within the system of interadministrative relations. In Thorbecke's scheme, the actual power of local authorities is balanced by the constitutional power of other authorities (Boersema 1949; Toonen 1987).

Under the influence of the German historical school of law, Thorbecke included in his unitary-state model features that manifestly belong to an organic-state model. He established general competences for local, provincial, and national authorities, which were thus accorded partly overlapping and mutually limiting remits. Regional government in the Netherlands is often a matter of co-government. The value placed on consensus gives considerable leverage to each power-sharing partner, which can provide incentives to seek creative solutions that satisfy all parties, but may also lead to frustrating dead-locks. The 'joint decision trap' that Scharpf has described in Germany also applies to the Netherlands.

The permanent search for consensus produces a pattern of intensive inter-actions where each of the three levels of government has relative advantages and disadvantages. Local authorities can use their local knowledge and operational experience. Provinces can turn their intermediary 'lynchpin' position to account. And national authorities can act as a final arbitrator of conflicts, while preferring to reach agreements with provinces and local authorities rather than to impose their will on them (Rieken and Baaijens 1986).

2. The Institutional Expression of Democracy

2.1 The National System

The political scientist Lijphart distinguishes between two models of democracy, which he breaks down into different institutional dimensions. The first is the Westminster model of democracy, which in its purest form is found in the United Kingdom (before devolution). The second is the consensus model of democracy, which is clearly inspired by Lijphart's earlier search for 'conso-ciational' democracy in the Netherlands. The former model is characterized by concentration and centralization of power, and the second by power-sharing and decentralization.

Lijphart and other authors who assume that there is a continuum between the Westminster model and the consensus model generally situate the political system of the Netherlands at the most consensual end of the continuum (Anderson and Guilory 1997). This is partly a case of formal institutions expressing democratic relations, and even more a case of informal institutions expressing democratic norms and values.

The formal institutions that determine the national system can be outlined quite briefly. The Netherlands has a party and voting system without thresholds and with straightforward proportional representation. In a country like the Netherlands that is pluralistic socially and culturally, this produces a fragmented and pluralistic party system dominated by more than just one consideration—in contrast with the United Kingdom, for example, where the socio-economic dimension has been all-important.

Unlike in the United Kingdom, the parliamentary majority is not the prevailing force in national government. The system of government is protected by the constitution: any political player or group that wishes to make changes to the established system must amend the constitution by a qualified majority of two-thirds of the Members of Parliament. In addition, both houses of parliament—upper and lower—must agree. This is part of the reason why there have been only incremental changes to the decentralized unitary state designed by Thorbecke since 1848. Power-sharing has remained an important feature of national government.

It is virtually impossible for one party to accede to power in the Netherlands. The political system is set up in such a way that power is usually exercised by a coalition of parties. However, the government is not fused with parliament. The relationship between government and parliament is in theory relatively dualistic. Although this is less the case in practice, dualism is certainly more institutionalized at the national than at the local level. The two houses of the Dutch parliament are less of a match to each other than the two houses in Germany, but more so than the two houses in the United Kingdom. The lower house is the more important of the two and is directly elected. The upper house is elected indirectly via the twelve provinces. However, the link with the provinces is weak; in Germany the link between the *Länder* and the *Bundesrat* is much stronger.

In respect of formal institutions, the Dutch system is organized to be relatively, but not excessively, consensual. It is above all the informal instruments of government, whose origins must often be traced back many centuries, that gives the Netherlands its place among the most consensual democracies. The administrative culture of the republic was one of improvisation, and today its style of government is still described in terms of the 'three Cs': consultation, consensus, and compromise (Duyvendak 1998). The three Cs permeate every level of the Dutch system. They are evident in the (neo-)corporatist economic system that is based on formal cooperation between employers, employees, and government. They are also evident in local politics, where joint policy-making and interactive planning are the modern equivalents of persuasion and consultation during the time of the Republic of the Seven United Provinces.

The Dutch government system is based on a culture of dialogue. It is a system of discussions and gatherings (Van Vree 1994). W. Frijhoff, a Professor of Modern History, remarked on this subject in an interview: '... nobody is in charge here, everybody is in charge, and ... in every possible way'.

Frijhoff referred to the typical Dutch culture of dialogue, which certainly dates back at least twelve generations and proved its worth above all during the time of the republic: 'The Dutch republic had an ill-defined structure. Power was exercised at local level, by the town councils and the states and regions. The States General were just an offshoot of this system, and this still has an effect today'.

Where culturally determined traditions and mores are concerned, it is interesting to compare the Netherlands with Belgium. On the one hand, the Netherlands has many similarities with Belgium, which is also a consensus democracy, even more so since federalization; on the other hand, substantial differences can be observed between Belgium and the Netherlands with respect to models of citizenship. This has to do with the difference between the Latin and northern (political) cultures. According to Hofstede's research (1991), the Netherlands clearly fits the northern model, whereas Belgium is much closer to the Latin model. The Latin model is characterized by distanced and often distrustful relations between government and citizens. In the Netherlands the northern cultural model is manifest in the so-called 'high-tolerance' and 'high-trust' culture. Authority and state do not have the negative connotations that they have in Belgium.

2.2 The Subnational Level

2.2.1 Local Government

Local authorities are generally seen as the most important level of subnational government in the Netherlands. In the constitutional set-up, as it has developed since Thorbecke's Constitution, local authorities have general competences, subject to certain conditions. They are free to develop activities that they consider important for the well-being and welfare of the local community, but this freedom is not unlimited: it is conditional (Toonen 1991).

Local-government activities must not conflict with rules and requirements set by higher levels of government. Local authorities are also subject to administrative control, which has traditionally been broken down into preventive (a priori) and disciplinary (a posteriori) control. Over the course of time, disciplinary control, which was unpopular with local authorities, has been reduced, and the role of preventive control has increased. The provinces are to a major extent responsible for administrative control (see below).

Another actor whose formal task is to assess the broader implications and merits of local government is the mayor. Mayors are appointed for this task by the national government. Unlike Belgian mayors, who are also appointed, Dutch mayors usually have no links with local politics. They are expected to be impartial. Larger cities often have mayors who have won their spurs in national politics. National concerns—geographical distribution of political parties, political rotation, and political 'outplacement'—are very relevant here. Local political parties can help to choose candidates and give their views. Local views are increasingly being taken into account, but it still regularly happens that the Minister for Home Affairs bypasses the preferred local candidate.

The possibility of introducing a system of elected mayors has been discussed for some time, but it is unlikely that this will ever happen. Although the current system has disadvantages, it also has considerable advantages. The fact that mayors are appointed by central government means that they are often well connected at this level, and this has positive implications for the management of local authorities' external relations. The fact that the mayor is not a direct political player and does not have to worry constantly about being re-elected and can, therefore, concentrate on his or her most important task—quality control—is an advantage for the political process in the local council and the municipal executive. Research has shown that mayors in the Netherlands have considerable influence compared with other local political players. They are also by far the most familiar actors on the local political scene.

Apart from being responsible for public order, Dutch mayors have few policy-related duties. Responsibility for policy is shared among the aldermen, who sit with the mayor on the municipal executive, which is in charge of the day-to-day management of the local authority. The aldermen are elected by and from the local council. It is much less common than in Belgium for the aldermen to come from a homogeneous political majority in the council; the executive more often reflects the political composition of the council, with several political parties forming a coalition.

The local council is the highest administrative organ of the local authority and is formally a unitary system. The municipal executive is meant to be the executive branch of the council but, in practice, the situation is much more dualistic, with the aldermen playing an active, shaping role in local politics and the councillors an evaluating and monitoring role (Tops 1994). The work of the aldermen is as much driven by the councillors as vice versa. Of all the political positions in the local authority, that of councillor has become the most pressurized. The local council is officially the most important body, but in practice it is bypassed in various spheres: in the political domain the councillors are overshadowed by the aldermen, and in the public domain the councillors feel themselves to be increasingly sidelined by civil servants and interest groups who are increasingly connected through interactive decision-making arrangements.

2.2.2 Provincial Government

The most important institutions in Dutch provincial government are the royal commissioner, the provincial council (the province's elected body), and the provincial executive (day-to-day management). Relations between these three institutions have much in common with those between the local bodies, as described above: the system is officially unitary, but in practice shows many dualistic characteristics; the commissioner is also not legitimized through elections, but is nevertheless the most influential player. However, there are also differences, which have to do with the particular role and position that provincial government has acquired in the Dutch system over time.

Historically, the provinces are the building blocks of the Dutch state. Between 1588 and 1795 there was a confederal republic in the Low Countries, in which the provinces enjoyed a considerable degree of autonomy. During the next few decades, however, the power of the provinces was substantially eroded. Reforms during the Batavian French period (1795–1813) aimed to curtail the provinces' power and incorporate the provincial layer of government into a uniform and indivisible unitary state. After the Netherlands regained its independence (1813), the authors of the new Constitution of the Kingdom of the Netherlands (1814–15) did their utmost to steer the provinces into an unimportant minor role as administrative offshoots of central government.

The Thorbeckean constitutional system restricted the authority of the provinces less than is usually assumed (Toonen 1987). But the scope given, in theory, to the provinces was certainly not taken full advantage of in practice. During the second half of the nineteenth century and in the twentieth century, the provinces lost administrative authority in a way that has not always been understood by outside observers—who look first at the constitutional status of the middle layer of government. Central government and local authorities rather than the provinces have become the face of public administration, to the extent even that over time the provinces have been described as 'the authorities' authority', that is an authority that was only visible and relevant to the authorities and civil servants of central government, provinces, and local authorities.

Today, the provinces' remit can be broadly subdivided into three categories. First, there are matters affecting the general public. The provinces' role in this sphere is limited. Second, there is the real authorities' authority. This is the classic role of the province as the watchdog of local authorities and water boards, particularly as regards their finances, and as the intermediary between central and local government, which is apparent, for example, in the role played by the royal commissioner in appointing mayors.

Third, are the activities of provincial government in the sphere of social policy. Over the past ten years, this has expanded considerably in areas such as the environment, agriculture, nature conservation, economic development, communications, and transport. An active, organizing role is increasingly often aspired to, with the emphasis on mobilizing the relevant players and putting them in contact with each other.

2.3 Institutionalized Interdependencies

Starting with Thorbecke's concept, which emphasizes the conditional autonomy of government bodies, actual developments since the mid nineteenth
century can be seen as a steady increase in both the amount and intensity of
interaction between the levels of government. In order to operate effectively
today, local authorities and higher levels of government must coordinate their
activities.

Administrative autonomy (mutual independence between levels of government) is a feature of the Dutch government system that has become increasingly important over time. Since the establishment of the decentralized
unitary state by Thorbecke, interdependence has become increasingly *institutionalized*. In this light, an open-minded view must also be taken of the so-
called 'nationalization of local government'. Of course, local government has
become more and more affected by national government over time. On the
other hand, national government has in turn become increasingly dependent
on local-government activities and sources of power. The number of central-
government instruments certainly increased in number over the years, but
quantity is not always reflected in quality. Circulars, information services, and
planning requirements seem in practice to be irritating, but not very effective.
The reorganization of administrative instruments in the 1980s and 1990s
must, therefore, be seen rather as a recognition of failure than as an abandonment of central-government authority.

The scope of legislation on co-government (*medebewind*)—under which
central government calls on local authorities for help in providing public
services—has increased considerably since the beginning of the twentieth
century. The balance between autonomy and co-government has been
reversed compared to the situation in the middle of the nineteenth century.
The vast majority of local-authorities activities covered by legislation are currently governed by the co-government system (RBB 1988; Derksen 1995: 13).
On the other hand, the nature of co-government has changed substantially.
In many areas, local authorities are now allowed to regulate in a certain matter
as opposed to simply implementing rules imposed by a higher authority.

By international standards, Dutch local authorities have relatively limited
own tax revenues. Even when income from duties and levies is added to these
revenues, local authorities' own resources amounted to no more than 16 per
cent of their total resources in 1995. In 1986 this percentage was less than 8
per cent (RGF 1996: 60). On the other hand, total revenues are relatively high
by international standards (WRR 1990: 202; OECD 1996: 7).

Local authorities in the Netherlands are largely dependent on central
government for their resources. Most of central government's contribution
to local budgets takes the form of specific transfers that are tied to departmental spending provisions. In 1985, over 70 per cent of local government

TABLE 6.1   Local expenditure as a percentage of total
public expenditure in the Benelux countries, 1980–92

Country	Year			
	1980	1984	1988	1992
Belgium	15.2	12.8	12.4	11.7
Netherlands	32.9	34.4	31.0	28.9
Luxembourg	15.2	12.9	—	—

Source: Maes (1997: 8).

revenue consisted of specific transfers. Over 400 different specific transfers existed at that time (Ministerie van Binnenlandse Zaken 1996: 4; RGF 1996: 60). Under decentralizing measures, the number of specific transfers was reduced to just over 140 in 1995. The proportion of local authorities' total revenue represented by specific transfers was also reduced, although not to the same extent as the number of such transfers, which was still amounting to over 50 per cent in 1995 (Ministerie van Binnenlandse Zaken 1996; RGF 1996: 60).

While local authorities are financially dependent on central-government departments, these departments are dependent on local authorities to implement policy. In most cases, it is local authorities, rather than central-government field units, that implement policy. Central-government departments depend on local authorities to put 'their' policies into effect. Comparisons with other countries show that a relatively large proportion of total public spending is carried out through local authorities. Belgium also provides a interesting comparison: Dutch local authorities have substantially more public money to disburse, despite the fact that they have fewer of their *own* resources to spend (see Table 6.1).

Dutch government departments are dependent on local authorities in the battle for scarce government funding, since good budget management requires that allocated appropriations should actually be spent, and here government departments rely heavily on local authorities as providers of 'financially viable projects'.

Local-authority autonomy in the purely constitutional sense has been affected by the institutionalization of interdependence, but this does not mean that Dutch local authorities have become powerless. Local authorities in the Netherlands have developed from a situation of 'measured autonomy' to 'modified co-government'. The dependence of local authorities on higher levels of government is offset by the dependence of these levels of government on them. While national government undeniably has resources, so do local authorities (cf. Table 6.2).

TABLE 6.2 Institutionalized interdependence

Type of resource	National	Local
Constitutional status	Unitary state Supervision Legislative hierarchy	Autonomy *Medebewind* (co-government) Decentralization
Policy status	Planning Budgeting	Content Implementation
Information and knowledge	Overview Bureaucratic competence	Insight Local presence
Political support	National parties National pressure groups	Citizens' initiatives New social movements
Legitimacy	Elections Represents the whole *vis-à-vis* the parts	Elections Represents an authentic part Within

3. The Practice of Subnational Democracy

3.1 The Role of Political Parties

Political parties represented in national government—the *Partij van de Arbeid* (PvdA, Labour Party), *Christen Democratisch Appèl* (CDA, Christian Democratic Party), *Volkspartij voor Vrijheid en Democratie* (VVD, People's Party for Freedom and Democracy), *Democraten 66* (D66, Democrats 66), *Groen Links* (Green Party) and a host of smaller parties in the very variegated Dutch party system—are also active at lower levels of government. There have always been a large number of political parties in the Netherlands. When the country was divided along socio-political lines, political power at subnational level—particularly in local authorities—was more often in the hands of one or a few parties. As such barriers have broken down and local political parties have developed, political power has become more splintered (Denters 1998).

The rise of local political parties has been very evident during the local council elections of recent years. Figure 6.1 shows how the seat gains of local parties parallels the seat losses of the big political parties, such as CDA and PvdA. The increase in local lists is striking in the southern, Catholic part of the country, possibly because the more personal and patronage-based style of local lists does better here (Depla and Tops 1998). The advent of new, local political parties is often associated with the decreasing importance of the

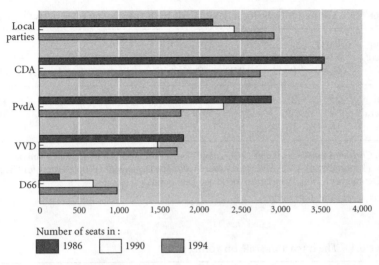

F I G. 6.1 Number of council seats obtained by local parties versus traditional parties, 1986–94. CDA, *Christen Democratisch Appèl* (Christian Democratic Appeal; PvdA, *Partij van der Arbeid* (Dutch Labour Party); VVD, *Partij voor Vrijheid en Democratie* (People's Party for Freedom and Democracy); D66, *Democraten '66* (1966 Democrats).

Source: ANP election service.

traditional type of politics with which people have become familiar during the post-war period. Membership of the established political parties has fallen dramatically since the 1950s. A stable, but small, group of people wants to be involved in party activities. Outside this circle, the established political parties have limited, and steadily diminishing, appeal. This manifests itself for example in the advent of the non-party-affiliated 'new social movements' while established political parties are losing members, organizations like Greenpeace and Amnesty International are growing rapidly—and also in phenomena such as floating voters, abstaining voters, and voting for local political lists.

The rise of local political parties is often criticized as producing a 'trivialization' of local politics, with too many inexperienced politicians with limited horizons. However, this trend has also a moderating effect on a persisting problem of local democracy: the nationalization of local-council elections. This problem is now somewhat moderated, but it continues to exist.

Depla and Tops (1998) compare local elections with a football match where the players (or candidates) have very little control over the ultimate result, which is largely determined by political skirmishing at national level and by national political players. Local elections continue to be placed in the national context, by political parties, by the media, and—let us not forget—by voters. Research shows that still relatively few people vote for a different party in local

TABLE 6.3   Voting motives: local, general, or both (percentages per party)

Voting motive	Party						
	CDA	PvdA	VVD	D66	Green Party	Local party	Other
Local	23	25	17	19	35	86	45
General	59	59	74	69	53	9	39
Both	18	16	9	2	12	5	15

CDA, *Christen Democratisch appèl* (Christian Democratic Appeal); PvdA, *Partij van der Arbeid* (Dutch Labom Party); VVD, *Volks partij voor Vrijheid en Democratic* (People's Party for Greedom and Democracy); D66, *Democraten '66* (1966 Democrats).

Source: Depla and Tops (1998).

TABLE 6.4   The impact of scale on voting

	Inhabitants				
	<10,000	10,000–19,999	20,000–49,999	50,000–99,999	>100,000
Party switchers	26	18	22	12	13
Local voters	17	6	9	2	2
Voting motive					
Local	43	32	33	31	24
General	45	51	58	57	65
Both	12	17	9	12	11

Source: Depla and Tops (1998).

elections than they vote for in national elections: less than one in five voters chooses to support a different party at local level than at national level.

It is not just actual voting behaviour, but also what motivates that behaviour, that reflects the national determination of local elections. Only one-third of voters in local elections are guided in their choice by local issues; national issues determine the choice of two-thirds (Depla and Tops 1998). Table 6.3 shows that parties may vary in this respect. People who vote for the VVD in local elections are relatively often motivated by general issues that are largely national in scope. People voting for local parties are least influenced by national issues.

Table 6.4 shows that the size of the municipality has a small, but perceptible, effect. In smaller municipalities the percentage of people voting for local candidates is higher, the percentage of party switchers is higher, and voters are less influenced by national issues (local issues play a larger role in smaller municipalities).

3.2 Citizens' Attitudes

Most research on people's position and attitudes to subnational levels of government in the Netherlands has looked at local authorities rather than provincial government. The rationale for this is the view that local authorities are closest to the general public, while provincial government is above all the 'authorities' authority'.

Denters and Geurts (1998*a*) conducted an interesting study on people's satisfaction with local government. The study first showed satisfaction with *local services* to be high. No less than 69 per cent of service beneficiaries were always satisfied with the services provided, 19 per cent were usually satisfied, and 11 per cent were almost always satisfied. The authors then looked at the perceived responsiveness of local authorities. Were they sufficiently aware of matters brought to their attention? Did people feel their concerns were being taken seriously? A small majority of respondents (54 per cent) were found to have brought something to the attention of the local authorities during the previous five years. Only 28 per cent of these people felt that their concerns had not been taken seriously enough. A majority of 72 per cent felt that they had been taken seriously by the local authorities. It was not just those whose petition had been successful who felt they were being taken seriously. Of those people who felt that their petition had been unsuccessful, 51 per cent still felt they had been taken seriously. In these cases, the local authorities had evidently been able to provide a 'well-reasoned no' (Tops 1995). Those whose efforts were successful were more likely to feel that they were being taken seriously: 85 per cent of these had this feeling after a successful appeal.

Denters and Geurts (1998*a*) asked people to rate their general satisfaction with their local authority on a scale of 1 to 10 (with 1 the lowest, 10 highest, and 6 satisfactory). Dutch local authorities were given relatively high scores by their citizens. Only 16 per cent of respondents gave scores below 6. The rest gave 6 or more to their local authority, with 31 per cent giving 6 and 53 per cent giving more than 6. The largest group (43 per cent) gave 7. The study of Denters and Geurts is relevant to the debate about increasing the size of local authorities, since it shows that satisfaction does not correlate positively with increase in size. Indeed, there seems to be greater dissatisfaction in the largest local authorities.

The same authors investigated people's perceptions of their political powerlessness *vis-à-vis* local authorities, and then compared this with their perceptions of political powerlessness *vis-à-vis* national government

(Denters and Geurts 1998*b*). Two aspects of political powerlessness were distinguished:

- a sense of one's own political power (subjective);
- confidence in the responsiveness of the local authority.

As far as the first aspect was concerned, the survey produced a less than positive overall picture. Three-quarters of the respondents rated their own power in local politics as low (34 per cent) or very low (41 per cent). But this overall finding is misleading, because it hides wide variations. Better educated people rate their own local political power significantly higher than people with less education. Men also rate their local political power significantly higher than women. The characteristics of the locality and of the local party system have virtually no effect on people's sense of political power.

It is very apparent that people feel they have more political power in national politics than in local politics. This is striking, given that local politics is closer and, therefore, easier to influence. The perceived difference in power is greater in large municipalities, where people are more focused on national media and national issues.

Confidence in the responsiveness of local authorities is considerable in the Netherlands: 60 per cent of respondents had high (26 per cent) to very high (34 per cent) confidence in the authorities' responsiveness; 40 per cent had low (19 per cent) to very low (21 per cent) confidence. There is a noticeable difference between older and younger respondents, with younger people often having greater confidence, and between large and small municipalities, with substantially more confidence felt in smaller municipalities. There seems to be a strong correlation between confidence in local authority responsiveness and the general opinion of the authority: if there is a positive general opinion of the authority, then people are more likely to have confidence in its responsiveness.

Confidence in the responsiveness of local authorities is noticeably greater than confidence in the responsiveness of national government. People from smaller municipalities are more inclined to make such a distinction than people from larger municipalities, who are more likely to put local and national government in the same category.

There seems to be less interest in politics in large municipalities than in smaller ones (Denters 1998). As far as political involvement in local affairs is concerned, there still seem to be differences between men and women (Leije-naar and Niemöller 1998). Readiness to vote is about the same among men and women. But differences are apparent in other respects, particularly in smaller municipalities:

- women are generally less interested in politics than men; this difference is less pronounced for local politics than national politics, especially in smaller municipalities;

- women make less use of local means of participation than men, except when it comes to taking part in local action committees;
- women have less subjective and objective political power at local level, especially in larger municipalities.

3.3 Patterns of Public Participation

Individuals do not often come into contact with provincial government. Direct involvement is often limited to the most traditional form of participation (i.e., in elections), in this case elections for the provincial council. Turnout at these elections is typically quite low—an average of 50 per cent on 8 March 1995—and strongly 'nationalized'; the results being determined only to a small extent by provincial issues and politicians. These elections are sometimes referred to as 'elections without a mandate'.

A recent survey by the provincial government of Limburg showed that people's familiarity with, and interest in, provincial politics is generally limited. People can only be said to be interested in concrete, specific issues with which provincial government is involved, but they are not always aware of the role played by the province in such matters.

Turnout at local council elections is usually higher. However, at the last three elections the turnout percentage was such as to raise doubts in many people's minds. In particular, turnout at the 1990 local-authority elections (at 62 per cent) was a great shock, which then lead to an intense debate about the need for political renewal. The shock was especially severe in large cities, where turnout in some cases fell below the symbolic 50 per cent threshold. At the same time, it should be noted that large cities have always tended to have a low turnout, certainly compared with rural authorities. Turnout was poorer in the southern, Catholic cities than in the more rural, Protestant east (Denters 1998).

Figure 6.2 shows why political scientists describe local-authority elections in the Netherlands as 'second-order elections'. Smeets *et al.* (1998) investigated intention to vote at local authority elections and parliamentary elections. Some 78 per cent of respondents said they would definitely vote in local-authority elections, 13 per cent were not sure, and 8 per cent said they would definitely not vote. For parliamentary elections these percentages were 87 per cent, 8 per cent, and 5 per cent, respectively. The size of the local authority seems to have little effect on intention to vote.

Table 6.5 shows quite a large variety of types of participation in Dutch local government. Voting is still the most common form of participation, followed by contacts with the local officials, addressing letters or complaints to the competent authority, and submitting petitions (what might be considered the 'respectable' methods of participation). 'Public discussion', or formal consultation at a public meeting, scores relatively low. This form of participation

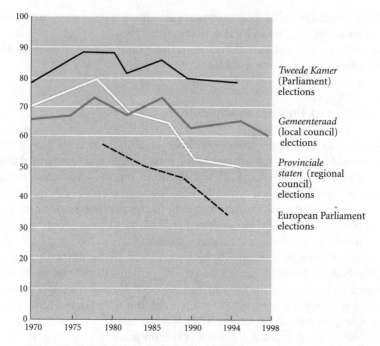

FIG. 6.2 Voter turnout at four elections in the Netherlands, 1998.
Source: Volkskrant, 5 March 1998.

TABLE 6.5 Participation in local government: types, percentages, inequalities, 1997

	% participation[a]	Score[b]	Odds ratio[c]	Score[d]
Public discussion	16	7	0.474	1
Neighbourhood campaigns	20	5	0.723	8
Actions	15	8	0.644	7
Party contact	11	9	0.544	2
Contact with politician	18	6	0.638	6
Contact with administration	31	2	0.628	4
Letters/complaints	24	3	0.632	5
Voting	77	1	0.589	3
Petition	23	4	0.834	9

[a] 20% of respondents claimed to have been involved in neighbourhood activities over the past 5 years.
[b] Neighbourhood activities rank fifth in the list of the most popular types of participation.
[c] The higher the odds ratio, the higher the degree of representative participation; participation in neighbourhood actions is thus fairly representative.
[d] Neighbourhood actions rank eighth in the list of non-representative participation; only petitions are more representative.

Source: Denters and Geurts (1998c: 174–6).

requires a lot of effort, while it is often perceived as yielding relatively low returns. The diminishing appeal of this approach is accompanied by an energetic search for new ways of consulting the general public in public decision-making processes (cf. section 5 below).

Denters and Geurts (1998c), from whom Table 6.5 has been taken, have investigated more closely the social representativeness (the extent to which the participating population mirrors the population at large) of the different forms of participation (see last two columns of Table 6.5). Social representativeness is highest in the case of petitions, followed by neighbourhood and other public campaigns; it is lowest in the case of public discussions, followed by party contacts and voting. The study findings for voting are notable in the sense that relatively high social representativeness could be expected here. In general, it can be said that social representativeness is higher in the case of specific activities that address problems than in the case of more general or political activities.

The size of the local authority does not affect the use of formal means of participation (voting, public discussions, party contacts), but it does affect the amount of direct contacts with local politicians: the smaller the municipality, the more often these are used. Size also correlates with social representativeness, especially when it comes to establishing personal contacts: the social representativeness of contact-seekers is greater in the smallest municipalities than in the larger ones. However, in the largest municipalities the social representativeness of two formal participation channels (voting and party contacts) is even greater.

The degree of parochialism of the local political system does not affect the extent to which different channels of influence are used, but it does affect the extent to which those using those channels can be defined as socially representative. More parochial political systems show greater social representativeness, especially in respect of establishing contacts with politicians and officials, but also in respect of election turnout and public discussions (Denters and Geurts 1998c).

People who become involved in local politics are relatively often satisfied with the way in which local authorities deal with their wishes and demands, even when these are not met (Denters and Geurts 1998a). However, people involved in local political affairs are not significantly more satisfied than those who are not involved. There is no causal relationship between participation and satisfaction. Denters and Geurts suggest that the causal relationship is rather the reverse: dissatisfaction leads to participation.

The political system in the Netherlands has a relatively favourable 'political-opportunity structure' for new social movements and their stock of action-oriented participation forms (Kriesi *et al.* 1992). Van der Eijk, Pennings, and Wille (1992) have observed that action-oriented types of participation are becoming increasingly popular. They are slightly higher in urban

TABLE 6.6 Willingness to protest, acceptance of various forms of protest, and desire for more say in subnational government (percentages), 1975–95

	Year				
	1975	1981	1985	1991	1995
Protest against unjust law	35	31	42	41	51
Accept sit-in	38	42	46	62	67
Accept parents occupying school	34	36	47	52	57
Accept squatters	n.a.	42	37	35	40
Accept blockade of nuclear plant	n.a.	42	45	58	65
Accept strike against social benefits cut	n.a.	37	46	56	62
Want more say in subnational government	70	63	60	66	70

Source: SCP (1996: 492–4); see also Denters (1998).

than non-urban municipalities, where traditional forms of electoral participation are a little more popular (Denters 1998).

Table 6.6 shows that acceptance of most types of political protest has increased noticeably over the years. The need for 'more say in subnational government' is as great as ever.

There is not only a good 'political-opportunity structure' for action-oriented forms of participation, but also a good basis for action-oriented 'new social movements'. In 1970, 70 per cent of the Dutch population had a materialistic political approach (aimed at traditional values such as safety, shelter, order, economic stability, etc.), a low proportion by international standards. In 1993, this percentage had fallen further to 14 per cent. During the same period, the proportion of the population with post-materialist political views (focusing on quality of life values) grew from 15 per cent to 22 per cent (Abramson and Inglehart 1995). The rise in post-materialist values seems to have slowed in the 1990s, remaining at a high level by international standards.

4. Challenges and Opportunities for Subnational Democracy

It is sometimes hypothesized that since the Netherlands no longer has any really serious problems public policy has become mainly 'administration'. This is thought to be particularly the case at subnational level. Compared with the problems experienced, for example by the southern European Union member states, those faced by subnational authorities in the Netherlands indeed appear to be relatively trivial. There are nevertheless substantial challenges, at least in the view of the provincial and local officials who are confronted with the following developments and phenomena.

- *De-pillarization* (Ontzuiling): Since the 1960s, the social 'pillars' on which national and subnational politics had rested for a long time have been substantially undermined. The pillars on which authorities were previously able to rely are much less strong. Many of these pillars continue to live on in name, but their external and internal orientation has changed a great deal. In the middle ground between public administration and ordinary citizens (civic society), vertical pillars have lost much of their significance whilst horizontal lines have increased in importance. For the authorities this represents a major challenge in that a society with a more horizontal structure requires an approach that is radically different from what is needed when a society is based on vertical pillars (Hendriks 1996).
- *Dehierarchization*: The horizontal lines are also visible in the new structures emerging today in the area lying between government, market, and the citizen. What these structures have in common is a non-hierarchical character. They are either loose networks of individuals cooperating with one another for pragmatic reasons or else new social and political movements that form relatively solid links and set great store by social involvement and political equality. The new organizations and groups promote models of citizenship that are noticeably different from the passive models characteristic of the old vertical structures. The new citizenship model is, on the one hand, individualistic, discerning, consumer-oriented, assertive, and quality-conscious, and, on the other, egalitarian, receptive to alternative lifestyles, geared to participation, and ecologically aware.
- *Rising demands and expectations*: Studies carried out by the Social and Cultural Planning Office show that the erosion of traditional social structures has not been accompanied by less social involvement on the part of ordinary citizens. Instead, involvement in public affairs has merely taken on a different form. National and subnational authorities can see that every day. The individual is now more critical, more assertive, and more active than ever before. Compared with the period of vertical pillars, citizens now make not only more extensive, but also more concrete demands on the authorities. For the authorities concerned this development raises administrative problems to which no satisfactory solution has been found. On the one hand, much more is expected of the authorities, whilst, on the other hand, intervention by the authorities in society is less easily accepted.
- *Meso-government*: Pillarization has been at least as important for subnational authorities in the Netherlands as it has been for national authorities. The fact that Dutch provinces this century have been confined to playing a

subordinate, supporting role is attributed by Toonen (1996) to the fact that the vertical pillar system has, *en passant*, been an effective system for coordinating interprovincial relations and solving interprovincial conflicts. The social foundations of the vertical pillars have been concentrated heavily in the regions, and because the pillar system has worked reasonably well as a framework for achieving consensus and framing policies, the provinces have been reduced increasingly to a technical and legal supporting role. With the decline of the vertical pillars, the Netherlands has shed itself of an implicit meso-government arrangement—a state of affairs that has led to the quest for functional equivalents. For a long time this quest has bypassed the provinces. Recently, however, the provinces have taken up the challenge in an effort to prove themselves fully fledged organs of meso-goverment.

- *Metropolitan regions*: Because of the poor reputation of the provinces, regional administrative solutions have for a long time been sought elsewhere, particularly in the supralocal framework of cities where interadministrative conflicts are most pronounced. Outside the Netherlands, answers to the regional question are being sought in territories such as Flanders, Catalonia, Scotland, or Bavaria. When talking of the 'regional question' in the Netherlands, one is thinking first and foremost of towns such as Rotterdam, the Hague, and Amsterdam. Frequent efforts have already been made to find an administrative solution to the problems of major urban areas. At the beginning of the 1990s, it seemed that a solution had been found in the creation or 'city regions' or 'city provinces'. However, after the referendums in Amsterdam and Rotterdam (see section 5 below), it would seem that things are once more uncertain. Regional urban questions thus still remain unsolved.

- *The 'abyss' between politicians and citizens*: Developments in the post-war period have led to major changes in political relations. Individuals are on the whole better educated and better able to defend their own interests. Politicians have been forced to accept that authority is no longer self-evident, but has to be continually earned through interaction with and between those who are governed. Earning such respect, however, is not so simple in a situation characterized by the displacement of politics (moving into areas lying outside the ken of the politician), the fragmentation of political life, and the dwindling power of politics to act as cement (see also section 3.1 above). There are many indications that political authority and trust are on the wane rather than on the increase. In this context, there is much talk of the widening gap between citizens and politics, particularly in large towns. Politicians, leaders of society, and opinion-makers attach great importance to the closing of this gap. Others—including political scientists such as Van Gunsteren and Andeweg (1994)—compare the situation with the Loch Ness monster, which no one has yet really seen, and have less confidence in the 'problem' being solved.

• *The extreme right*: The council elections of 1986, 1990, and 1994 saw the growing influence of extreme right-wing parties, and seats fell into the hands of their politicians, particularly in town-council elections. In the council elections of 1998, however, extreme right-wing parties were almost wiped off the map. An explanation for this has not yet been found, but it is highly unlikely that the breeding ground for the extreme right has simply disappeared in the course of a few years. Generally speaking, the extreme right is still a focal point for malcontents and a phenomenon to be kept under constant surveillance.

5. Innovative Approaches to Improving Subnational Democracy

5.1 Macro Trends

The specific features of any given trend often become clear when placed in a comparative perspective. As far as the reform of regional and local government in the Netherlands is concerned, a comparison with Belgium and Germany makes interesting reading. By comparison with Belgium, it is striking how few institutional reforms have actually been carried out in the Netherlands, even though there has never been a lack of planned reform. Under the recent proposals there would be five national areas, forty-four socio-economic regions, thirty-seven new-style provinces, seven city provinces, etc. Needless to say, none of the proposed institutional reforms has actually seen the light of day although this does not mean that there have been no changes of any note in the system of Dutch regional and local government.

We shall see below that the major changes carried out in the Netherlands concern processes rather than structures, whereas in Belgium the situation is the other way round. The necessary changes in terms of processes have undoubtedly been made in Belgium, but most of the conspicuous reforms there have been concerned with structures. In fact, whilst the Netherlands basically remains the same decentralized unitary state, Belgium has turned into a regionalized federal state within a few decades.

Comparisons with Germany are particularly interesting, with local government reforms in the two countries moving in opposite directions. What was fashionable in the Netherlands in the 1980s—New Public Management (NPM)—is now at the heart of discussions in Germany in the 1990s, whilst the German obsession with co-productive policy-making in the 1980s is now, in the 1990s, the centre of attention of the Netherlands.

In the 1980s, NPM, which had come to fruition in the Anglo-Saxon world, took firm root in Dutch local government, with municipal experiments taking place all over the country in self-management, contract management, and related private-enterprise type ventures. The examples of Delft and Groningen are well known. The most famous example of private-enterprise type local administration was, however, to be found in the municipality of Tilburg, leading to the so-called Tilburg model and the international furore surrounding it. In the 1980s, Germany was left well behind in the move to introduce NPM techniques. German municipalities were themselves in the throes of a development termed *Die Erneuerung der Politik von Unten* (The Renewal of Politics from Below) (Hesse 1986), which sought to institutionalize participatory and communicative forms of administration from the bottom up. New Public Management was introduced in Germany only slowly, but eventually broke through with unprecedented force. Local authorities in Germany now look with special interest at the Netherlands, and particularly the Tilburg model, which appears to have acquired a cult status in Germany (Klages and Löffler 1996).

During the same period, the municipality of Tilburg set in motion a process of change that has led to a situation where the municipality is less interested in the logic of internal production and more in the external environment. In many other municipalities, one can observe comparable trends involving interactive district administration, communicative decision-making, policy co-production, etc. Generally, local administration in the Netherlands in the 1990s has been going down a path already trodden by Germany in the 1980s.

The 1980s were years when the concept of New Public Management was accepted with enthusiasm in Dutch local government. During that decade, local administrations had to adjust first and foremost to tighter public purse strings, with substantial savings having to be made in local government expenditure. This requirement was all the more powerful as Dutch local authorities were dependent on the central authorities for a substantial part of their income. The pressure to make savings was also an opportunity to make considerable changes in administrative practice. A politico-administrative culture characterized by growth-sharing now had to be turned into a culture characterized by savings and structural cutbacks in funds available. The development of a new set of instruments was influenced by the *Zeitgeist* of neo-liberalism and market thinking. There was a favourable climate for this in the Netherlands, although less so than in the United Kingdom and the United States. Terms such as 'deregulation' and 'privatization' began to crop up in discussions. Classical bureaucratic modes of operation were observed with growing scepticism. The idea of New Public Management was taken up in writing and in discussions with growing enthusiasm, and the culture and instruments of private enterprise became a shining example for the authorities (Hood 1991). Concepts such as contract management, product-oriented budgeting, management evaluation, quantifiable policy goals, indicators, and benchmarking began to seep into the vocabulary of local administration. The reference points for discussions lay outside the higher authorities and were to be found in business life and business administration. The rapprochement between public and private sectors stemmed from an admiration for the 'codes' of private enterprise, whilst private investors were also badly needed by public players to develop ambitious, large-scale urban schemes. Attractive inner-city designs, buildings with a strong identity, and innovative architecture became the common denominators of this planning approach. They became the expression of a new urban enthusiasm shared by a wide spectrum of politicians. In the Labour Party, which held a strong position in city councils during the 1980s, there was even talk of a 'return to alderman socialism' (Depla and Monasch 1994).

The 1990s have seen Dutch local authorities once more going in search of the forgotten citizen. The local-council elections of 1990 created shock waves. In a number of local authorities, urban regeneration projects had been severely criticized, and this was reflected in the outcome of those elections. The Labour Party lost ground everywhere, but particularly in municipalities where it had championed urban-renewal schemes. The turnout was also less than expected, falling on average throughout the Netherlands from 73 per cent to 62 per cent. In some municipalities less than 50 per cent of the electorate came to the ballot box. As a further aspect of the reaction, great importance was attached to plans to change the way politics and the administration were run (Gilsing 1994; Depla 1995). Efforts of every description were made to win back the ordinary citizen. The focus of attention was not on formal institutions, but on actual decision-making processes (within a given institutional structure). Attempts were made to give citizens (or, at any rate, the views of citizens) a prominent place in the decision-making process. One of the methods of achieving this was via all sorts of civic polls and surveys that had been developed in many municipalities in the recent past (Depla and Schalken 1996). Instead of, or in addition to, consultation procedures, which had given citizens a say in public affairs, the Dutch authorities now frequently turned to 'interactive' decision-making, 'open-plan procedures', co-production, and so on. The role of the local government became primarily that of a *process* manager. The intention was largely to leave the process of reaching a consensus to the parties concerned.

These concepts fitted in perfectly well with the ancient Dutch traditions of improvisation, consultation, compromise, consensus, and a heavy reliance on civil society. For the rest, we have to remember that a number of cherished objectives are not attainable without the active involvement of ordinary citizens, particularly in respect of the implementation of public affairs.

In the meantime, the growing tendency in some municipalities to resort to co-production and interactive decision-making led to a review of the forms of local administration that developed in the 1980s. Even in Tilburg, which for many people was a shining example of successful New Public Management at local level, a permanent development process (POP) got under way, whereby local authorities became less obsessed with their own product-oriented philosophy and more concerned with questions of civic participation (Hendriks and Schalken 1997).

5.2 Micro-level Experiments and Practices

In addition to the general trends described above, there are many cases of micro-level practices and experiments at subnational level that deserve to be mentioned.

- *Public marketing*: The view has been taken that competition in different areas has increased because of the creation of the European internal market and the revolution in information and transport technologies. Dutch towns have in particular become increasingly aware that they are now in competition with one another as well as with other towns in Europe. With this awareness of competition, more and more attention has been paid to public marketing, that is, the intensive monitoring of, and response to developments in, those markets in which towns are active. Public marketing policy has often been carried out under advertising slogans such as '*Het Nieuwe Rotterdam*' (The New Rotterdam) or '*Tilburg Moderne Industriestad*' (Tilburg—Modern Industrial City).
- *Social regeneration*: Public marketing is certainly 'biased' in favour of those local-government policy areas that can be termed 'hard', because of their crucial importance to the competitive position of towns. This does not mean that the 'soft' edges of the urban fabric have been neglected. Ever since the third Lubbers Cabinet (which came into office in 1989), a great deal of attention has been paid to social regeneration in Dutch towns. The pathfinder in this area has been Rotterdam, which has blazed a trail with its so-called '*Opzoomeracties*'. The name *Opzoomer* refers to a street in Rotterdam where citizens have mobilized themselves in constructive, concrete ways to improve their living environment. Supported by the Rotterdam authorities, Opzoomeren has, literally and figuratively, infiltrated every part of the city of Rotterdam and won subsidies from the national policy on social regeneration.
- *Large city policy*: What social regeneration was to the third Lubbers Cabinet, large city policy is to the first and second Kok Cabinets. This is a strategy of local regeneration stimulated and aided by the national authorities; it finds expression and applications in rundown city areas and urban districts with special needs. It is in reality an extension and expansion of the policy on social regeneration. Whilst social regeneration focused on poor social conditions, the large city policy also lays great emphasis on economic potential. It thus aims at a combination of social and economic revitalization, with

economic revitalization taking pride of place. In July 1995, the four large cities together signed an agreement with the government (GSB) to promote the policy. The agreement covers the 1996–9 period. To be able to benefit fully from the GSB, the local authorities have had to develop plans over a short period of time and submit these to the central government.

• *Debates on the future and scenario workshops*: At the beginning of the twenty-first century, Dutch municipalities are showing a marked tendency to look into the future and project scenarios or visions of the future into the next few decades. Examples of this are *Rotterdam 2005*, the futuristic *Arnhem 2015*, and the *Local Agenda 21 Velsen*. In planning debates on the future and in scenario workshops, the process has often been considered as important and sometimes even more important than the result. The fact that social-interest groups have been holding discussions with one another and with the local authorities on matters of public importance for the future is considered to be of value in itself. In towns such as Deventer, scenario workshops have been set up to reflect on long-term policies. In Delft, use has been made of a simulation game to launch an unorthodox discussion between city councillors and top officials on teamwork. In Zaanstad and Alkmaar, but also in Amsterdam and Rotterdam, attention has been focused on round-table discussions and on broad-based public discussions.

• *Interactive project development*: This differs from the scenario workshops and debates on the future described above regarding the extent to which the topics discussed are open or closed. With interactive project development, it is generally clear that a given project or provision is going to be implemented. The interaction consequently concentrates on how best to implement the project or provision from a social point of view. An example of this is the development of the *Kop van Zuid* in Rotterdam. Inhabitants and organizations have been expressly invited to take part in discussions on the building of this new district in Rotterdam. Creative thinking has also gone into ways in which adjacent areas of the city might likewise benefit from the 'social return on investment'. Another example is the traffic plan for inner-city Delft, which is likewise being developed interactively. Interaction between individuals and the authorities in Delft has led to a plan being drawn up on the management and control of urban traffic. A third example—the north–south underground line in Amsterdam—is of interest, because this special project has been set up with the help of a relatively powerful and influential forum, the *Amsterdam Forum*. The *Amsterdam Forum* has brought together groups of citizens, supported by local-planning and university experts, to discuss the north–south underground line. The topic has been discussed from different angles—first minifora, then clusters of minifora, and finally round-table discussions. The *Amsterdam Forum*'s drive to win support has been so successful that the project has survived a referendum, which in itself is significant for a city where there has been much opposition to, and justifiable criticism of, underground planning in the past (see below).

- *Experiments with referendums*: The Netherlands has no experience of refer- endums at national level, at least not yet. At local level, however, there have already been twenty or so experiments in recent years. Subjects vary from the closing times of cafés (Leiden) and building on green polder land (Haarlem), to the establishment of city provinces (Amsterdam and Rotter- dam), restricted car access to inner-city areas, the building of a new resi- dential area, and the construction of an underground line (Amsterdam). There have so far been more local referendums in the Netherlands than in Belgium, although the 'rules of play' of the former have not yet been legally established. This makes Dutch referendums experimental in nature. Many local authorities have drawn up their own rules on referendums. There are big differences in turnout thresholds, required yes/no votes, the presenta- tion of questions, reasons for not holding a referendum, etc. What the different rules on referendums have in common, however, is that they are designed to ensure that advice is given and corrective measures taken. In practice, efforts have frequently been made to ensure that non-binding refe- rendums become more binding. This is to be achieved through a commit- ment to voluntarily accept the findings of a referendum; in other words, a local council may formally disregard the advice of the people, but it promises not to do so provided certain conditions are met (a considerable turnout and a considerable majority). However, when a local authority, moves too far away from the representative democratic institutions already in existence, the Ministry of Home Affairs may still annul the referendum provisions in question (as happened with the referendum provisions of Arnhem in 1994 and Amsterdam in 1996). The city where the practice of holding referendums is most discussed is undoubtedly Amsterdam. The practice began, unhappily, with the 1992 referendum on limited car access to inner-city areas: a low turnout accompanied by a close vote on the two options meant that the dilemma of political choice became greater rather than smaller as a result of the referendum. Against this, the 1995 referen- dum on a 'city province' was nothing if not clear. Ninety-two per cent of those voting were against; and, if any problems arose, it was because the state authorities had maintained at the outset that the matter could not be solved by a local referendum. In the referendum on the IJburg residential area, the turnout was even higher, but the results were declared null and void, because the Minister of Home Affairs had in the meantime introduced a rather com- plicated voting threshold that was not reached in the referendum. Well over 60 per cent of registered voters (out of a total of 130,000 votes) had voted against the residential area, but this did not lead to a political decision, since a minimum of 155,000 no-votes were required. In the fourth referendum, this time on the above-mentioned north–south underground line, the turnout was extremely low (only 22 per cent showed up) so that, although there was a majority of no-votes, this once more failed to secure a political decision on the grounds that too few votes had been cast.

- *Opinion polls and consumer surveys*: A referendum carries with it expectations and hence (political and moral) obligations. If the rules of the game are not clear or do not carry the seal of official approval, this can lead to great frustration and tensions. Opinion polls and consumer surveys do not have this disadvantage. They exist to find out precisely what the opinions and tastes of citizens are without this leading to expectations. However, despite their non-binding nature, opinion polls and consumer surveys can be of real influence in decision-making and in the provision of services to the public. Local authorities that set great store by market and customer trends cannot simply ignore the signals being sent out by the public. An institutionalized form of consumer survey is the *stadsmarktonderzoek* (urban market survey) of the municipality of Tilburg. Consumer surveys fit neatly into the philosophy of the Tilburg New Public Management model. Nijmegen, on the other hand, has experimented with the idea of the *stadsraadpleging* (town-council consultations), where the opinions of around 2,000 randomly selected persons are sought on tricky problems. Questions are framed in such a way that answers are not squeezed into a rigid yes/no schema. The *Kabelexperiment Hoogvliet* (a borough of Rotterdam) is our final example. In this experiment, soundings were taken via cable, on reactions to certain positions. Participants in this cable experiment were able to give their reactions via a so-called *Huis Informatie Toetsenbord* (House Information Manual). The reactions were picked up and stored electronically, although there was no question of push-button democracy. The cable experiment did not seek to eliminate options, but to spark off debates and float ideas.

6. Conclusions

For assessing democratic reform at local and regional level in the Netherlands a distinction should be made between 'institutional democracy' and 'everyday democracy'. On the institutional or structural level, the reform record is not very impressive. Efforts to reform the Thorbeckean system at the subnational level (efforts to create more or less or different types of provinces, metropolitan authorities, etc.) have all failed. Pre-Thorbeckean institutions like the appointed mayor, the appointed Queen's Commissioner, the collegial decision-making structure seem to be even more resistant to change.

If one redirects attention from the institutional structure to the everyday process of subnational democracy a different picture appears. Everyday democracy at the local and regional level in the Netherlands has seen several marked changes and innovations (see section 5). The most important one is the reinvention of interactive policy-making, sometimes also described as participative decision-making, open planning, and co-production of policy. Under the heading of the 'polder model' the reinvention of interactive policy-making in the Netherlands has recently also received foreign interest and acclaim.

If the success of a trend in subnational democracy is measured by the amount of imitation and dissemination it enjoys, then the trend towards interactive policy-making is very succesful in the Netherlands. Even the city of Tilburg, internationally acclaimed for its lean and mean business-like 'Tilburg model' has initiated a drastic reform intended to lead to less reliance on the internal business process, and increased reliance on the external interaction process.

The reinvention of interactive policy-making should not be understood as a version of the reinvention of government (à la Osborne and Gaebler), but as a matter of the reinvention of tradition (Hendriks and Toonen 1998). The Netherlands have a long administrative tradition of interactive 'accomodation and pacification' reflected in the famous three Cs of Dutch politics (consultation, consensus, and compromise). The present practice of interactive policy-making reconnects with this long tradition. But it adds new elements to it as well, as section 5 of this chapter has shown.

References

ABRAMSON, P. and INGLEHART, R. (1995). *Value Change in Global Perspective*. Ann Arbor: University of Michigan Press.

ANDERSON, C. J. and GUILORY, C. A. (1997). 'Political Institutions and Satisfaction with Democracy: A Cross-National Analysis of Consensus and Majoritarian Systems'. *American Political Science Review*, 91/1: 66–81.

BOERSEMA, K. H. (1949). *Johan Rudolf Thorbecke: een historisch-kritische studie*. Leiden: Brill.

BREUNESE, J. N. (1982). 'Twee eeuwen Nederlandse provincie'. *Bestuur*, 1/7: 14–19.

DENTERS, S. A. H. (1998). 'Urban Democracies in the Netherlands: Social and Political Change, Institutional Continuities?'. Unpublished paper.

——and GEURTS, P. A. TH. M. (1998a). 'Tevredenheid over het gemeentebestuur', in S. A. H. Denters and P. A. Th. M. Geurts (eds), *Lokale democratie in Nederland, burgers en hun gemeentebestuur*. Bussum: Uitgeverij Coutinho.

——and GEURTS, P. A. TH. M. (1998b). 'Opvattingen over politieke machteloosheid tegenover de gemeentelijke en de nationale politiek', in S. A. H. Denters and P. A. Th. M. Geurts (eds), *Lokale democratie in Nederland, burgers en hun gemeentebestuur*, Bussum: Uitgeverij Coutinho.

——and GEURTS, P. A. TH. M. (1998c). 'Politieke gelijkheid: de sociale representativiteit van participatie in de lokale politiek', in S. A. H. DENTERS and P. A. Th. M. GEURTS (eds), *Lokale democratie in Nederland, burgers en hun gemeentebestuur*. Bussum: Uitgeverij Coutinho.

DEPLA, P. (1995). *Technologie en de verniewing van de lokale democratie.* 's-Gravenhage: VUGA Uitgeverij.

——and MONASCH, J. (1994). *In de buurt van de politiek: Handboek voor vernieuwing van de lokale democratie.* Amsterdam: WBS.

——and SCHALKEN, K. (1996). 'De sprekende burger', in *Jaarboek overheidskommunikatie 1996.* 's-Gravenhage: VUGA Uitgeverij.

——and TOPS, P. (1998). 'De lokale component bij raadsverkiezing/de invloed van de gemeentegrootte', in S. A. H. Denters and P. A. Th. M. Geurts (eds), *Lokale democratie in Nederland, burgers en hun gemeentebestuur*. Bussum: Uitgeverij Coutinho.

DERKSEN, W. (1995). *De bereikbare overheid.* 's-Gravenhage: VUGA Uitgeverij.

DETH, J. VAN and VIS, J. (1995). *Regeren in Nederland. Het politieke bestuurlijke bestel in vergelijkend perspectief.* Assen: Van Gorcum.

DUYVENDAK, J. W. (1998). 'De souplesse van stroperigheid', in F. Hendriks and Th. Toonen (eds), *Schikken en Plooien. De stroperige staat bij nader inzien.* Assen: Van Gorcum.

EIJK, C. VAN DER, PENNINGS, P., and WILLE, A. C. (1992). 'Politieke betrokkenheid: is de burger afgehaakt?', in J. J. M. van Holsteyn and G. A. Irwin (eds), *De Nederlandse kiezer 1989.* Amsterdam: Steinmetzarchief.

GILSING, R. (1994). 'Bestuurlijke vernieuwing in Nederland'. *Acta Politica*, 29/1: 3–36.

GUNSTEREN, H. VAN and ANDEWEG, R. (1994). *Het grote ongenoegen: over de kloof tussen burgers en politiek.* Haarlem: Aramith.

HENDRIKS, F. (1996). 'Ontzuiling, onthierarchisering en de veranderende relatie tussen burgers en bestuur', in Chr. Balje *et al.* (eds), *De ontzuiling voorbij: Openbaar bestuur en individualistisch burgerschap.* Den Haag: SDU.

——and SCHALKEN, K. (1997). 'Local Government and the New Public Management: the Case of the Tilburg Model', in D. Grunow and H. Wollman (eds), *Verwaltungsmodernisierung in Aktion.* Basel: Birkhauser.

——and TH. TOONEN (eds) (1998). *Schikken en Plooien. De stroperige staat bij nader inzien.* Assen: Van Gorcum.

HESSE, J. J. (ed.) (1986). *Erneuerung der Politik von Unten? Stadtpolitik und kommunale selbstverwaltung im Umbruch.* Opladen: Westdeutscher Verlag.

HOFSTEDE, G. (1991). *Allemaal andersdenkenden: omgaan met cultuurverschillen.* Amsterdam: Contact.

HOOD, C. (1991). 'A public management for all seasons'. *Public Administration*, 96/2: 3–19.

KLAGES, H. and LÖFFLER, E. (1996). 'A New Steering Model in Germany: The Ideal Solution to the Problems of Guaranteeing a Self-Sustaining Development of New Public Management?', paper presented at the IIAS Annual Conference, Beijing.

KRIESI, H., KOOPMANS, R., DUYVENDAK, J. W., and GUIGNI, M. (1992). 'New social movements in Western Europe'. *European Journal of Political Research*, 22: 223–46.

LEIJENAAR, M. H. and NIEMÖLLER, B. (1998). 'Politieke betrokkenheid van vrouwen en mannen op lokaal niveau', in S. A. H. Denters and P. A. Th. M. Geurts (eds),

Lokale democratie in Nederland, burgers en hun gemeentebestuur. Bussum: Uitgeverij Coutinho.

MAES, R. (1997). 'Het profiel van de lokale politiek'. *Res publica*, 39/1: 3–26.

MINISTERIE VAN BINNENLANDSE ZAKEN (1996). *Overzicht specifieke uitkeringen 1997, Een uitgave van de beheerscommissie gegevensbestand specifieke uitkeringen.* 's-Gravenhage: Ministerie van Binnenlandse Zaken.

OECD (Organization for Economic Co-operation and Development) (1996). *Managing across Levels of Government: Conclusions, Public Management Committee.* Paris: OECD.

RBB (Raad voor het Binnenlands Bestuur) (1988). *Medebewind: van autonome waarde.* 's-Gravenhage: RBB.

RGF (Raad voor de Gemeentefinancien) (1996). *Jaarboek Gemeentefinanciën.* 's-Gravenhage: RGF.

RIEKEN, J. G. P. and BAAIJENS, J. M. J. (1986). *De provincie als bestuurlijk midden.* Deventer: Van Lochum Slaterus.

SCP (Sociaal en Cultureel Planbureau) (1996). *Sociaal en cultureel rapport 1996.* Rijswijk & 's-Gravenhage: Sociaal en Cultureel Planbureau & VUGA Uitgeverij.

SMEETS, I. S. M. A., DENTERS, S. A. H., and GEURTS, P. A. TH. M. (1998). 'Stemintentie bij verkiezingen', in S. A. H. Denters and P. A. Th. M. Geurts (eds), *Lokale democratie in Nederland, burgers en hun gemeentebestuur.* Bussum: Uitgeverij Coutinho.

TOONEN, TH. (1987). *Denken over binnenlands bestuur, theorieën van de gedecentraliseerde eenheidsstaat bestuurskundig beschouwd.* 's-Gravenhage: VUGA Uitgeverij.

——(1991). 'Change in Continuity: Local Government and Urban Affairs in the Netherlands', in J. J. Hesse (ed.), *Local Government and Urban Affairs in International Perspective: Analysis of Twenty Western Industrial Countries,* Baden-Baden: Nomos.

——(1996). 'On the Administrative Condition of Politics'. *West European Politics,* 19/3: 609–32.

TOPS, P. (1994). *Moderne regenten: over lokale democratie.* Amsterdam: Atlas.

——(1995). *Gemeenten en gezag: het verschuivende politieke moment in het lokale bestuur.* Amsterdam: Atlas.

VREE, W. VAN (1994). *Nederland als vergaderland: opkomst en verbreiding van een vergaderregime.* Groningen: Wolters-Noordhof.

WRR (Wetenschappelijke Raad voor het Regeringsbeleid) (1990). *Van de stad en de rand.* 's-Gravenhage: WRR.

7

Luxembourg: Change and Continuities in the Local State

Frank Hendriks*

1. History and Concept of Democracy

Luxembourg is a unitary state with a single legislative chamber and a single tier of subnational, that is municipal, government (consisting of 118 municipalities). Below, subnational/municipal democracy in Luxembourg is described in the context of the central-state structure.

1.1 Historical Background

In 1815, at the Congress of Vienna, the territories of present-day Belgium and Luxembourg were united with the Kingdom of the Netherlands in order to create a buffer state against France. Belgium gained independence in 1830. Luxembourg became independent nine years later, even though the personal union between Luxembourg and the Dutch crown ended only in 1890. In that year, the Dutch King William III died without leaving a male heir in Luxembourg and succession passed to the present Luxembourg dynasty. This furthered the eastward orientation of Luxembourg, which had been boosted earlier by the inclusion of Luxembourg in the German *Zollverein* (Customs Union) in 1842, which lasted until 1918.

Notwithstanding this unmistakable eastward orientation, the tiny state has always tried to create and strengthen economic and political ties in all directions. It formed an economic and monetary union with Belgium and institutionalized its relations with the Netherlands and Belgium under the Benelux treaty. It has wholeheartedly supported cooperation with other European countries in the context of the European integration process.

* I would like to thank Alphonse Cruchter for commenting on this chapter.

1.2 Luxembourg: The Local State

Luxembourg is tiny with a surface area of just 2,586 square kilometres—smaller than some European subnational regions—and has a population of approximately 415,000 inhabitants—similar to many medium-sized cities (Statec 1996). These scales mean that there the national and the local levels of government are closely intertwined and it is difficult to speak of local democracy without also referring to national democracy.

Luxembourg is a representative democracy with some of the features of a constitutional monarchy. The role played by the Grand Duke of Luxembourg is, however, more than just ceremonial. He is head of state and, together with the government, forms the executive. All of the Grand Duke's governmental acts require the countersignature of a responsible minister, but he still retains substantial room for manoeuvre should he so wish. He has the right of initiative in legislative matters, and no bill can be enacted and become binding unless he signifies his assent to it and orders it to be promulgated and carried into effect (Thill and Frieden 1993: 453). The constitution allows him a maximum of three months within which to sanction a bill after the final vote is taken in the Chamber of Deputies. However, this right of sanction, although effectively used in the past, is steadily becoming more and more of a formality (Majerus and Goerens 1995: 13–20). The Grand Duke may still adjourn the chamber, but not for a period exceeding one month. He is allowed to make the regulations and orders necessary for carrying laws into effect (but he may at no time suspend the laws themselves or dispense with their enforcement). He is also authorized to organize and supervise administrative services, including the army, the *gendarmerie*, and the police. His role in public administration must, however, always be related to the executive power.

In theory, the Grand Duke chooses the government. In practice, he chooses only the prime minister, who in turn selects the other members. Although, constitutionally speaking, the Grand Duke is the most prominent figure in the Luxembourg government, in practice it is the prime minister who holds this position. The other members of government must enjoy the confidence of the Grand Duke, but also, as could be expected in a parliamentary democracy, of the Chamber of Deputies. In theory, the Grand Duke can dissolve government at any moment, but in practice he only dissolves government when it ceases to enjoy parliamentary support. The backbone of almost all governing coalitions since 1915 has been the *Chrëstlech-Sozial Vollekspartei* (PCS, Christian Social Party), with other members alternating from the *Parti Démocratique* (Liberal Party) to the *Parti Ouvrier Socialiste* (Socialist Party). Exceptions to the rule were the years 1925–6 and 1974–9 (Thill and Frieden 1993: 458–63). The sixty members of the chamber are supposed to represent the Luxembourg people. The chamber shares the exercise of legislative power with the Grand Duke and the chamber, like him, has the right of initiative in legislative matters. The constitution assigns to the chamber certain powers in financial matters and invests it with the right to supervise the acts of the government. In international affairs, the consent of the chamber is required before a treaty can come into effect on the territory of the grand duchy.

Seats in the chamber are allocated according to the rules of proportional representation and the principle of the smallest electoral quota. The country is divided into four electoral districts. The number of deputies is determined by the constitution, which prescribes sixty deputies:

• twenty-three from the South;
• twenty-one from the Centre;
• nine from the North;
• seven from the East.

Each Luxembourg voter has as many votes as there are deputies to be elected in his constituency. The vote can be cast either under the party-list system or on a name basis. The elector who votes under the party-list system may not cast any other vote under pain of cancellation of his ballot paper, unless the chosen list comprises a smaller number of candidates than the number of deputies to be elected in the given constituency. Electors who vote on a name basis may select their candidates from the same list or from different lists, but must take care not to cast more votes than there are seats available (Majerus and Goerens 1995: 24–5). Like Belgium, but unlike the Netherlands, Luxembourg allows more than one office to be held by the same person (*cumul des mandats*). More than half of the Members of Parliament are also mayors or members of municipal councils.

For bills to become law, a majority of 51 per cent is necessary in the Chamber of Deputies. The moderating influence of a second assembly, or senate, is absent. The authors of the constitution, being aware of this, tried to mitigate it by introducing the procedure of the second constitutional vote, that is a 'cooling-off' period. After voting on a bill as a whole, the chamber is in principle required to vote a second time on the same bill within a specified interval allowing for further reflection. Another safeguard against immature legislation is the Council of State, consisting of twenty-one councillors required by constitution to examine government bills and any amendments proposed to them. No bill is to be submitted to the Grand Duke or presented to the chamber before the Council of State's opinion has been heard. If, however, the government considers the presentation of a bill to be a matter of urgency, it may consult the chamber directly. If the chamber shares the government's view as to the urgency of the matter, discussion may be opened without the Council of State first having to give its opinion. On no account, however, may the chamber proceed to a final vote on the bill before the council's opinion has been made known to it.

Democracy in Luxembourg is basically representative democracy: the people choose deputies who participate instead of, and on behalf of, the people in the policy-making process. In certain cases the electorate may take part directly in government by way of a referendum. The referendum, provided for in the constitution, is left to the discretion of the legislator. It can be used, if the need arises, to ascertain the views of the people on specific issues of national importance.

1.3 The Luxembourg Model: Consensus and Dialogue

Keywords describing the institutional relationship between Luxembourg society and the state are consensus and dialogue. In the social-economic field, clear traces of corporatism can be found. The so-called 'Luxembourg model' is based on cooperation and consensus between employers and workers, with the state playing an important role as broker. Within the Luxembourg model, an important role is ascribed to the Social Economic Board, consisting of thirty-five members representing different social bodies. The SEC is an advisory body in matters of economic, financial, or social importance. The SEC can act on its own initiative or on the request of government. In the Luxembourg consensual political culture, statements of such a corporatist advisory body are taken very seriously.

The Luxembourg model allows for controlled innovation and for stable social relationships. Stability and caution are characteristic of the Luxembourg political system as a whole. This is demonstrated not only by a relatively steady pattern of policy-making, but also by the fact that changes in government occur smoothly. The three main political parties (Christian Social, Socialist, Liberal) alternate as coalition partners without difficulty.

2. *Subnational Democracy in Luxembourg*

The subnational system of Luxembourg has neither provinces, departments, nor counties and the municipality is the only form of territorial decentralization. From the administrative point of view the municipality is an autonomous territorial authority, possessing legal personality. It administers through local representatives, under the supervision and control of central government (Majerus and Goerens 1995: 54). At present there are 118 municipalities in Luxembourg.

An important role in the supervision and control of local government is played by the district commissioner, who is supposed to act as hierarchical intermediary between central government and municipal authorities. District commissioners are appointed for three administrative districts: Luxembourg, Diekirch, and Grevenmacher. Each municipal authority, with the exception of the city of Luxembourg, is placed under the immediate supervision of district commissioners and may deal with the higher authority only through them, save in serious and exceptional cases. District commissioners are appointed by the central government (formally the Grand Duke). They are civil servants under the direct authority of the Minister for Home Affairs in particular, and the government more generally. Each municipality has its own municipal council elected by the inhabitants who are qualified to vote. The municipal council corresponds on the local level to what the Chamber of Deputies is on the national level. Municipal authority is exercised by the municipal council and by the corporate board of burgomaster and aldermen. The relation between these two bodies is similar to that between parliament and government at the national level. The municipal council is required by law to draw up regulations concerning internal administration and the maintenance of law and order in the municipality. The competence of the municipal council is unlimited with respect to the internal administration of the municipality, municipal property, revenue and expenditure, work to be done, the public establishments of the municipalities, and the appointment of the municipal secretary, municipal collector, and municipal employees.

In principle, local elections are held under the absolute-majority system. However, in municipalities that have 3,500 or more inhabitants or whose sections include at least one section comprising 3,000 inhabitants, elections are held on a party-list system with proportional representation as for the legislative elections. In boroughs where the proportional system is used, they constitute only one constituency even if they comprise various separate localities (Majerus and Goerens 1995: 54–60). Members of the municipal council are elected for a six-year term, commencing from the first day of January following their election. Their number varies with the population of the municipality, but is always an odd number. Voting is compulsory in Luxembourg. The last local elections were held in 1993, resulting in an 87.96 per cent turnout—a little lower than in 1987, when the turnout was 88.51 per cent.

There is also the possibility of organizing local referendums. This is either decided by the municipal council, or it may come about on the request of a fixed percentage of voters.

The board of burgomaster and aldermen of the municipality must be chosen from among the municipal councillors. This corporate body forms the executive and administrative body of the municipality's day-to-day affairs. It corresponds at the local level to the government at the national level. As an executive body, the board of burgomaster and aldermen is responsible for a number of tasks. These include: publishing and implementing the resolutions of the municipal council, administering the municipality's property, handling revenue and authorizing expenditure, keeping a check on the municipal treasury and accounts, governing municipal establishments, administering rural police work, and exercising supervision over municipal employees, the fire brigade, the keeping of records, etc. In addition, the board of burgomaster and aldermen is responsible for supervising municipal works and judicial proceedings at the local level. The issuing of birth, marriage, and death certificates and the keeping of their registers fall exclusively within the domain of executive local authority. The board of burgomaster and aldermen performs not only purely municipal tasks, but in certain cases it also acts as an organ of central authority. As such, the board of burgomaster and aldermen is responsible, on the territory of the municipality, for enforcing laws and regulations and central-government's decisions. The burgomaster is also responsible for enforcing laws and police regulations under the supervision of the district commissioner.

Local government in Luxembourg is entangled in a pattern of central–local relations that approach the ideal type of the centralized unitary state. Compared to a (decentralized) unitary state such as the Netherlands, central government in the Luxembourg unitary state operates remarkably close to local government. This is true, not only in a physical sense (the state operates on a smaller scale, with a total population not exceeding that of the Hague), but also in an institutional sense. Significant in this context is also the fact that the Grand Duke, as head of state, has been given the right to dissolve the municipal council (which is still an expression of local democracy). No less significant is the fact that communal charges cannot be imposed when the Grand Duke withholds his authorization.

To prevent the municipal autonomy from constituting a threat to national interests, the constitution requires the legislator to regulate the composition and organization of the municipal council and has invested the higher authority with the right to exercise continuous administrative supervision over municipal affairs. Lines of control between national and local government are relatively short and well organized with the support of the above-mentioned district commissioners. The municipal council may draw up regulations concerning internal administration and maintenance of law and order in the municipality, but such regulations may on no account conflict with general administrative laws and regulations.

3. *Change in Continuity*

On a continuum with institutional stability on the one hand, and institutional change on the other, the Luxembourg system of local democracy would certainly tend towards the former. Continuity is a core element of the Luxembourg system in general and of the local political system in particular. The continuity of the local-government system in Luxembourg is reflected in Table 7.1. Here we can see that Luxembourg has developed a rather cautious policy of local-government fusion and upscaling. Between 1950 and 1992 the total number of municipalities in Luxembourg was reduced by only 7 per cent, while in the Netherlands and in Belgium this number was reduced by 36 per cent and 78 per cent, respectively.

Stability and continuity are relative matters, of course. In contrast to other countries, Luxembourg exhibits a stable local-government system. That does not, however, mean that nothing ever changes. Compared to previous decades, some interesting processes of 'stabilized innovation' can be discerned. Seven items should be mentioned in this respect: interactive planning in rural areas; co-production of social housing projects; installation of special committees for women and immigrants; growth of single-issue parties; consultative local referendums; extension of municipal cooperation; and—most notably—the reappraisal of local self-government, articulated in the 1988 Municipal Act.

• *Self-government*: The 1988 Municipal Act has made central-government control over municipalities less extensive. The Act gives municipalities the right to bring central-government decisions concerning local government before the court, and coincides with a growing awareness of the importance of administrative decentralization and local self-government. Luxembourg was the first country to ratify the Charter of Local Self-Government of the Council of Europe (Committee of the Regions 1996).

TABLE 7.1 Total number of local authorities, 1950 and 1992

Country	Year		Evolution	
	1950	1992	No.	%
Luxembourg	127	118	−9	−7
Netherlands	1,015	647	−368	−36
Belgium	2,669	589	−2,080	−78

Source: Toonen and Raadschelders (1997: 109).

- *Municipal cooperation*: In order to compensate, in some way, for the absence of local-government fusion, links among municipalities have been intensified significantly during recent years. Intermunicipal cooperation takes form within so-called *syndicats communaux*. These syndicates may deal with all kinds of matters—including transport, waste disposal, education, social programmes—that a single municipality is not able to administer.
- *Local referendums*: The 1988 Local Government Act made possible the organizing of consultative local referendums. Under this Act, a referendum has to be organized when a particular number of inhabitants ask for it. The quorum is 25 per cent of the electorate for municipalities with less than 3,000 inhabitants and 20 per cent of the electorate for municipalities with more than this number. Thus far there have been two referendums in small municipalities: in 1990 on the construction of a cultural centre, and in 1991 on the location of a tar plant. Both schemes were rejected and followed by identical decisions of the city council. There have been no further referendums since these.
- *Single-issue parties*: The Luxembourg political make-up has been changed in recent years by the growth of single-issue parties. Two green parties, which fused subsequently, won five of the sixty seats in the Chamber of Deputies in 1994. The 'Five-Sixths Pensioners Action Committee'—now known as the ADR (Action for Democracy and Fair Pensions)—also won five seats.
- *Consultative committees*: Special committees have been created to improve the position of immigrants and women in the local public domain. Municipalities with an immigrant population of more than 20 per cent are obliged to create a consultative committee to deal with questions of integration. Half of the members of the committee must be immigrants and the other half Luxemburgers but the chair is a Luxemburger. Most municipalities now have such a committee, which is generally viewed favourably. Consultative committees (five to seven members) can be created for women's issues, but this set-up is not compulsory. Instead of installing a committee, many municipalities have set up special posts (not necessarily filled by women) for dealing with women's issues.
- *Co-production in social housing*: The cooperative social housing policy, which has developed in Luxembourg over a period of more than ten years, can be put in the category of 'best practice'. Under this policy, Luxembourg municipalities together with national organizations have 'co-produced' many new housing projects, which are generally of a high quality.
- *Interactive planning in rural areas*: A strong trend towards co-productive relationships between governmental organizations and citizens in urban areas and neighbourhoods, such as the ones discerned in Belgium and the Netherlands, cannot be discerned in Luxembourg. The notion of co-production is more influential in rural areas, where local authorities, in the

context of the EU LEADER programme, try to develop rural programmes in cooperation and dialogue with the rural population. Interactive programming is specifically required by the LEADER programme.

4. Conclusions

Luxembourg can be viewed as a 'local state'. Subnational democracy in Luxembourg can only be properly understood in connection with national government, which operates remarkably close to the local level. Luxembourg is a relatively centralized unitary state, with strong echoes of the French model, combined with several elements that can also be found in the Dutch and the Belgian systems. Consensus and dialogue are keywords describing the institutional relationship between Luxembourg society and the state. Compared to other countries, Luxembourg has a relatively stable local government system, which is not to say that nothing ever changes. Interesting processes of 'stabilized innovation' can be discerned in the Luxembourg local system, as shown in section 3.

References

COMMITTEE OF THE REGIONS (1996). *Regional and Local Government in the European Union: Luxembourg*. Brussels.

MAJERUS, P. and GOERENS, J.-M. (1995). *The Institutions of the Grand Duchy of Luxembourg*. Ministry of State, Luxembourg.

STATEC (1996). *Le Luxembourg en chiffres*. Luxembourg: Statec.

THILL, J. and FRIEDEN, L. (1993). 'Het Groothertogdom Luxemburg', in L. Prakke, C. A. J. M. Kortmann, and M. C. Burkens (eds), *Het staatsrecht van de landen der Europese Gemeenschappen*. Deventer: Kluwer.

TOONEN, T. A. J. and RAADSCHELDERS, J. C. N. (1997). Public Sector Reform in Western Europe. Unpublished manuscript, Leiden University.

Part 3

THE NAPOLEONIC TRADITION

8

France: Between Centralization and Fragmentation

John Loughlin and Daniel-L. Seiler

1. History and Concept of Democracy

France has been a model of state organization that has been copied time and again. Many of the countries mentioned in this book were inspired by the French system and imported the French departmental model.[1] At the end of the nineteenth and beginning of the twentieth century France was regarded as being at the forefront of institutional design particularly for states such as Greece, Italy, Finland, and Ireland emerging after a period of nationalist struggle. The French model embodies a republican vision of the nation-state, which promotes the equal treatment of citizens as well as of territory. Until recently, the French state was among the most centralized in Europe and was built on the famous Jacobin notion of 'the one and indivisible Republic' (Hayward 1983). This was interpreted in the past and to some extent is interpreted to this day as meaning uniformity enforced through the system of prefects set up by Napoleon I as a way of consolidating the centralizing processes of the French Revolution. This picture of a highly centralized and uniform state needs to be modified, however, by the sociological and cultural diversity that characterizes France right up to the present day (Braudel 1986). In some ways, the notion of 'the one and indivisible Republic' dear to Jacobins such as the late Michel Debré or the current Minister of the Interior, Jean-Pierre Chevènement, was invented in many respects as a way of compensating for, and overcoming, this diversity. Furthermore, sociologists have pointed out that the

We would like to thank Alistair Cole, Robert Elgie, and David Hanley for comments on early drafts of this chapter.

[1] The Benelux countries and Finland as well as the countries of South Europe, Portugal, Spain, Italy, and Greece. Loughlin and Peters (1997) describe this as the Napoleonic model of the state in contrast to the Anglo-Saxon, Germanic, and Scandinavian models.

French politico-administrative system did not simply destroy the 'local' or the 'periphery' but incorporated them into the centre through the *notabiliaire* system with its *cumul des mandats* (multiple holding of offices) and the representation of localities in the Senate. Previous scholars dubbed this *le pouvoir périphérique* (Grémion 1976).

Centralization remained for many years the 'ideal-type' of the French state and this notion was inculcated into French citizens, whether they lived in isolated villages in Corsica or Ardèche or were Parisian *Enarques* being trained to run the state. The decentralization reforms of the 1980s have modified this excessive administrative centralization by changing the role of the prefects and creating new bodies such as elected regional councils. It is less certain that either traditional centralization or more recent decentralization reforms have enhanced the practice of democracy at the regional or local levels in France. It is also true that the spirit of decentralization has taken a long time to penetrate into the political and administrative cultures of France's ruling elites.

1.1 Historical Background

The French state was gradually built up by the Capetians whose power was centred on the Île-de-France. By the end of the eighteenth century, following several centuries of centralization, the monarchy controlled a territory whose boundaries corresponded almost exactly with modern France.[2] The monarchy was overthrown during the French Revolution (1789–94), which laid the foundations of modern France as well as developing the concept of the nation-state. This is the key to understanding the French tradition of democracy: it occurs in a state wherein the Republic is in essence the nation. On the eve of the Revolution, the Kingdom of France boasted an efficient public administration, parts of which have survived to this day. Decisions were taken in Paris, the state was absolutist, the army and the navy were considerably improved under Louis XVI, the centralized road network was the best in the world, and the police system was the envy of Jeremy Bentham. Colbertism had laid the foundations for a state-controlled economy, with a number of royal factories building ships and also producing carpets and porcelain, among other products.

Meanwhile, alongside the centralized administrative and police machinery, there was an equally powerful network of counterbalances. There was no single judicial structure; France had two different legal systems: Germanic

---

[2] The outlines of the 'Hexagon' were already clear: only Savoy and Nice remained to be incorporated in 1860, while Alsace-Lorraine would become definitively French, and not German, in 1945.

common law north of the Loire, and written Roman law in the south.[3] The high judicial courts (*parlements*) were independent and guarded their autonomy jealously. Local government existed in diverse forms with powers varying from one area to another. Likewise, there were several systems of weights and measures, varying between regions and even towns. The Kingdom was divided into provinces, some tiny (such as Bigorre) others much larger (such as Normandy), the size of the present-day regions. Most were governed from Paris. A sizeable minority were *pays d'États* (provinces), which had provincial assemblies, some with tax-raising powers. Each of these early regional councils had a specific and unique status. Meanwhile, power at *commune* (municipal) level was even more diverse and varied. Titles—*maire, mayeur, syndic, jurat, consul, échevin*—varied from one place to another. The same was true of the form and degree of participation, which, while ranging from oligarchy to representation and even democracy, was widespread.

The changes wrought by the Revolution centred on reducing that far-reaching and supposedly feudal diversity. For the senior civil servants in the royal government, the streamlining effected by the Revolution was a dream come true, and many of them played an active role behind the scenes. The Revolution continued the authoritarian tradition and achieved what had also been the objectives of the royal government, breaking through the barriers of tradition and local customs that were an obstacle to the reforming zeal of the lawyers and administrators of the Enlightenment. The objective of state rationality was achieved at every level and across the board. Every level was affected, as the past was swept away—a true revolution—and rebuilt from scratch. The reformers targeted the complex structure and tangled networks of jurisdictions, provinces, *bailliages, prévôtés*, elections, and other *parlements*. The country was divided into *départements* (departments), which Saint-Just wanted to be exactly equal in size and demarcated by meridians and parallels. The *constituants* preferred geography as a criterion of pure geometry.

In the Republican tradition, public authorities were rationalized across the board, since in a sense, according to Pierre Rosenvallon (1992), the state determined society. During the Third Republic (1870–1939) the state took responsibility for national education, relegating the Church to the private sector: education was made free, secular, and compulsory, the same for everyone everywhere—at least in principle—and in one language (French). The government also established a new social order by abolishing the old intermediate tiers and entering directly into contact with the individual, the 'citizen' during the Republic, the 'subject' during the two empires, and Vichy France.

---

[3] Interestingly, this is the reverse of the situation in Great Britain where, to the present day, England and Wales have English common law, while Scotland has a system of Roman law.

As a result, the 'nation' became synonymous with the population, governed by the state within a defined territory. Sovereignty is vested in the nation and the nation is indivisible.[4] The state established the nation, and the nation is, in a sense, incarnated by the Republic. The Republic is the cornerstone of French democracy and can be defined by three concepts: secularism, equality, and representative democracy.

1.2 Democracy at the Subnational Level

From what has been said above, it can be seen that the practice of democracy differs between the national level on the one hand, and the local and regional levels on the other. Republican democracy appears to be essentially monistic, as all power emanates from the nation, is embodied in the state, and exercised by the central government. The relationship between central government and local territorial authorities can be summed up neatly as follows: political democracy is exercised primarily at the national level, at the local level there is primarily administration. Thus, France, at least until recently, has not possessed local *government* as is the case in the United Kingdom or the Scandinavian countries but, more accurately, a system of local *administration*. Nevertheless, there has been a slow development of the injection of an element of democratic governance[5] since the period of the Third Republic (1870–1939) with the roles of local actors changing from mere conduits of national policies to actors in their own right within regional and local public spaces (Balme, Faure, and Mabileau 1999). This has accelerated as a result of the decentralization reforms of the early 1980s which radically transformed the relations between the prefect, or representative of the governement, and the presidents of the organs of regional, departmental, and local government. Decentralization also became intermingled, in France as in other western

---

[4] Recent judgments of the *Conseil constitutionnel* have reaffirmed this understanding of state and nation and their relationship to the individual: in 1991, it struck down a reference to the 'Corsican people, a component part of the French people' in a Bill revising Corsica's special status; and, in June 1999, it declared that parts of the European Charter of Regional and Minority Languages are contrary to Articles 1 and 2 of the Constitution which emphasizes that '*le principe d'unicité du peuple français*' (see *Le Monde*, 25 June 1999). And again: '*La Charte . . . en ce qu'elle confère des droits spécifiques à des "groupes" de locuteurs de langues régionales ou minoritaires, à l'intérieur de "territoires" dans lesquels ces langues sont pratiquées, porte atteinte aux principes constitutionnels d'indivisibilité de la République, d'égalité devant la loi et d'unicité du peuple français*'. The Republican Constitution only recognizes the French people and the French language and the 'citizen' is an abstraction without gender, colour, religion, or distinct culture and language.

[5] The concept of 'governance', translated as '*gouvernance*' has been popularized in the French academic literature by Jean Leca (1996), who applies it to the national level, and Patrick Le Galès (1995), who applies it to cities.

countries, with the 'retreat of the state' following the fad of privatization and deregulation which swept across these countries in the 1980s (Wright 1994). These reforms have created windows of opportunity for regional and local actors and new bases of political legitimacy (Biarez 1999). Nevertheless, it is a moot question as to whether these changes have strengthened 'democracy' in either its representative or participatory forms. Some commentators have argued that in fact this is a new expression of elitism rather than democracy which has strengthened the position of the *maire* and the traditional *notables* rather than the citizen who remains passive (Paoletti 1999; Sadran 1999).

2. The Institutional Expression of Democracy

Until 1982,[6] when the new socialist government introduced the decentralization reforms, France, as stated above, was one of the most centralized countries of the industrialized world. At least this was true in a formal and constitutional sense. In practice, the situation was rather more complicated, as sociologists showed that central–local relations in France were governed by a complex system of relationships between the prefect and his administrators and *les notables* (the local politicians) (Crozier and Thoenig 1975; Grémion 1976). This was a two-way process through which the local political system functioned as a system of mediation between the local society and the state. The *notables* ensured the loyalty of the local populations while the state ensured that resources were channelled through them to the locality. The prefect, in turn, represented his territory as much as he did the state (Machin 1977). This system of interlocking relationships (sometimes called the 'honeycomb structure') between the centre and the local level was reinforced by the *cumul des mandats*, whereby national politicians hold several political posts at the national and local levels simultaneously (Sadran 1999).

It has been argued that the 1981 decentralization reforms were *le sacre des notables* (a consecration of the *notables*) (Rondin 1985; Mény 1992). According to this argument, the power of the *notables* has been reinforced by the transfer of competencies from the prefect to the presidents of the *Conseil*

---

[6] The basic law which launched the decentralization reforms was promulgated on 2 March 1982 and between this and 1986 there followed an avalanche of around 40 laws and 300 decrees. Michel Verpeaux has described the law of 2 March 1982 as the 'locomotive' which has pulled along the subsequent laws and decrees which he describes as the 'carriages' (Verpeaux 1999).

général (departmental council) and the *Conseil régional* (regional council). This analysis has been carried further by Mabileau, who sees a new hierarchy of *notables*: the *grands notables* (usually the mayors of the large cities) at the summit; next the *barons intermédiaires* (those holding the position of *député* and, at the same time, mayor of a medium-sized town, for example); and, at the bottom of the hierarchy, the *vassaux* (ordinary local politicians who operate as a 'clientele' of the middle group) (Mabileau 1997). Neverthe-less, the initial scepticism expressed by authors such as 'Rondin'[7] needs to be tempered as it gave the impression that decentralization really did not change very much of the old system. A more prudent analysis suggests that the reforms, while consecrating some previous practices, did indeed introduce some significant changes as well (Loughlin and Mazey 1995; Jouve and Lefèvre 1999; Négrier 1999). Michel Verpeaux (1999) summarizes the main results of the decentralization reforms as follows: the suppression of prior administrative control (*la tutelle a priori*) by the prefect over local authorities; the transfer of executive powers from the prefect to the presidents of the regional and departmental councils; and the creation of the region as a *collectivité territoriale*, that is, an entity with the same legal status as the communes and departments. Nevertheless, he also recognizes the persistence of certain traditional features of French local politics such as the system of *cumul des mandats* and also that these reforms have been carried out largely without the involvement of ordinary citizens—'*les grands absents de la décentralization*'.

Perhaps the most important change resulting from the decentralization reforms has been the fragmentation of the French politico-administrative system at the local level (Mabileau 1997). There is now less planning at the central level, and the state has to some extent disengaged from public policy areas, leaving a situation of competition and even chaos ('*un démarche chao-tique et bricolage institutionnel*', according to Mabileau) among the different levels of local government. Mabileau's judgement might be somewhat exag-gerated. What is significant are the new intergovernmental relations between the state and the subnational, especially the region, implied by the 'contrac-tualization' approach. Regions now sign with the state a *contrat de plan* which is, in essence, a programme of economic development over a number of years (Balme and Bonnet 1995; Négrier 1999). While the state has, in some respects, reinforced its power through these contracts, there now exists a new process of bargaining and negotiation which is producing new types of relationship between the centre and the locality. It is also interesting that the state now feels the need to use contractual procedures to ensure compliance with its objectives, reflecting, from the point of view of the state, a real dispersal of

---

[7] It seems that 'Rondin' is the nom de plume of several authors who contributed to this volume.

power.[8] The levels that have gained most from the reforms are the big cities and the departments, since they have acquired new functions and also the resources to meet them. The regions have not gained as much as regionalists had hoped and are weak bodies compared to the Spanish Autonomous Communities or the Italian regions (Dupoirier 1998). Nevertheless, they do exist, and this has added an extra layer of complexity to the administrative and political system alongside the *départements* and the thousands of small municipalities. Thus, the French politico-administrative should be regarded as in a state of flux and has moved beyond the old system of cross-regulation analysed in terms of organization theory by Grémion, and Crozier and Thoenig in the 1970s. Contemporary analysts are coming to terms with the effects of decentralization using 'actor-centred' and 'public policy' approaches (Mabileau 1999; see also Négrier 1999).

2.1 The National Level

Although France may be regarded as the founder of the concept of the nation-state, at the time of the French Revolution, it has had enormous difficulties in adopting a political regime that gives political and institutional expression to this concept. Since the Revolution, it has tried several systems, each one succeeding the other by either a revolution or a regime crisis: two Empires, two constitutional monarchies, and five Republics of which the present regime is the Fifth. There has been a tendency to swing between an authoritarian plebiscitary democracy along Napoleonic lines and a fragmented and unstable parliamentary system as during the Third and Fourth Republics. The current Fifth Republic was designed by Charles de Gaulle to stress the plebiscitary approach. In 1962 there was a referendum changing the constitution to permit the direct election of the President of the Republic. De Gaulle wished to use this as a way of 'taming' parliament. Under the constitution of the Fifth Republic, it is the president who is head of state and nominates the prime minister. The latter is the head of the government but the president chairs meetings of the cabinet (*conseil des ministres*). He is also responsible for several policy issues, including foreign affairs. However, each succeeding president has tempered this presidentialism and there has been an increasing acceptance of the role of parliament and the importance of the opposition. This has finally resulted in the situation of cohabitation whereby we have seen a socialist president (Mitterrand) govern alongside a prime minister from the right (Chirac), and a right-wing president (Chirac) alongside a socialist prime minister (Jospin). Thus, the current French political system may be categorized as 'semi-presidential' (Duverger 1963; Duhamel 1993). After the election

---

[8] I would like to thank Alistair Cole for pointing this out to me.

of the socialists to power in 1981, following twenty-three years in opposition, France has also seen the development of a Westminster-style polarization in which there has been an alternation of government power between two party 'blocs' on the left and right of the political spectrum.

The French Parliament is composed of two houses: the lower house is the *Assemblée Nationale* (National Assembly) and the upper house is the *Sénat* (Senate). The National Assembly has 577 *députés* elected by universal suffrage (Stevens 1996). Elections are held under a constituency-based two-round system. If a candidate receives 50 per cent of the valid votes cast in the first round, he or she is elected. However, more often, there is a run-off to the second round when the candidate who wins a simple majority of the votes is elected. In 1986 a system of proportional representation was introduced by the socialist government, apparently to try to stave off electoral defeat (Stevens 1996). However, this did not prevent a right-wing government being elected who then reverted to the original electoral system.

The senate consists of 321 members representing France's local authorities: each electoral constituency consists of one *département* (department) and its electoral college is made up of the deputies, the *conseillers généraux* (departmental councillors), the mayors, and the *conseillers municipaux* (town councillors) of that department. The senate is important from the point of view of local democracy (or at least from that of the representation of the locality by its *grands notables*) as it represents the interests of the local authorities (around one-third of its members in 1995 were also mayors), and it is able to influence legislation even if it cannot block this completely.

2.2 The Local Level

It could be argued that local democracy in France consists of little more than some functions of government being assigned to territorial communities and managed by elected members, whom the state provides with resources. The Jacobin system did not, however, rule out local elections: mayors and municipal, district, and departmental councillors were elected and the *commissaires de la République*—who were later replaced by prefects—represented the nation. The principle of election extended even to judges and prosecutors. In short, this was centralized democracy, which Napoleon was to convert into an authoritarian regime, replacing elected representatives with officials. The prefect, with greater powers, managed the *département*, the sub-prefect managed the *arrondissement* (district), and the mayor managed the municipality. They were advised by *notables* (local politicians) appointed by the state. The monarchy of July 1830 reintroduced the election of municipal councillors, and the Third Republic set up the *conseils généraux*—elected departmental councils—and restored the election of the mayor by municipal councils. Despite the centralization of the French state, it could, however, be also argued that the existence of a '*compétence générale d'administration*' allows localities—within limits—to engage in local public policies as is clear from the competition between communes, departments, and regions where there are overlapping competencies. In this sense, the French localities can be considered as having even greater freedoms than exist at this level in the United Kingdom, allegedly the land of self-government.

2.2.1 The Commune

The basic unit of local government in metropolitan France is the *commune* (municipality), of which there are 36,755. These entities were the parishes and communities of the Middle Ages, and French people have shown a great attachment to them. This explains why so many have survived. However, the vast majority of them are tiny and completely unviable, from the technocratic point of view of their capacity to carry out the tasks of modern government. Of the *communes*, 22,000 have less than 500 inhabitants, and 10,000 have between 500 and 2,000 inhabitants (Stevens 1996). Half of the population of 57 million in metropolitan France live in the 2 per cent of municipalities with over 10,000 inhabitants while thirty-six municipalities are cities of over 100,000 people (ibid.). Even more striking is the political, economic, and demographic domination of Paris among French cities which is unique in Europe ('*la macrocéphalie de Paris*' according to Hoffmann-Martinot 1999).

Communes have two aspects: they are both levels of state administration obliged to carry out tasks assigned to them by the state and they are also institutions of representative government entitled to exercise competencies not specifically forbidden by law. The *conseil municipal* (municipal council) is the legislative organ of the municipality while the *maire* (mayor) is its executive. In municipalities of more than 3,500 inhabitants, councils are elected by a list system in two rounds whereby the list that obtains an absolute majority in the first round or a simple majority in the second receives half of the seats; the other half are distributed proportionately among the winning list and the other lists. The municipal council administers the affairs of the municipalities as well as voting its budget and administering its finances.[9]

The key figure in the municipality is the mayor. One commentator described him/her as 'the gentle autocrat of the municipality, its principal arbitration officer, its father confessor and the guardian of its interests' (Wright 1983). The mayor has two tasks: first, he/she is the representative of

---

[9] Its financial resources come largely from the central government in the form of *dotations globales de fonctionnement* (DGF); *dotations globales d'équipement* (DGE); and *dotations globales de décentralization* (DGD).

the state in the municipality, responsible for implementing legislation emanating from Paris and for public safety within the municipality; second, he/she
is the executive officer of the municipal council. Indeed, it has been remarked
that the principal task of the almost half a million local councillors in France
is to elect the mayors. Under the system of *cumul des mandats*, many mayors
hold other positions at prefectoral, regional, and national level (see Table 8.1).
Many are also members of the government, and usually the president and the
prime minister are also mayors of sometimes tiny villages. Many national
political figures have been, and are, identified as mayors of large cities:
Defferre in Marseille, Chaban-Delmas in Bordeaux, Lecanuet in Rouen,
Mauroy in Lille, etc. Several attempts have been made to reduce the number
of offices that any one politician may hold (Sadran 1999). Table 8.1 shows that
this has been largely unsuccessful with 48.4 per cent of deputies and 50.8 per
cent of senators holding three offices; 83.4 per cent of deputies and 68.6 per
cent of deputies hold a position at communal level. Prime Minister Jospin has
requested that the ministers of his government give up the position of mayor
should they hold that position.[10]

French politicians, administrators, and academic commentators have long
been aware of the problems resulting from the '*éparpillement communale*'—
the fragmentation resulting from the huge number of communes (Regourd
1999). A law adopted in February 1992 pointed out that France had more
communes than existed in all of the other member states of the European
Union added together! Two approaches have been adopted to try to remedy
this problem. The first, attempted in the *Loi Marcellin* of 1971, followed the
example of other European countries and tried to suppress most of the small
communes to create larger and more viable entities. This proved a complete
failure given the attachment of the French to their communes as an expression of 'local democracy' and 'local autonomy'. The second approach has been
more successful and consisted in encouraging intercommunal cooperation
through the voluntary setting up of *syndicats* such as the *syndicats intercommunaux à vocation unique* (single purpose syndicates, SIVU) or the
syndicats intercommunaux à vocation multiple (multipurpose syndicates,
SIVOM). This approach, however, has been a victim of its own success and
has resulted in 16,500 SIVU and 2,500 SIVOM in which communes can cooperate on an *ad hoc* basis but where there is a lack of coherence and rationality over the entire territory. The 1992 law referred to above was an attempt to
put some order into the situation by bringing the associations of communes
withing the framework of a wider programme of territorial development covering the entire territory but under the aegis of the departmental prefect. The

---

[10] Sometimes, mayors of towns will nominate their deputy mayor to replace them while
they exercise the position of minister—in effect, they continue to run the commune by
proxy!

TABLE 8.1 *Cumul des mandats* (multiple office-holding) in France (data collected after parliamentary elections of 1997 and before regional and department elections of 1998)

No. of offices	Deputies		Senators		Presidents of regions		Presidents of departments		Mayors of municipalities with >2,500 inhabitants	
	Total	%	Total	%	Total	%	Total	%	Total	%
1	53	9.2	50	16.2	5	19.2	8	8	2,313	65.4
2	225	30.0	101	32.7	13	50.0	37	37	960	27.2
3	279	48.4	157	50.8	8	30.8	55	55	248	7.0
4	20	3.5	1	0.3	0	0	0	0	13	0.4
Total	577		309		26		100		3,534	
Also having the office of:										
Deputy					6	23.1	18	18	262	7.4
Senator					4	15.4	41	41	76	2.2
MEP	3	0.5	1	0.3	0	0	1	1	7	0.2
Regional councillor	98	17.0	38	12.3			12	12	241	6.8
Department councillor	261	45.2	167	54	1	3.8				
Municipal Councillor	481	83.4	212	68.6	18	69.2	75	75	909	25.7

MEP, member of the European Parliament.

Source: P. Sadran (1999: 28).

law also defined in which areas cooperation should occur rather than leaving this to the free choice of the communes themselves but it also furnished the syndicats with their financial resources. Despite some failings, these developments have been considered a success and formed the basis of further reforms along the same lines (Regourd 1999). The Chevènement Law of 12 July 1999 dealt with '*l'organization urbaine et . . . la simplification de la coopération inter-communale*'. This law follows the French 'voluntarist' tradition of non-coercion, but provides important financial incentives to create '*communautés d'agglomération*' (i.e., in the large cities).

2.2.2 *The* Prefecture *and the* Conseil Général

The French departments were set up in 1790 during the French Revolution and were conceived as a 'rational' organization of the territory to break from the system of the *Ancien Régime* with its great variety of customs and regimes. The size of the department was determined by the distance covered in a day's horse ride to reach its principal city. However, despite the vast demographic and socio-economic changes that have taken place in France over the last 200 years, the boundaries of the departments remain largely the same today as they were then although the number has slightly increased.[11] Napoleon retained the departmental structure, but instituted the system of prefects to ensure central control of this territory.

Before 1871 there was an appointed *conseil général* (advisory council), but after that date this was changed into a unit of local democracy through direct elections with the cantons (sub-departmental territorial units) as the constituencies. However, the prefect remained the executive of the council and was responsible for drawing up the agenda of meetings, for controlling the budget, and for executing the decisions of the council. This remained the case until the 1981–2 decentralization reforms that transferred these functions to the council president (Loughlin and Mazey 1995).

The departmental system is closely identified with the Jacobin conception of the state as 'the one and indivisible Republic', and those French people who cherish this conception are reluctant to see it changed. This explains why the decentralization reforms left this system untouched while at the same time setting up the new regions. In practice, the departments are in a much stronger position than the regions given the range of functions they perform,[12] the

---

[11] There were originally 89 departments, a number that was later increased to 90; however, today there are 96 in metropolitan France, following the division of Paris into 5 departments in 1966 and the division of Corsica into 2 in 1976. There are also 4 overseas departments (DOM): Guadeloupe, Martinique, French Guyana, and Réunion.

[12] These functions include various social-welfare services, some health services, responsibility for most roads and some bridges and ports, building and maintenance of *collèges* (secondary schools for pupils between the ages of 11 and 16), and some cultural activities.

budgets for which they are responsible, and the number of staff that they employ.[13]

2.2.3 The Region

The regions are the 'poor cousins' of the local-government system.[14] Each region is headed by a *conseil régional* (regional council), elected by universal suffrage using proportional representation. The president of the region is chosen by the council and he or she appoints the executive. However, 'regionalism' has fitted uneasily into the French politico-administrative system and was for a long time seen as contrary to the principles of the Jacobin state. After the Second World War, regionalism did develop but was primarily concerned with cultural and economic issues and less with the political organization of the state. In the 1950s, there was some regionalization of the national plan, and functional regions were set up in the 1970s with a responsibility for economic development and some administrative functions. The 1981–2 reforms did strengthen the regions by upgrading their juridical status and setting up directly elected regional councils (Loughlin and Mazey 1995). However, the implementation of the regional aspects of the reforms was delayed by the socialist government for political reasons, and elections were not held until 1986. Furthermore, the elections were held on the same day as the parliamentary elections, and this diluted the importance of the region. In general, although all of the main political parties in France now accept the regions, central governments of both left and right have been reluctant to strengthen them. To a large extent this problem is related to the continuing influence of the departmental system. The original regions were designed to be mainly a union of departments without territories of their own. This idea was retained in the electoral arrangements of the new regions. These arrangements are still based on the departmental constituencies (Nay 1998).

Nevertheless, the regions do exist and are now part of the French politico-administrative system changed by the decentralization programme. Their functions are still mainly related to economic development, which is achieved through agreements signed by them and the central state in the form of *contrats de plan État-Région* (Balme and Bonnet 1995). However, they have also acquired a number of other functions for which they are either solely responsible or share responsibility with the central state.[15] There is today a wide

[13] In 1990 there were 142,264 people employed by departments compared to 4,490 employed by regions.

[14] Until 1991 they included Corsica, but with the new Joxe Statute of that year, the island became a *collectivité territoriale* with a different (and more powerful) legal status than the other regions.

[15] For example, they can now fund research and technology programmes, have responsibility for the building and maintenance of *lycées* (upper-level secondary schools), and have subsidized university development.

variety among French regions in their capacity to assert themselves on the national and international scenes. Some, such as Rhône-Alpes, have considerable economic clout and are active on the European scene through organizations such as the 'Four Motors' group (which also includes Baden-Württemberg, Catalonia, and Lombardy). Some have also developed cross-border programmes such as between Aquitaine and the Basque Country or the West Mediterranean Euro-region (including Languedoc-Roussillon, Midi-Pyrénées, Catalonia). In general, the French regions have tried to develop an orientation towards Europe, although the central state still acts as a restraint on these activities (Mazey 1995). Despite their constitutional limitations, some contemporary scholars have argued that the French regions have, since 1986, managed to assert themselves as important actors in the French politico-administrative landscape and, alongside the large cities, are beginning to squeeze the departments out of their position within the subnational governance system.

2.2.4 Special Status Regions and Cities

A number of cities and regions have been given a special status either because of their size or for cultural and geographical reasons.

The city of Paris is both a municipality and a *départment*, and its mayor is an important national figure (until recently and for many years the post was held by the current French president, Jacques Chirac). Paris, Lyons, and Marseille are divided into *arrondissements*, each of which has an elected mayor and council.

Corsica is an island with a strong cultural specificity and has experienced serious political disorder and violence since the 1960s (Loughlin 1989; Loughlin, Olivesi, and Daftary, 1999). In 1982 under the decentralization reforms, it received a *statut particulier* (special statute) that was meant to give the islanders a greater amount of autonomy than the other French regions and to take into account their cultural and geographical specificity. However, this arrangement failed to work and, in 1991, it was given a new statute drawn up under the Minister of the Interior, Pierre Joxe (Hintjens, Loughlin, and Olivesi 1995; Loughlin, Olivesi, and Daftary, 1999). This transformed Corsica into a *collectivité territoriale*, which has greater powers than the regional councils of the mainland. The *collectivité territoriale* also differs in that it has both an assembly and an executive, each of which is headed by a president. It is the president of the executive who is the effective head of the *collectivité*. However, the Joxe bill also contained a recognition of the *peuple corse*, a demand of the autonomists and nationalists on the island. The French parliament accepted this clause, but it was struck down as unconstitutional by the *Conseil constitutionnel*, which ruled that there is only one people, *le peuple français*, and only one language, *la langue française*.[16]

The four *Départements d'Outre Mer* (DOM, overseas departments—Guadeloupe, Guyane, Martinique, and Réunion) are almost identical to the mainland departments except that they may develop *mesures d'adaptation* (special measures that take into account their situation). Each DOM is also a region, but the *Conseil constitutionnel* did not permit a single council for each DOM, insisting instead that there be separate departmental and regional councils. The paradox is that Corsica now benefits from a statute that recognizes a much greater degree of specificity than is the case with the distant DOM (Duhamel 1993).

The *Territoires d'Outre Mer* (TOM, overseas territories) are in a completely different situation from Corsica or the DOM. The French Constitution recognizes a distinction between the French people and the overseas peoples who have a right to self-determination. The latter category includes some archipelagos in the Pacific, New Caledonia, French Polynesia, and Wallis and Futuna. These territories have a high degree of autonomy, have their own assemblies, and participate in the legislative process since they must be consulted by parliament if their interests are affected. They may accede to independence if they so desire.

2.3 The Role of Parties

Political parties are virtually non-existent in small localities and are only really active in the 2 per cent of towns with more than 10,000 inhabitants; those towns do, of course, account for half of the population of France. However, partly owing to the electoral system, the lists are based on cross-party coalitions, including a number of independent candidates. It is only in towns of over 30,000 inhabitants that the national parties exert real control over those coalitions and that applies more to the left than to the right.

Decentralization has involved a transfer of real power and resources to French local authorities. As a result, there has been an attempt at colonization of these levels of government by the political parties, even if parties remain weak at this level. However, this has involved less a 'localization' or 'regionalization' of the national parties than a 'nationalization' of the local and regional (Mabileau 1997). French politicians have traditionally tried to build a support base at the local level through the system of *cumul des mandats*. In recent years there has also been a tendency for the party apparatuses to develop at the local level (at least in the larger towns), to organize local and regional elections, and

---

[16] See footnote 3 above.

to choose the candidates for these elections (ibid.). The regions especially have become important arenas of political activity for the opposition, which may attempt to win them as an important base from which to attack the government. The right-wing parties [*Rassemblement pour la République*, RPR (Rally for the Republic), and the *Union pour la Démocratie Française*, UDF (Union for French Democracy)] had largely opposed the 1981–2 decentralization reforms, but quickly came to accept them and, following the 1986 regional elections, won majorities in twenty out of the then twenty-two councils. The extreme right *Front National* has also used the region as a way of gaining a foothold in the mainstream political system.

However, the parties still continue to see the department and the big cities, rather than the region or the myriad of small municipalities, as the primary foci of political activity. It was significant that, when a law was passed limiting the number of offices that may be held under the *cumul des mandats*, most national politicians chose to retain their presidency of the departmental council rather than the presidency of the regional council. This continuing 'departmentalism', as well as the system of proportional representation, have caused problems for the regional councils, since they have led to fragmentation and unstable coalition majorities (Nay 1998). The difficulty of forming stable majorities is compounded by the fact that the elected regional councillors have a primary loyalty to the department for which they were elected rather than to the party to which they belong.

3. The Practice of Subnational Democracy

3.1 The Role of Policy Networks and Pressure Groups in Local Government

The French political tradition has tended to be suspicious towards 'pressure groups' or 'intermediary associations'. In drawing up the Constitution of the Fifth Republic, Michel Debré wished to eliminate them from any influence over either politics or policy-making. De Gaulle, on the other hand, wished to see them excluded from politics, but was willing to allow them a role in policy-making (Wright 1983). However, unlike the countries of northern Europe, interest groups in France, such as trade unions, business associations, farmers' organizations, or student organizations, have tended to be fragmented and fractious. As a result it has proved difficult to bring them into the policy-making system (ibid.), although there are some exceptions such as large-scale farmers and secondary school teachers who have shown greater cohesiveness and have exercised some influence on policy-making.

This has also been true at the local level, although at this level there is a certain imbrication of political and business elites through the *notable* system outlined above. These may sit together in the *sociétés d'économie mixte* (semi-state bodies), which are responsible for areas such as urban planning and housing. There are also the various chambers, such as the *Chambres de Commerce et d'Industrie*, the *Chambres d'Agriculture*, and the *Chambres de Métiers*, that exist at the regional and departmental levels and in the large towns. Little research has been carried out on the power and influence of these bodies, but some studies have suggested that through them powerful local (or national) interests may have a strong influence, such as in the Chamber of Commerce in Rennes that made possible the building of a giant Citroën car plant near the town (Wright 1983). Cole and John (Cole and John 1995) have conducted extensive research on the role of policy networks in Rennes and Lille, comparing them with the English cities of Leeds and Southampton. The authors found in the French cases quite a complex picture involving several different kinds of network. These were either individual or organizational. The individual networks revolved around well-known politicians such as Pierre Mauroy in Lille, who accumulated a great number of political offices. These individuals exercised great influence and patronage in the process of decision-making. The organizational networks were broken down into distinct types: (Anglo-Saxon type) public policy networks; politico-economic networks; spatial networks; and political networks. There were important differences in these networks depending on the sector (e.g., local development or education). The main conclusion of the authors is that networks do play an important role in decision-making but that the French state remains omnipresent and continues to shape the context in which they operate although this has changed as a result of decentralization.

3.2 Critiques of Local Democracy in France

The most severe critique of the French system of democracy is that it exists in a purely formal sense and was is on the abstract notions of citizenship and the state, which exist in a direct relationship with each other. The attempt to destroy the intermediary bodies between the citizen and the state led, in practice, to an excessive centralization of power. This excessive centralization was expressed graphically in the title of the book by the French geographer Jean-François Gravier, *Paris et le Désert Français* (1958). The local political system existed primarily to administer the decisions taken in Paris. Relations between the centre and the periphery were mediated by the *notables* as outlined above. While, from the time of the Third Republic onwards, elections were held at both the departmental and communal levels, and from 1986 onwards, at the regional level, it has been argued that this simply was the legitimation of the exercise of power by the *notables* rather than the expression of the will of the people.

This critique intensified from the 1960s onwards, especially after May 1968. Groups such as the *Parti Socialiste Unifié* of Michael Rocard promoted the notions of *autogestion* (autonomy) to be applied at different levels of society (in factories and schools but also on the territorial level). There was also an upsurge of regionalist movements in regions such as Brittany, Corsica, and Occitanie, demanding the liberation of the *forces vives* of local societies through a restructuring of the centralized state. Some of these themes were later incorporated into the programme of government of the left [Socialist Party, *Parti Communiste Français* (French Communist Party), and *Parti Radicale de Gauche* (Radical Party of the Left)] in 1981 and can be found in the *110 Propositions du candidat Mitterrand*. Although the more radical of the proposals were watered down after the left came to power,[17] some of them, such as a special statute for Corsica, did come to fruition in the 1981–2 decentralization programme. In fact, the programme itself was a fruit of this way of thinking and was justified as way of strengthening democracy in general.

However, it has since been claimed that decentralization did not fully realize this goal. Mabileau (1997) argues that, '*il faut bien admettre que la décentralization s'est effectuée sans la démocratie locale*' ('one must admit that we have had decentralization, but without local democracy'). Many commentators note that decentralization has, in fact, simply consecrated the *notable* system (Rondin 1985; Mény 1992). Nevertheless, it could be argued that the *système notabiliaire* itself has changed and that decentralization has effected a transformation of the French politico-administrative system. It has also been pointed out that the reorganization of local government through 'intercommunality' has been carried out with the participation of citizens and that the new bodies created such as the *communautés d'agglomération* have little democratic legitimacy. The key question is how to ensure that this transformation is given a democratic dimension and to define what this dimension might entail.

These critiques of the practice of democracy have been explicitly accepted by governments of both left and right. Indeed, a law in 1992, on the *administration territorial de la République* (ATR), began to address the problem of citizen participation by permitting the creation of consultative committees bringing together elected representatives and representatives of local associations. This law, completed by a further law in 1995, also allowed local referendums on any question concerning the commune, although such referendums were non-binding on the council (Verpeaux 1999: 10). In 1995, Lionel

---

[17] For example, the promise to create a single Basque *département* instead of the present two, or the promise to promote regional languages.

Jospin, then chair of the socialist party, told the party that '*le renouveau de la démocratie*' was now one of its priorities. In 1996, the former minister Jack Lang told a party annual congress that '*La France connaît aujourd'hui un malaise démocratique*' and French people were either turning away from, or turning against, democracy. It is not difficult to see here a veiled reference to the successes (at that time) of the extreme-right party, the *Front National*. According to Lang, this was a consequence of the economic crisis and social exclusion which accompanied it. The text adopted almost unanimously by the congress promised to promote democracy by combating social exclusion but also, by encouraging local democracy and reducing the number of accumulated offices (*cumul des mandats*). In 1997, the *Parti Socialiste* programme for the parliamentary elections of that year declared, quite simply, '*la démocratie française reste archaïque*' (*Le Monde*, 7 April 1998).

3.3 Citizens' Attitudes to Local Government in France

French people are among those most rooted in their locality and show a marked reluctance to move out of it. In 1963, 80 per cent of French people lived in the region they were born in, and in 1990 this figure stood at 70 per cent (Percheron 1992). This characteristic is a probable explanation for the degrees of identification with local levels of government rather than with the state: 90 per cent of the population feel close to the municipality, 76 per cent to the department, 63 per cent to the region, and only 22 per cent to the state (ibid.). They also believe that a certain number of services are better delivered by local authorities, including the regions, than by the state.[18] On the other hand, they are more concerned that services be provided than with the government level that provides them. In recent years, there has been a worryingly high level of abstentionism in local elections. In the regional and cantonal elections in March 1998, the abstention rate actually increased from the first (39.5 per cent) to the second (45 per cent) round (*Le Monde*, 14 March 1998).

3.3.1 Attitudes towards Decentralization, Regionalization, and Europe

With regard to the decentralization reforms, a poll conducted in 1991 showed that 65 per cent of French people were favourable towards them (SOFRES, *Institut de la décentralization*, quoted in Mabileau 1997). Furthermore, despite

---

[18] An opinion poll taken in 1991 showed that majorities thought that decisions concerning large infrastructural works would best be made by the state: e.g., TGV (high-speed train) routes (45%) and motorways (32%). Decisions with regard to other issues would be best made by regions: creation of universities (35%), training (31%), creation of industrial zones (30%). Communes were best suited to decision-making with regard to rural development (36%), local economic activity (37%), or housing (58%).

the limited nature of the regional dimension of the reform, there has been a very positive attitude towards the regions, increasing as time has gone on (Percheron 1992). Since the 1986 regional elections, the majority of citizens regard the region rather than the department as the political and administrative entity of the future: in 1986, 59 per cent thought this of the region and 26 per cent of the department; in 1991 the figures were 70 per cent for the region and 20 per cent for the department. These opinions were true of all social categories, political orientations, and residential situations (from small municipalities to the Parisian conglomeration). When asked why they place such confidence in the region, respondents answered that it is not because of regional identity (only 12 per cent thought this), but because they viewed the region in functional terms. For some, generally those from lower social and educational backgrounds, it was an extra source of state subsidies. For those of higher social and educational background, it was viewed favourably because of its European dimension (ibid.). This optimism toward the region is also illustrated by other data collected by the *Observatoire Interrégional Politique* (OIP) in Paris (Dupoirier, 1998*b*) which showed that in 1997 only 33 per cent of those polled were 'very' or 'rather' optimistic about the future of France, while 49 per cent felt this about the region. It is true that in 1989 these figures stood at 52 per cent optimistic about France and 62 per cent optimistic about the region, but they still illustrate the superiority of the region in this regard.

However, this positive attitude toward the region does not mean that French people wish the departments or the state to disappear. On the contrary: 78 per cent wish to maintain the status quo in this regard (Percheron 1992). On the other hand, 65 per cent are in favour of amalgamating the municipalities. There seems to be, however, a certain amount of confusion in French people's minds with regard to the region. An opinion poll conducted in 1997 showed that 54 per cent of those polled thought there were too many levels of government. When asked a further question as to which level ought to be removed, 38 per cent thought it should be the region, 32 per cent the department, 15 per cent the municipality, and 15 per cent did not know (*Le Monde*, 27 February 1997). In this same poll, respondents were asked to judge which centre of decision-making was most important today and which would be the most important in twenty years time. With regard to the current most important centre, 44 per cent thought it was the state, 30 per cent thought it was Europe, and 21 per cent local authorities. In twenty years time, 68 per cent of the population think that it will be Europe, 15 per cent the state, and 7 per cent local authorities.

3.3.2 Attitudes towards Local Politicians

Fifty-five per cent of French people think that decentralization has enhanced the role of local politicians, 7 per cent think it has reduced it, while 28 per cent think it has left it unchanged (*Le Monde*, 27 February 1997). Forty-eight per cent thought it had had a positive effect on the effectiveness of local politicians, while 13 per cent thought it had not. When asked which of their politicians they trusted most, a huge majority (68 per cent) chose the mayor. The prefect came next (26 per cent), followed by the deputy (23 per cent), the president of the *conseil général* (23 per cent), the president of the *conseil régional* (16 per cent), and the *sénateur* (6 per cent), while only 6 per cent trusted none of these (ibid.). There was generally a positive attitude toward local politicians, although a slight majority (51 per cent) thought they were not close to the people. A majority (50 per cent) also felt that local bureaucrats were competent.

Summarizing these findings, we might note that French people are strongly devoted to the locality and are most conscious of the presence of the mayor and the prefect at the local level. There is generally a positive attitude toward local politicians, especially the mayor, who is the most trusted by far. Many believe that the region has a bright future and there seems to be a growing awareness and acceptance of its importance. More would prefer to remove the department than the region if they had to choose should there be a restructuring of subnational government, although the difference between the two positions was not great. Finally, there is an awareness of the importance of 'Europe' and a feeling that this would be the most important level of all in the future.

4. Challenges and Opportunities for Subnational Democracy

4.1 The European Challenge

France is one of the founding members of the European Community and, with Germany, has been the driving force behind European integration. However, this has been principally the prerogative of the central state and, in particular, of the president of the Republic who works also with the prime minister. Subnational levels of government have been, until recent years, largely excluded from the European scene. This is true even within the field of EU regional policy, where the *Délégation à l'aménagement du territoire et à l'action régionale* (DATAR) has been more important than the regions in drawing up and implementing the Community Support Frameworks (CSFs). Nevertheless, decentralization has given the French regions an opportunity to act on the European level, while the notion of a 'Europe of the Regions' has provided further justification for this (Delcamp 1992; Mazey 1995). First,

French regions, like other European regions, have established offices in Brussels that act as information-gathering centres. Second, a number of regions have established cross-border associations. Third, French regions are members of, and indeed, are sometimes the driving forces behind interregional associations such as the Conference of Peripheral Maritime Regions (including the Atlantic Arc and the Latin Arc) and the Assembly of European Regions. Within this context of extraterritorial activity, Rhône-Alpes is a part of the Four Motors group (see section 2.2.3 above). Finally, French local politicians have been active in the Committee of the Regions, whose first president was Jacques Blanc, the president of the Languedoc-Roussillon region.

The close result in France in the referendum on the Treaty on European Union shows, nevertheless, that there is still a certain apprehension with regard to European integration even if the results of the opinion poll quoted above (section 3.3.1) show that most French people think that Europeanization is inevitable. The task and opportunity, therefore, is to ensure that it strengthens democratic governance at the regional and local levels rather than the inverse. In many ways 'Europe' remains an affair of the political elites, including the local elites who are clearly using it as a means of consolidating their hold on local society (Négrier 1999). Nevertheless, the growing importance of Europe has widened the horizons of French citizens beyond the 'Hexagon' and opened them up to other political experiences.

4.2 Socio-Economic and Demographic Changes

France has undergone a dramatic transformation since the Second World War. At the end of the War it was still a country with a large population engaged in agriculture and where traditional rural values still dominated life, even in the towns. Since then, there has been a massive exodus from the countryside and a corresponding growth in the towns and cities. However, France still retains the political and administrative system inherited from the nineteenth century with the addition of the new regions. Basically, the large number of municipalities and the size of the departments do not correspond with the changed socio-economic and demographic realities. The vast majority of the municipalities are too small to be viable, while the existence of both the department and the region means there is probably one layer of government too much.

There is clearly a need for a rationalization of this system. The profound attachment of French people to their municipality has made this difficult. However, beginning in the 1950s, there have been some attempts at voluntary amalgamation of municipalities, using a variety of arrangements (Mabileau 1997).[19]

4.3 Strengthening Local Democracy in the 1980s and 1990s

One of the purposes of the decentralization reforms of the 1980s was to strengthen democracy in the French state as a whole by bringing government and administration closer to the people. It might be remarked that this aim has been largely achieved. However, it is less evident that it has brought the people closer to the state in the sense that they are more *administrés* than active and participatory citizens.

According to Mabileau (1997), the attempt to achieve true local democracy (i.e., participatory rather than representative democracy) by decentralization has been diluted by the introduction of other less radical approaches. These include the search for *transparence* ('openness'), better communications, allowing citizens easier access to local government, institutionalizing negotiation and concertation, opinion surveys, rebuilding local citizenship. The 1992 Act on 'the territorial administration of the Republic' contained a chapter on 'local democracy' and the Pasqua Act of 1995 attempted to involve citizens more fully in the form of popular initiatives with regard to planning questions (see section 3.2 above) However, the attempt to build a participatory democracy in France, as elsewhere, has, according to Mabileau, foundered on the rock of massive citizen indifference; a conclusion also reached by several of the authors in the work edited by Balme, Faure, and Mabileau (1999).

5. *Conclusions*

France has inherited from the nineteenth century a political system whose chief feature was its highly centralized character, although this model was regarded a hundred years ago as the most advanced form of state and was adopted by newly emerging national states such as Greece, Italy, and Finland.

---

[19] *Syndicats intercommunaux à vocation multiple* (SIVOM) were set up in 1959; *districts urbains* were set up in 1959, and *districts ruraux* in 1970; *communautés urbaines* were set up in the large cities in 1966; *communautés de communes* and *communautés de villes* were set up by the 1992 law on the territorial administration of the republic. The Pasqua law of 1995 introduced 'an organization of territory based on the notion of the *pays*' to devise local development plans. According to Mabileau (1997), this might be interpreted as a new form of centralism given the role of state officials such as the sub-prefect in this organization.

Democracy, however, was seen as involving the exercise of citizenship, interpreted in an abstract manner as the exercise of certain rights and the possibility of voting in elections. The state dominated everything, and local societies were seen as the recipients of state administration rather than as autonomous self-governing communities as in the Anglo-Saxon and Germanic traditions; even so, the French people remain profoundly attached to their locality and are reluctant to see the communal system reformed. In the 1980s, the position of the state changed with the decentralization laws that caused a profound upheaval of the French politico-administration system. The state is no longer the omnipresent and omnipotent state of the past, but is more fragmented and dispersed, although it remains an important (probably the most important) collective actor. There has been a real transfer of power to local governments, and regions have been enhanced. The nature of policy-making has also changed from a vertical and hierarchical approach to one that is more characterized by horizontal networks of decision-makers operating across administrative boundaries. However, although decentralization is viewed positively by French citizens, it has not made it easier for them to participate in decision-making, which still remains the affair of either central or local elites. In other words, the *notable* system has remained intact. The challenge for the future, therefore, is to involve French citizens in the quite considerable reforms that are affecting their systems of local and regional governance, such as the drive towards intercommunality or the new activities of regions at the European level.

References

BALME, R. and BONNET, L. (1995). 'From Regional to Sectoral Policies: The Contractual Relations between the State and the Regions in France', in J. Loughlin and S. Mazey (eds), *The End of the French Unitary State: Ten Years of Regionalization in France, 1982–1992*. London: Frank Cass.

——, FAURE, A., and MABILEAU, A. (eds) (1999). *Les Nouvelles Politiques Locales: Dynamiques de l'action publique*. Paris: Presses de Science Po.

BIAREZ, S. (1999). 'Incertitudes et caractère composite des gouvernements locaux en Europe', in Balme *et al.* (eds), op. cit.

BRAUDEL, F. (1986). *L'Identité de la France*, 3 vols. Paris: Arthand-Flammasion.

COLE, A. (1997). 'Governing the Academies: Sub-central Secondary Education Policy-making in France'. *West European Politics*, 20/2: 137–56.

——and JOHN, P. (1995). 'Les réseaux locaux de politique public, le cas de la métropole lilloise'. *Les Cathiers du CRAPS*, 21: 7–22.

CROZIER, M. and THOENIG, J.-C. (1975). 'La régulation des systèmes organisés complexes. Le système de décision politico-administratif local en France'. *Revue française de Sociologie*, 16/3.

DELCAMP, A. (1992). 'La décentralization française et l'Europe'. *Pouvoirs*, 60: 149–60.

DUHAMEL, O. (1993). *Le pouvoir politique en France*. Paris: Seuil.

DUPOIRIER, E. (ed.) (1998*a*). *Régions, la croisée des chemins: perspectives françaises et enjeux européen*. Paris: Presses des Sciences Po.

——(1998*b*). 'L'offre identitaire des régions françaises et la construction des identités régionales'. *Revue Internationale de Politique Comparée*, 5/1: 21–34.

DUVERGER, M. (1963). *La Cinquième République*, 3rd edn. Paris: Presses Universitaires de France.

GRAVIER, J.-F. (1958). *Paris et la Désert français*, Paris: Flammasion.

GRÉMION, P. (1976). *Le pouvoir périphérique. Bureaucrates et notables dans le système politique français*. Paris: Seuil.

HAYWARD, J. E. S. (1983). *Governing France: The One and Indivisible Republic*, 2nd edn. London: Weidenfeld & Nicolson.

HINTJENS, H., LOUGHLIN, J., and OLIVESI, C. (1995). 'The Status of Maritime and Insular France: the DOM, TOM and Corsica', in J. Loughlin and S. Mazey (eds), *The End of the French Unitary State: Ten Years of Regionalization in France, 1982–1992*. London: Frank Cass.

HOFFMANN-MARTINOT, V. (1999). 'Les grandes villes françaises: une démocratie en souffrance', in O. Gabriel and V. Hoffmann-Martinot (eds), *Démocraties urbaines: L'Etat de la démocratie dans les grandes villes de 12 pays industrialisés*. Paris: L'Harmattan.

JOUVE, B. and LEFÈVRE, C. (1999). 'Des leaders en quête d'institutions territoriales', in Balme *et al.* (eds), op. cit.

LECA, J. (1996). 'La gouvernance de la France sous la Cinquième République', in F. d'Arcy and L. Rouban (eds), *De la Cinquième République à l'Europe*. Paris: Presses de Science Po.

LE GALÈS, P. (1995). 'Du gouvernement des villes à la gouvernance urbaine'. *Revue française de Science Politique*, 45 (1).

LOUGHLIN, J. (1989). *Regionalization and Ethnic Nationalism in France: A Case-study of Corsica*. Florence: European University Institute.

——and MAZEY, S. (eds) (1995). *The End of the French Unitary State: Ten Years of Regionalization in France, 1982–1992*. London: Frank Cass.

——, OLIVESI, C., and DAFTARY, F. (eds). (1999). *Autonomies Insulaires: vers une politique de différence pour la Corse*. Ajaccio: Albiana.

LOUGHLIN, J. and PETERS, B. G. (1997). 'State Traditions, Administrative Reform and Regionalization', in J. Loughlin and M. Keating (eds), *The Political Economy of Regionalism*. London: Frank Cass.

MABILEAU, A. (1997). 'Les genies invisibles du local. Faux semblants et dynamiques de la décentralization'. *Revue française de Science Politique*, 47/3–4: 340.

——(1999). 'Les perspectives d'Action Publique autour d'un Local Reconsideré', in Balme *et al.* (eds), op. cit.

MACHIN, H. (1977). *The Prefect in French Public Administration*. London: Croom Helm.

MAZEY, S. (1995). 'French Regions and the European Union', in J. Loughlin and S. Mazey (eds), *The End of the French Unitary State: Ten Years of Regionalization in France, 1982–1992*. London: Frank Cass.

MÉNY, Y. (1992). 'La République des fiefs'. *Pouvoirs*, 60: 17–24.

Nay, O. (1998). 'La reforme du scrutin régional: l'hypocrisie politique'. *Pouvoirs locaux*, 36: v.

Négrier, E. (1999*a*). 'Échange politique territorialisé et intégration européenne', in R. Balme *et al.* (eds), op. cit.

——(1999*b*). 'The Changing Role of French Local Government', *West European Politics*, 22/4: 120–40.

Paoletti, M. (1999). 'Les maires. Communication et démocratie locale'. In Balme *et al.* (eds), op. cit.

Percheron, A. (1992). 'L'opinion et la décentralization ou la décentralization apprivoisée'. *Pouvoirs*, 60: 25–40.

Regourd, S. (1999). 'Organization et fonctionnement des collectivités locales: nouveaux enjeux. L'intercommunalité au coeur d'une spécificité française', in *Les Collectivités Locales en Mutation*. Paris: La Documentation française, 41–6.

Rondin, J. (1985). *Le Sacre des Notables. La France et la décentralization*. Paris: Fayard.

Rosanvallon P. (1992). *Le sacre du citoyen histoire du suffrage universel en France*. Paris: Gallimard.

Sadran, P. (1999). 'La Vie Politique Locale', in *Les Collectivités Locales en Mutation*. Paris: La Documentation française, 25–32.

Stevens, A. (1996). *The Government and Politics of France*, 2nd edn. Basingstoke: Macmillan.

Verpeaux, M. (1999). 'La Décentralization depuis les lois en 1982', in *Les Collectivités Locales en Mutation*. Paris: La Documentation française, 3–11.

Wright, V. (1983). *The Government and Politics of France*, 2nd edn. London: Hutchinson.

——(ed.) (1994). *Privatization in Western Europe: Pressures, Problems and Paradoxes*. London: Pinter.

9

Italy: The Crisis of the Second Republic

John Loughlin

1. History and Concept of Democracy

1.1 Historical Background

Italy was a relative latecomer to the club of nation-states in the nineteenth century, being created only between 1860 and 1870 as a union of many 'Italies': the economically developed North with its great cities and political traditions close to those of northern Europe; the backward South characterized by a feudal-type system of large-scale landowners and non-politicized peasants with traditions of patronage and clientelism; and the Centre, once dominated by the Papal States and, like the South, with little experience of liberal constitutional democracy. The Piedmontese elites who created the new state saw their primary task as being to weld these very different territories and societies into a single territorial unit. Only a very small percentage of the population of Italy spoke the Italian language while the majority spoke dialects that were mutually incomprehensible (Putnam, Leonardi, and Nanetti 1993: 18).

The political regime chosen for the new Italy was a monarchy with a centralized state administration modelled on the French Jacobin state. In the debate leading up to unification, some public figures, such as Cattaneo and other figures of the Risorgimento, had advocated a federal design for the new state. However, an alliance of Piedmontese industrial and political elites and the great landowners of the South thought that federalism would encourage the centrifugal tendencies of the new Italy while Jacobinism would better hold the different parts together. This uncomfortable alliance between North and South gave rise to the major political, social, and economic problems of Italy since its foundation: the glaring disparities between the North (including the Centre), which, in terms of economic development and democratic

I would like to thank Mark Donovan and James Newell for commenting on this chapter.

practice, is relatively modernized and developed, and the South, which is more backward economically and whose social and political system is marked by clientelism and institutional incapacity (Putnam, Leonardi, and Nanetti 1993). The crucial problem in the South was the failure of a new entrepreneurial middle class to emerge. This allowed the state to become omnipresent as a substitute. This overbearing state was used by the southern elites to protect themselves in a situation of acute social conflict and to use the already existing divisions in southern cities to establish their hegemony. This eventually led to collusion with the Mafia and the encouragement of further division (Davis 1996). Undoubtedly, these broad statements need to be further nuanced as recent work on the South has shown that it is not a homogeneous whole but consists of a variety of situations and degrees of development (Bagnasco 1998). Nevertheless, the general picture of the North–South divide holds good.

The Italian state went through three historical experiences each of which profoundly affected the nature of its democratic system: (*i*) unification, (*ii*) Fascism, and (*iii*) the Resistance and reconstruction (Hine 1993).

At the time of unification (1860–70), and in the subsequent period of Liberal Italy (until the Fascist period that began in 1922), democratic practice in the form of political parties and parliamentary politics was very rudimentary. The country continued to be divided along North–South lines, with the state lacking legitimacy for the southern peasants, but also along secular–religious lines as the Catholic Church at first refused to recognize the new state. Liberal Italy was ill-equipped to cope with the arrival of mass politics and was opposed by the three most important political movements that emerged during this period: socialism, clericalism, and nationalism (Hine 1993). In 1912, men's suffrage with a system of proportional representation was adopted, and this gave a voice and a power to these movements thus threatening the Liberal rulers. Unable to control the political and social unrest after the First World War, the Liberal leaders asked Mussolini to assume the office of prime minister. He soon dismantled the liberal-democratic state and installed the Fascist state. This, however, was far from totalitarian, but rather 'a shambling, inefficient, inordinately corrupt and multi-centred state bureaucracy' (Hine 1993: 20).

The reconstruction of the Italian state that took place immediately after the Second World War was carried out by the Committee of National Liberation (CNL), which consisted of six parties of which four would survive into the contemporary period. These were the Christian Democrats (DC) and the Italian Liberal Party (PLI) on the centre-right of the political spectrum and, on the left, the Socialists (PSI) and the Communists (PCI). These parties were responsible for restoring democracy after the Second World War when the monarchy was abolished in a referendum and a new constitution adopted in 1948 that turned Italy into a republic.

The 1948 Constitution resulted from a compromise between the principal forces that had participated in the Resistance: communists and Catholics. It reflected a balance between these different ideologies: concern for the individual person as well a number of rights guaranteed by the state; setting up countervailing forces such as regions and a strong judiciary to guard against excessive centralization and authoritarianism; and a strong parliament. However, the onset of the cold war and the exclusion of communists from government ensured that most of these principles were not fully respected (Portelli 1998). The Christian Democrats became the centre of a political system dominated by the political parties—the *partitocrazia*—that would eventually collapse in ignominy in the 1990s.

These developments also made it difficult for Italians to construct a strong national identity. In fact, the concept of 'nation' had been recuperated by Mussolini's Fascists and many groups in Italian society (intellectuals, the trade unions, left-wing political parties) were reluctant to appeal to it (Rusconi 1998). Communists and the extreme left in general appealed rather to internationalism. Christian Democrats, on the other hand, were conscious of belonging to a universal Catholic Church and also were keen advocates of the growing European Community. The only party which strongly advocated a sense of nationhood were the MSI (*Movimento Sociale Italiano*), the neo-Fascist successors of the Fascist Party. As a party excluded from participation in Italian politics they were not likely to be a strong influence. However, as Rusconi comments, 'In Italy, we have a Republic, but we do not have a republican culture able to create a sincere attachment to democratic institutions' (1998: 17). This he attributes to a weak sense of nationhood on the part of Italians in contrast to the French republican tradition of citizenship. Harbingers of the crisis of the Italian state appeared in the *anni di piombo* (the leaden years) from the late 1960s until the 1980s when right- and left-wing terrorism appeared to destabilize the state itself. During these years, the existence of shadowy groups, such as Gladio (a group set up by the Italian secret services close to NATO) and the secret masonic lodge P2, within the state apparatus itself was revealed. These right-wing groups may have been behind some of the worst terrorist outrages of this period. All of this led to a profound crisis of Italian identity the fruits of which would appear in the outburst of popular anger in the 1990s.

In constitutional terms Italy is a liberal democracy, like other western states, while economically it is one of the advanced industrial societies. However, the nature of Italy's political institutions and of its economic features is rather different from other western democracies and has a number of special characteristics:

• The predominance of a *legalistic* approach to administration and politics in which individual acts assume a great importance (Dente 1985: 80).

- The predominant role of political parties—pejoratively known as the *par-titocrazia*—and their domination of public administration, economic, and social life (ibid.).
- The existence of Catholic and Communist *subcultures* whereby society was organized through associations, networks, and activities controlled by the Christian Democrats (DC) or the Italian Communist Party (PCI), respectively (Mannheimer 1991: 18).
- A *territorialization* of the two subcultures with the Communist Party particularly strong in the so-called 'red belt' regions of Emilia Romagna, Tuscany and Umbria, and the Christian Democrats in the 'white belt' regions of the North East (but also the South, although their presence in the latter was considerably different from the North).
- Widespread *clientelism* whereby patrons distribute resources to their clients—in recent years this took the form of *party clientelism* (Graziano 1980).
- *Corruption* and the penetration of the political and administrative system by organized crime, not just in the South but also in the Centre and North (Della Porta 1996; Allum 1996).

1.2 Democracy at the Subnational Levels

Despite the creation of an Italian nation-state that is now over one hundred years old, Italians remain more attached to, and identify more fully with, the local rather than the national level. Formally, at least, there is no specific tradition of democracy at the local level that is different from what occurs at the national. Both levels have tended to be dominated by the parties even if the provincial and regional party organizations have tended to behave in an autonomous manner. Central–local relations in Italy have been conflictual, with the central state showing a great reluctance to cede extensive powers to the subnational levels of government (Dente 1985). Nevertheless, a somewhat distinctive style of politics has developed at the regional level at least in the regions of the North and Centre, after the 'ordinary' regions were established in 1970 (Putnam, Leonardi, and Nanetti 1993). In many cases, this was the result of successful communist domination of certain regions who used this position as a kind of compensation for their exclusion from government at the national level. In practice, these regions become models of democratic practice in contrast to national politics. This strategy was also successfully applied to some of the large cities run by the left. The recent wave of reforms to some extent had their origins at the regional and local levels where movements such as the Northern Leagues or the mayors' movement developed. To this extent, it could be argued that democratic practice has been different from, and, in many cases, stronger than, that at the national level.

2. The Institutional Expression of Democracy

2.1 The National Level

Italy is a parliamentary democracy that, until 1993–4, used a system of proportional representation for its elections. In comparison with other European states, the legislature has been relatively powerful *vis-à-vis* the executive, thanks to the powerful role of parties in the system (Hine 1993). The parliament is based on bicameralism with the senate and the chamber of deputies performing identical functions (ibid.). However, the parliament is constrained by the judiciary, the constitutional court, and the use of referendums by the electorate. Referendums may be used to repeal both constitutional and ordinary legislation and have been used forty-five times since 1974 (Donovan 1998).

2.2 The Regional and Local Levels

The position and powers of regional and local government (the provinces and the municipalities) are entrenched in the constitution (Arts. 114–33) and not simply by legislation. This means they cannot be abolished or altered except through constitutional change, which must follow strict rules. However, the constitutional description of regional and local powers does not exactly correspond with the reality, especially since financial relations are not laid out in constitutional form. Important reforms of local government were passed in 1990 and 1993 (see below).

2.2.1 The Region

The 1948 Constitution provided for the setting up of regions as 'autonomous territorial bodies with their own powers and functions' (Art. 115). The constitution distinguished between the fifteen 'ordinary' regions and five regions with special statutes: Sicily, Sardinia, Trentino-Alto Adige (South Tyrol), Val d'Aosta, and Friuli-Venezia Giulia. Four of the special regions came into existence immediately in 1948, while Friuli-Venezia Giulia was set up only in 1964. The nature of the statute accorded to Trentino-Alto Adige changed over time because of agitation by the German-speaking minority who were supported by the Austrian government (Lapidoth 1996).[1] The fifteen ordinary regions

---

[1] Mussolini had tried to Italianize the region with measures that disadvantaged the German-speaking population. The problem was solved by creating German- and Italian-speaking provinces each with extensive powers.

only began functioning after direct elections in 1970,[2] as a result of political pressure from the left, which had been excluded from power and which saw regional government as an arena where it could exercise influence (Putnam, Leonardi, and Nanetti 1993). Nevertheless, despite their late start and the financial limitations imposed by the central state and the party system, the regions, especially those in the North and the Centre, managed to acquire an important position in the Italian politico-administrative landscape (Putnam, Leonardi, and Nanetti 1993). They are represented in national policy-making through the *Conferenza permanente stato-regioni*.

Regions are organized along the same lines as central government. Each region has an aassembly that, until 1995, was elected every five years by proportional representation (PR). After 1995 a new electoral system based on a combination of PR and a 'bonus' system to encourage the formation of majorities was adopted. The assembly passes regional legislation and elects a *giunta* (executive) consisting of a president and *assessori* (ministers) to implement the legislation. A number of committees cover different policy sectors.[3]

2.2.2 The Province

The province dates from the Piedmontese state and is the equivalent of the French *département*, performing a similar role as the basic unit of field admin-istration. It has a *giunta* (council) elected (since 1993) by a system based on a combination of proportional representation and a 'bonus' system, and a president elected by means of a double-ballot system. The province has few functions and, in the 1980s, there was some talk of abolishing it. However, there has been a tendency for regional governments to devolve some policy functions to the provinces (Hine 1993).

2.2.3 The Municipality

The *comune* (municipality) has a directly elected council whose members vary between fifteen and eighty in number, and a *giunta comunale* (executive)

---

[2] It was not until the late 1970s that the regions began exercising most of their powers.
[3] Art. 117 of the constitution specifies the areas for which the region may legislate: municipal boundaries; urban and rural police forces; fairs and markets; public charities; hospital assistance and health; vocational training and financial assistance to students; local museums and libraries; urban planning; tourism and the hotel industry; regional trans-port networks (excluding railways); regional roads, aqueducts, and other public works; lake navigation and ports; mineral and spa waters; extractive industries; hunting; inland fish-eries; agriculture and forestry; and artisanship. However, there have been many conflicts with central government over the exercise of these powers, especially as there have been many changes in Italian society and economic life since the constitution was promulgated in 1948 (Hine 1993: 267).

whose members are known as *assessori*. *Assessori* head particular departments. The *sindaco* (mayor) heads both the council and the *giunta*. Mayors have two principal roles: (*i*) they are the political heads of the coalition running the municipality, and (*ii*) they are the administrative representatives of the government (Hine 1993). Mayors of the big cities such as Milan and Rome are also important figures at the national level. Since the local government reforms of the 1990s, mayors are now directly elected and appoint the executive (see below). Municipalities have been gaining strength in terms of power and influence at the expense of the regions, which have been badly affected by the anti-corruption drive.

2.3 The Role of Political Parties

The party domination that operates at the national level is also to be found at the subnational level. The vast majority of councillors have traditionally belonged to a political party (Dente 1985: 98). This has led to a tendency towards centralization and nationalization of local politics. Tarrow, comparing the role of French and Italian mayors in the 1970s, noted that the French mayor obtained resources for his or her commune through the state administrative institutions, whereas his or her Italian counterpart did so through party channels (quoted in Dente 1985). However, subsequent studies have somewhat modified this picture of central-party control over the local level. To some extent, these would suggest a rather complex set of central–local relationships in which the parties were more an alternative system for channelling resources between the centre and the periphery.

It is generally recognized that the setting up of the regions in 1970 has somewhat modified the traditional party system by allowing the parties of the left a role in the political system (Dente 1985; Putnam, Leonardi, and Nanetti 1993). On the one hand, these parties, in some regions, were able to pursue at the regional level policies that were more programmatic and less based on ties of clientelism (Putnam, Leonardi, and Nanetti 1993). Nevertheless, according to this same research, there have been changes in *all* of the Italian regions as a result of regionalization.

There are also a number of regionalist parties some of which also participate in national elections. The most important of these are: *Partito Sardo d'Azione* (PSdA, Sardinian Action Party), the *Südtiroler Volkspartei* (South Tyrolean People's Party), and the *Lista Valle d'Aosta* (List Aosta Valley). We might also add the *Lega Nord* (Northern League), which, in some senses, may be regarded as a regionalist party. These parties have gained seats at the national level.

3. The Practice of Subnational Democracy

3.1 The Role of Policy Networks and Pressure Groups in Local Government

The form that policy networks and pressure groups has tended to take in the Italian case is clientelism (Dente 1985: 105). Clientelism is not unique to Italy and exists in different European countries, such as France, the United Kingdom, and Ireland. Furthermore, the Italian politico-administrative system is also marked by rational bureaucratic and professional-technocratic features (ibid.). Nevertheless, what distinguishes clientelism in Italy is its widespread nature and the role of the party system in its perpetuation (Graziano 1980). The Italian political parties gradually adopted a clientelistic approach between themselves and specific social groups as a method of exchange whereby they provided resources for these groups and in return received electoral support. Some authors have claimed that this system was not 'corrupt' as such, but simply another way of democratic government—the specifically Italian method (LaPalombara 1987). However, as the '*mani pulite*' ('clean hands') investigations have demonstrated in recent years, the thin line between clientelism and corruption, sometimes involving links with organized crime, disappeared in the 1980s. These features of the Italian system were also present at the subnational level and, in the early 1990s, many regions found themselves leaderless as regional politicians were incriminated in the anti-corruption drive (Dente 1997).

3.2 Critiques of Regional and Local Democracy in Italy

The critique of democracy at the regional and local levels in Italy must be placed within the critique of the general political system in Italy, which gathered pace in the 1980s (Bull and Rhodes 1997). Comparing attitude surveys taken in 1967 and 1980, it can be seen that there was a sharp decline in confidence in the government: in 1967, 32.8 per cent of the general population thought the Italian government did not act with *serietà e onestà* (seriousness and honesty) and 21.8 per cent thought it lacked *capacità e competenza* (ability and competence); in 1980 these figures had risen to 84.8 per cent and 69.4 per cent respectively (quoted in Mannheimer 1991: 27). Italians became increasingly dissatisfied with the functioning of their democratic system. On the other hand, political parties are intimately connected to the democratic system, and an opinion poll, comparing attitudes in Italy with those in other European states reported in 1993, shows that a higher percentage of Italians remain attached to a party (Table 9.1). This suggests a rather

TABLE 9.1   Attitudes on the functioning of democracy in four European countries (percentages), 1991

	Italy	France	UK	Germany
Satisfied with functioning of democracy	28.4	56.8	61.3	75.7
Interested in politics	32.2	51.3	59.8	62.4
Associated with a party	37.7	22.4	28.6	27.6

Source: Biorcio (1991: 44).

complex set of relationships between society, political parties, and the state. Neverthless, in the 1990s the Italian political system entered a state of crisis in which the old system of parties came under attack both for its corruption and for its inefficiency.

This crisis was engendered by changes both within Italian society that affected the support base of the parties and by the geo-political changes that accompanied the collapse of the Soviet Union and the end of the cold war (Mannheimer 1991; Biorcio 1991). The internal changes were related to the rapid secularization of Italian society that saw the old Catholic subculture diminish in importance. The external changes brought about changes within the communist subculture as a result of the ending of the cold war, although Italian communism had already begun to distance itself from the Soviet Union even before this. Nevertheless, the events of 1989–90 completed this process, and the communist subculture no longer had a reference point in the struggle against capitalism. It also meant that the Christian Democrats and those within the Catholic subculture were deprived of the enemy, which had been a means of reinforcing their solidarity with each other (Mannheimer 1991). In the 1980s the old certitudes of Italian politics and the left–right divide had considerably weakened, and this allowed the development of either simple abstentionism or the emergence of new political forces such as ecologists, feminists, the new regionalists such as the northern autonomist leagues, and new anti-corruption parties such as *La Rete*, founded by a former Christian Democratic mayor from the South. A series of referendums on issues such as the public financing of political parties and on the electoral system, from the late 1970s onwards, gave the general public an opportunity to express their discontent with the Italian political system and to initiate the process of change (Pasquino 1993). In the 1992 general elections these forces came to fruition, and, as Pasquino remarks, they mark the end of the post-war political regime based on the political parties (ibid.). The 1994 elections confirmed these trends, and as some authors remarked, 'the Italian earthquake rumbled on' (Bull and Newell 1995).

The severest critique of the Italian system came from the territorially-based movements such as the Northern Leagues and La Rete. These attacked both the political parties (with the exception of the Radicals) and the Roman central administration. Furthermore, the Northern Leagues attacked the very foundations of the Italian state as a unified republic and advocated the establishment of a federal system (Mannheimer 1991; Piccone 1992). The heartland of the Leagues' support is in the North and North East. However, they have failed to establish bases elsewhere.

3.3 Citizens' Attitudes to Territorial Government

There is a certain paradox evident in citizens' attitudes to territorial government in Italy. Despite the collapse in confidence in central government and in the national political system, there has been a growing identification on the part of young people with Italy as a country. In the 1980s, almost half of all young Italians between the ages of fifteen and twenty-four identified primarily with their locality while just over a quarter identified with Italy as a whole (Table 9.2). Barely 10 per cent chose the region and 13.5 per cent 'the world/Europe' as their primary identification. By 1992 these attitudes had changed. While identification with the locality dropped to just over a third, that with Italy had risen to about the same figure. There was a slight increase in support for the region (12.4 per cent) and a somewhat larger increase for the world/Europe (17.4 per cent). Support for the region was highest in the

TABLE 9.2 Feelings of belonging among young people between 15 and 24 years old (percentages), 1986 and 1992

Feeling of belonging to:	Place of residence			
	North	Centre	South and Islands	Total
1986				
The locality	46.9	53.7	52.3	49.6
The region	11.4	7.1	9.9	10.3
Italy	28.2	26.8	23.8	26.5
The world/Europe	13.5	12.4	14	13.5
1992				
The locality	31.5	34.9	38.8	35
The region	15.1	8.6	11.5	12.4
Italy	35.3	37.8	33.7	35.2
The world/Europe	18.1	18.8	16.1	17.4

Source: Sondaggi IARD 1986 and 1991 (quoted in Biorcio 1997: 122).

North (15.1 per cent). The importance of identifying with Italy was borne out in another national survey which indicated that 71.9 per cent were *molto orgoglioso* (very proud) to be 'Italian' (Limes 1994: 17). In the same survey, 66.4 per cent indicated they were very proud to be 'Europeans/citizens of the world', 62.4 per cent were very proud to be members of their region, and 50.9 per cent very proud to be members of their city.

Although the majority of Italians have a sense of national pride as reported above, they are evenly divided with regard to the future structures of the Italian state. Around one-third (34.9 per cent) wish to maintain the status quo, but around two-thirds seek a more or less radical decentralization of the state along either regionalist/localist (33.5 per cent) or federalist (31.6 per cent) lines. Among those who advocated some kind of federalist structure, 6.7 per cent would like to see a federal Italy with three large macro-regions (the North, the Centre, and the South), 4.9 per cent a confederation with the possibility of independence for the three macro-regions, and 20.9 per cent a federal state with the present regions as the sub-federal entities with increased powers (Limes 1996). These findings are consistent with another survey, which indicated that 78 per cent of Italians would like to see the municipalities have greater powers in the economic and social fields, 71 per cent thought these powers ought to increase for the regions, and only 44 per cent wished to see the central state have an increase in powers in these areas (Limes 1994).

It might be pointed out here that the rather pessimistic analysis of Ruscone (1998) with regard to Italians' sense of nationality is not completely supported by these findings. At least among the younger generations there is a growing sense of pride in Italy as a country despite the scandals and crisis of its political system. It could be that the upheavals resulting from this crisis have given young Italians, especially, a sense of confidence that change can come about and that all is not lost. Many of the old guard of politicians have disappeared and new political leaders have appeared— not just the Leagues but other reformers such as those found in the mayors' movement.

4. Challenges and Opportunities for Subnational Democracy

4.1 The Crisis of the Italian State

The most serious challenge to, but also the greatest opportunities for, regional and local democracy in Italy comes from the crisis of the Italian state itself (Bull and Rhodes 1997). According to D'Alimonte and Bartolini (1997: 110), there have been four fundamental changes with respect to the past: (*i*) a new vitality in the field of electoral reform, entailing significant changes to all electoral laws apart from those regulating European elections; (*ii*) a high turnover of political and parliamentary elites with a distancing of many (but not all) sectors from the influence of the parties and pre-1994 governments; (*iii*) a reorganization of the old centre parties, substituted by new formations or presented under new names, winning minimal shares of the vote and split into different groups; (*iv*) a radical realignment of electoral coalitions and of the experimental coalitions of 1994 to 1996—the most innovative element of which was the entry into government of the two parties which historically had been excluded from power, namely, the Democratic Party of the Left (PDS)—the former Italian Communist Party (PCI)—and National Alliance (AN), the former Italian Social Movement.

This has been described as a transition from the *partitiocrazia*, which was based on the power (and, eventually, the corruption) of the old political parties, to a new democratic system less dependent on the parties and more grounded on institutions and institutional leadership (Pasquino 1997). A Bicameral Constitutional Committee was set up in 1997 with four subcommittees, each of which was to tackle one of four questions: (*i*) the nature of the state; (*ii*) the form of government; (*iii*) the type of parliament; and (*iv*) the 'system of guarantees' (i.e., the judicial system). With regard to the form of government the options are: presidential, semi-presidential, neo-parliamentary, classical parliamentary. With regard to the form of the state the issue is whether it ought to be federalist or otherwise and, if federalist, what kind of federalist structure (ibid.). Some of the opinions of Italian citizens on these questions have been outlined above (section 3.4).

4.1.1 The Transformation of the Italian Parties

With the 1994 elections, a new configuration of parties had come into existence with most of the older parties transformed. Competition for government now focuses on electoral alliances. There are over forty parties in parliament, defined as being in receipt of state funding, and about eleven parliamentary groups. The right-wing alliance, the *Polo della Libertà* (Freedom Pole), comprises primarily: *Forza Italia* (Berlusconi), the *Alleanza Nazionale* (National Alliance, formerly the neo-Fascist MSI), and the *Centro Cristiano Democratico* (Christian Democratic Centre, conservative former Christian Democrats). The Northern League was briefly a member of this alliance in 1994. The centre-left is now organized around *L'Ulivo* (the Olive Tree) alliance; it comprises primarily: the *Democratici di Sinistra* (Left Democrats—ex-PDS, formerly PCI) with minor left-wing allies, the *Partito Popolare Italiano* (Italian People's Party, centre-left former Christian Democrats), and *Rinnovamento Italiano* (Italian Renewal, a movement of reformist technocrats led by L. Dini). The Olive Tree has formed a minority government and is supported by *Rifondazione Communista* (Communist Refoundation—the more orthodox successor to the PCI).

The impetus for initiating reform did not come from the government or parliament, but instead from an Electoral Referendum Movement that, in two referendums (1991 and 1993) succeeded in changing the electoral system in such a way as to reduce the element of proportionality (Pasquino 1997: 44). This has had the effect of creating two large political blocs of the left and the right that might alternate in the exercise of government, rather than the previous system of the same parties exercising power in an endless variety of coalitions while permanently excluding the left and the extreme right. However, while the old party system has been largely destroyed and the *partitocrazia* will not reappear, its replacement with a more adequate system of democracy has so far largely eluded the decision-makers in the government, and the crisis of the system continues to lurch onwards: 'the Italian transition is still mid-stream and all its political actors and institutions are under stress' (Pasquino 1997: 51).

4.2 Central–Local Relations and Strengthening Local Democracy in the 1990s

The territorial question is at the heart of these developments in the Italian political system. First, the challenge from the Northern League has called into question the North–South relationship that is the very foundation of the Italian state. Many of the grass-roots movements of reform originated at the local and regional level: the leagues in the North (especially in the regions of Piedmont, Lombardy, and Veneto), and *La Rete* in the South. Second, the constitutional overhaul of the Italian political system also involves changes at the regional and local levels, the kind of changes depending on whether the overhaul consists in strengthening the regions, or adopting federal or confederal reforms. It is more likely that change will occur along regionalist rather than along federal lines, at least according to the wishes of the electorate mentioned above and of the political parties (Dente 1997: 182).

4.2.1 The Reform of the Laws Governing Local Authorities and Provinces

Law 142 was adopted in 1990, and through it a series of transfers of powers occurred: from the *consiglio comunale e consiglio provinciale* (municipal and provincial councils) to the *giunta* (executive), from political organizations to the administration, from the organizations of local government to external agencies (such as *le società per azioni a capitale pubblico locale incaricate della gestione di pubblici servizi*), and from local government to either individual citizens or citizens' groups (through different mechanisms such as local referendums, petitions, popular action) (Pitruzella 1994).

In 1993, Law 81 introduced a system of direct election of mayors and of the presidents of the provincial councils in two rounds of voting, with only the first two candidates going to the second ballot. The members of the executive are appointed directly by the mayor (Dente 1997: 184). In effect, this means that the leadership of these levels of local government has ceased to be so dependent on the political parties and the position of mayor especially has been strengthened. The result of these changes was a complete renewal of municipal politicians after 1993, with the election of mayors completely new to politics (as in Turin, Genoa, Trieste, and Bari) or different from the usual politicians (as in Venice, Rome, Palermo, and Catania) (Dente 1997). Many of these new leaders were re-elected in 1997.

4.3 The Impact of Europeanization

Italy is a founder member of the European Community and has generally tended to be one of the states whose citizens are most favourable to European integration (Desideri and Santantonio 1996). However, relations with the European institutions and with other member states have tended to be mediated by the Ministry of Foreign Affairs. The Constitutional Court adopted an extremely restrictive definition of what constituted 'international relations', and, as a result, there was little development of direct contacts between subnational levels of government with Brussels or with other subnational authorities. In general, the Italian regions remained within their national boundaries (ibid.). This began to change in the 1990s, under pressure from the regions, when the Constitutional Court redefined international relations as those cases where the state's 'external power' was exercised (principally through signing of treaties). After this, regions could engage in 'promotional activities abroad' and 'activities merely of international significance' (ibid.). This allowed regions to engage more fully at the European Union level. In a presidential decree of 31 March 1994, a distinction was made between international relations and activities within the EU. With regard to the latter, regions can establish direct relations without requiring the approval of the government. This is also formalized by the participation of Italian subnational authorities in the Committee of the Regions. Italian regions have also been involved since the 1970s in interregional associations: Arge-Alp (involving Lombardy, the provinces of Bolzano and Trento, and a number of German and Austrian *Länder* and Swiss cantons), Alpe Adria (involving authorities from Italy, Austria, Slovenia, Croatia, and Hungary), and Cotrao (involving Piedmont, Valle d'Aosta, and authorities from France and Switzerland). Lombardy is a member of the 'Four Motors of Europe' association (with Rhône-Alpes,

Catalonia, and Baden-Württemberg), and regions along the Ligurian coast are members of the Latin Arc.

However, perhaps the most important impact of the EU on the Italian political system is the attempt by Italy to be part of the first wave of entrants into the Single European Currency group. This has involved considerable reform of Italian economic policies and the acceptance of the necessity of reforming the large and inefficient Italian administrative system. Romano Prodi, now President of the European Commission, was a key actor while Prime Minister in introducing the reforms necessary to ensure Italy's entry into the Eurozone. It must be remarked that the negative attitudes of northern countries such as Germany and the Netherlands to Italian efforts and their distrust of the results merely reinforced the latters' determination to succeed.

4.4 The 'Federalization' of the Italian State

The subcommittee of the Bicameral Constitutional Committee dealing with the reform of the state (see section 4.1 above) presented a set of proposals to parliament, which were accepted on 30 April 1998. These proposals were as follows:

- the republic will now consist of local authorities, provinces, metropolitan cities (i.e., of at least 1 million inhabitants),[4] regions, and the state;
- the fifteen ordinary regions can acquire special-region status by negotiation with parliament following regional referendums, and the institutional 'model' for each region need not be uniform;
- the state retains exclusive legislative competence in the following ten areas (but will specify the legislative framework in twelve others):
  - foreign policy, international relations, and immigration;
  - defence and the armed forces;
  - currency, competition policy, and taxation;
  - public order and security;
  - justice and civil and criminal law;
  - culture and the environment;
  - electoral laws for all levels of the state and referendums;
  - the institutional forms of local government;
  - weights and measures, statistics, and information on public administration;
  - the indication of the minimum levels of social rights (e.g., health and education);

---

[4] In effect, this means Rome, Naples, Milan, and Turin.

- the regional elections of 2000 will see the direct election of regional presidents, which conforms to the trend toward directly elected executive authorities;
- the senate will be elected on a regional basis and, when a regional council falls, with early elections, there will also be an election for the relevant senate constituency.

These proposals are subject to referendum. In effect, they transform the nature of the Italian state into something similar to the Spanish autonomic state model, which seems to have influenced the proposal to allow ordinary regions to achieve special status following a referendum in the region.

5. Conclusions

Italy emerged from the period of Fascism determined to build a democratic system that would prevent a return to authoritarian rule. The 1948 Constitution was admirable in its principles and design which balanced central government with regional democracy and strengthened the role of parliament. Unfortunately, the onset of the cold war and the conflict between Christian Democrats and Communists led to the deformation of these principles. Parliamentarianism and the growing power of the parties ensured that the principles of the constitution were never fully applied. On the contrary, *partitocrazia*, corruption, and criminality came to dominate the Italian political system including at the regional and local levels. The exceptions to this were those regions run by the Communists. The North–South divide became even greater and a sense of fatalism set in concerning the possibility of bringing about a balanced and harmonious Italian Republic. The years of right-wing and left-wing terrorism in the 1970s and 1980s were symptomatic of the crisis of the state itself and revealed the existence of shadowy and subversive organizations, such as Gladio and P2, in the heart of the system itself. Finally, Italian citizens had had enough and there was an explosion of anger against the system taking different forms in the 1990s: the magistrates' '*mani pulite*' investigations, the Northern Leagues, the referendum movement, the mayors' movement.

The '*mani pulite*' investigations have meant that many politicians, including ministers and party leaders, have been removed from public life, because of their involvement in corruption and bribe taking. Popular movements have rejected the party state and changes instituted in the system through a series of referendums which changed the national and subnational electoral systems and the mode of financing of parties. By the mid 1990s the old party system had collapsed but without a fully consolidated new system being put in its place. Italy might be said, therefore, to be still in the midst of a regime transition, the outcome of which is still unclear.

These aspects of the Italian democratic system have also affected subnational government. Provincial and municipal government were dominated by the party system and centralization remained strong. The regional system, although guaranteed by the 1948 Constitution, was applied in a gradual and piecemeal manner and, with the exception of some of the regions of the North and Centre, tended to follow the same pattern as the national system. Research has indicated that some of these regions were able to develop a different style of politics, although many of the regional leaders were also caught up in the anti-corruption drive of the 1980s and 1990s.

Law 59/97, passed in March 1997, provided, among other things, for the delegation of a number of administrative functions to the regions and the local authorities. The law emanating from the Bicameral Constitutional Committee on the reform of the state does advance a kind of 'federal' solution. Nevertheless, this reform could be seen as a strengthening of the regionalist system rather than the inauguration of a truly federal system. The central government still retains control over many policy areas that are the responsibility of sub-federal authorities in other federal systems. The second significant reform is the direct election of mayors, which has led to what has been dubbed 'the mayors' movement'. This has led to the emergence of a new political class at the municipal level. This new group of politicians is reform-minded and likely to push forward a new type of democratic politics at the local level.

References

ALLUM, P. (1996). 'From Two into One: The Faces of the Italian Christian Democrats'. *Party Politics*, 1/3: 23–52.

BAGNASCO, A. (1998). 'Changement social dans une période de changement politique', *Italie: la Question Nationale. Hérodote: revue de géographie et de géopolitique*, 89/2 (Special Issue): 55–69.

BIORCIO, R. (1991). 'La Lega come attore politico: dal federalism al populismo regionalista', in R. Mannheimer (ed.), *La Lega Lombarda*. Milano: Feltrinelli.

——(1997). *La Padania Promessa*. Milan: Il Saggiatore.

BULL, M. and NEWELL, J. (1995). 'Italy Changes Course? The 1994 Elections and the Victory of the Right'. *Parliamentary Affairs*, 48/1.

——and RHODES, M. (eds) (1997). *Crisis and Transition in Italian Politics. West European Politics*, 20/1 (Special Issue).

D'ALIMONTE, R. and BARTOLINI, S. (1997). '"Electoral Transition" and Party System Change in Italy'. *West European Politics*, 20/1: 110–34.

DAVIS, J. (1996). 'Changing Perspectives on Italy's "Southern Problem"', in C. Levy (ed.), *Italian Regionalism: History, Identity and Politics*. Oxford: Berg.

DELLA PORTA, D. (1996). 'Political Parties and Corruption: Reflections on the Italian Case'. *Modern Italy*, 1/1: 97–114.

DENTE, B. (1985). *Governare La Frammentazione*. Bologna: Il Mulino.

——(1997). 'Sub-national Governments in the Long Italian Transition'. *West European Politics*, 20/1: 176–93.

DESIDERI, C. and SANTANTONIO, V. (1996). 'Building a Third Level in Europe: Prospects and Difficulties in Italy'. *Regional and Federal Studies*, 6/2: 96–116.

DONOVAN, M. (1998). 'The 1997 Referendums: Failure due to Abuse?', in M. Rhodes and L. Bardi (eds), *Italian Politics*. Boulder, CO: Westview.

GIBLIN, B. (ed.) (1998). *Italie: la Question Nationale. Hérodote: revue de géographie et de géopolitique*. 89/2 (Special Issue).

GRAZIANO, L. (1980). *Clientelismo e sistema politico-Il caso dell'Italia*. Milan: Franco Angeli.

HINE, D. (1993). *Governing Italy: The Politics of Bargained Pluralism*. Oxford: Oxford University Press.

LAPALOMBARA, J. (1987). *Democracy: Italian Style*. New Haven: You University Press.

LAPIDOTH, R. (1996). *Autonomy: Flexible Solutions to Ethnic Conflicts*. Washington, DC: United States Institute of Peace.

LIMES (1994). *Rivista Italiana di Geopolitica*, no. 4.

——(1996). *Rivista Italiana di Geopolitica*, no. 1.

MANNHEIMER, R. (ed.) (1991). *La Lega Lombarda*. Milano: Feltrinelli.

PASQUINO, G. (1993). 'Introduction: a Case of Regime Crisis', in G. Pasquino and P. McCarthy (eds), *The End of Post-War Politics in Italy: The Landmark 1992 Elections*. Boulder, CO: Westview.

——(1997). 'No Longer a "Party State"? Institutions, Power and the Problems of Italian Reform'. *West European Politics*, 20/1: 34–53.

PICCONE, P. (1992). 'Federal Populism in Italy'. *Telos*.

PITRUZELLA, G. (1994). 'I poteri locali', in P. Gingsborg (ed.), *Stato dell'Italia*. Milano: Mondadori.

PORTELLI, H. (1998). 'La réforme de l'Etat: les avatars du projet constitutionnel'. *Italie: la Question Nationale. Hérodote: revue de géographie et de géopolitique*, 89/2 (Special Issue): 209–15.

PUTNAM, R., LEONARDI, R., and NANETTI, R. (1993), *Making Democracy Work: Civic Traditions in Modern Italy*. Princeton: Princeton University Press.

RUSCONE, G. (1998). 'Question nationale et question démocratique'. *Italie: la Question Nationale. Hérodote: revue de géographie et de géopolitique*, 89/2 (Special Issue): 17–37.

10

Spain: Nation, Nationalities, and Regions

Eliseo Aja

1. History and Concept of Democracy

In historical terms, Spain is a young democracy, coming into being with the 1978 Constitution. It lacks a liberal past worthy of the name: most of its nineteenth- and twentieth-century regimes were highly authoritarian and oligarchical, frequently relying on states of emergency and the army to maintain order. There are only a few exceptions. The 1868–73 period culminated in the First Republic, a general political crisis, and army intervention to restore the monarchy. The Second Republic (1931–6), came to a tragic end with a military rebellion and bloody civil war. This was followed by forty years of Franco's authoritarian regime with no representative institutions or freedoms of any kind. As a result, the present-day democracy has adopted many of its institutions from other European constitutions. It represents a full-blown reaction against the past.

1.1 Authoritarianism and Centralism as Constant Factors of the State in Contemporary Spain Prior to the Present Constitution

Authoritarianism and centralism were two constant factors of the contemporary Spanish state up until the current 1978 Constitution. From the first Constitution of Cadiz (1812) onwards, and following the lengthy absolutist period of Ferdinand VII (1814–33), the liberal Spanish state displayed a number of common characteristics throughout most of the nineteenth and twentieth centuries and was dominated by conservative cliques representing a closed economic and social oligarchy. Despite the numerous changes of constitution and government, most of the period was dominated by two constitutional texts: the 1845 Constitution, in force during the moderate decades (1844–68); and the 1876 Constitution, during the lengthy Restoration period (1875–1931). Each of these constitutions was inspired by a doctrine that denied national sovereignty but granted substantial powers to the king. They held out against parliamentarianism by restricting or manipulating suffrage and preventing the creation of a party-political system such as those existing elsewhere in Western Europe.

On the rare occasions that saw the beginnings of a truly liberal or democratic process, that seemed to escape the control of conservative groups, the army would step in to guarantee the hegemony of the oligarchy. This is quite clearly shown by the experience of the First Republic (1873), the Primo de Rivera dictatorship (1923–30), and the Francoist period (1939–75).

This conservative and authoritarian domination resulted in continuity in nearly all components of the state, but above all in its highly centralized power structure: this was crucial during the moderate periods and was extended during periods of authoritarian rule. Centralism guaranteed the domination of the ruling clique, chiefly through the civil governors, the leading government authority in each province, who were in charge of the forces of law and order, coordinated local ministerial offices, and had a decisive influence on election results in each province. Predictably, the brief intervening periods of freedom invariably triggered vigorous attempts at decentralization, such as those under the First and Second Republics.

Decentralization in the first part of the nineteenth century focused on reviving municipalities and provinces in the belief that encouraging the *forces vives* at the local level would help weaken the system of oligarchy and local strongmen that flourished under centralism. However, nationalist movements sprang up in Catalonia, Galicia, and the Basque Country in the late nineteenth and early twentieth centuries, demanding regional self-government and recognition of their traditional languages and law.

None of the various decentralization projects discussed in the early years of the twentieth century met with success, with the exception of Catalonia's embryonic autonomous government, the *Mancomunidad* (1914–23), which brought administrative autonomy to the four Catalan provinces. Primo de Rivera's dictatorship shut down the *Mancomunidad* together, of course, with all other decentralization projects.

The only solid precedent for the present autonomy system was in fact the experience of regional autonomy under the, short-lived, Second Republic (1931–6). The only autonomous institutions that actually worked under the republic were the Catalan ones, since the Basque Statute was adopted in July 1936, days after the Civil War had broken out, and the Galician Statute was put to a referendum, but was never endorsed by the *Cortes* (national parliament); and clearly, autonomy could not be expected to work in a country cut in two by civil war.

1.2 Autonomy during the Transition to Democracy and the Constituent Parliament

Forty years of Francoism took state centralism to such extremes that restoring democracy necessarily entailed drastic changes to the territorial organization of power. For Catalonia and the Basque Country in particular, but also to a lesser extent for other regions, democracy could only be consolidated if accompanied by substantial autonomy in one form or another.

Demands for autonomy spread throughout the country after the first democratic elections of June 1977, either on account of a general desire for self-government to offset the economic imbalances caused by centralism, or with the aim of bringing the institutions closer to the grass-roots. In practice, this was formalized in two very different, but ultimately complementary, ways: the immediate establishment of provisional, or 'pre-autonomy', arrangements; and the drafting of a new constitution, which was to define the territorial structure of the state.

The Adolfo Suárez government, which emerged from the first democratic elections of 1977, was immediately faced with the need to devise a practical form of autonomy, in order to respond to the demands of the Catalan and Basque majorities and to halt the spread of the decentralization movement throughout Spain. Against this backdrop, the Suárez government undertook a highly ambitious initiative: to enter into an agreement with Josep Tarradellas, then living in exile in France as the president of the Republican *Generalitat* (autonomous Catalan government), to restore autonomy to Catalonia on a provisional basis, pending its definitive inclusion in the new constitution. Introducing this republican and pro-autonomy element into the new monarchy presented a major challenge, but it succeeded in defusing autonomist demands by postponing the decision on its final shape until the future constitution was drawn up and by wresting the initiative away from the political opposition, which had won the elections in Catalonia. Autonomy was provisionally restored to Catalonia by the Decree of 29 September 1977 and was progressively extended to other regions, resulting in a total of seventeen pro-autonomy arrangements. Despite its provisional nature, this structure had a definite and strong influence on the subsequent development of the *autonomous communities* or self-governing regions.

The constituent parliament tackled all the main problems to be resolved by the new constitution in a spirit of consensus: in other words, basic agreement was sought between political forces so as to avoid having to settle them by strict application of the majority rule. It is fair to claim that several historical taboos were thus broken, for example, the polarization of pro-monarchy versus pro-republic and religious versus secular positions.

Consensus was of special importance, however, in determining the territorial structure of power and organizing the autonomous communities, since the positions of the parties, and popular aspirations, varied widely from region to region.

1.3 The Current Concept of Democracy

The weak tradition of liberalism and the recent arrival of democracy explain why there is no guiding idea that structures every aspect of democracy in Spain. A wide-ranging declaration of citizens' rights, embracing economic and social as well as individual freedoms, representative institutions (at three levels: central, autonomous regional, and local), and the intrinsic importance of self-government are most probably the elements shared by the differing conceptions of democracy.

The exemplary way in which the transition from Francoism to democracy was accomplished, culminating in the adoption of the constitution with the agreement of all parties, has given the constitution itself a very special place in Spain. This view has been strengthened by the work of the Constitutional Court which, in many and very different cases, has brought the constitution directly to bear in opposition to government decisions and laws, in order to safeguard democratic criteria. In the past, Spanish constitutions were always of a party-political and programmatic (that is not directly applicable) nature: the universally agreed and directly applicable nature of the present constitution confers particular prestige upon it. In the absence of a strong notion of democracy, confidence in the constitution has perhaps been the most prominent trait.

2. The Institutional Expression of Democracy

2.1 The State (National) Level

In Spain the words 'national' and 'state' have two meanings, which have to be made clear each time they are used: 'nation' may refer either to Spain as a whole, or to Catalonia, Galicia, and the Basque Country, which also consider themselves to be 'nations' or 'nationalities'. 'State' is sometimes used to describe the institutions as a whole, including the autonomous communities, but on other occasions means the central institutions only, especially as distinct from the autonomous communities. It should also be pointed out that since the constitution is a young one, most general state institutions are regulated by it and have not undergone substantial change through custom or constitutional convention. Moreover, since its promulgation, there has been only one constitutional reform, incorporating the right of European Union citizens to stand for election in accordance with the Maastricht Treaty.

The king is head of state and a constitutional monarch without independent political powers: these belong to the government or parliament. He is the symbol of the country's unity and permanence, and represents Spain at the highest level in international relations. Constitutional law has framed the present monarchy along the lines used in the countries of northern Europe, and this approach has been scrupulously adhered to by the king, in clear contrast with the Spanish tradition of disruptive political interference by monarchs.

The *Cortes Generales,* or parliament, comprises two chambers, the Congress of Deputies and the Senate, the latter having far fewer powers. The Congress, which comprises 350 deputies, is elected under the d'Hondt system of proportional representation. The Senate has 207 members elected to represent the provinces and islands, and another fifty or so appointed by the autonomous communities' parliaments (one for each community plus one more for each million of population). The parliamentary groups, which correspond to the political parties, have the decisive say in how it is organized and works. An important feature of legislation is the wide variety of types of law, which are classified by subject matter and are passed under special conditions. Fundamental rights, the electoral system, and other particularly important subjects, for example, must be enshrined in *organic laws,* which, unlike ordinary laws, must be approved by an absolute majority of the Congress of Deputies in a comprehensive vote on the law as a whole.

The prime minister is the key figure in the executive and the entire institutional system, corresponding to the British prime minister or German chancellor. He or she is elected by the Congress of Deputies by either an absolute majority in the first vote, or by a simple majority in the second. This allows minority governments to be formed. The prime minister is generally also the leader of the largest party in the Congress of Deputies and appoints and dismisses the other government ministers.

The constitution set up two bodies that were new to Spain and important for its democratic consolidation: the General Council of the Judiciary, which approves most government decisions on judges and courts, and the Constitutional Court, which may annul laws, settle disputes between the central state and the autonomous communities, and, ultimately, protect citizens' fundamental rights. The Constitutional Court, which had a short-lived predecessor during the Second Republic, not only possesses many important powers, but has also exercised them vigorously, especially during the early years of democracy.

2.2 The Autonomous Communities

The present Spanish constitution grants autonomy to the 'nationalities and regions' (Art. 2), but this dual denomination has no *direct* legal consequences as the constitution does not specify which territories fall into which category and all subsequent rules and regulations use the term 'autonomous communities'. Title VIII of the constitution enshrines the general principles, procedures, and limits to be observed both in creating autonomous communities and in their subsequent day-to-day working, but the constitution did not draw up a 'map' of possible autonomous communities, nor specify a definitive model for a new type of state. This has allowed the autonomous communities themselves to decide upon their responsibilities and institutions when approving their statutes, in accordance with the route to autonomy chosen by each of them—either the ordinary or the reinforced procedure.

By 1983, following adoption of all the autonomy statutes, two groups of autonomous communities had emerged, distinguished by level of authority: seven were on the higher tier and the remaining ten on the lower but all possessed similar institutions and enjoyed a single constitutional status. These definitions, which were presupposed by the constitution but not put in explicit form, were the result of the first autonomy pacts of 1981, which were signed by the two largest parties in the *Cortes* at that time, the governing *Unión de Centro Democrático* (UCD, Union of the Democratic Centre) and the opposition *Partido Socialista Obrero Español* (PSOE, Spanish Socialist Workers' Party).

2.2.1 The Components of Federal-type Autonomy

Once the autonomous communities had been organized in their final form, they presented a number of aspects comparable to those displayed by the German *Länder* or the federal states, together with other more specific ones. Prominent among the former are the following features.

- *The constitutional guarantee of autonomy and the function of the statutes as the constitution of each autonomous community.* Constitutional recognition is decisive in insulating autonomy from changing parliamentary majorities. There is no room for ambiguity over this in Spain, as the situation is set out in Article 2 and the entire Title VIII of the constitution: consequently, self-government cannot be cut back by any central law. The autonomy statute of each region is of a secondary constitutional nature, as acknowledged by the Constitutional Court, and may only be amended by procedures determined by itself, prevailing over the laws of the central state and the autonomous community, both of which would be acting unconstitutionally if they were to contravene it.

- *The division of powers between the state and the autonomous communities, and the settlement of disputes by the Constitutional Court.* The division of powers can be accomplished by means of various legal techniques, as all federal constitutions show. The outcome is currently a distinction between exclusive state powers, concurrent powers (framework legislation by the state and secondary legislation by the autonomous communities), shared powers (legislation by the state and direct implementation by the autonomous communities), and exclusive autonomous-community powers. In the event of discrepancies between the faculties of the state and the autonomous communities, the Constitutional Court decides.

The basic institutions of the autonomous communities have common features, required by Article 152 of the constitution: a democratically elected parliament under proportional representation, the president of the community and of the government to be appointed by the parliament, with the community government to be nominated by the president, with the relations between them reflecting what the Constitutional Court has described as 'rationalized parliamentarianism'. Their composition and titles are stipulated by the autonomy statute of each autonomous community. The institutions of the autonomous community reflect the approach of the majority as expressed in the community's elections, with no hierarchical dependence upon central institutions. The autonomous presidents represent the head of state within their regional territories. The varying political orientations followed by the autonomous governments in recent years bear witness to this independence (Table 10.1).

The autonomous communities are financed in two different ways: the Basque Country and Navarre have a special system rooted in their historical rights—the *foras*—while general arrangements apply to all the others. In Navarre the regional government regulates and collects almost all taxes and transfers a part of the total revenues to the central government, equivalent to the amount of state expenditure on the autonomous community. In the Basque Country the same legal and management powers for taxation are vested in each of the three provincial administrations (Vizcaya, Alava, and Guipúzcoa), which also transfer portions of the revenues to the Basque government and to the central government to offset expenditure on the tasks they perform. Both systems, which in practice produce greater resources than the average for the other self-governing regions, are regulated by two special laws, the *Agreement* and the *Covenant*, entered into by the central government and the regional bodies and ratified by the *Cortes*.

The general funding system, known in Spanish as the *Ley Orgánica de Financiación de las Comunidades Autónomas* (LOFCA, Organic Law on the Financing of the Autonomous Communities), draws on three sources: tax revenues raised by the autonomous communities; a share of central-state

TABLE 10.1   Autonomous governments, 1983–95: parties, majorities, and coalitions

Region	Year			
	1983	1987	1991	1995
Andalusia	**PSOE**	**PSOE**	**PSOE**	**PSOE + PA**
Aragon	**PSOE**	PAR	**PAR + PP** PSOE	**PP + PAR**
Asturias	**PSOE**	**PSOE**	**PSOE**	PP
Canary Islands	**PSOE**	CDS + AIC + AP CDS + AIC	AIC + PSOE CC	**CC + PP**
Cantabria	**AP** AP	**AP** **PSOE + PP + PRC + CDS**	UPCA	**PP + PRC**
Castile-Leon	**PSOE**	AP	**PP**	**PP**
Castile-La Mancha	**PSOE**	**PSOE**	**PSOE**	**PSOE**
Catalonia	**CíU**	**CíU**	**CíU**	**CíU**
Community of Valencia	**PSOE**	**PSOE**	**PSOE**	**PP + UV**
Extremadura	**PSOE**	**PSOE**	**PSOE**	**PSOE**
Galicia	AP	CP **PSOE + CG + PNG**	PP	**PP**
Bearic Islands	AP	**AP + UM**	PP/UM	**PP**
La Rioja	**PSOE**	AP PSOE	**PSOE**	**PP**
Madrid	**PSOE**	**PSOE**	**PSOE**	**PP**
Murcia	**PSOE**	**PSOE**	**PSOE**	**PP**
Navarre	**PSOE**	**PSOE**	UPN (PP)	CDN + PSOE + EA
Basque Country	PNV	PNV + PSOE	PNV + EA + EE PNV + PSE + EE PNV + PSE	PNV + PSE + EA

Notes: **Bold** type, absolute majority; medium type, largest single group; +, post-electoral pact; /, pre-electoral pact.

AIC, *Agrupación Independiente de Canarias* (Independent Group of the Canary Islands); AP, *Alianza Popular* (Popular Alliance); BNG, *Bloque Nacionalista Galego* (Galician Nationalist Bloc); CC, *Coalición Canaria* (Canary Islands Coalition); CDN, *Convergencia de Demócratas de Navarra* (Navarre Democrats' Grouping); CDS, *Centro Democrático y Social* (Democratic and Social Centre); CG, *Coalición Galega* (Galician Coalition); CíU, *Convergència i Unió* (Convergency and Union); CP, *Coalición Popular* (Popular Coalition); EA, *Eusko Alkartasuna* (Basque Solidarity); EE, *Euskadiko Ezkerra* (Basque Left); PA, *Partido Andalucista* (Andalusian Party); PAR, *Partido Aragonés Regionalista* (Aragonese Regionalist Party); PNV, *Partido Nacionalista Vasco* (Basque Nationalist Party); PP, *Partido Popular* (Popular Party); PRC, *Partido Regionalista de Cantabria* (Cantabrian Regionalist Party); PSOE, *Partido Socialista Obrero Español* (Spanish Socialist Party); UM, *Unión Mallorquina* (Mallorcan Union); UPCA, *Unió para el progreso de Cantabria* (Union for Cantabrian Progress); UPN, *Unión del Pueblo Navarro* (Union of the People of Navarre); UV, *Unión Valenciana* (Valencian Union).

resources; and income from solidarity funds, either at national (Interterritorial Compensation Fund) or EU level, the latter being of particular importance in recent years for certain regions. The bulk of resources is generated by distributing central-state revenue, which since the 1993 and 1996 reforms is done by drawing on the proceeds of personal income tax within the autonomous community in question. The reforms have not been accepted by all the regions, and the dispute has been taken to the Constitutional Court.

Under both systems, the autonomous communities enjoy considerable spending powers, and the central state has progressively transferred to them the subsidies for devolved services (education, social services, etc.), since the Constitutional Court has expressed the view that the central state does not have United States-style spending authority, and cannot maintain subsidies in areas that are the responsibility of the autonomous regions, without involving them.

Relations among the autonomous communities, by means of formal agreements or other horizontal cooperation instruments, are relatively undeveloped; and although region–state relations are far more intensive, the entire field of intergovernmental relations (especially sectoral conferences) is regulated on a rather shaky basis, because of the absence of an explicit constitutional foundation and of the predominance of bilateral relations between the different governments.

2.2.2 The 'Differentiating Factors'

In addition to this initial, two-tier system of responsibility, the constitution introduced other, more qualitative criteria to distinguish the autonomous communities themselves on the basis of history, law, and language and allowed the autonomy statutes to express these in practical form.

Article 3.2 of the Spanish Constitution accepts that some languages can have joint official status within the relevant autonomous communities. This is the case in the Basque Country, Catalonia, Galicia, the Community of Valencia, and the Balearic Islands. The continuation of regional, historical charter-based, or special civil law in certain regions is directly accepted by Article 149.1.8 of the constitution, under which the 'conservation, amendment, and development' of such law may be established as an exclusive power of the relevant autonomous regions (Navarre, Catalonia, etc.) by their statutes. The First Additional Provision (by which the Constitution safeguards and complies with the historic rights of the regional privileges or charters) underpins the Basque Country's and Navarre's differing financial and tax system. The economic and tax arrangements of the Canary Islands are also given special treatment in the constitution. Finally, there are certain issues of outstanding political importance that fall within the remit of certain autonomous communities only, such as the ability of the Basque Country, Galicia, Navarre, and Catalonia to set up their own police forces.

These special features of some autonomous communities are generally known as 'differentiating factors' (Table 10.2); their immense political importance stems first from the fact that they closely reflect the underlying causes of the respective popular demands for autonomy and second that they impact upon a wide range of areas of responsibility. In Catalonia, for example, the language is the principal issue historically justifying the claim for autonomy. It is a vital element in the Catalan people's sense of identity, and it affects the way the Catalan authorities discharge their functions in areas like education, culture, public administration, etc. It even has an impact on central-state responsibilities such as justice, since individuals are entitled to speak Catalan in court.

In short, the autonomous communities share some features with other European federal systems—although this term is never used—to the extent that they are ultimately regulated by an autonomy statute, they possess powers that cannot be altered by law, they have institutions that answer only to the directives of their own electorates (with no hierarchical obligations towards the central government), they are financed through an objective system that cannot be tampered with, and their disputes with the government are resolved by the, central, Constitutional Court. Furthermore, some autonomous communities have special faculties that are incorporated as 'differentiating factors', which set them apart from the traditional equality of states and *Länder* in European federal systems.

TABLE 10.2   Summary of 'differentiating factors' of the autonomous communities

Region	Factors				
	Language	Civil law	Special funding arrangement	Intermediate institutions	Autonomous police force
Aragon	✓	✓			
Canary Islands			✓	✓	
Catalonia	✓	✓			✓
Community of Valencia	✓	✓			
Galicia	✓	✓			
Balearic Islands	✓	✓		✓	
Navarre	✓	✓	✓		✓
Basque Country	✓	✓	✓	✓	✓

2.3 Local Powers

The constitution also triggered decisive changes at the local level, essentially by introducing elections for the membership of all local-government bodies, by removing the political controls that central-state bodies exercised over their local counterparts, and by certain forms of safeguard for their autonomy, even in the face of laws. However, local authorities have had something of a 'Cinderella' role in contrast with the strong development of the autonomous communities, and many of their long-standing problems remain unresolved. This is clearly illustrated by comparing the growth of economic resources at the two levels (Table 10.3).

The main local body is certainly the municipality, which is the first tier at which the popular will is expressed as well as a public administration responsible for providing services. Its governing body, the *ayuntamiento* (municipal council), consists of councillors directly elected by the local population, also under the d'Hondt proportional system, and of the mayor, who is in turn elected by the councillors. In some cases, there are also an executive committee and other sectoral committees.

The traditional intermediate link is the province, covering a number of municipalities and having a governing body, the *Diputación*, which is indirectly elected from among municipal councillors. This tier does not, however, exist in the single-province autonomous communities (Asturias, Cantabria, La Rioja, Navarre, and Madrid), in the islands, which each have an individual governing council (called *Consejos* in the Balearics and *Cabildos* in the Canaries), or in the Basque Country, where each of the three provinces is organized as a *historic territory* with its own highly robust institutions and resources.

The basic problem of municipalities in Spain lies in their geographical fragmentation and their highly diverse circumstances, which do not easily fit under a single set of rules and arrangements. It is worth recalling that there

TABLE 10.3 Public expenditure trends by tier of administration (as a percentage of the total), 1981–97

Year	Central government	Autonomous communities	Local authorities
1981	87.33	2.9	9.72
1985	73.15	14.12	12.73
1990	65.78	20.21	14.01
1995	65.01	23.12	11.87
1996	62.58	24.73	12.68
1997	61.10	25.93	12.98

are more than 8,000 municipalities in Spain, 86 per cent of which have less than 5,000 inhabitants and account for only 16 per cent of the total population. At the other end of the spectrum, 42 per cent of the population is concentrated in only 54 municipalities with populations of more than 100,000. Such diversity results in glaring inequalities between municipalities in terms of provision of services and local-government efficiency (Table 10.4).

In Spain, local authorities' organization, responsibilities, funding, etc. are regulated partly by the central state, partly by the autonomous communities. The central state may adopt framework legislation (Law 7/1985 regulating the bases of local government), and the autonomous community may adopt secondary legislation as well as holding the relevant regulatory and management powers. However, in addition to direct legislation concerning local authorities, a whole range of sectoral laws emanating from both the state and the

TABLE 10.4   Number of municipalities by population band and by autonomous community, with Ceuta and Melilla

Community	Population						Total municipalities
	<5,000	5,000–20,000	20,001–50,000	50,001–100,000	100,001–500,000	+500,000	
Andalusia	531	176	42	9	8	2	768
Aragon	709	17	2	—	—	1	729
Asturias	45	25	3	3	2	—	78
Balearic Islands	40	20	6	—	1	—	67
Canary Islands	28	44	11	1	3	—	87
Cantabria	85	14	1	1	1	—	102
Castile-La Mancha	854	48	7	5	1	—	915
Castile-Leon	2,211	35	4	4	4	—	2,248
Catalonia	797	103	24	9	8	1	942
Extremadura	337	36	5	1	1	—	380
Galicia	179	117	10	4	3	—	313
Madrid	139	19	9	5	6	1	179
Murcia	10	24	8	1	2	—	45
Navarre	253	13	1	—	1	—	268
Basque Country	184	45	9	5	4	—	247
La Rioja	167	6	—	—	1	—	174
Community of Valencia	409	88	33	5	3	1	539
Ceuta and Melilla	—	—	—	2	—	—	2
Total	6,968	829	176	55	49	6	8,083

Source: Directorate-General for the Legal Structure, Ministry for Public Administration.

autonomous communities also come into play, further complicating the picture. This plurality of systems is reflected in the various intermediate tiers (districts, provinces, etc.), although less so at the municipal level. Despite the differences of scale, they are largely governed by the same rules, which fail to cater for the widely differing problems of large cities, metropolitan areas, rural and tourist municipalities, etc.

2.4 Nationwide and Autonomous Community-based Political Parties

There have been two major parties on the right and the left in Spain since the inception of democracy [first, *Unión de Centro Democrático* (UCD, Union of the Democratic Centre) and PSOE; subsequently PSOE and *Partido Popular* (PP, Popular Party)], as well as the smaller *Partido Comunista de España* (Communist Party of Spain), which, in recent years, has combined with other forces of the left to make up the current *Izquierda Unida* (United Left). A small party—the *Centro Democrático y Social* (Democratic and Social Centre), founded by Suárez after the break-up of the UCD—was on the scene for a few years.

These parties have equivalents in other European countries. The main distinguishing feature of the Spanish party system, however, is the presence of political parties who operate only in the autonomous communities and do not extend beyond them (although certain Basque parties are represented to some degree in Navarre) (see Table 10.5).

Most of these parties are nationalist or regionalist, in the sense that over and above any other ideological aspect, their declared primary aim is to defend the interests and political standing of their respective autonomous communities (in order to avoid frequent repetition of the expression 'nationalist and regionalist parties', and because there are numerous differences between them, the more neutral term 'autonomous-community-based parties' (ACBPs) will generally be used henceforth).

The ACBPs' importance stems initially from their strength within the autonomous communities. *Convergència i Unió* (CiU, Convergence and Union) and the *Partido Nacionalista Vasco* (PNV, Basque Nationalist Party)

TABLE 10.5   Political parties, 1996

Party	% votes	No. of seats
Partido Popular (Popular Party)	38.6	156
Partido Socialista Obrero Español (Spanish Socialist Party)	37.4	141
Izquierda Unida (United Left)	10.5	21

have headed their respective regional governments ever since the first elections in 1980. More recent parties are now achieving comparable scores. The *Coalición Canaria* (CC, Canary Island Coalition) has been in government for more than five years, holding the presidency since before the latest elections, although it now rules in a coalition with the Popular Party. The *Bloque Nacionalista Galego* (BNG, Galician Nationalist Bloc) has been the main opposition party since the 1997 elections, overtaking the PSOE. The *Partido Aragonés Regionalista* (PAR, Aragonese Regionalist Party) took the presidency of its region in 1987 and is now a junior party in a government headed by the Popular Party. The *Unión del Pueblo Navarro* (UPN, Union of the People of Navarre), which merged with the Popular Party, is the biggest party in Navarre. Other, smaller parties play an important role in their autonomous communities, either because larger parties need them in order to form a government or because, despite their small size, they can tip the balance in electing presidents or ensuring absolute majorities within the autonomous community. More parties than might be expected are in this position. Table 10.6 describes the main ACBPs on the basis of the last regional election results.

The ACBPs do not only contest autonomous-community elections, but regularly stand for national and European parliamentary elections. Some ACBPs have a significant presence in the *Cortes*, being assisted by the territorial concentration of votes. The number of seats won in the Congress of Deputies by the ACBPs in the 1996 elections are set out in Table 10.7.

Using their presence in the Congres of Deputies, the CíU, PNV, and CC have played an important role in central government, by pledging their votes to the Socialist and Popular Party governments (1993–6 and 1996 to present, respectively) and holding the balance of power at national level.

2.5 Autonomous Community Developments and the Major Themes for Discussion in Recent Years

The initial difference in the powers of the two groups of autonomous communities, the higher tier and the lower tier, was seen by some as a reflection of historical and political differences, summed up in the 'nationalities and regions' dichotomy of Article 2 of the constitution. However, this did not apply to the seven autonomous communities of the first group, and it appeared more appropriate to view the more modest powers of the second group simply as a 'running-in' stage, which the constitution would allow to be extended after the first five years of autonomy. At the end of the 1980s some autonomous communities (Castile-Leon, the Balearics, etc.) did indeed begin to call for reform of their statutes to give them greater powers. In the end, the

Table 10.6 Principal autonomous-community-based parties (ACBP) obtained in the regional elections, 1995

Region	Party (% votes)
Andalusia[a]	**PA** (5.8)
Aragon	**PAR** (20.3), Chunta Aragon (5)
Asturia	Partido Asturias (3.3)
Balearic Islands	PSM-EN (12.5), UM (5.3)
Basque Country[b]	**PNV** (29.8), HB (16.3), **EA** (10.3), UA (2.7)
Canary Islands	**CC** (32.9)
Cantabria	UPCA (16.5), **PRC** (14.4)
Catalonia	**CíU** (40.8), ERC (9.5)
Community of Valencia	UV (7)
Extremadura	CE (3.8)
Galicia[c]	BNG (24.7)
Navarre	**UPN** (31.1), CDN (18.4), HB (11.3), EA (4.5)
La Rioja	PR (6.7)

Note: **Bold** type, ACBP in regional government.

[a] 1996. [b] 1994. [c] 1997.

BNG, *Bloque Nacionalista Galego* (Galician Nationalist Bloc); CC, *Coalición Canaria* (Canary Islands Coalition); CDN, *Convergencia de Demócratas de Navarra* (Navarre Democrats' Grouping); CíU, *Convergència i Unió* (Convergency and Union); EA, *Eusko Alkartasuna* (Basque Solidarity); ERC, *Esquerra Republicana de Catalunya* (Catalan Republican Left); HB, *Herri Batasuna* (People's Unity); PA, *Partido Andalucista* (Andalusian Party); PAR, *Partido Aragonés Regionalista* (Aragonese Regionalist Party); PNV, *Partido Nacionalista Vasco* (Basque Nationalist Party); PRC, *Partido Regionalista de Cantabria* (Cantabrian Regionalist Party); PSM-EN, *Partido Socialista de Mallorca-Entesa* (Socialist Party of Mallorca-Agreement); UA, Unidad Alavesa (Alavesan Unity); UM, *Unión Mallorquina* (Mallorcan Union); UPCA, *Unió para el progreso de Cantabria* (Union for Cantabrian Progress); UPN, *Unión del Pueblo Navarro* (Union of the People of Navarre); UV, *Unión Valenciana* (Valencian Union).

Table 10.7 ACBP representation in the Congress of Deputies

Party	No. of seats
Convergència i Unió (Convergency and Union)	16
Partido Nacionalista Vasco (Basque Nationalist Party)	5
Coalición Canaria (Canary Islands Coalition)	4
Bloque Nacionalista Galego (Galician Nationalist Bloc)	2
Herri Batasuna (People's Unity)	2
Esquerra Republicana de Catalunya (Catalan Republican Left)	1
Eusko Alkartasuna (Basque Solidarity)	1
Unión Valenciana (Valencian Union)	1

argument over extending their remit was settled by a series of new autonomy pacts between the Socialist Government and the Popular Party in February 1992. Organic Law 9/1992 on the transfer of powers to autonomous communities provided a rapid solution, with ten more autonomy statutes being reformed in the same way in 1994 (the Canary Islands' statute was adopted two years later).

Without going into detail, all the statutes may now be said to contain equivalent substantial powers, except for the health sector, due to the management and financial problems it raises.

With this one exception, the autonomous communities' powers in areas directly affecting citizens are identical for practical purposes. In contrast, the most important differences of substance lie in the specific historical, legal, and linguistic aspects of some autonomous communities, and these do not apply across the board. The first set of powers, which are applicable to all, may therefore be described as substantial, while the second set might be termed 'specific' or inherent to the 'differentiating factors'.

The reaction of many nationalist parties to this 'levelling-up' has been to demand further powers. In 1998 in particular, and following *Euzkadi ta Azkatasuma's* (ETA's) ceasefire declaration, a series of proposals for major political reforms (including the right to self-determination, the creation of a confederation, etc.) has generated debate at a level such that it is hard to predict what direction the autonomy arrangements will eventually take, or to predict the final balance between what makes the autonomous communities similar and what makes them different.

3. The Practice of Subnational Democracy

3.1 Critiques of Regional and Local Democracy

The serious problem of excessively small municipalities—86 per cent of Spain's 8,000 municipalities have populations of less than 5,000—is a practical barrier to any general or sectoral policy that is strongly decentralized and based on local administration. The result is strong centralization within the autonomous communities. A policy of encouraging mergers or groupings of municipalities, or even of compulsorily redrawing the municipal map, is indeed a primary duty of the autonomous communities, but to date they have simply offered mild encouragement for setting up voluntary joint associations.

Structures at the tier above municipalities are relatively undefined. Some autonomous communities clearly support the role of the provinces, while others seek to empty them of any real substance and prefer to back other institutions instead, such as districts in the case of Catalonia. The result is a general tendency to view the provincial, or equivalent, level as a support measure for municipalities, providing assistance and cooperation and filling gaps in their services, but on a scale that varies widely from region to region. In the vast majority of cases, the provincial or district levels are organized through a system of indirect representation, with the exception of the Basque provinces and the islands. This serves to diminish their credibility and social accept-ability, as they are operated in purely party-political interests.

In practice, municipalities enjoy a very low level of organizational inde-pendence, since the powers of the municipal assembly, the executive commit-tee, and the mayor are strictly bound by basic state legislation. The few areas in which local authorities have some modest scope for devising their own solutions are their advisory information committees, popular participation, and internal devolution within the municipality. Municipal authorities usually set up parallel bodies to provide certain services and functions: these fre-quently take the form of bodies established by private law.

As pointed out earlier, neither the constitution, nor the autonomy statutes, nor the law governing the bases of local government guarantee any spe-cific powers to municipalities. All the law does is to draw up a list of public services that municipalities must provide to the local population, in line with their size. It is, therefore, up to the central or regional legislator, depending on the subject in question, to assign specific powers to local authorities.

The prevailing conception of local autonomy, enshrined in the local-government law and constitutional case law, would suggest that recognition of local authorities' right to take part in running affairs of concern to them, particularly those listed in the local-government law, is sufficient. In practice, this means that the laws governing these areas do not usually grant full public decision-making powers to municipalities for entire sectors of activity. The local authorities possess virtually no exclusive powers; in many areas in which they should, according to the local-government law, enjoy some powers, they are only allowed to act on a subordinate and non-decision-making basis: they can only involve themselves in procedures that are ultimately decided by the autonomous community or the central state.

Dissatisfaction with this state of affairs is evident in all municipalities that have a minimum of operational capacity, since they cannot implement their own policies in important sectors of popular demand, such as housing, social services, education, etc. As a result, a movement has emerged from the con-federation of local authorities, demanding a 'local pact' with central and regional governments, seeking an undertaking that they will be granted more powers.

The system of local law in Spain has opted to make all supervision of local-authority business subject to decision by the courts: both the central state and

the autonomous communities are specifically empowered to bring local agreements that they deem to be unlawful, or to infringe their powers, before an
administrative court, and they can apply for a court order obliging a local
authority to annul an agreement. Local agreements can only be rendered inef-
fective by the administrative courts, apart from in highly exceptional circumstances that seriously threaten Spanish national interests.

A wide range of circumstances, however, still exists in which sectoral
legislation requires prior authorization or subsequent endorsement of local
agreements by the central state or the autonomous communities. This is constitutionally permissible only in so far as they do not constitute general controls, but occur in specific cases in which interests at a level higher than the
purely local, which may be affected by a municipal decision, can be demonstrated. These are in fact situations where powers are shared between the local
authority and the next level of administration, in areas where coordinated,
consistent action is required (urban planning offers a multitude of instances).
The latter offers a way of restoring what amounts to regulation in areas where,
legally, this is not possible.

The constitution does not specifically acknowledge the principle of
financial autonomy for local authorities, as this is considered to be part of
their general political autonomy, but the principle of adequate resources is
explicitly guaranteed. Nevertheless, the current legal system, largely in the
form of the 1988 Local Finance Act, does not allow either principle to be fully
upheld.

Municipal tax revenues derive essentially from property and business taxes,
both of which are highly inflexible. Local authorities also levy charges and
special contributions for works and services. Overall receipts from Spanish
municipalities' own sources provide about 40 per cent of their total income.
The remainder is made up of a share of national taxes, through various state
economic-cooperation programmes, either in the form of unconditional
general subsidies under multi-annual programmes, or specific conditional
investment subsidies provided by either the state or the autonomous community. Finally, borrowing accounts for nearly 25 per cent of local budgets,
which has a considerable impact on how local finances are balanced.

Some autonomous communities have created their own funds or economic-cooperation programmes with municipalities. This boosts local
resources and increases local autonomy by reducing the proportion of overall
local financing derived from conditional subsidies.

Local-authority spending represents 14 per cent of total public spending in
Spain: the corresponding figures for the autonomous communities and the
state are 30 per cent and 56 per cent, respectively. More than 30 per cent of
municipal expenditure is spent on general services and pensions.

The autonomous cities of Ceuta and Melilla (Spanish enclaves in North
Africa) are special cases. While being cities, they enjoy autonomy statutes

conferring powers far greater than those of any mainland city, falling not far short of the autonomous communities' (non-legislative) management powers. They differ institutionally, and enjoy certain financial advantages.

3.2 Citizens' Attitudes

Democracy is quite firmly established in Spain today, and there is little contestation of the democratic system and little nostalgia for the previous authoritarian regime of Franco. Attitude surveys of the *Centro di Investigaçiones Sociologicas* (CIS) show a consistent pattern of support for the democratic transition. In 1995, 79 per cent of Spaniards thought that the form and manner of the transition to democracy was a source of pride (Estudio CES 2201, December 1995). Seventy-nine per cent thought that democracy was preferable to any other political system, against 9 per cent who thought that an authoritarian system was better, and 8 per cent who felt that there was little difference between the two systems (ibid.). However, although a very high percentage were happy with the democratic system, fewer were satisfied with the way in which the system actually functions (about 50 per cent). Forty-six per cent wished to see reforms, while 33 per cent wished to maintain the status quo. With regard to the form of the Spanish state, the system of autonomous communities, there was a great deal of satisfaction. Only a tiny and declining minority wished to see a unitary state: 9 per cent in November 1984, 7 per cent in December 1990, and 3 per cent in March 1996. Majorities were in favour of the autonomic system: 51 per cent in November 1984, 60 per cent in December 1990, and 69 per cent in March 1996. However, this last category contained sizeable minorities that wished the autonomous communities to have more powers than they do at present. Small minorities wished to see the possibility of independence for the autonomous communities, although in March 1996, 40 per cent thought that they had contributed to the development of separatism. In this same poll, 61 per cent thought that the autonomous arrangements had brought public administration closer to the citizens. It is sometimes claimed that there is a high degree of apathy among Spanish citizens. Indeed a CIS survey taken in March, April, and May 1996 showed that only 24 per cent were interested (highly or quite) in politics; 36 per cent were only slightly interested, and 37 per cent not at all interested. On the other hand, another poll taken at the same time showed 87 per cent of the electorate always or nearly always use their votes. In terms of the political level of greatest interest to citizens, 62 per cent were interested (highly or quite) in the activities of the local authority (*ayuntamiento*), 49 per cent in those of the autonomous government, and 48 per cent in the activities of the national government. Only 29 per cent were interested in the discussions of the national parliament.

4. Challenges and Opportunities for Subnational Democracy

4.1 Some General Issues of Democracy Concerning the Central State, the Autonomous Communities, and Local Authorities

The *political parties* were developed—to some extent artificially—during the early years of democracy, to compensate for their weakness after forty years of prohibition. They were granted significant public funding accordingly (as parties, as parliamentary groups, and as electoral candidates) as well as free, large-scale access to the mass media during election campaigns. Moreover, party management was strengthened by the introduction of the fixed, closed-list electoral system, which allows all candidates to be screened. However, both the lack of a democratic tradition, reflected in authoritarian attitudes to any expression of dissent, and the uncovering of a number of corruption scandals have brought serious discredit upon the political parties. As a result, reforms to both parliamentary regulations and legislation are in the pipeline.

A recent attempt at renovation is represented by the 'primary' elections held by the PSOE among its members (thus not 'primaries' in the American sense) to choose candidates for the main mayorships, regional presidencies, and the prime ministership. A turning point came when the PSOE's Secretary General, entirely unexpectedly, lost to a candidate who enjoyed great popularity within the party, but had been kept at arm's length by its centres of power. Juan Borrell will now be the next socialist candidate for the post of prime minister in the general elections. Official candidates were also defeated in a number of autonomous communities and major municipalities, such as Madrid; these events have raised an expectation of renewal that is beginning to spread to other parties.

The autonomy arrangements present a paradox: while the autonomous communities' position has been consolidated, the state as a whole appears much weaker. There is no official body integrating the political ambitions of the autonomous communities (no progress has been made on reform of the Senate, although agreement was reached in 1994), and relations between the autonomous communities themselves and with the central state are not stable. This is at a time when ever greater efficiency is required in intergovernmental relations in general. Furthermore, the Spanish autonomy arrangements have been challenged in recent years, primarily by initiatives stemming from governing nationalist parties in the autonomous communities. This is especially the case with the PNV and CiU, which have raised the issue of recognition of the right of self-determination, joint sovereignty, and even confederation. The Northern Ireland peace agreement has had a considerable impact, particularly in the Basque Country, although the Basque Country is now running into difficulties (Letamendia and Loughlin 2000).

4.2 The European Dimension

Autonomous-community involvement in the European Union enjoys important two-way recognition, through the Conference for EU-related affairs, bringing together all the autonomous communities and the central government, and through the establishment of autonomous-community offices—recognized by the Constitutional Court—in Brussels, in addition, of course, to the forum provided by the Committee of the Regions. In 1998 a further agreement was reached under which the autonomous communities would be represented within the Spanish delegation to the EU Council of Ministers.

4.3 Trends Affecting Regional and Local Authorities

One of the universally recognized shortcomings facing municipalities is the absence of guarantees for their autonomy and, more generally, the scarcity of the resources available to them, in terms of both powers and finance. A local pact between the state, the autonomous communities, and municipalities to remedy this problem has been under discussion for years: in 1998 the central government eventually submitted a bill introducing various reforms, one of the main features of which is the ability of municipalities to go to the Constitutional Court to defend their independence. However, the autonomous communities, which possess powers in most areas of local demand, seem reluctant to engage in any further decentralization.

5. *Innovative Approaches to Improving Subnational Democracy*

5.1 Semi-direct Democracy

'Semi-direct' forms of democracy (referendums and popular legislative initiatives, in particular) are regarded with great suspicion by the constitution, and this attitude has been transmitted to the other institutions. Referendums can only be held in the autonomous communities to reform certain autonomy statutes, and municipal authorities hardly ever take advantage of their greater legal opportunities to conduct popular consultations. Even when they do so, the consultation is conducted informally as an opinion poll, not in the official, legally established form. Good examples of this are the consultations carried out in the Treviño area, to gauge whether the population would prefer to be included in the Basque Country or to remain within Castile-Leon, and in Palamós, on the plan to build a housing estate on a beach outside the municipality (El Castell).

Almost all the autonomous communities provide for popular legislative initiatives, but regard them with mistrust (as at national level), and they are rarely employed. Of the more than forty initiatives submitted during these years in the seventeen autonomous communities as a whole, only five have been adopted. Most of the autonomy statutes allow a cluster of municipalities to submit proposals for legislation to the regional parliament: this faculty has scarcely been used either.

5.2 Direct Democracy

Forms of direct democratic participation, in contrast, appear to have a brighter future, although they are as yet at an early stage. The most widespread of these—probably because it is expressly sanctioned by the constitution—is the involvement of individual citizens and relevant associations in drafting government regulations. Virtually all the autonomous communities have made official provision for this procedure, and the idea that regulations drawn up without such involvement are invalid is gaining ground. The involvement of relevant associations in drafting legislation, on the other hand, is at a far more embryonic stage of development, although the Asturian and Andalusian Parliaments have recently introduced this option.

5.3 Autonomous Community Initiatives for Social Integration

A wide range of sectoral advisory committees have been set up in nearly all the autonomous communities, facilitating negotiations between economic operators and the regional authorities. This presupposes a certain amount of lobbying, which is permitted under law. The regional government-promoted economic and social pacts between trade unions and employers' bodies are generally of greater importance, especially in years when comparable national pacts at national level have broken down. The economic and social councils set up in most autonomous communities, bringing together workers, employers, and the authorities themselves, put this dialogue onto an even more developed institutional level.

5.4 Metropolitan Areas and Elected Mayors

There are no clear and specific rules for large metropolitan areas; the autonomous communities, which might have some powers in this regard, have not adopted any positive policies to address the issue. As a result, an initiative has emerged from among the larger municipalities, aiming to introduce specific legislation covering the biggest cities, which would herald a shift away from the traditional legislative uniformity that has been a feature of local-government organization in Spain.

At present, mayors are elected by municipal councils, but discussion is beginning to focus on the idea of officially enabling the direct election of mayors by the general electorate; a procedure that is explicitly permitted by Article 140 of the constitution. This would match the current legislative trend to reinforce the position of the mayor, which has also benefited from the 1991 reform of the electoral law, designed to boost local-government stability by limiting the scope for motions of censure directed against mayors.

5.5 Other Initiatives

Other innovative experiments are still too rudimentary or recent to be evaluated. For example, the Catalan Parliament, with the support of a foundation, has launched a programme (*Parlament Obert*, Open Parliament) to disseminate news of its activities and to draw in citizens (initiatives, suggestions, opinions, etc.) through the Internet. The government of Castile has begun to draw up 'citizens' rights charters', which might help narrow the gap between citizens and their institutions, and possibly even offer a more active role for regional government in exercising citizens' rights; something that is not usually seen as a primary function of the autonomous communities.

The most recent forms of democracy have included the experiments with the *Núcleos de Intervención Participativa* (NIPs, local teams seeking to stimulate popular involvement). These were put into action by some local authorities, such as Rubí in Catalonia and, on a larger scale, in the Basque Country, as a means of sounding out public opinion on possible public decisions. In the area of immigration, another issue of growing sensitivity over recent years, some municipalities are beginning to set up fora or participatory consultation bodies. These bodies are important, because non-EU foreigners do not have voting rights and are generally subject to fairly harsh general laws. In another, very different area, there are several projects to enhance communication between local councils and inhabitants, such as the Barcelona grouping that is running the *Local-red* ('Local Network') programme, or Valencia's 'Infoville' programme, aiming to equip every household with a terminal, in the belief that providing Internet access should be considered as a basic, statutory service.

6. Conclusions

Democracy in Spain is closely related to the transition from Francoist dictatorship and to the setting up of the 'autonomic state'. The latter is seen as an essential component of democratization. On the whole, the transition to democracy in Spain must be regarded as a success given the scant historical traditions of democracy that existed hitherto. Most Spaniards are clearly content both with the transition and with the functioning of democracy at all levels. Some questions, however, are still unresolved. One is the position of the nationalities within the Spanish state and, especially, that of the Basque Country. There continues to exist tensions betweeen the centre and the autonomous communities over a range of questions ranging from finance to language. Only in the Basque Country, however, has this led to a serious challenge to democracy as such and to the democratic settlement of 1978. In the rest of Spain, and, for example, in Catalonia there has been no serious armed challenge to the state. On the contrary, the rest of Spain has shown a capacity to deal with problems in a democratic and non-violent way. Perhaps the best recognition of this is in the form of a paradox. Spain's democratic credentials are shown by the fact that it is converging with the trends of other European countries—including the switch-off from politics shown by ordinary citizens.

Bibliography

AJA, E. *et al.* (1990). *El sistema jurídico de las Comunidades Autónomas.* Madrid: Tecnos.

BUSTOS, GISBERT, R. (1996). *Relaciones internacionales y Comunidades Autónomas.* Madrid: Centro de Estudios Constituciónales.

FANLO LORAS, A. (1990). *Fundamentos constitucionales de la autonomía local.* Madrid: Centro de Estudios Constituciónales.

FERNÁNDEZ, T. R. (1985). *Los derechos históricos de los Territorios Forales.* Madrid: Centro de Estudios Constituciónales.

FONT Y LLOVET, TOMÀS (ed.) (1990). *Informe sobre el gobierno local.* Madrid: Ministerio para las Administraciones Publicas Fundació.

GARCIA, A., APARICIO, B. C. *et al.* (1989). *El Gobierno en la Constitución y en los Estatutos de Autonomía.* Barcelona: Diputació de Barcelona.

GARCIA ROCA, J. (1993). *Los conflictos de competencias entre el Estado y las Comunidades Autónomas.* Madrid: Centro de Estudios Constituciónales.

Gomez Ferrer, R. (ed.) (1991). *La provincia en el sistema constitucional*. Madrid: Civitas Barcelana Diputació de Barcelona.

Letamendia, F. and Loughlin, J. (2000). 'Peace in the Basque Country and Corsica', in A. Guelke, M. Cox, and F. Stephen (eds), *A Farewell to Arms: From 'Long War' to Long Peace in Northern Ireland*. Manchester: Manchester University Press.

Martín Rebollo, L. (ed.) (1991). *El futuro de las Autonomías territoriales*. Santander: Universidad de Cantabria.

Pallarés, F. (1994). 'Las elecciones autonómicas en España (1980–92)', in P. del Castillo (ed.), *Comportamiento político y electoral*. Madrid.

Perez Calvo, A. (ed.) (1997). *La participación de las Comunidades Autónomas en las decisiones del Estado*. Madrid: Tecnos.

Perez Tremps, P. (1987). *Comunidades Autónomas, Estado y Comunidad Europea*. Madrid: Ministerio de Justicia.

Rodriguez Arana, J. (1996). *Autonomía y administración pública. Reflexiones sobre la administración única*. Barcelona: Práxis.

Tomas y Valiente, F. (1988). *El reparto competencial en la Jurisprudencia del Tribunal Constitucional*. Madrid: Tecnos.

Tornos, J. (ed.) (1997). *La administración del Estado en las Comunidades Autónomas*. Barcelona: Institut d'Estudís Autonòmics.

Trayter, J. M. (1992). *¿Son nulos los reglamentos elaborados sin respetar el trámite de audiencia?* Madrid: Tecnos.

Generautat de Catalunya (1995). *Uniformidad y diversidad de las Comunidades Autónomas*. Barcelona: Institut d'Estudís Autonòmics.

——(1997). *Función ejecutiva y administración territorial*. Barcelona: Institut d'Estudís Autonòmics.

For monitoring of the autonomous communities, see the *Informe de las Comunidades Autónomas*, edited by E. Aja, which has been published annually since 1989; for local authority activities, see the *Anuario del Gobierno local*, edited by T. Font y Llovet, published since 1995. Both these publications are compiled by the *Instituto de Derecho Público* (Public Law Institute), Barcelona and include comprehensive bibliographies.

11

Portugal: The Difficulties of Regionalization

John Loughlin

1. History and Concept of Democracy

1.1 Historical Background

Compared with the other member states of the European Union, Portugal is a country of contrasts. On the one hand, it is one of the most centralized of the unitary states, but, on the other, it has one of the most participatory and most modern local democracies. Linguistically, it is one of the most homogeneous nations. Sociologically, it is divided along north-south or north-centre-south dimensions. Portugal's territorial development was among the earliest in Europe and its present borders were already fixed by the Middle Ages. It could be argued that a sense of national identity developed as early as the break away from the Kingdom of Spain. Portugal was a small country, but became an important imperial nation and, histori-cally, it belongs to the group of great powers such as England, France, and Spain. It too is at the centre of a large linguistic community—the lusophone. Portuguese comes fourth among the European languages spoken in the world—after English, French, and Spanish, but before German. Portugal is thus one of the four European states that are at the centre of a global network of solidarity and cultural exchange. After decolonization in the 1970s, only the archipelagos of the Azores and Madeira remain from this imperialist and maritime past.

However, despite this early national and state development, there is little evidence that democracy in Portugal has deep historical roots. Taking the long historical view, this seems to have been created *ex nihilo* at the time of the Revolution of Carnations in 1974. Previously, Portugal was influenced by corporatist traditions, especially during the period of the dictatorship (Wiarda 1989). However, it has shown a remarkable capacity for change and modernization.

I would like to thank Jose Magone for commenting on this chapter.

When democracy was established during the Revolution of Carnations in April 1974, it borrowed from several other national experiences: the Basic Law of Germany; the presidential tradition of the French Fifth Republic; Westminster-type parliamentarism; and, at the local level, direct or participatory democracy (Opello 1991). Similar to what happened in Spain, democratization was also encouraged by the accession of Portugal to the European Community in 1986. According to a Portuguese political scientist, José Magone, the European Union 'is an important agent to change mentalities and the improve the quality of life in Portugal. The process of Europeanization is a twin of democratization' (1997).

1.2 Democracy at the Subnational Level

During the period of the *Estado Novo* (1926–74), local government was totally dependent on central government at both the administrative and financial levels (Nunes Silva and André 1994). However, the Revolution of Carnations became a kind of laboratory of democratic experimentation in which Portugal, after many years of dictatorship, explored new and innovative forms of local democracy. The debate centred around whether this should be representative democracy or *autogestion*, whether Portugal should be considered as part of western Europe or as emerging from the Third World, whether it should follow its unique path, or whether it should join the European Community. In the end, the country adopted the forms of liberal democracy that existed in other European states. Nevertheless, the country did retain elements of the experimentation with *autogestion*. Indeed, the post-revolutionary constitution emphasized local government as a major factor of democratization (Magone 1997). In effect, there exist in Portugal today two types of democracy. At the national level, there is what the Dutch political scientist Arend Lijphart has termed 'majoritarian democracy', which follows the Westminster model (although, unlike the latter, it uses a system of proportional representation). At the local level, there remain from the post-Revolution period the tradition of direct democracy and a tradition of consensus that does not exist at the national level.

2. The Institutional Expression of Democracy

2.1 The National Level

The organization of democratic Portugal follows the model laid down in the constitution that was approved by the constituent assembly on 2 April 1976.

The constitution established a semi-presidential republic similar to that of the French Fifth Republic. In this system, the president is directly elected and appoints a prime minister who is responsible to parliament. Another important feature of the first version of the Constitution was its strong socialist orientation: Article 2 spoke of 'the transition toward socialism through the creation of conditions for the democratic exercise of power by the working classes'. The constitution created a unicameral parliament (the Assembly of the Republic) with 250 members. Deputies are elected from party lists, and seats are allocated according to the d'Hondt system of proportional representation. According to the constitution, deputies are meant to represent the whole country and not their individual constituencies.

The first version of the constitution reflected the dominance of the Socialist and Communist left at the time of the revolution. However, in the 1980s, as the centre-right and the right returned to power, there were important constitutional revisions. The most important of these was in 1982 when a revision limited the powers of the president and strengthened those of the parliament, which was henceforth seen as the major instrument of national policy-making (Oppello 1991). The socialistic elements were also modified by giving greater protection to private enterprise.

2.2 The Local and Regional Levels

Local and regional government (Table 11.1) in Portugal are guaranteed by the constitution, which establishes (in sect. VIII, pt. III) the principles of government and decentralization (Council of Europe 1993). There exist *municipios* (municipalities), *freguesias* (parishes), and administrative regions (the latter, although provided for in the constitution, have not yet come into existence—see below). *Comissões de Coordenaçãos* (CCRs, Regional Coordinating Commissions) have existed since the revolution, but these are coordinating bodies directed from the centre with no democratic basis. There are

TABLE 11.1 Total number of local and regional government units, 1993

	Municipalities	Parishes
Mainland	275	4,005
Azores	19	149
Madeira	11	53
Total	305	4,207

Source: Council of Europe (1993).

also two autonomous regions on the island archipelagos of the Azores and Madeira.

Local authorities are elected by proportional representation in secret elections and have two kinds of body: deliberative and executive (Table 11.2). Portuguese local government makes a division between the deliberative assembly and the executive, which is accountable to the former. This structure has also been adopted in the statute for Corsica that was adopted in 1991, and the division also underlies the reforms of local government currently taking place in the United Kingdom. The Portuguese might be seen, therefore, to have been quite innovative in this approach.

However, some of the local-authority assemblies consist of a mixture of directly and indirectly elected representatives, while others consist entirely of directly elected representatives. The municipal assembly is made up of the chairs of the executive committees of the parishes as well as directly elected members. The latter equal the number of parishes plus one, and are elected using the d'Hondt method of proportional representation. If the administrative regions were to come into existence they would consist of fifteen to twenty members representing municipal assemblies plus directly elected members. The municipal representatives will be elected by an electoral college consisting of directly elected members of the municipal assemblies. The rest will be directly elected by the population using the d'Hondt method of proportional representation. Members of the parish assembly are directly elected. In parishes of less than 200 voters there is no assembly, but decisions are taken by a plenary meeting of the residents of the parish (Council of Europe 1993).

There is also a variety of arrangements for the election of the different executives. Members of the *câmara municipal* (municipal chamber) are directly elected by the d'Hondt method from party lists. Their numbers vary between five and seventeen, depending on the size of the electorate. The *junta regional* (regional government), on the other hand, would have been elected by the regional assembly from lists using the system of majority votes. In regions of more than 1.5 million voters it would have consisted of a chairman and six other members and, in other regions, of a chairman and four other members.

TABLE 11.2   Local authority bodies

	Deliberative	Executive
Freguesia (parish)	Parish assembly	*Junta de frueguesia* (parish committee)
Municipio (municipality)	Municipal assembly	*Câmara municipio* (municipal chamber)
Region (region)	Regional assembly	*Junta regional* (regional government)

Sources: Council of Europe (1993); Nunes Silva and André (1994).

Parish committees have a chairman and other members depending on the size of the electorate. In parishes with more than 200 residents, committee members are elected by the assembly using a list system; in those with less than 200, they are elected directly by the plenary session.

2.3 The Autonomous Regions: The Azores and Madeira

The two island archipelagos of the Azores and Madeira have the special status of *autonomous regions*, accorded to them by the 1976 Constitution. This recognizes their specific geographical, social, and cultural characteristics, as well as the existence of autonomist movements on the islands (Oliveira Mendes 1996). The islands have much wider powers of self-government than would have had the administrative regions of the mainland. They have the power to legislate within the framework of the constitution and the laws of the republic on all matters that are of concern to them unless these are within the exclusive domain of the national government. The national government is represented by a minister of the republic, appointed and dismissed by the president of the republic (Council of Europe 1993). The autonomous regions have their own flags, stamps, and national anthems.

2.4 The Metropolitan Areas: Lisbon and Oporto

Because of the size, population, and economic and administrative importance of Lisbon and Oporto, they have been accorded the special status of 'special association of municipalities' (Council of Europe 1993). They are territorial bodies that aim to promote the interests of their inhabitants.

2.5 The Role of Political Parties

The existence of political parties is guaranteed by the constitution. At the national level, elections take place according to party lists using the d'Hondt system. The party system is bipolar with power alternating between two big parties: on the left, is the *Partido Socialista* (PS, Socialist Party), representing the interests of workers, and on the centre-right is the *Partido Social Democrata* (PSD, Social Democratic Party) representing the interests of capital and espousing free-market ideologies. Each of the big parties is flanked by more extreme parties: the *Partido Communista Português* (PCP, Portuguese Communist Party) on the left and the conservatives of the *Partido Popular* (PP, Popular Party), which used to be the *Centro Democrático e Social* (CDS, Democratic and Social Centre) and the Popular Monarchist Party (PPM) on the right. These right-wing parties formed the Democratic Alliance in the

1980s and sought, successfully, to bring about the constitutional revisions mentioned above. The conservatives of the CDS once adopted Christian-Democratic positions, but have now abandoned these and are resolutely nationalist, centralist, and anti-regionalist.

There is a regional dimension to party implantation in Portugal (Nunes Silva and André 1994). First, there is a strong division between the North and South of the country, with the North favouring right-wing parties and the South, parties of the left. Other factors also influence voting behaviour. There is a strong correlation between religious practice and the choice of right-wing parties. Peasants also favour the right, while farm workers support the Communist Party. Urban populations are divided between supporters of the Socialist Party, on the one hand, and of the Social Democrats, on the other. They will also sometimes support new political formations. In the industrial regions of the South the Communist Party is dominant, while in those of the North and Centre it is traditionally the Socialist Party.

The party system at the local level displays a number of important differences compared to the national. In local elections, lists of independents as well as party lists may present themselves. Traditionally, the *municipios* of the North and Centre have been dominated by parties of the centre and the right, PSD and CSD (see Table 11.3). The Socialist Party has had weak representation at the local level, but, in 1989, it made a significant number of gains in these areas of the North and Centre (Table 11.3). In the industrial suburbs of the cities the Communist Party has a strong position. However, at the local level there is also a somewhat different political culture that is based more on consensus politics than is the case at the national level (Nunes Silva and André 1994). This consensus may be a result of close interpersonal relations that occur at the level of the *câmara* and a more pragmatic approach to politics. The important role of the president of the *câmara* also leads to a personalization of the vote. Another factor is the *vote utile*: parties which have little chance of being elected are not chosen. Finally, local elections are sometimes used as a judgement (often negative) of the policies pursued at the national level.

An important feature of these elections is the declining turnout. This was 64.6 per cent in 1976 and 60.9 per cent in 1993. However, it did reach the seventies in 1979 (73.8 per cent) and 1982 (71.4 per cent), although this is still lower than the turnout in national elections.

2.6 The Autonomous Regions

The Portuguese national parties are represented in the Azores and Madeira, with the centre-right parties being dominant. There are autonomist parties but these have little electoral support (Tables 11.4 and 11.5).

TABLE 11.3 Party representation in local elections, 1976–93

Year	Party	No. of votes	%	Municipal chamber	Municipal assembly	Parish assembly
1976[a]	CDS	692,869	16.6	317	48	5,104
	FEPU	737,586	17.7	267	674	2,336
	GDUPS	104,629	2.5	5	—	—
	PPM	7,496	0.2	3	—	—
	PS	1,386,362	33.2	691	1,700	8,407
	PSD	1,012,251	24.3	623	1,259	9,086
1979[b]	AD	1,272,058	25.5	436	2,186	10,368
	APU	1,021,486	20.5	322	1,786	5,086
	CDS	344,902	6.9	165	862	4,267
	PDC	6,616	0.1	2	—	—
	PPM	6,162	0.1	6	—	—
	PS	1,380,134	27.7	523	2,749	10,939
	PSD	733,384	14.7	480	2,255	9,806
	UDP	64,355	1.3	3	—	—
1982[c]	AD	1,004,065	19.6	332	1,656	7,863
	APU	1,061,492	20.7	325	1,781	5,086
	ASDI	7,156	0.1	7	—	—
	CDS	386,527	7.5	191	1,019	4,532
	PPM	11,293	0.2	5	—	—
	PS	1,595,723	31.1	628	3,203	12,848
	PS/UE	37,102	0.7	14	—	—
	PSD	750,295	14.6	442	2,159	9,585
	UP	30,941	0.6	6	—	—
	UDP	31,937	0.6	3	—	—
1985[d]	APU	942,197	19.4	305	1,062	3,675
	CDS	471,838	9.7	224	1,019	4,532
	PDC	7,863	0.2	2	—	—
	PPM	233,897	0.5	3	—	—
	PRD	230,177	4.7	51	270	726
	PS	1,330,388	27.4	571	1,817	9,044
	PSD	1,649,560	34.0	822	2,539	13,117
	UDP	28,701	0.6	3	—	—
1989[e]	CDS	451,163	9.1	179	698	3,434
	CDS/PS	947	—	1	—	—
	MDP	11,354	0.2	1	—	—
	MDP/PRD	3,585	0.1	2	—	—
	PCP/PRD/PEV	22,972	0.5	5	—	—
	PCP/PEV	633,682	12.8	252	848	—
	PDC	5,662	0.1	1	—	—
	PPM	2,765	0.1	1	—	—
	PRD	38,452	0.8	4	25	59
	PRD/MDP	710	—	1	—	—

TABLE 11.3 (cont.)

Year	Party	No. of votes	%	Mandates		
				Municipal chamber	Municipal assembly	Parish assembly
	PS	1,598,846	32.3	728	2,445	11,201
	PS/PCP/MDP/ PEV	180,635	3.7	9	—	—
	PS/CDS	34,866	0.7	15	—	—
	PSD	1,552,846	31.4	781	2,582	13,261
	PSD/CDS	31,548	0.6	4	—	—
	PSD/CDS/PPM	161,420	3.3	9	—	—
	UDP	16,093	0.3	4	—	—
1993[f]	CDS/PP	455,357	8.4	133	557	2,719
	MDP	1,386	—	1	—	—
	MPT	23,408	0.4	14	—	—
	PCP/PEV	689,928	12.8	300	803	2,747
	PRD	—	—	—	2	10
	PS	1,950,133	36.1	795	2,445	12,312
	PS/CDS-PP	11,482	0.2	7	—	—
	PSD	1,552,846	31.4	807	2,582	13,679
	PS/PCP/PEV	95	—	2	—	—
	PS/PCP/PEV/ PSR/UDP	200,822	3.7	11	—	—
	PS/PCP/PEV/ PSR/UDP/PDA	10,221	0.2	4	—	—
	PSD	1,822,925	33.7	807	—	—
	PSN	28,922	0.5	3	—	—

[a] Electoral constituencies: 304; registered voters: 6,457,440; voters: 4,170,494 (64.6%).
[b] Electoral constituencies: 305; registered voters: 6,761,751; voters: 4,987,734 (73.8%).
[c] Electoral constituencies: 305; registered voters: 7,191,084; voters: 5,131,483 (71.4%).
[d] Electoral constituencies: 305; registered voters: 7,594,753; voters: 4,853,529 (63.9%).
[e] Electoral constituencies: 305; registered voters: 8,121,045; voters: 4,946,196 (60.9%).
[f] Electoral constituencies: 305; registered voters: 8,121,045; voters: 4,946,196 (60.9%).

Ad, *Aliança Democrática* [AD-C, *Aliança Democrática dos Açores* (loose electoral alliance based on the CDS/PP)]; APU, *Aliança Povo Unido*; ASDI, *Associação de Social-Democratas Independentes*; CDS, *Centro Democrático e Social* [CDS/PP, *Partido Popular* (formerly CDS)]; CDU, *Coligação Democrática Unitária*; FEPU, *Frente Eleitoral Povo Unido*; GUDPS, *Gabinete de Dinamização da Unidade*; MDP, *Movimento de Esquerda Socialista*; MPT, *Movimento Partido de Terra*; PCP, *Partido Comunista Português*; PDA, *Partido Democrático do Atlântico*; PDC, *Partido Democracia Cristã*; PEV, *Partido Ecolistica os Verdes*; PPD/PSD, *Partido Social Democrata* (formerly PPD, *Partido Popular Democrático*)]; PPM, *Partido Popular Monárquico*; PRD, *Partido Renovador Democrático*; PS, *Partido Socialista*; PS/UE, *Partido Socialista/União de Esquerda*; PSR, *Partido Socialista Revolucionário*; UDP, *União Democrático Popular*; UP, *União Popular*; UPT, *União Popular de Trabalho*.

Source: Secretariado Técnico, quoted in Magone (1997).

TABLE 11.4   Electoral results in the Azores regional elections, 1976–96

Party	Year					
	1976	1980	1984	1988	1992	1996
PPD/PSD	53.8	57.3	56.3	48.6	53.6	41
PS	32.8	27.3	24.2	35.5	36.4	45.8
CDS-PP	7.5	4.5	7.9	7	—	7.3
PCP-PEV, APU, CDU	2.2	3.2	5.3	3.8	2.3	3.5
PDA	—	2.3	1.6	1.3	1.4	0.3
AD-A	—	—	—	—	4.6	—
Abstentions	32.2	23.9	37.6	41.2	37.6	41

Note: See Table 11.3 for full names of the political parties.
Source: Comissão Nacional de Eleições, *Resultados Eleitorais*.

TABLE 11.5   Electoral results in Madeira regional elections, 1976–96

Party	Year					
	1976	1980	1984	1988	1992	1996
PPD/PSD	60.40	65.33	67.65	62.36	56.86	56.87
PS	22.63	15	15.33	16.79	22.51	24.84
CDS-PP	9.62	6.46	6.13	8.19	8.09	7.31
CDU	—	3.13	2.73	—	2.96	4.04
UDP	5.16	5.48	5.51	7.73	4.63	4.03
Autonomists	—	—	—	—	2.41	0.64
Abstentions	25.2	19.15	28.57	32.35	33.47	34.74

Note: See Table 11.3 for full names of the pontical parties.
Source: Comissão Nacional de Eleições, *Resultados Eleitorais*.

Political representatives at the local level reflect reasonably faithfully the characteristics of the general population (Magone 1997). However, there are differences between the municipal and the parish levels. At the municipal level, according to two surveys undertaken by the Ministry of Home Affairs in 1982 and 1989, the majority of elected members to the municipal chamber and the municipal assembly originated from the higher social classes of the population: 'higher and middle technical and scientific cadres' and 'landowners, directors and entrepreneurs' (quoted in Magone 1997). At the parish level, on the other hand, the elected members were recruited evenly from all social strata with a relative majority coming from 'industrial and agricultural workers'. However, it is also the case that almost one-third of all presidents and members of local government were elected from the 'industrial and agricultural workers' group of society (ibid.).

Women are seriously under-represented at the local level, perhaps because Portugal continues to reflect traditional attitudes of male domination; only 7 per cent of representatives are women. They are slightly better represented in the assemblies than in the executives; 11 per cent of municipal assemblies and 7 per cent of the members of parish assemblies are women. Six per cent of the members of municipal chambers and only 4 per cent of the members of parish boards are women. Four per cent are presidents of local bodies (ibid.).

3. The Practice of Subnational Democracy

3.1 The Role of Policy Networks and Pressure Groups

Little research has been carried out on the role of policy networks in the practice of Portuguese local democracy, and how these might affect the policy-making system at this level. However, as has already been pointed out above, there are dense interpersonal relations among politicians and citizens at this level, which sometimes lead to cross-party collaboration and pragmatism on local issues. Furthermore, the operation of the Commissions of Regional Coordination (CCRs) stimulated the formation of interest groups at the regional level, and these have been intensified by the attempts by international organizations such as the EU and OECD to develop what is known as the 'partnership approach'. This is based on a recently developed model of regional and local development predicated on a bottom-up approach to development, involving the mobilization of regional and local actors in a clearly defined development project (see also Chapter 3).[1] In Portugal, initiatives in the 1980s to promote this model have included the Local Employment Initiatives (ILEs) of the OECD and the Local Employment Development Action (LEDA) of the EU (Syrett 1997). Other initiatives include the Regional Development Plan of Portugal, approved by the EU, which seeks the creation of Agencies for the Promotion of Regional Development as well as the European Commission's LEADER programme (ibid). Undoubtedly, these initiatives are leading to the development of new interest groups and policy

---

[1] This approach has been criticized by Syrett (1997) who points out correctly that the OECD and EU approaches to 'partnership' are different, the former being based on a neo-liberal approach, the latter on a neo-corporatist approach. However, Syrett thinks that both approaches consecrate existing power differences between partners: in fact, there may not be qualified 'partners' to enter into these relationships in rural areas of Portugal thus leaving the leadership to already existing powerful interests.

networks or the development or the strengthening of existing ones at the regional and local levels.

3.2 Critiques of Regional and Local Democracy

It has been argued that 'Portugal remains characterized by a strongly centralized and bureaucratic state system poorly suited to respond to local difference' (Syrett 1997). The setting up of the administrative regions has also been delayed because of an interminable debate about the number and the geographical boundaries of these regions. A bill has been implemented in a vain attempt to set up the new regions (see below). Syrett (1997) has also pointed out the absence of all types of local-level community groups (indispensable for local development based on 'partnership'), although this is now changing with the coming into existence of local cultural associations and a range of voluntary and Church-based groups.

3.3 Citizens' Attitudes to Local Government

There is a dearth of indicators on citizen's attitudes, but participation in, and abstention from, elections may be used as indicators of attitudes. The Portuguese are also among the top four states (with Ireland, Greece, and Sweden) whose citizens are the most attached to their own countries (97 per cent). Citizens of these four states also show the highest attachment to their own town or village, with Portugal at 94 per cent (*Eurobarometer*, 44, 1996). Another striking indicator of attitudes and behaviour in relation to local government is the higher rate of abstention in local elections compared to national elections (Table 11.6).

TABLE 11.6   Abstention rates in local and national elections, 1976–95

Year	National Assembly	Municipal Chamber
1976	16.5	34.8
1979	12.9	26.2
1983	20.9	28.4[a]
1985	24.6	36.5
1987	27.4	38.8[b]
1991	31.8	36.6[c]
1995	33.7	39.9[d]

[a] 1982 figures.   [b] 1989 figures.   [c] 1993 figures.   [d] 1997 figures.

Sources: Nunes Silva and André (1994); Ministério da Administração Interna.

Commentators such as Nunes Silva and André (1994) argue that these differences do not necessarily reflect a lack of interest in local politics on the part of Portuguese citizens. Rather is it a case that the party system that operates at the national level is not completely appropriate for politics at the local level. At this level there is an absence of partisanship and a greater degree of 'personalization' of politics. For example, the president of the municipal chamber is often an individual who adopts a consensual approach even towards those from other parties. The latter also recognize this characteristic of the president and work closely with him. The municipality of Lisbon is a good example of this approach. Since the 1988 local elections there is an alliance between Communists and Socialists in the city, which is a far cry from the situation at the national level.

A survey carried out in 1992 gives some indication of the attitudes of politicians and interest-group leaders with regard to a number of issues including regionalization (Opello 1993). More than half of the politicians thought that the regional level was the most appropriate for the delivery of a number important services: health (60 per cent), agriculture (78.7 per cent), secondary education (63.8 per cent), industrialization (70.2 per cent), credit (60.6 per cent), and transport (60.6 per cent). In only three areas did a majority feel the central state was the most appropriate: foreign trade (54.3 per cent), scientific research (55.3 per cent), and employment (77.4 per cent). The interest-group leaders generally agreed with these opinions. However, there was a great deal of dissatisfaction with regional functioning (Table 11.7). Of the elected politicians, 74.6 per cent, and 79.4 per cent of interest-group leaders were either little or not satisfied with regional functioning. Nevertheless, the author of the report concludes that the answers to the questionnaires show

TABLE 11.7   Degree of satisfaction with regional function (percentages), 1992

Degree of satisfaction	Region*						
	Azores	Madeira	Norte	Centro	Lisboa e V. Do Tejo	Alentejo	Algarve
Very satisfied	5	8	3	1	0	3	0
Somewhat satisfied	20	35	32	17	13	11	5
Little satisfied	61	42	49	57	54	54	36
Not satisfied	14	10	15	24	33	32	59

* With the exception of the two autonomous regions, the Azores and Madeira, these refer to the planning regions administered by the regional coordinating committees (CCRs).
Source: Opello (1993: 176).

that there is 'a strong desire to gain decision-making autonomy *vis-à-vis* the central government' even if the latter does administer EU policies efficiently (Opello 1993: 185).

4. Challenges and Opportunties for Subnational Democracy

4.1 The European Challenge

Portugal, along with Spain, acceded to the European Community in 1986. There is little doubt that this event was highly important in the consolidation of democracy in both countries (Magone 1998).[2] Portuguese people are overall quite positive about Europe, a feeling that is growing. According to a Eurobarometer survey (no. 43, 1995), 63 per cent said that the EU made them feel 'hopeful', compared to 43 per cent in 1994. The Portuguese were also among the least adamant with regard to keeping decision-making at the national level: 47 per cent compared to 69 per cent of Danes, 67 per cent of Greeks, and 62 per cent of Austrians. This positive attitude toward the EU was confirmed by the 1996 Eurobarometer report that showed the Portuguese among the top five member states supporting the Union, 48 per cent (although an equal 48 per cent did not support it).

The EU has also been a challenge in terms of the implementation of the various Community funds and programmes that have arrived in Portugal. At first, these were strictly controlled by the central government (as in Ireland). However, it soon became evident that the central government alone could not implement these funds effectively (Reis and Négrier 1998). This has resurrected the debate on regionalization and was an important influence on the decision by the Socialist government elected in 1995 to finally pass legislation to implement the constitutional provision for administrative regions (see below). The European dimension has also been important in facilitating links between Portuguese local authorities and other bodies outside Portugal. These include cross-border links with Spanish regions as well as membership of pan-European associations such as the Conference of Peripheral Maritime Regions, especially its Atlantic Arc Commission (Reis and Négrier 1998). These developments have played an important part in widening the perspectives of at least some of Portugal's local politicians outside that of the

---

[2] In the case of Portugal, it meant that the country moved towards the western capitalist model of liberal democracy rather than toward the more left-wing and Third-Worldist versions that also had their supporters at the time of the Revolution of Carnations in 1974.

nation-state. On the other hand, the European dimension has also stimulated the formation of anti-European sentiments on the part of some of the centre and centre-right parties that fear that Portuguese national sovereignty will be eroded. Such parties also tend to oppose regionalization.

4.2 Central–Local Relations and Strengthening Regional and Local Democracy

The pressure to set up administrative regions came from the functional imperatives of the implementation of European funds as well as from those regions with strong cultural identities (Reis and Négrier 1998). The Socialist Party saw regionalization as a way of bringing about administrative modernization and also of enhancing democracy by bringing decision-making closer to citizens (Magone 1999). They also argue that thirteen out of the fifteen EU member states are now regionalized. In 1995, the newly elected Socialist government promised to implement the constitutional provisions for administrative regions on mainland Portugal. Finally, a Law of 28 April 1998 created eight regions: Entre Douro e Minho, Trás-Os Montes e Alto Douro, Beira Interior, Beira Litoral, Estremadura e Ribatejo, Alentejo, Algarve, and Lisboa e Setúbal.

The administrative regions would have been territorial authorities with administrative and financial autonomy (Art. 1, Law 56/91). Their main task was to coordinate the activities of local authorities and to mediate between local and central government. They would have followed the pattern of other local authorities with a regional assembly and a regional executive. The centre and centre-right, although they approved a Law on Regions in 1991, opposed the current proposals because of fears that they would endanger national unity as well as increase bureaucracy. They proposed instead a programme of decentralization, but not regionalization (*El Pais*, 7 September 1998). The regionalization reform was put to the test in a referendum of all Portuguese voters held on 8 November 1998. The reform proposal was rejected.

5. Innovative Approaches to Improving Subnational Democracy

Portugal has been quite innovative in exploring approaches to strengthen regional and local democracy. The following are some of the methods used (Council of Europe 1993).

- *Local/regional referendums*—these have existed since 1990 and are held on issues within the exclusive powers of the local authorities. Certain subjects, however, such as financial matters may not be subject to referendum.
- *Public Meetings*—meetings of the deliberative bodies of the local authorities are open to active participation by the public. The executive bodies must organize monthly meetings to answer questions of local interest.
- *Extraordinary meetings*—these may occur on the initiative of local residents.
- *Publication of minutes of meetings*—these are produced by local authorities and made public.
- *Publication of decisions*—before decisions are enforced they must be published in public places.
- *Associations of local residents*—the constitution allows for the formation of 'local people's organizations'. These associations enjoy certain rights in local authorities, especially at parish level, such as taking part in meetings or exercising some responsibilities delegated by the authority.
- *Groups of citizens as candidates in elections*—these may stand in parish elections alongside the political-party lists.
- *Plenary assemblies of voters*—this is a system of direct democracy that occurs in parishes with less than 200 voters where there is no elected deliberative body.
- *Right to organize petitions*—the Constitutions permits Portuguese citizens to organize petitions, make representations, submit protests, and lodge complaints in writing.

6. *Conclusions*

Portugal, like Spain, although following a rather different trajectory, has passed within the space of twenty years from a non-democratic, authoritarian regime to one characterized by a healthy practice of liberal democracy. This transition to democracy was greatly assisted by Portugal's accession to the European Community in 1986. This allowed the country to take its place among the nations of western Europe as a fully fledged democratic country. Local democracy has also taken time to develop as the local was completely dominated by the centre during the dictatorship. However, the national and local levels of democracy have rather different characteristics. The national level is dominated by the bipolar competition between the two big parties of the right and left and the parties gravitating around them. The local level is more characterized by 'personalization' and party consensus as well as by close relations between local politicians and the electorate. There is a certain amount of territorial differentiation in Portugal with some regions more strongly identified with some parties than with others.

Perhaps the biggest lacuna in the Portuguese subnational system has been the lack of a regional tier of government, with the exception of the two island archipelagos of the Azores and Madeira despite the provision for these in the constitution. An attempt to rectify this was the regionalization programme, launched by the Socialists after their election in 1995 with a view to strengthening administrative modernization but also regional democracy. This was rejected in a referendum in November 1998.

References

COUNCIL OF EUROPE (1993). *Portugal: Structure and Operation of Local and Regional Democracy*. Strasbourg.

MAGONE, J. (1997). *European Portugal: The Difficult Road to Sustainable Democracy*. Basingstoke: Macmillan.

——(1998). 'Portugal and the European Union', in D. Dinan (ed.), *Encyclopaedia of the European Union*. Basingstoke: Macmillan.

——(1999). 'European Union Governance and National Territorial Politics: Rewriting Marginality in Spain and Portugal', in N. Parker (ed.), *The Margins of Europe*. Basingstoke: Macmillan.

NUNES SILVA, C. and ANDRÉ, I. M. (1994). 'Portugal: Le Pouvoir Local'. *Peuples Méditerranéens*, 66: 91–102.

OLIVEIRA MENDES, J. M. DE (1996). 'O regionalismo como construção identitária. A caso dos Açores'. *Rivista Critica d Ciências Sociais*, 45: 127–41.

OPELLO, W. (1991). *Portugal: From Monarchy to Pluralist Democracy*. Boulder, CO.: Westview.

——(1993). 'Portuguese Regionalism in the Transition from the *Estado Novo* to the Single Market', in R. Leonardi (ed.), *The Regions in the European Community: The Regional Response to the Single Market in the Underdeveloped Areas*. London: Frank Cass.

REIS, J. and NÉGRIER, E. (1998). 'Territoires économiques et échanges politiques', in E. Négrier and B. Jouve (eds), *Que Gouvernent les Régions d'Europe? Échanges politiques et moblisations régionales*. Paris: L'Harmattan.

SYRETT, S. (1997). 'The Politics of Partnership: The Role of Social Partners in Local Economic Development in Portugal'. *European Urban and Regional Studies*, 4/2: 99–114.

WIARDA, H. (1989). *The Transition to Democracy in Spain and Portugal*. Washington, DC: Institute for Public Policy Research.

12

Greece: Between 'Henosis' and Decentralization

John Loughlin

1. History and Concept of Democracy

1.1 Historical Background

Greece became part of the Ottoman Empire, along with the rest of the Balkan peninsula, in the fifteenth century and lived under Turkish rule for some four centuries (Legg and Roberts 1997). After the uprising that started in 1821 against Turkish occupation, they were the first of all the Balkan peoples to win partial liberation, with the London Protocol of 7 May 1832, which recognized the independence of a new Greek state, though only for part of Greece. The newly independent Greek state established a centralized government along the lines of the French Napoleonic state. Before and after Greek independence there was a division among nationalists as to whether the new state should adopt the institutions of western states (modernizers) or whether it should return to the institutions of Byzantine Greece (traditionalists). In the end, both had their wishes to some extent. Greece adopted the institutions and administration of representative democracy well before many western states did so. However, these institutions were informed by the culture and mentality of the Ottoman period and its political culture owed much to the practices of clientelism and patronage that had developed during that period. Thus, the Greek political system has been marked by the concentration of power at the centre and a less than satisfactory system of public administration. The question of modern Greece's national identity, and whether the country is 'western' or 'non-western' has never been finally resolved and still affects the nature and practice of democracy in the country.

At independence, the surface area of the state consisted of only 36 per cent of the present Greek territory. The remainder was added in a piecemeal way; the most recent addition being in 1947. This territorial expansion sometimes brought Greece into conflict with neighbours, such as Turkey, where some politicians made claims on the Aegean Islands and the Dodecanese. There were also disputes with Bulgaria over Macedonia and Thrace (Verney 1997). Some of these historical conflicts are still alive or, in the case of Macedonia, have again arisen as a result of the break-up of Yugoslavia. This history of irredentism and national liberation struggles and the presence of military threats in a hostile neighbourhood have led Greek nationalism to emphasize territorial unification and centralism summed up in the political ideology of *henosis*. It has also acted as a catalyst for a high degree of centralization, which, nevertheless, has been characterized by institutional and organizational fragility. This combination in turn led to intensified clientelistic relations between different levels of government. A strong civil society did not develop (Legg and Roberts 1997), but rather one that has been dominated by the political parties. The Greek state and political traditions tended to look back to the glorious past of the Hellenic period, sometimes stressing what made Greece different from the rest of Europe (sometimes called 'Hellenism' or 'Grecianism') (Wenturis 1997). Other Greeks were conscious of the contribution this civilization had made to European history.

The development of the concept of democracy in modern Greece must be seen within a context whereby the government was dominated by a ruling elite that saw itself as embodying the values and legitimacy of the nation (Wenturis 1997). This ruling elite tended to view any opposition, even that found in parliament and at the local level, as a threat to the integrity of the nation. Thus, there developed a distance between government and parliament and between the state and society, with the central organs of the state exercising a tight control over all other levels of administration and politics. The Greek political system of the nineteenth and early twentieth centuries has been called 'oligarchic parliamentarism' (Mouzelis 1995). A small number of families of notables controlled the parliament and dominated the political parties during this period. The notables had their power bases in specific areas and operated a system of 'decentralized clientelism' (ibid.). However, after the military coup in 1909, the Liberal Party of Eleuthérios Venizelos rose to power, and this led to the break-up of the grip of the traditional notables over the political system and facilitated the emergence of centralized political parties. Nevertheless, these parties continued to have a particularistic/clientelistic character right up to the 1967–74 military dictatorship (ibid.). The Civil War (1946–9) fought between Communists and anti-Communists left bitter memories and accentuated the suspicion of the conservative ruling elites of any form of dissent. It was only in 1974, after the fall of the colonels' dictatorship and the rise to power of *Panellinio Sosialistiko Kinima* (PASOK, Pan-Hellenic Socialist Movement) led by Andreas Papandreou that there was some movement toward a democratic system marked by a left–right alternance in government.

1.2 Democracy at the Subnational Levels[1]

In the democratic system of ancient Athens, Cleisthenes created the *deme* (municipality) as a unit of local government. According to some modern Greeks, this tradition of local self-government continued uninterrupted in Greece, and the communities of the Middle Ages were just a variation on the ancient autonomous city states adapted to the new situation in which Greece found itself. All the occupying powers accepted Greek self-government in many parts of the country, either because they had no choice or in order to reduce administrative costs and more effectively exploit their subjects. The community thus became a small ethnic pocket in which the subject peoples moved and acted freely, helping each other, showing solidarity, maintaining ethnic traditions and self-government, and joining forces in the concerted fight for freedom until the great national uprising against the occupying power was launched in 1821. This, at least, is the mythology of contemporary Greek nationalism held by many politicians and citizens but clearly which needs to be accepted with a great deal of caution.

In 1912, the government of Eleutherios Venizelos came to power and passed a law on the establishment of municipalities and communities (Official Gazette 58/1912). According to one interpretation, the basic aim of the Venizelos government at the time was to create a modern state by strengthening the central political system, with particular emphasis on parliamentary government. Local centres of power—the municipal mayors—therefore, had to be weakened. The 1912 Law also formalized the division into municipalities and communities on the basis that the administration of rural and municipal areas had to be organized differently. Municipal and community authorities have almost always been elected by the people. This, though, was not the case during the period from the establishment of dictatorship in 1936, through the Second World War (1940–4) and the civil war (1945–9); thus municipal and community authorities were elected normally on 11 February 1934 and not again until 15 April 1951. Throughout this time, municipalities and

---

[1] The following section contains two interpretations of the history of local democracy in modern Greece. The first was supplied to the author by the Greek national delegation to the Committee of the Regions who disagreed with the excessive criticism of the first drafts of this chapter. In fact, one Greek delegate wrote a counter chapter and the national delegation wished this glowing account of Greek democracy to be included in the study. Naturally, this was unacceptable to the author as the study was meant to an independent and critical survey of the issue. The second interpretation, much less benign than the first, is drawn from a number of contemporary scholars of modern Greece, for the most part Greek themselves. It seems to us that this is a more accurate reflection of reality but it is interesting to include the benign interpretation if only to see how myth-building is not totally dead in Greece today.

communities were run by authorities appointed by the government in power at the time.

Another exception was the junta period from 1967 to 1974, when the elected municipal and community authorities were replaced by government appointees. The last elections before the dictatorship were held on 5 July 1964, and the first elections after the fall of the junta took place on 30 March 1975. Since then, municipal and community authorities have been directly elected every four years by the local population on the basis of a secret ballot and universal suffrage. Since the foundation of the Greek state, the prefecture has been a level of local government covering the whole country. Until 1994, prefectures were governed by a prefect appointed by central government.

Another, less benign, interpretation found in the literature written by Greek historians and social scientists sees Greek local government as having its origins in the administrative system that existed during the Ottoman Empire. According to this view, it has been dominated by local magnates and operated in a clientelistic manner, but controlled by the centre. The right-wing governments that ruled Greece after the civil war regarded local government with suspicion, as this became a stronghold of the left, especially of the Communists who were on the losing side of this war. During the military dictatorship (1967–74) the colonels abolished the post of elected mayor and replaced it with government appointees. It was only restored with the transition to democracy. Another factor limiting the democratic character of local government is that many of those registered on the electoral rolls of the municipalities live outside them in the large cities. While they vote in local elections they take little direct interest in what happens in their commune (Verney 1997).

Until very recently there has been no regional level of government or administration in Greece and no regionalist movements demanding this. This is true even of large islands such as Crete. In fact, this is unusual in European terms in so far as most European islands are governed by special statutes of autonomy (political, administrative, or fiscal) which take account of their insularity. In Greece the pressures of centralization and the threat to the islands from some of Greece's neighbours have meant that regionalism as a political movement, even on the islands, is almost non-existent.[2] Only in recent years have there been some moves towards regionalization as a result of Europeanization, although this has occurred primarily for pragmatic reasons rather than out of a concern for improved democratic governance.

---

[2] There are 220 inhabited islands with a surface area of 25,042 km^2 and 1,384,110 inhabitants (1981 census). This represents 13% of the population and 19% of the territory.

2. The Institutional Expression of Democracy

2.1 The National Level

After the fall of the military dictatorship, the monarchy was abolished following a popular referendum held in December 1974, and a new constitution was promulgated in 1975 (Mahaira-Odoni 1995). Greece became a parliamentary republic whose president is head of state and whose prime minister is the head of government. In June 1986 an amendment to the constitution reduced the powers of the president. The political system formally follows that of other western liberal democracies: sovereignty rests with the people, and the executive, legislative, and judicial branches of government operate according to the principle of checks and balances. Every adult citizen has the right to participate in the affairs of the country, and the constitution guarantees the protection of a full range of human rights (ibid.). Although there is freedom of religion, the Orthodox Church has a special status and is closely linked to the state. Parliament consists of a unicameral assembly of 300 deputies. The government consists of the prime minister who appoints ministers and deputy ministers. The latter do not need to be members of the assembly. The Greek legal system is based on Roman civil law, but is influenced by French and German sources as well as classical Greek philosophy (ibid.).

2.2 The Regional and Local Levels

The Greek state was organized, as we have seen above, as a centralized system, with ministries and central government departments at national level, prefectures at regional level, and municipalities and communities at local level. The intermediate level was the prefecture, but this was a level of administration and, until recently, existed primarily as a means by which the prefects exercised power on behalf of the central government. As one author comments: 'the concept of popular involvement in local affairs was remote at best and failed to take any firm root in Greek governance' (Mahaira-Odoni 1995: 213).

At local level, public administrative authority lies with the first-tier organs of local government (i.e., the municipalities and communities). Here, the basic authorities are the mayor and municipal council in the case of municipalities and the community president and community council in the case of communities. All these bodies are directly elected every four years on the basis of a secret ballot and universal suffrage by the people of each municipality or community.

2.2.1 The Region

Even before Greece joined the European Community, there had been some concern that its lack of regional structures would hinder it from receiving European Regional Development Fund (Verney 1997). As a result, a regional development plan was drawn up just before accession in 1980. In March 1982 the PASOK Government submitted a memorandum to the European Commission requesting special treatment for Greece's 'economic peculiarities'. The result was the Integrated Mediterranean Programmes (IMPs) based on an integrated programme approach and the principles of subsidiarity and partnership. The most important consequence for Greece in administrative terms was that, under the terms of the IMP regulation, these programmes necessitated setting up a level of regional administration that had not existed before. Greece was divided into six geographical areas[3] for purposes of the IMPs and, subsequently, Law 1622/86 created thirteen regions (Papageorgiou and Verney 1992).[4]

These regions were a decentralized level of the state administration and not a level of regional government (Council of Europe 1993). Each region was headed by a regional governor representing the government. He or she was assisted by a regional council responsible for 'democratic planning' and made up of representatives of local government. However, the regions had no budgets and no allocated personnel of their own. There is no hierarchical relationship with other levels of local government and administration. Nevertheless, despite these limitations and the fact that the regions have little legitimacy as organs of subnational democratic practice, they did represent a break with the previous highly centralized Greek tradition and constituted a major innovation (Verney 1997).

From 13 July 1994, the regions have also become areas of state administration, each headed by a general secretary. The regional general secretary represents the state and central government in the region. Each region has a regional council with responsibility for democratic planning and regional development. The members of the regional council are elected representatives of first- and second-tier local authorities and of business and professional circles, who are meant to speak for all citizens and thus ensure maximum social consensus in the process of regional development.

In 1997, the Greek Parliament passed a law that made the region a deconcentrated administrative entity with its own organization, its own budget, and

---

[3] The Aegean Islands, Attica, Central and Eastern Greece, Crete, Northern Greece, and Western Greece/Peloponnese. A seventh Greek IMP covered the entire national territory (Verney 1997).

[4] Attica, Central Greece, Central Macedonia, Crete, Eastern Macedonia and Thrace, Epirus, the Ionian Islands, the North Aegean Islands, the Peloponnese, the South Aegean Islands, Thessaly, Western Greece, and Western Macedonia.

its own staff. The region gains new responsibilities as well as those field services already operating within its territory. The regional council is mainly responsible for democratic planning and most of its members are still drawn from local government.

2.2.2 The Nomoi

The *nomoi* (prefectures) are the administrative divisions of Greece. Originally, under Decree 3/15 of April 1833, the country was divided into ten prefectures and forty-two provinces. In 1866, after the Ionian Islands had been reunited with the rest of Greece, another three prefectures and eleven provinces were added. Under an 1899 law the country was divided into twenty-six prefectures. When the rest of Greece was liberated and the new territories annexed, the number of prefectures increased to fifty-one, which is the present number.

The prefectures were each headed by a *nomarch* (prefect or governor), who was the principal agent of the central government with responsibility for coordinating the activities of the central departments in his or her territory. In the 1950s there was some administrative decentralization that made the prefectures into a level of planning and implementation when each prefecture was allocated a separate public works budget (Verney and Papageorgiou 1992). In the 1980s, after Greece's accession to the EC, the prefecture acquired more responsibilities, such as health and education (ibid.). However, these attempts at decentralization were generally judged to be a failure as the prefectures were too numerous and too small and, in some areas, hardly functioned at all.

In 1982 the PASOK Government, which had promised to initiate a programme of political decentralization before it came to power, enacted Law 1235/1982 on the Exercise of Government Policy and Establishment of Popular Representation in the Provinces (Mahaira-Odoni 1995) which relaunched the consultative prefecture councils. The councils remained largely advisory, but were explicitly allocated a role and decision-making powers in the planning process. They were to meet more frequently (at least once a month) and had a stronger representation from local interests. Local government representatives were to make up half the membership. The other half are elected by prefecture-level professional organizations, agricultural cooperatives, and chambers of commerce. However, the councils still did not constitute a genuine, popularly elected level of local government, although clearly interest groups now had a greater input into this level of decision-making. Law 1235/1982 explicitly stated that the prefecture councils were a transitional institution to prepare the way for new tiers of local government (ibid.). Law 1622, passed in 1986, did provide for upgraded prefecture councils with 75 per cent of their members to be directly elected and 15–20 per cent to be chosen by interest groups. However, when *Nea Demokratia* (ND, New

Democracy) returned to power in 1989, the law was not implemented and they renewed the emphasis on centralization. When PASOK came back to power in 1993, they took up once again the decentralization programme. The key change here was the upgrading of the prefectures to 'second-level territo-rial authorities' with the direct election of the prefects and the prefecture councils. In October 1994 the prefects were elected for the first time. Until 1994 the prefect acted as a one-member state regional authority with general responsibilities, exercising considerable power within the prefecture; under the laws on decentralized administration, prefects carried out important tasks on their own account and—under delegating legal provisions—on behalf of most government ministries, with a few exceptions, such as the Finance Min-istry, the Foreign Ministry, and the Ministries of Justice, Defence, and Mer-chant Shipping.

Since 1 January 1995, the prefecture has functioned as the second tier of local government, with legal personality and governed by a prefect and council whom citizens elect directly every four years on the basis of a secret ballot and universal suffrage. The elections take place on the same day as the elections for the mayors and councils of municipalities and for presidents and councils of communities throughout the country.The prefectures are now run by elected prefects and an elected prefectoral council. Greece is the only country with a system of elected prefects, which, according to members of the Greek delegation to the Committee of the Regions, has been a complete success during the first four-year term!

2.2.3 The Local Level—Demes and Koinotites

Greece was divided into municipalities after its unification. In 1834, a total of 457 municipalities were established throughout the country. There were three types of municipalities, according to the size of their population: those with a population of over 10,000; those with a population of over 2,000; those with a population of under 2,000. In 1912, a basic change took place in local self-government. The municipalities that had existed since 1834 were abolished, and a system of *demes* (municipalities) and *koinotites* (communities) was introduced. Urban areas became municipalities and rural areas communities. This system of municipalities and communities came into effect from 1914 and has continued until today.

In practice, the original criteria for distinguishing municipalities and com-munities have gradually become obsolete. Of the 457 municipalities today, 223 (48.45 per cent) have a population of less than 5,000 inhabitants. Of the 5,318 communities, 4,491 (84.44 per cent) have a population of less than 1,000 inhabitants; 3,164 (59.49 per cent) have a population of less than 500; and 1,995 (37.51 per cent) have a population of less than 300 inhabitants (Table 12.1).

TABLE 12.1   Size of local authorities, 1992

No. of inhabitants	No. of local authorities	% of total no. of authorities
<1,000	4,704	79
1,000–5,000	1,201	17
5,000–10,000	74	1.2
10,000–50,000	98	2
50,000–100,000	17	0.3
>100,000	8	0.1

Source: Council of Europe (1993).

Thus, local government in Greece has been extremely fractionalized. In 1981 there were around 6,000 local government units for a population of 9.7 million (Verney 1997). There is also a monastic community of about 1,500 monks (in about twenty monasteries) on Mount Athos, which has administrative and economic autonomy within the Greek state.[5] In 1981, there were around 300 munipalities and 5,700 communes. Municipalities were supposed to have a minimum of 10,000 inhabitants and communes a minimum of 1,000. However, over 3,000 communes had less than 500 inhabitants (ibid.). It is obvious that these tiny communes could not possibly perform many of the functions allocated to them. Instead, they became completely dependent on the prefecture. Indeed, in constitutional terms, the prefecture exercised an a priori legal control over their actions.

The PASOK reforms of the 1980s curtailed prefectoral controls over local government, and the municipalities now send representatives to sit on the prefectoral councils. There were also attempts to strengthen democratic processes at the local level (Christofilopoulou 1987). A new proportional electoral law was introduced to allow more representation of minority parties. Neighbourhood councils were elected in Athens, Piraeus, and Salonika, while in the smaller towns municipal councils may decide to hold elections for community councils. These councils are purely advisory and have no resources of their own, but were meant to encourage grass-roots involvement in decision-making. However, the councils have become dominated by the political parties, while the general public has tended to be increasingly absent (ibid.). Other attempts have been made to encourage the voluntary amalgamation of some of the tiny municipalities. This has been largely unsuccessful. However, some new institutions have managed to establish themselves: *development syndicates* are voluntary associations of municipalities, which form in order to

---

[5] Although, spiritually, the peninsula is subject to the jurisdiction of the Patriarch of Constantinople (Istanbul in Turkey).

obtain a special grant from the Public Investment Programme; *planning contracts* are drawn up between local authorities and public sector bodies with a view to coordinating the provision of a service or other aspect of a development programme; *municipal enterprises* are an attempt to develop a more flexible way of providing municipal services jointly with other entrepreneurs and outside the usual bureaucratic controls (ibid.). Although these efforts at reform have been regarded by most commentators as piecemeal and failing to dent the excessive centralization of the Greek political system, one author has commented that '[n]onetheless, there is an effort at a progressive democratization and devolution of powers to local councils and a potential for a radical developmental and participatory role of local authorities' (Christofilopoulou 1987: 10). Furthermore, the PASOK decentralization law of 1986 went much further and would have considerably strengthened local democracy and decentralized democratic planning, but, unfortunately, was not implemented.

More than ten years of experience with voluntary cooperation between municipalities and communities, which began in the 1980s, was extremely valuable, because it made people aware, especially in rural areas, that the problem of strengthening the municipalities must be tackled in a completely different way. In other words, communities and municipalities must be required to merge. Central government legislation in 1997 created strong first-tier local government in Greece by merging municipalities and communities. The 457 municipalities and 5,318 communities are being merged to make 133 municipalities and 900 communities.

There have been no changes in the cities of Athens-Piraeus and Thessaloniki, or in Attica, since a uniform metropolitan administrative system is being set up for these areas.

The 133 municipalities and 900 communities that have been set up under Law 2539/1997 started operating on 1 January 1999, on which date the mayors, municipal councils, community presidents, and community councils were inaugurated and took office, having been elected in general municipal and community elections on 11 October 1998.

The municipalities and communities that will disappear by being subsumed into a larger municipality are recognized as geographical and administrative subdivisions of the new municipality, or 'municipal districts'. These are decentralized administrative bodies, each of which has an elected local council.

2.3 The Role of Political Parties

The Greek political system is dominated by political parties (Legg and Roberts 1997). The parties follow what has been described as 'party clientelism' with ideological considerations coming behind personal patronage in their priorities. As a general rule, politicians seek to win elections not to implement a political or policy programme but to gain control over a state system which can provide various kinds of favours to their clients. This is not to say that the party system has remained static. On the contrary, it has evolved from a situation of multiparty instability characteristic of the post-Second World War period to a fairly predictable and stable three-party system: 'during the entire period, one major party has been associated with the right, another with the centre or centre-left, and a third, much smaller than the other two, with the left or the extreme left' (ibid: 132). Another important change has been in the organization of the political parties, if not their ideology or relationship to the old political elites, in the sense that they have now found it necessary to develop as mass organizations (Spourdalakis 1996).

The main party associated with the right is New Democracy, the centre-left is represented by PASOK, and the third important, albeit small, party is the Communist Party of Greece. Other Greek parties revolve around these three. After the fall of the junta and the change of political system in 1974, Greece was governed by New Democracy until 1981. Karamanlis, leader of New Democracy and the first post-authoritarian prime minister, devised a political system in which the political parties would have a key role (Spourdalakis 1996). There was a consensus on the transition to democracy held by several parties, including some in opposition: Centre Union/New Forces; United Democratic Left; and the Communist Party (interior). A. Papandreou's newly founded PASOK was also committed to the transition to democracy but objected to certain features of Karamanlis's design. After PASOK came to power in 1981, the new government made important changes to the country's centralized system of government; it succeeded since 1994 in implementing a decentralized administrative system by transferring government responsibilities to the prefectures. The remit of the municipalities and communities was broadened at the same time. Changes to the municipal and community electoral system (Law 1270/1982) ensured that all political leanings of the electorate were represented in municipal and local councils and that a viable majority was formed on the political basis of the mayor or president of the community. The same system applies in the prefectures.

3. The Practice of Subnational Democracy

According to members of the Greek delegation to the Committee of the Regions, Greece has made great strides in this area over the past few years and, in practice, local democracy is now stronger than it has ever been.[6] Government is no longer centralized. The decentralized system is fully operational at local and prefectoral level, with power being exercised by bodies directly elected every four years on the basis of a secret ballot and universal suffrage. These are not central government authorities, but bodies of first-tier (municipalities and communities) and second-tier (prefectures) local government with separate legal personalities. State powers at the centre (government and ministries) and in the regions have been restricted; the regions are the only discrete decentralized administrative branches of central government, run by a general secretary who is responsible for implementing government policy on regional issues.

Under the Greek Constitution (Art. 82) the government determines and directs the general policies of the country, in accordance with the constitution and the laws. Citizens, nevertheless, have an unconditional right to participate in politics at local and prefectoral level. Every four years all citizens who are legally entitled to vote may directly elect, by secret ballot: (*i*) mayors, (*ii*) members of municipal councils, (*iii*) presidents of community councils, (*iv*) prefects, and (*v*) members of prefectoral councils. Any citizen who is able to vote and has reached the age of twenty-one on the date of the election may stand for election and vote for all the above-mentioned offices of first-tier local government. Any citizen who is able to vote and has reached the age of twenty-three on the date of the election may stand for election and vote for the above-mentioned offices of second-tier local government (prefectures).

It is clear from what has been said above that the practice of local democracy in Greece has passed from being a highly centralized system to one that now seems to be changing. This is true at least in a formal sense. However, it usually takes some time for institutional changes to influence political culture and practice and, in the Greek case, according to Legg and Roberts (1997), there is a large gap between constitutional statements and on-the-ground realities.

3.1 The Role of Pressure Groups

The undeveloped nature of Greek civil society has meant that pressure groups have also been very weak. There are few powerful business or other kinds of associations at the national level and even fewer at the regional or local levels (Legg and Roberts 1997: 88–91). Instead, the state is omnipresent, dominat-

---

[6] The following paragraphs reproduce the benign interpretation of local democratic practice supplied to the author by the Greek national delegation to the Committee of the Regions. This needs to be treated with some caution and verges on propaganda although, in fairness, one must recognize that some progress has been made.

ing civil society and relations between pressure groups, interest associations and the state tend to follow the patron-client pattern outlined above. This is borne out in a study of the Europeanization of Greece by Lavdas (1997), which attempts to apply a neo-corporatist framework to the country but which concludes that this is, in fact, 'disjointed corporatism'.

3.2 Citizens' Attitudes to Regional and Local Democracy

There are little data on citizens' attitudes to territorial government. However, a series of Eurobarometer polls conducted in the 1980s and early 1990s give some idea of attitudes to Greek democracy as such (Table 12.2). This shows a remarkable decline in satisfaction beginning in the late 1980s. In 1990, only 34 per cent declared themselves very or fairly satisfied with democracy against 63 per cent who were not very or not at all satisfied. The latter category contained no less than 38 per cent. By 1993, there was a slight recovery but still 59 per cent declared themselves not very or not at all satisfied.

Another survey conducted in the early 1990s and published in 1992 does reveal some of the attitudes of political, administrative and other key elites towards the functioning of the prefecture councils (Verney and Papageorgiou 1992). This survey suggested that the role played by councillors in their prefectures was chiefly determined by their other political posts (e.g., mayor or

TABLE 12.2 Satisfaction with democracy (percentages), 1980–93

Year	Very satisfied	Fairly satisfied	Not very satisfied	Not at all satisfied	No response
1980	20	33	23	22	2
1981	24	28	18	23	7
1982	19	41	21	11	8
1983	19	40	21	13	7
1984	19	41	21	13	6
1985	19	40	21	13	8
1986	18	38	17	20	7
1987	20	41	20	15	4
1988	14	37	20	24	5
1989	17	35	20	22	6
1990	7	27	25	38	3
1991	5	32	35	25	3
1992	6	30	39	21	4
1993	5	34	41	18	2

Source: *Eurobarometer Trends*, 1974–1993 (May 1994) quoted in Legg and Roberts (1997).

president of the local labour centre). The councillors themselves did not rate their political influence very highly: 40.3 per cent thought it was 'medium', and 33.1 per cent thought it was 'little'. Those groups that had 'great' or 'very great' influence on the life of the prefecture were: national party leaders (85.1 per cent), government ministers (69.4 per cent), the press (65.6 per cent), the prefect (61.1 per cent), and members of parliament (55.2 per cent). At the lower end of the scale in this category are local party leaders (34.4 per cent), prefecture councillors (18.8 per cent), and senior civil servants at regional, prefecture, and local levels (14.2 per cent).

Despite the weak political influence of the prefecture and of prefectoral politicians and administrators, 94.8 per cent *dis*agreed that the creation of the prefecture councils had been an error. Eighty-six per cent believed this had led to more positive than negative results. However, when asked to point out two successes and two failures of the councils, only 2 per cent indicated 'issues of popular participation and information' among the successes. When asked to list the priorities of the councils only 0.7 per cent thought these were to 'aid individual citizens in dealings with the public administration', while 36.2 per cent thought they were to defend the interests of the prefecture at the national level.

These data confirm the picture of a highly centralized system in which sub-national government continues to be dominated by the national political parties and the central government and feels it necessary to defend itself against these rather than to promote grass-roots participation by citizens. It is not surprising, therefore, that there was overwhelming support for decentralization. In almost all policy areas huge majorities favoured giving the prefectoral councils greater powers: cultural affairs (95.4 per cent), taxes for local projects (93.2 per cent), small and medium enterprises/artisanry (90.1 per cent), environment (98.8 per cent), agriculture (85 per cent), health (82.4 per cent), public works (82.1 per cent), employment (79.5 per cent), police (78 per cent), transportation (73.7 per cent), and school education (72.4 per cent). Only in a few areas did a minority wish to see greater powers: scientific research (41.9 per cent), exports (40.7 per cent), and university education (32.9 per cent).

4. Challenges and Opportunities for Subnational Democracy

Undoubtedly, the greatest challenge as well as opportunity for regional and local democracy in Greece is Greece's membership of the European Union (Lavdas 1997). This has led to what has been described as an 'uneasy interdependence' (Tsinisizelis and Chryssochoou 1996). Greece's entry into the European Community in 1980 had little to do with its economic readiness but was rather a consequence of political decisions by the then EC leaders (Legg and Roberts 1997: 2). It had been a faithful member of the Western Alliance and had undergone the period of dictatorship of the colonels. It was felt at the time both that Greece should be rewarded for the first and that membership would help consolidate the newly emerging democracy. There was also a sense at the time among some of the EC leaders (who had had a classical education) that it was important to include Greece for cultural and historical reasons as a key element of 'western' civilization. Economic considerations were low on the list of reasons for inclusion. There is little evidence that membership of the Community has led to the political and institutional reforms necessary to ensure some kind of economic development as has happened in Portugal, Spain, and Ireland—other countries starting membership with a low economic base. Legg and Roberts (1997: 2) attribute this to a failure in political leadership in Greece compared to these other countries where the leadership was willing to make the changes and sacrifices necessary to lay down the conditions for development.

Nevertheless, the application of the Integrated Mediterranean Programmes and their successors has been the direct cause of the establishment of a regional level of administration as mentioned above. The present administrative reforms have a strong element of deconcentration and decentralization and are closely related to the strengthening of the regional entities, the upgrading of the prefecture councils, and the attempts to amalgamate the fragmented system of communes.

There is overwhelming support for increasing the Community's scope and powers as was revealed in the 1993 study quoted above (Verney and Papageorgiou 1992). When asked whether the EC should acquire more functions after 1992, 70 per cent agreed that this should happen in ten out of twelve sectors with over 85 per cent agreeing in nine sectors. The two sectors with only a minority were on promoting integration of immigrants (47 per cent) and financing a European defence policy (35.1 per cent). These pro-European attitudes were shared across the parties although the parties to the left of the PASOK were somewhat less enthusiastic. Large majorities were also in favour of various forms of 'interregional cooperation' on a range of policy issues: environmental protection (96.7 per cent), culture and tourism (95.5 per cent), applied research (95.4 per cent), creation of a pressure group to lobby the European Commission (78.4 per cent). As far as 'interregional cooperation' is concerned, one example is the Environment Centre of the European Mediterranean Regions, which was set up on 10 March 1995 in the framework of the sixth meeting in Marsëilles of the Inter-Mediterranean Committee at the Conference of Peripheral and Maritime Regions (CPMR) in the European Union. This centre is based in Athens and its founding members include the thirteen regions of Greece together with the Mediterranean regions of Spain, France, Italy, and Portugal. The centre is specifically concerned with the quality of the environment in the Mediterranean region, which faces particular ecological problems.

However, this enthusiasm for European integration is not matched by an equally positive assessment of the ability of the prefecture councils to meet the challenge. Asked specifically whether their councils were ready for the Single Market programme of 1992, there was no single area, ranging from the level of technological innovation in industry to the state of the health service, where a majority thought the prefecture was 'satisfactory' (Verney and Papgeorgiou 1992: 133). There was a certain amount of anxiety about the effects of the Single Market programme on their prefectures. Nevertheless, large majorities thought the overall impact would be positive.

5. Conclusions

Greece originally had a centralized system of government, its political institutions dating back to the country's liberation and the setting up of an independent Greek state in 1833 after some four centuries of occupation by the Ottoman Empire. The administrative system was centralized after the country's liberation. This was necessary at the time because the new state was set up from scratch in a country that had been destroyed and devastated following the Greeks' ten-year armed struggle to free themselves from the occupying power. Within this system, first-tier local government (there effectively being no second tier) was weak and depended to a large extent on central government.

As in Italy, the Greek political parties are dominant. Political parties, once in power, tended to reinforce centralization and dominated subnational levels of administration and government. In this system, local government was fragmented, weak, and highly dependent on the centre. PASOK introduced political decentralization reforms in the 1980s, but these were only partially implemented both by the Socialists and also by the conservative *Nea Demokratika* which has generally opposed decentralization.

In recent times, membership of the European Union has had the effect of encouraging the setting up of a regional level of administration and has led to a consciousness of the inadequacies of Greek local government to meet the challenges of membership. Laws currently going through parliament are attempting to redress this situation by strengthening the regional authorities and democratizing the prefecture councils. Both prefects and mayors are now directly elected although still on the basis of party lists. They will also compulsorily amalgamate the huge number of fragmented communes. This is being accompanied by administrative reforms that are being drawn up and carried out in conjunction with the European Commission. All of these developments may lead to a strengthening of regional and local democracy in Greece.

References

CHRISTOFILOPOULOU, P. (1987). 'Decentralization Policy in Post-dictatorial Greece'. *Local Government Studies*, 13/6.

COUNCIL OF EUROPE (1993). *Structure and Operation of Local and Regional Democracy—Situation in 1992—Greece.* Strasbourg.

LAVDOS, K. (1997). *The Europeanization of Greece: Interest Politics and the Crises of Integration.* Basingstoke: Macmillan.

LEGG, K. and ROBERTS, J. (1997), *Modern Greece: A Civilization on the Periphery.* Boulder, CO.: Westview Press.

MAHAIRA-ODONI, E. (1995). 'Government and Politics', in G. E. Curtis (ed.), *Greece: A Country Study.* Washington, DC: Library of Congress.

MOUZELIS, N. (1995). 'Greece in the Twenty-First Century: Institutions and Political Culture', in D. Constas and T. Stavrou (eds), *Greece Prepares for the Twenty-First Century.* Baltimore & London: The Johns Hopkins University Press.

PAPAGEORGIOU, F. and VERNEY, S. (1992). 'Regional Planning and the Integrated Mediterranean Programmes in Greece'. *Regional Politics and Policy*, 2/1–2: 139–61.

SPOURDALAKIS, M. (1996). 'Securing Democracy in Post-authoritarian Greece: The Role of the Political Parties', in G. Pridham and P. Lewis (eds), *Stabilising Fragile Democracies: Comparing New Party Systems in Southern and Eastern Europe.* London & New York: Routledge.

TSINISIZELIS, M. and CHRYSSOCHOOU, D. (1996). 'Images of Greece and European Integration: A Case of Uneasy Interdependence?' *Synthesis*, 1/2: 22–33.

VERNEY, S. (1997). 'Central State–Local Government Relations', in K. A. Lavdas (ed.), *The Europeanization of Greece.* Basingstoke: Macmillan.

——and PAPAGEORGIOU, F. (1992). 'Prefecture Councils in Greece: Decentralization in the European Community Context'. *Regional Politics and Policy*, 2/1–2: 109–37.

WENTURIS, N. (1997). 'Political Culture', in K. A. Lavdas (ed.), *The Europeanization of Greece.* Basingstoke: Macmillan.

13

Belgium: Federalism and Subnational Democracy in a Divided Country

Frank Hendriks

1. History and Concept of Democracy

From its birth in 1830 until the first state reform of 1970, Belgium was a decentralized unitary state, similar to the Netherlands, with a subnational government divided into provinces and municipalities. The four state reforms that have been enacted since 1970 (in 1970, 1980, 1988, and 1993) have altered the relationships between the various tiers of government, transforming the country from a unitary state into a federation (Ministerie van de Vlaamse Gemeenschap 1993; Veldkamp 1993; Alen 1995; Gouvernement Wallon 1998). The first article in the most recent version of the Belgium Constitution reads 'Belgium is a federation, consisting of communities and regions'.

1.1 Historical Background

Belgium became an independent state in 1830 when, after a rebellion, the southern provinces broke away from the United Kingdom of the Netherlands. For a long time afterwards, Belgium was a unitary state until, after a series of reforms, it became a federation in 1993. The origin of Belgium's transformation into a federation lies in the ancient boundary between Germanic and Romance languages that splits the country into a Flemish-speaking north (Flanders) and a French-speaking south (Wallonia). In the early nineteenth century, French was the language of government and Belgium seemed to be on the way to becoming a French-speaking country. But opposition started building up in Flanders from the mid nineteenth century onwards. After

I would like to thank Philip de Rynck, Johan Ackaert, and Stefaan Walgrave for commenting on this chapter.

various protracted political battles, language laws were passed giving the Flemish language official status in education (1932), government (1932), and the courts (1935), and in 1963 the language frontier was finally defined. This has now become a political and administrative frontier. Belgium has been divided up into four language areas: the Flemish-speaking area (Flanders, with a population of 5.7 million), the French-speaking area (Wallonia, 3.1 million), the German-speaking area (66,000 inhabitants), and the bilingual capital, Brussels (consisting of the city of Brussels and eighteen of the surrounding municipalities, with a total population of 970,000), where Flemish and French have equal status.

With the establishment of the language frontier and the recognition of Flanders as a monolingual area, the idea of cultural autonomy grew in that part of Belgium. Wallonia too had an autonomist movement, but this had a largely economic character. Above all, Flanders achieved a strong demographic and economic ascendancy after the Second World War, which led to the Walloon demand for control over their own economic destiny (Ministerie van de Vlaamse Gemeenschap 1991).

Slowly, the idea grew on both sides of the language frontier that the unitary state structure was no longer viable in the long term. This led eventually to the reforms that transformed Belgium.

1.2 Democracy at the Subnational Levels

With the fourth state reform of 1993, based on the 'St. Michael's Agreement', Belgium has become a full-blown federation. (A federation is a group of states in which power is shared between the central government and the sub-federal states, with the aim of granting the latter a high degree of autonomy.) The idea in Belgium is to have a form of federation known in constitutional law as 'dual federalism'. Sovereignty is formally divided among three authorities— the federal government, the regions, and the communities—which each have their own exclusive powers and which, in principle, must not encroach on the prerogatives of the others. The national government, with its own powers and responsibilities, exists not above but alongside the regions and communities. Hence, there is no hierarchy between the federal and the regional and community governments (Alen 1995).

Notwithstanding the dual-federal basic structure, there is also, in practice, 'cooperative federalism', similar to the German federal system. This is expressed in the organization of 'community-to-community talks' when working out cooperation law and, more generally, in a high level of government interpenetration. Because of the lack of hierarchical relationships, community affairs (of which there are naturally many in a compact country like Belgium) must be discussed in great detail, and often at great length. The former Belgian prime minister, Jean-Luc Dehaene, did not hesitate to call the new Belgian government structure a form of 'federal cooperative'. Even the Flemish government, which is undoubtedly leaning towards independence, acknowledges that cooperation across administrative boundaries is still of great importance (Ministerie van de Vlaamse Gemeenschap 1993).

Cooperative federal tendencies rely significantly on the arts of accommodation and 'coming to an arrangement' that have long typified Belgian administration; but cooperation is also enshrined in the law. The principle of federal loyalty is laid down in Article 107 of the constitution. This calls, for instance, for cooperation and consultation in order to monitor the integration of different policies. Cooperation agreements are one facet of this. Administrative bodies that have authority over the same field have a statutory duty to consult with each other. If any conflicts of interest still arise, the senate is the body empowered to decide on a solution.

2. The Institutional Expression of Democracy

2.1 The National Level

Sovereignty in the Belgian federation is now spread over three political levels: central government, the regions (*gewesten/régions*), and the communities (*gemeenschappen/communautés*).

There are three linguistic communities: the French-speaking, Flemish-speaking, and German-speaking communities. The communities are empowered to pass laws and have their own governments. There are also three regions: the Flemish, Walloon, and Brussels Capital regions. All three have their own parliaments with authority to pass laws and their own governments.

The regions and communities came into being in response to the different political priorities in the North and South. The communities were conceived as a way of meeting Flemish cultural and linguistic demands for self-government; the regions as an answer to French-speakers' demands for more economic autonomy.

At the federal level, legislative power is exercised by the head of state and the two elected houses of parliament. The federal legislative authority operates through a controlled bicameral system and is exercised by the House of Representatives (Lower House) and Senate (Upper House) jointly with the king. The distribution of duties between the House and the Senate is based on the following basic principles:

- the Lower House exercises political control over the government and monitors public finances;
- both houses are responsible, on an equal footing, for institutional lawmaking and relations between the federal government and the communities and regions;
- the Senate provides a forum for reflection;
- it is also the meeting place between the federal government and the federal states.

The Lower House has 150 members, who are directly elected every four years. The Senate has seventy-one members, of whom forty are directly elected. The Flemish Council and the French Community Council each send ten members to the Senate, the Council of the German-speaking Community sends one member. The other ten senators are co-opted.

The executive consists of the federal ministers, who are responsible to the Lower House, and the head of state who cannot be held responsible to anyone.

Given political realities, the primacy of the legislature has given way to to a *de facto* ascendancy of the executive. Draft laws initiated by it take precedence over draft laws initiated by the legislature. Amendments have little chance of being adopted, in view of existing parliamentary majorities (De Ridder 1994).

Obviously, not everything has changed in the Belgian system with the advent of federalism. Belgium can still be described as a hereditary, constitutional, and parliamentary monarchy. The monarchy is regulated and limited by the constitution. The king possesses no powers other than those specifically vested in him by the constitution and special legislation. The monarchy is thus also anchored in the parliamentary democracy. The king cannot act on his own in his capacity as head of state. Every act or position with political repercussions must be endorsed by the minister (or by the whole government), who is answerable for it to the Lower House.

The substance and significance of the king's role have declined in the course of political history. Nowadays the monarchy exercises influence rather than authority. This influence is exerted mainly through confidential discussions between the king and his ministers. The ministers inform the king and advise him. The king advises, exhorts, and warns. Occasionally the monarch acts as a bridge between the parliamentary majority and the opposition, and between the different communities and regions. Finally, he carries out ceremonial duties and is the symbol of Belgian sovereignty (De Ridder 1994).

2.2 Political Institutions

In addition to the above-mentioned institutions, several other sustained patterns of behaviour have had a fundamental influence on Belgian politics and democratic practice.

2.2.1 Consensus-building

In the terminology of Lijphart (1984), Belgian democracy can clearly be described as a consensus democracy, which grew out of, and was a response to, the deep divisions that have riven the country. These divisions were institutionalized in society as separate worlds or 'pillars': Catholic or Christian-democratic, socialist, and liberal. In addition, there are the divisions between Flemish- and French-speakers. Belgium is thus a fragmented country that survived as a democracy because of this tradition of consensus.

It could be argued that federation has pushed Belgium even further towards Lijphart's ideal-type model of consensus democracy. On the other hand, one could object that, with federation, power-sharing has been 'organized out of existence': dividing up the goods seems to be a more important principle than power-sharing. However, as has been already pointed out, cooperation across administrative boundaries is still a central feature of Belgian government. The combination of a greater spreading of power and solidarity ensures that the consensual political culture of Belgium survives.

2.2.2 Pragmatism

'Fixing', the art of concluding (creative) *ad hoc* agreements, is highly esteemed in the Belgian political system. In practice, this goes hand-in-hand with a large dose of pragmatism.

The contrast between Belgium and the Netherlands is particularly striking on this last point. The former Belgian prime minister, Wilfried Martens, is alleged to have said: 'The Dutch are more rational. First they make memoranda, then they get down to business. The Flemish are more emotional and spontaneous. We go and negotiate first and then we put something down on paper' (Donkers 1996). Planners and other professional problem-solvers play a more important role in the Netherlands than in Flanders, where political fixers are more predominant. The cobbling together of a workable arrangement is generally considered to be more important than adhering to previously determined standards and principles.

Political dexterity is at least as important as analytical skills in a country where political decisions have from time immemorial been taken in 'conclaves' of political and administrative elites. The state structure seems like a labyrinth to political and administrative outsiders. This impression has not diminished since Belgium became a federation. Political and administrative insiders, on the other hand, have no such difficulty. Personal contacts create the Ariadne's thread that enables them to find their way through the 'Belgian labyrinth' (Van Istendael 1993).

2.2.3 Clientelism

This is now under pressure, although it still has considerable influence in Belgian politics. It has long been an important feature of Belgian political culture. The services that politicians provide are, in principle, free and have no strings attached, but that does not stop politicians hoping that their 'clients' will give them something in return, such as a preferential vote. In the run-up to elections, politicians send out letters in which they remind their 'clients' of the services they have provided and ask for their vote. Electoral research shows that at least four out of ten voters who have used the services of a politician actually do give a preferential vote to that politician. Hence, the political exchange of a preferential vote for a service is a reality, although it is not a necessity (De Winter 1994: 428–30).

Even if clientelism does not always deliver the desired preferential vote, it can be a useful exercise for politicians, as it is often a source for them of information about issues of concern to citizens. Research also indicates that this 'rendering of services' can have a very positive psychological impact.

There are, nevertheless, many disadvantages in clientelism. The link between the citizen and the politician becomes more and more a customer–service provider relationship. This creates a dependency situation between them (De Winter 1994: 528–30).

Clientelism entails a risk of a separate system being set up for case treatment, whereby cases supported by politicians get faster, better treatment than those that have to go through the normal administrative channels. Because of their overblown concern for the interests of individual citizens, public representatives may have too little time to think of general solutions and formulate legislation for the greater good.

2.2.4 Particracy

Closely linked to the practice of clientelism is that of political appointments. A political appointment can be effective as a service or as a reward for a service. But for some time there has been a growing political will to drastically curtail this practice (De Winter 1994: 428–30).

'Particratic' tendencies in the Belgian system are often described as problematic. However, the practice of partisanship also has features that are more positive. For example, as a small country, Belgium has largely avoided becoming a hostage to decision-making by an omnipotent bureaucracy. One of the reasons for this is the party politicization of the civil service and especially the existence of powerful ministerial staffs.

2.2.5 Elitism or the 'Pyramid of Power'

Earlier in this text the image of the 'Belgian labyrinth' was evoked. Another popular image used to describe the decision-making culture in Belgium is that of the 'pyramid of power'.

Dewachter and Das, in a survey of the Belgian political elite, identified the major decision-makers in six policy areas during the period 1988–90 and the significance of twenty political positions in the entire political decision-making process in Belgium. The findings were summed up as follows: 'Instead of institutions and bodies that stand alongside one another, inequalities appear in the share out of decision-making power, as well as hierarchical relationships, involving individuals and positions' (Dewachter and Das 1991).

In practice, the Belgian set-up suffers relatively little interference from awkward citizens or otherwise competitive forces. In this elitist political structure, government is a rather 'elusive' phenomenon: '[it] is like a slippery eel that always slips out of the net. Decision-making is well-nigh impossible to monitor', states Dewachter (1995: 353–6).

3. The Practice of Subnational Democracy

The communities and regions are the constitutive parts of the federal Belgian state established in 1993. As a rule of thumb one can say that the communities are responsible for 'individual-related matters' (language, culture, education, health care, social aid, etc.), while the regions are responsible for 'territorial matters' (such as road infrastructure, water, the environment, land division, housing, spatial planning, and regional economic affairs). The Flemish preference for the community and the French-speaking preference for the region have led to an asymmetrical federal structure.

There are separate Walloon and Brussels regions and a separate German-speaking community.

In 1980, Flanders decided to amalgamate region and community. In practice, this means that the Flemish community exercises both community and regional powers and, therefore, has a budget comprising both regional and community funds. The Flemish community is empowered to issue decrees that can amend, supplement, or abolish existing Belgian laws in so far as these come under the Flemish authorities' terms of reference.

French-speakers chose a different direction: the powers of the French community can be wholly or partially transferred to the French-speaking faction in the Brussels Capital Council and to the French-speaking area of the Walloon region (which also includes the German-speaking community!). The French-speaking faction in the Brussels region, the French Community Commission of Brussels (COCOF), has the power to issue decrees. In practice, the French community delegates sport, tourism, vocational training, and school transport to the Walloon region or, as regards French-speakers in Brussels, to the Brussels region.

Constitutional law specialists point out that there are in fact eight sub-federal entities: the three regions, the three communities, the Brussels

Communal Community Commission, and the French Community Commission of Brussels (COCOF).

3.1 The Communities

The Flemish-speaking, French-speaking, and German-speaking communities each have their own legislative bodies: the Flemish Council (which is also the legislative body of the Flemish region), the French Community Council, and the Council of the German-speaking Community.

The Flemish Council has 124 members: 118 members directly elected by voters in the Flemish region and 6 Flemish members of the Brussels Regional Council. The French Community Council comprises 75 members from the Walloon Regional Council and 19 French-speaking members from the Brussels Regional Council, making a total of 94 members. The Council of the German-speaking Community has 25 directly elected members.

The executive of the communities is elected by the councils and forms the community government.

The most important responsibility of the communities is education and science policy. Another important area of responsibility is what is known as personal affairs. This includes social and legal youth protection, family policy and help and assistance for children, social welfare, the integration of immigrants, and policies on the disabled and the elderly. Cultural policy is also a responsibility for the communities. Finally, the Flemish- and French-speaking (but not the German-speaking) community are empowered to regulate the use of languages in administrative affairs, education, industrial relations, and the statutory acts and documents of companies. However, decrees in this area are not applicable in Brussels or in the so-called 'facility municipalities'. (These are municipalities where speakers of the minority language, whether French or Flemish, may have services proided in that language.)

3.2 The Regions

The Flemish, Walloon, and Brussels Capital regions each have their own legislative institutions: the Flemish Council (also the legislative body of the Flemish community), the Walloon Regional Council, and the Brussels Capital Council. The executive authority of the regions is the regional government, whose members are elected by the appropriate council.

The Flemish government, which is both the regional and community government, has a maximum of eleven members. The Walloon regional government has a maximum of seven members. The Brussels regional government has five members, plus three regional junior ministers.

The regions are responsible for spatial planning, the environment, land allocation, conservation, and water policy. In the economic sphere, they are responsible for economic development, industrial renewal, public industrial initiative, foreign trade, natural resources, and energy policy. The regions are obliged to carry out their economic policy within the framework of the Economic and Monetary Union. Other regional responsibilities include employment policy and public works and transport.

The regions are responsible for the general funding and supervision of the municipalities and the provinces (except for the municipalities in the German-speaking area, which come completely under the central government, and the six 'facility municipalities', which theoretically come under the federal level but are effectively supervised at regional level) (Deweerdt 1994b: 191–4).

Under the 1993 Constitution, the regions and communities will in future be responsible for all matters that are not expressly vested in the federal government. However, it is still not clear when this allocation of responsibility will take place as this must still be decided by a special legislator, and the federal government's responsibilities must still be enshrined in the constitution.

3.3 The Subregional Levels

Despite federalization, the traditional subnational system of government in Belgium, consisting of provincial and local authorities, has remained largely unchanged, although the context within which it finds itself has, of course, drastically changed since 1993. The most obvious difference from the earlier situation is that responsibility for the municipalities and provinces and for specific payments to these subnational authorities has been transferred from the old central government to the new regional authorities. Other differences will be dealt with in more detail below, along with areas where there is no change.

3.3.1 The Institutions of Local Government

The most important institutions in Belgian local government are the municipal council and the municipal executive consisting of the mayor and aldermen. The municipal executive is responsible for the day-to-day running of the municipality. In principle it is a collegial body, but tasks are shared out within it in the interests of efficiency. Meetings of the executive are held behind closed doors. Decisions require, in principle, an absolute majority. Aldermen are elected, by an absolute majority, by the municipal council from among its members.

The municipal executive is chaired by the mayor, who is appointed by the monarch and is usually a member of the municipal council. The mayor-elect must enjoy the support of at least half of the municipal councillors. He or she is also the representative of central government. Hence, two levels of government come together in one person: the central and the local. Mayors tend to present themselves as promoters of their municipality; they try to attract public or private investments to their area and to operate social services for its inhabitants. At the same time the mayor must often operate as a broker to settle any conflicts within the municipal majority (Ackaert 1994: 538–44).

The municipal council, which is also chaired by the mayor, is the representative and legislative body of the municipality. A municipal decision is taken by an absolute majority of votes. Not all municipal council discussions are open to the public. The public may attend meetings about decisions that affect the financial situation of the municipality or that relate to the establishment of institutions of municipal interest. The municipal council must meet behind closed doors when identifiable persons are concerned, or if two-thirds of the members present decide that the meeting should not be open to the public in the interests of public order.

Article 41 of the constitution lays down that municipal interests are to be handled exclusively by the municipal council. It is largely the legislative body that defines what is a 'municipal interest'. This can be positive when a broad discretionary power is explicitly granted to the municipal authorities; or it can be negative when a certain power is withdrawn from the municipal or provincial authority, or is strictly regulated. In exercising their powers, the municipal authorities are subject to higher-level legislation.

As well as running their local government area, municipalities can also be called upon by higher tiers of government to undertake joint ventures with them. Examples include maintaining population registers, national service lists, organizing censuses, etc. The term 'joint administration' is used when the municipalities have virtually no room for manoeuvre to make their own contributions. Where municipalities (subject to minimum standards) have discretionary powers, the term 'tasks of joint interest' is used.

Municipalities are supervised by higher authorities, depending upon the task at hand. This administrative supervision is divided into general administrative supervision (suspension and annulment) and special administrative supervision (preliminary opinion, authorization, and approval). A distinction is also made between ordinary and specific supervision. This means in practice that ordinary administrative supervision is restricted to municipal actions to deal with municipal matters, whereas specific supervision deals with municipal action in the context of joint administration (Ackaert 1994: 533–5). Important in administrative supervision is that the supervisory authority cannot usurp the role of the decentralized government.

Compared with municipalities in other Western European countries, Belgian municipalities control a relatively small share of state spending (Table 13.1).

TABLE 13.1 Local expenditure as a percentage of total
government spending in the Benelux countries,
1980–92

Country	Year			
	1980	1984	1988	1992
Belgium	15.2	12.8	12.4	11.7
Netherlands	32.9	34.4	31.0	28.9
Luxembourg	15.2	12.9	—	—

Source: Maes (1997: 8).

Municipal expenditure amounts to around 12 per cent of all government spending. Municipal revenues include income from taxes and financial levies. The municipalities also receive money from the central municipal fund. They are also eligible for a number of specific payments from the federal government or the regions and communities.

3.3.2 The Institutions of Provincial Government

The key provincial institutions are the provincial council, the provincial governor, and the permanent deputation. The provincial council is the representative and legislative body of the province and decides on all matters of provincial interest. The number of members varies from forty-seven to eighty-four, depending on the province's population. The provincial governor is a 'liaison officer' between the provincial and national government and appointed by the crown for an indefinite period. As a political official, the provincial governor can receive instructions from both the central and regional government. As the administrative supervisory body, he or she can rule on the legality of decisions taken not only by the municipalities and public social welfare bodies, but also by the provincial council. The provincial governor is the voting chairman of the permanent deputation, the other members of which are appointed by the provincial council. The permanent deputation rules on all matters related to the day-to-day government of the province.

It is a matter of some surprise that the provinces have survived the Belgian constitutional reforms. The Belgian unitary state had nine provinces; the Belgian federation has ten: five Flemish and five Walloon. The nineteen Brussels municipalities, which used to be part of the province of Brabant, now come directly under the Brussels Capital region. The other municipalities of the former province of Brabant are now shared between the new provinces of Walloon Brabant and Flemish Brabant, hence there is one extra province (Deweerdt 1994a: 46–7).

The province is a largely independent political institution with a council elected directly every six years. It has a two-fold task. First, it is responsible for managing provincial affairs, including the day-to-day running of the permanent deputation. Second, it plays a role with the higher authorities in joint government. The provincial council, but especially the permanent deputation and the provincial governor, take important decisions on behalf of the central government on environmental licences, building and housing appeals, the settlement of municipal tax complaints, the approval of municipal budgets and accounts, security, and maintenance of law and order.

The province has a qualified right of initiative. This means that it can take initiatives in any matter that is either of provincial interest or does not clash with the legal terms of reference of the municipal authorities, provided that the higher authority has not taken it up. By making use of such a qualified right of initiative, provincial governments formulate policy on education, social affairs, culture, the environment, leisure, tourism and recreation, utilities, agriculture and horticulture, road building and maintenance, public health, and security (Coenen 1994: 520–1).

The value of the provinces lies above all in such low-profile but important activities as providing support, assistance, and encouragement. The provinces' low profile as a government body has even been called a 'blessing in disguise' (De Rynck 1992). This 'blessing' does not apply so much to the provincial council (the role of this provincial institution is now as good as over), but it does apply to those responsible for the daily running of the province: the governor and the permanent deputation.

These have few formal powers of decision, but informally they play an important role as middlemen in all sorts of interlocking administrative networks. Above all, the governors, who are appointed for life, can exert a great deal of political clout.

However, it remains the case that the value of the provincial tier of government is not evident to many people, especially now that the regional government is becoming increasingly prominent, while supraprovincial relationships (such as the Antwerp-Ghent-Brussels triangle) are becoming more important. Many think it absurd to maintain provincial boundaries alongside municipal and regional boundaries. Drawing attention to their own autonomous powers does not seem to be a viable option for the provinces. The best survival strategy for the Belgian provinces still seems to be to operate as a back-up for and 'subsidiary' to other government bodies (De Rynck 1994).

3.3.3 Other Institutions at the Subregional Level

- *Regional development corporations (RDCs)*: These are regional associations where representatives of employers, workers, provinces, municipalities, and joint municipal authorities (JMAs) come together. The RDCs work along

provincial lines and play an important role in framing regional programmes. They also lobby various bodies in a bid to strengthen the economic structure of an area.

- *Districts*: These are regional administrative bodies without policy-making
  powers, without any autonomy, and without any political or civil representation. The federal government appoints district commissioners with
  responsiblity for one or more administrative districts. They assist the governors and, therefore, have their residences in the provincial capital. Within
  their official areas, district commissioners are responsible, under the direction of the governor, for upholding the law and general government regulations as well as supervising all rural police services.
- *Joint municipal authorities (JMAs)*: Although mergers between municipalities have led to greater economies of scale and to more efficient administration, municipalities cannot perform all their allotted tasks completely
  efficiently. This problem is generally solved via cooperation between municipalities. The most detailed structure here is the joint municipal authority.
  This is a structure for cooperation between different municipalities, regulated by public law, that is set up and managed on the basis of voluntary
  rules adopted by the participants for the promotion of matters of municipal interest. Participation in a JMA is voluntary, in principle. The major
  policy areas are energy supplies and waste processing. JMAs are supervised
  by the regional governments.
- *College of provincial governors*: The college consists of the governors of the
  ten provinces and has a number of specific responsibilities confined to the
  facitiliy municipalities of Voeren and Komen-Waasten.
- *The governor and the deputy governor of the Brussels Capital administrative
  district*: After the province of Brabant was split up, the nineteen municipalities of Brussels were no longer attached to a province and were grouped
  together to form the Brussels Capital administrative district. In this district
  the commissioner has the title of governor and exercises the powers of a
  provincial governor.
- *Public centres for social welfare*: The public centres for social welfare are
  municipal institutions that enjoy municipal autonomy. Their organization
  and administrative supervision is carried out by the municipalities. The social
  welfare council consists of nine to fifteen members, depending on the population of the municipality. Members are elected by the municipal council.

3.4 Subnational Government: Complexity and Lack of Transparency

In accordance with the constitution, those directly elected by their relevant
constituency must defend the province's interests. The elector votes for

delegates to the provincial council, which defines policy in all openness and carries out the duties entrusted to it by its constituency.

In practice it has also been noticed that the municipalities often concern themselves with policy matters that are outside their remit. Countless non-profit bodies and JMAs with general objectives have been set up. These threaten to grow into supralocal bodies without a democratic basis recognized by the constitution.

The federalization of Belgium has not led to a devolution of power to subregional levels. Instead, it has in a sense further strengthened centralization but at the community/regional level. It is worth noting here the new administrative centres that have been set up by the Flemish government in the provincial capitals since 1985. These are simply more layers of official-dom between the citizens and the policies that continue to be forged in Brussels.

If the central authorities wish to secure more devolved input, they tend to set up more and more councils, commissions, or specific public law institutions. The creation of the Flemish community has not stemmed this trend; it has perhaps even accentuated it.

Against this background it is hardly surprising that there is now great concern about the opaque, uncontrollable meso-level of the policy-making system. This situation is generally described as a democratic deficit (Coenen 1994: 529–31).

3.5 Citizens' Attitudes

Previous research indicates that provincial administration is not held in high regard. The municipality is seen as the most relevant subnational administrative unit. Maes (1997) states that citizens identify closely with their municipality as a geographical entity. In a survey, Dutch and Belgian citizens were asked to state which geographical entity they identified with first and second. The results were as follows: both Dutch and Belgian respondents identified primarily with their municipality. When the first and second choices were added together, the Dutch respondents came out in favour of their nation, but Belgians continued to identify more closely with their municipality (Table 13.2).

Interviews suggest that knowledge of, and interest in, local political institutions is of a lower level than in the Netherlands, whilst knowledge of, and familiarity with, local politicians is greater in Belgium. This is because local politics is much more personalized in the latter country. In 1987 no fewer than 92 per cent of those polled knew the name of their mayor. Through the tradition of political favours, other local politicians (councillors) also have a relatively high profile.

TABLE 13.2 Geographical identification by Belgian and Dutch citizens: first and second choices (percentages), 1996

| Entity | Country | | | | | |
| | Belgium | | | The Netherlands | | |
	1st	2nd	1st & 2nd	1st	2nd	1st & 2nd
Municipality	45	16	63	43	23	66
Region	14	25	38.5	7	19	25.5
Country	21	29.5	51	35	34	69
Europe	16	23	4	144	19	8
World	10	6	16	9	8	17

Source: Maes (1997: 8).

The attitude of the Belgian public towards local government is strongly coloured by political and cultural factors. A comparative cultural survey shows that Belgian political culture exhibits strong Latin characteristics and differs clearly in this respect from Dutch political culture (Hofstede 1991). Flemish- and French-speakers may perhaps exhibit cultural differences, but these differences in values are much less pronounced than those between the Walloons and the French, or between the Flemish and the Dutch (Kerkhofs and Rezsochazy 1984: 214).

The Latin cultural model implies a certain kind of citizenship and certain expectations of government, including subnational government. In general this is a rather 'clientelistic' form of citizenship: the citizen has long played second fiddle to the client. Confidence in local government is not self-evident. Local politics achieves recognition to the extent that it meets the citizen's expectations.

The depillarization and individualization of society has certainly not made the consumer model of citizenship any less influential. And public confidence in traditional politics has certainly not broadened. This is clear from the results of the last elections, which showed a clear move away from traditional politics.

3.6 Patterns of Public Participation

Public participation can be divided into classical, conventional forms and new, unconventional forms.

3.6.1 'Conventional' Politics

If conventional participation is broken down further (voting, party membership, discussion of politics), and a comparison is made between Belgium and the Netherlands, the following picture emerges. Belgians talk less about politics and take less interest in politics than the Dutch. Belgians are also less likely to be members of a political party, but they vote more frequently than the Dutch (Heunks 1996: 222) although this is because voting is compulsory in Belgium and is not in the Netherlands. But, where local elections are concerned, the picture is more complex than this.

There is a general belief that local elections mean more, and make more of a difference in Belgium, than they do in the Netherlands. Belgian local elections are noticeably less 'nationalized' than Dutch local elections. Local politicians are judged by their own actions to a greater extent in Belgium than in the Netherlands, where this depends in the main on trends in national political preferences. In Belgium electors have two votes: one to be cast for a list and the other for a candidate on a list, which gives elections a personal touch. If one votes for the candidate at the top of a major party list, one effectively contributes to the election of the mayor. Although in Belgium mayors are appointed by the Crown, this is done, unlike in the Netherlands, on the basis of instructions from the ruling majority in the local council. Normally the head of the list of the largest party represented in the council becomes mayor. The influence of the Belgian voter on the governing majority is also much more direct, as in Belgium it is far more common than in the Netherlands for a relatively small, homogeneous majority to govern. Between 1988 and 1994 almost 60 per cent of Belgian municipalities were governed by a homogeneous political majority (and not by a broad-based coalition, as is often the case in the Netherlands). Usually one party had an absolute majority, or sometimes there was a lasting coalition of parties.

3.6.2 'Unconventional' Politics

Political opportunities for unconventional, participation-based 'new' politics—as often expressed through new social movements—are less favourable in Belgium than in the Netherlands (Walgrave 1995). With reference to the difference between materialistic 'old' politics and post-materialist 'new' politics, it can be stated that the 'old' politics is still relatively important in Belgium (Inglehart 1990: 91–5). Belgians are less interested than the Dutch in membership of new political movements such as the environmental, anti-nuclear, and peace movements (Inglehart 1990: 379). Belgians are less inclined than the Dutch to vote green/ecologist (Knutsen 1996: 172). The environmental movement is also perceived as less legitimate in Belgium than in the Netherlands (Kanji and Nevitte 1996: 288). The relatively low level of political mobilization around the 'new politics issues' in Belgium is linked by Kitschelt (1989) to competition from other fault lines or 'cleavages'. In Belgium, regional and socio-economic cleavages still command attention. Kitschelt concludes that the mobilizing potential of the post-materialist dimension is, therefore, low in Wallonia and no more than moderate in Flanders. Walgrave (1995) points to the effect of Belgian political culture, which does not take for granted the political involvement of individuals and groups. Involvement of this kind is not considered as particularly socially desirable, although it is not discouraged.

Grass-roots participation is not strongly encouraged by the nature of the existing institutions. This is connected with the underdeveloped opportunities for public enquiries and the protection of rights, and also, to a lesser extent, with the lack of transparency of the decision-making system. If citizens or groups of citizens wish to resist something, they tend to use political rather than administrative channels. By using political channels one can attempt to obtain access to the relatively closed 'conclaves' where political negotiations are traditionally conducted (Dewachter 1995: 353–6). (Table 13.3.)

TABLE 13.3 Results of local, regional, and national elections (percentages), 1988–99

	Local		Regional		National		
	1988	1994	1995	1999	1991	1995	1999
Flanders							
Participation	95.0	93.5	92.5	92.2	93.6	92.6	91.1
Blank/Invalid	4.3	4.7	6.6	5.3	6.1	6.4	6.2
CVP	37.4	29.9	26.8	22.1	26.9	27.6	22.8
SP	19.7	16.3	19.4	15.0	19.4	20.7	15.6
VLD	15.0	17.6	20.2	22.0	19.8	20.9	23.2
VU	8.5	4.3	9.0	9.3	8.6	7.3	9.1
AGALEV	4.7	5.9	7.1	11.6	7.8	7.2	11.4
VL Blok	2.5	6.7	12.3	15.5	9.8	12.3	15.8
Others	12.2	19.3	5.2	4.5	7.7	4.0	2.1
Wallonia							
Participation	92.8	91.6	90.5	90.1	91.8	90.5	90.1
Blank/Invalid	5.3	5.7	7.2	7.1	6.9	7.6	7.4
PS	39.4	34.9	35.2	29.5	34.9	33.7	27.6
PSC	23.8	24.3	21.6	17.1	22.8	22.5	15.9
PRL-FDF	19.9	20.4	23.7	24.7	23.1	23.9	27.4
RW	1.2	4.2	0.2	0	0.6	0	0
ECOLO	6.8	7.1	10.4	18.2	9.5	10.3	19.9
FN-AGIR-extr r	1.9	4.6	6.1	4.0	2.9	5.5	3.9
Others	7.0	4.5	2.8	6.5	6.2	4.1	5.3
Belgium							
Participation	93.5	92.3	91.5	91.1	92.7	91.1	90.6

CVP + PSC, Christian democrats; PS + SP, social democrats; VLD + PRL, liberal democrats; VU + FDF, national democrats; AGALEV + ECOLO, green parties; FN + AGIR + extr R + VL Blok, extreme nationalists.

4. Challenges and Opportunities for Subnational Democracy

The challenges faced by subnational government in Belgium are in some cases the same as those existing in other countries (see Chapter 1); in other cases, however, they are peculiar to Belgium, arising from the country's unique political and social situation.

4.1 'Glocalization', Europeanization, and Regionalization

The simultaneous processes of increasing and decreasing scale (glocalization = globalization + localization) are a general trend that is making itself felt in Belgium to some extent, as the country houses Europe's government institutions and is federalized at the same time. Belgian politicians, more so than many of their European counterparts, are pulled in two directions by the forces of Europeanization and regionalization ('Think European, act regional').

4.2 New Social and Political Movements

The rise of new social and political movements is a second general trend that is having a major impact on Belgium (Walgrave 1994; 1995) although, as remarked above, in comparison with the Netherlands, the rise of a cohesive network of new social movements with a clear post-materialist agenda is less pronounced. The Belgian movements are more diverse, and this is also true of their agendas, which makes the challenge to authority a complex one. In the Netherlands the rise of new movements is clearly correlated with the emergence of post-materialist preferences and demands. This is less clearly the case in Belgium. Traditional, regional, and materialist cleavages continue to play an important part, often in combination.

4.3 The Flemish–Walloon Divide

A look at the Flemish–Walloon divide reveals the connection between the various cleavages. The division is not just a purely linguistic one, but also socio-economic and politico-cultural. The economic decline of Wallonia has coincided with the economic rise of Flanders. Studies show that Flemish and French speakers occupy different positions along the traditional left–right divide: with the Walloons more to the left and the Flemish more to the right, although all kinds of subtle distinctions can be made (Delruelle-Vosswinkel 1984; Iker 1995).

Dealing with the Flemish–Walloon divide remains a major task for the Belgian government—a task complicated by the reversal of roles that has taken place. The former elite has grown dependent on a section of the population that used to be backward. This causes tensions on both sides of the language frontier.

4.4 Crumbling Legitimacy

Confidence in political and democratic institutions has come under pressure as a result of a number of scandals, including the Augusta and Dutroux affairs. *Ad hoc* action, including the sacking of individual members of the government, have not succeeded in turning the tide. The broad support for the White Movement has shown how brittle confidence is, and how strong the support for fundamental change.

4.5 Growing Consumerism

Students of Belgian government talk of declining support for advisory bodies and dwindling interest in the forms of participation set up in the 1970s and 1980s. In place of this, consumerist citizenship, which has always played an important part in Belgium, has taken on a new lease of life. In this way developments in the direction of partnership democracy are hindered.

4.6 The Rise of the Extreme Right

At recent local council elections the extreme right parties—the *Vlaams Blok* in Flanders, the *Front National* and *Agir* in Wallonia—made large gains. Between 1976 and 1994 support for the *Vlaams Blok* in Flanders as a whole rose from 0.7 to 6.6 per cent. In Wallonia support for the extreme right increased from 0.1 per cent in 1982 to 3.1 per cent in 1994. In the six municipalities of the Brussels Capital where the *Vlaams Blok* put candidates forward in 1988 and 1994, support increased from 1.8 to 3.9 per cent (Ackaert 1995).

4.7 Pressure on the Traditional Political Parties

The crumbling of the national political system, the first signs of which were seen in the 1991 parliamentary elections—in which socialists and Christian democrats lost on both sides of the language frontier—was confirmed by the 1994 local elections. Once again, the *Christelijke Volkspartij* (CVP, Christian People's Party) lists in Flanders and the *Parti Socialiste* (SP, Socialist Party) lists in Wallonia performed badly.

4.8 Breathing Life into the 'New Political Culture'

In reaction to the trends mentioned above, virtually all the traditional political parties have declared their willingness to work together on the development of a 'new political culture'. This is a promise that will be very difficult to keep, and it is still not at all clear how, in concrete terms, it is to be done. Ideas are in some cases vague and undeveloped, in other cases diverse and mutually contradictory. Thus, greater proximity of citizen and government is being urged (closing the notorious 'gulf'), as is an end to the practice of political favours for citizens (which would increase the distance between citizen and government).

4.9 The Provincial Legacy

The provincial layer of government is a legacy of the unitary Belgian state that is not seen in a uniformly positive light in a regionalized Belgium. Abolition is not planned at present, however, particularly since the creation of a new province, with the division of Brabant into a Flemish and a Walloon part. The institutions and operation of the Belgian provinces remain a source of continuing concern. The pressing questions are how the Belgian province can be made to function as an intermediate tier of government, and how the province can obtain legitimacy in the eyes of citizens (see also section 3.3.2).

4.10 Management of Change

The Belgian government has been undergoing change for a long time and this will continue for still some time to come, in the light of the situation outlined above (the need for change) and below (movements for change, see section 5). Whilst the institutionalization of state reform continues to be the focus of attention, the question of de-federalizing the law on municipalities and reforming the courts has also resurfaced. During the reconstruction (of the institutions), public 'business' (policy, public goods, and services) must, however, continue as normal. This is a particularly difficult task, even for the Belgians who have become past masters of change.

5. Innovative Approaches to Improving Subnational Democracy

Belgium differs sharply from its neighbour, the Netherlands, with regard to political and government reforms. In the Netherlands weighty reports and memos are written, but little changes in the end. In Belgium, however, less is written, but the changes are far greater. A watershed in the process of change in Belgium was the 1993 Constitution which made it absolutely clear that Belgium was no longer a unitary state, but rather a federal state.

However, the reforms do not stop at the federalization/regionalization of Belgium. It may be concluded that a new wave of reforms has started with regionalization, particularly in Flanders where an activist regional government has set to work. This has much to do with the fact that a new government has to carve out a niche for itself and differentiate itself from other parties. There has been sharp criticism of regional activism from some quarters, which, it is alleged, is excessively top-down and operated too much along functional lines. Others, however, have paid tribute to what has been achieved in a relatively short time and not solely on the initiative of regional government. Let us look at this in more detail.

5.1 Opening the 'Black Box'

Subnational government in Belgium has always been a relatively closed subject. Government has traditionally negotiated a lot with social actors, but the discussions tend to take place in restricted, closed, functionally delimited policy communities. The advisory councils, set up in large numbers in the late 1970s, have brought little fundamental change. The national government style has, as it were, been copied at local level. The advent of a new generation of advisory councils—above all in the field of environment policy—has, however, brought some changes. It is now less common for meetings of the advisory councils to be dominated by mainly retired middle class men. The new advisory councils are in theory more attractive to broader sections of society. However, practical involvement in the advisory councils has declined rather than increased. If citizens want to take an interest in public affairs, they look for deeds rather than words (a theme that will be developed further below).

An important factor in the opening up of a formerly closed system is the new Law on Open Government, adopted in 1994, which has since been making its influence felt. This law enables citizens and institutions to get to grips more effectively with the 'Belgian labyrinth'. If they, nonetheless, draw a blank and suspect foul play they may turn to the ombudsman. The ombudsman has recently enjoyed a spectacular ascendancy in Belgian government, including local government. Ombudsmen have been, or are being, appointed in many areas.

5.2 Reform of Democratic Procedures

In 1994, it was possible to vote electronically in 12 per cent of municipalities; this is not without practical significance, but it does little to alter the logic of local democracy.

The logic of local democracy has been changed, however, by the provision to hold local referendums, introduced by the Local Government Law of 1995. The referendum option adds a direct democratic element to a system of indirect democracy. To date, fifteen attempts have been made to force a referendum. The required conditions were met on three occasions. Of the three referendums held (in Ghent, Genk, and Begijnendijk), two produced no result because of low turnout (in Genk and Begijnendijk the turnout was below 40 per cent). In Ghent, however, the turnout was high enough to lead to the adoption of a policy measure: the withdrawal by the local authority of a draft decision to build an underground car park.

It was laid down in the 'St. Michael Agreement' that local and provincial council elections should be held on the same day. This happened for the first time in 1994. In this way it is possible to focus public attention simultaneously on these two levels of subnational government. In order to counter the low level of representation of women in local authorities the Minister for Internal Affairs introduced a legislative initiative aimed at ensuring that at least a quarter of party members sitting on local councils are women.

5.3 Towards a New Political Culture

The great confusion over the idea of a new political culture should not blind us to the fact that a number of initiatives have been taken in this area. There is, however, no generally accepted idea of what 'new' should mean, although there is a discernible trend away from the 'old'. Major initiatives for a new political culture have been taken by the liberal, Guy Verhofstadt. He has been responsible for a number of influential citizens' manifestos and has been the driving force behind the reshaping of the old *Partij voor Vrijheid en Vooruitgang* (PVV, Party for Freedom and Modernization) into the new *Vlaamse Liberalen en Democraten* (VLD, Flemish Liberals and Democrats). The VLD has turned away from the old political culture by severing all its links with liberal pressure groups and instead seeking direct dialogue with the individual citizen, from whom a new sort of citizenship is expected. He or she is treated less as a client/consumer than as a citizen.

The practice of political favours has fallen into disrepute. New parties such as *Agalev* have turned their backs on the favours system. And even the traditional parties have recently become more critical of it. On the initiative of the Flemish politician, De Winter, a code of conduct against political favours has been drawn up. Having the proper party card is less important than it used to be in obtaining positions and other favours. Politicians' 'meeting days' seem to be losing ground.

The contrast with the situation in the Netherlands is striking. One expert on Belgian government put it in a nutshell: 'Just when you [the Dutch] are trying to get politicians into the cafés, we are trying to get them out'.

5.4 Making Planning and Decision-making more Rational and Objective

In some areas the gap between Belgian and Dutch political and government culture is narrowing rather than widening. For a long time the process of making planning and decision-making more rational and objective was considered less important in Belgium than in the Netherlands. This is clearly changing, certainly in Flanders, which is looking to the northern European style of government. Thus, for example, government is now required to publish the reasons for decisions. This is a hindrance to the practice of political favours. There is also a move to rationalize (spatial) planning. Municipalities and provinces are making more and more use of outline planning documents. The 1997 spatial planning decree requires the drawing up of municipal structural plans. There are also tentative signs of the emergence of structural approaches. Inclusive planning is gaining ground at the expense of old-style (*ad hoc*) functional planning. The Dutch practice is being consciously imitated in implementing rationalization and introducing objective practices.

5.5 Trends in Intergovernmental Relations

As a reaction to the electoral successes of the *Vlaams Blok*, urban environment policy has become one of the top priorities of the Flemish government (Peeters 1997). By improving living conditions in urban areas it is hoped that the ground can be cut away from underneath the extreme right. The Flemish regional authority is taking initiatives in this area. It has drawn up a youth employment policy plan and a social stimulus fund, but is also urging town authorities to make their contribution. Working with covenants, and more 'horizontal' government in general, are considered positive. The practice of urban environment policy conforms to a great extent with the horizontal policy philosophy, but this certainly does not apply to all areas where covenants and agreements are used.

Maes (1997) asserts that interactivity in central–local relations only appears to have increased. In fact, he believes that there is still too much one-sidedness, uniformity, and hierarchy in relations. A municipal interest group writes that covenants are often a smokescreen. The VVSG (The Flemish Union of Towns and Communities) stated in December 1997 that 'certainly the first generation of covenants were more like one-sided contracts'. The VVSG is calling for an increase in the scope for local policy, which a number of developments have put under pressure. Examples quoted are the tendency to foist tasks on municipalities, increasing enthusiasm for regulation at regional level, the increasing number of planning requirements, and the development of many new forms of supervision that ensure that the expected lightening of the supervisory load (in the light of the 1993 supervision decree) is not actually materializing. The hierarchical mentality in intergovernmental relations—as expressed in concepts such as 'subordinate levels of government' and 'government under supervision'—has, many feel, not diminished with the regionalization of Belgium and the increasing concern for government renewal. One involved party felt that many acts of higher levels of government, ostensibly aimed at 'renewal of government', actually tended to accentuate the degree of control exercised (Suykens 1997b).

5.6 Towards a New Public Management

The growing interest in functional rationality and businesslike, efficient, and client-oriented working is generally grouped together in the international literature under the heading New Public Management (NPM). Subnational government in Belgium, and particularly in Flanders, is clearly in the grip of NPM and the values and practices associated with it. The foundation was laid with the relatively large-scale reorganization of municipalities between 1950 and 1992. During this period, the number of Belgian municipalities fell by no less than 73 per cent (for comparative purposes: in the Netherlands the number of municipalities declined by only 36 per cent). The reorganization made larger-scale government action possible, but also created problems in terms of external communications and internal management. Major financial interventions in the early 1980s accentuated the need for Management by Objectives (MBO). The first step in this direction was a new municipal accounting system that became operational in 1995. There are doubts in the municipalities as to the renewing qualities of this system: the system is said to bring automation, but little in the way of modernization (in terms of decentralization of government responsibilities, etc.).

In other areas, however, renewal is unmistakable. Examples springing to mind are the rise of competitive and entrepreneurial thinking in urban government, growing autonomy and privatization, the development of self-management and public–private partnerships and the emergence of performance management and human resources policy. During the current term of office a number of large municipalities—Ghent, Louvain, and Antwerp—have initiated a radical internal reorganization. The Antwerp municipality is now broken down into nine 'business units'. At the same time strenuous efforts are being made to increase the level of professionalism. Businesslike professionals—an example being the district managers in towns—are gaining ground at the expense of the dispensers of political favours, who for a long time dominated contacts with citizens.

5.7 The Beginnings of Partnership Democracy

Looking at the Netherlands, we can see that NPM and joint policy-making have enjoyed popularity at different times. In Belgium, the two are running in parallel, with a slight preference for NPM. Interactivity is not stressed so much in Belgium, as links between politicians and citizens have always been close and should, some feel, be given less emphasis. Interesting examples of businesslike joint policy-making can be found in Antwerp and Ghent. Genk provides illuminating examples of a combination of businesslike and district-oriented working methods. Government is being brought closer to citizens' lives, but at the same time also made more objective. The Genk approach is supported by structural discussions, steering groups, and district managers, and conditions for this are relatively favourable (a stable political situation combined with a strong mayor).

A similar combination can be found in Antwerp. For example, the municipality is pressing ahead with making the organization more businesslike. An example is the establishment of 'business units' referred to above, which undoubtedly contributed to the town secretary being elected government manager of the year 1997. At the same time, the municipality attaches great importance to grass-roots work, with a specific level of cooperation (joint policy-making) being sought between government and citizen. A number of sectors within the Antwerp organization are now working in a district-oriented way. And this is necessary since the Antwerp authority underwent a sharp increase in scale as a result of merger in 1981. For some time the development of district councils as a form of decentralization within the Antwerp urban area has been intensively discussed. In other towns this is not an issue.

It is typical of Belgium that calls for 'partnership democracy' often go hand-in-hand with calls for strong democratic leadership (Suykens 1997*a*). The Belgians are less inclined than the Dutch to shrink away from a central leadership role. There are, however, often different ideas as to who should fill this role. The phrase 'government by the municipality' is often bandied about. And yet the municipalities are still often seen as the implementers of regional policy.

In terms of reformist tendencies at the subnational level, Flanders has clearly progressed further than Wallonia. This coincides with the practice of political and government renewal in Belgium. In general, it can be said that Flanders wishes to reform itself faster and more radically than Wallonia, which in some cases is clearly applying the brakes to reform initiatives, such as the defederalization/regionalization of the law on municipalities, which commands a high level of support in Flanders.

6. Conclusions

Four subsequent state reforms (1970, 1980, 1988, 1993) have transformed Belgium from a decentralized unitary state into a federal state which spreads sovereignty over three basic institutions: the central state, the regions, and the communities. There is no hierarchical relationship between the three constituting elements of the Belgian federal state. Federal government is positioned among, and not above the regions and the communities.

The traditional subnational political system of Belgium, consisting of provinces and municipalities, has basically remained the same after the fourth state reform in 1993. The institutional environment of this system has, however, changed considerably because of federalization. An important difference in comparison to the previous period is that the administrative supervision of local and provincial government and the adjudication of policy-related grants to subnational government has been shifted from the traditional administrative centre to the new regionalized institutions of the federal state.

Democracy in Belgium inclines towards the consensual type distinguished by Lijphart (1984). Consensus building is traditionally a relatively closed and secretive activity. Public decision-making traditionally takes place in *conclaves*—relatively small and intransparent policy communities bringing together social and political elites in various fields. New practices and experiments at the subnational level (see section 5) are to a large extent geared at changing the elitist and intransparent aspects of consensual decision-making Belgian-style.

Making a distinction between formal democracy and everyday democracy, it is clear that democratic reform in Belgium has in the last decades been strongly focused on the formal-institutional aspect of democracy in its new federal shape and form. The cultural, informal-institutional aspect of democracy has received less attention. It is probably there where the biggest challenge for future democratic reform lies, as the recent calls for a 'New Political Culture' also underscore.

References

ACKAERT, J. (1994). 'De gemeenten', in M. Deweerdt, C. de Ridder, and R. Dillemans (eds), *Wegwijs politiek*. Leuven: Davidsfonds, 533–58.
——(1995). 'De gemeenteraadsverkiezingen van 9 oktober 1994'. *Res Publica*, 37/3–4: 351–88.
ALEN, A. (1995). *Handboek van het Belgisch staatsrecht*. Antwerp: Kluwer.

Coenen, O. (1994). 'De provincies', in M. Deweerdt, C. de Ridder, and R. Dillemans (eds), *Wegwijs politiek*. Leuven: Davidsfonds, 519–32.

Delruelle-Vosswinkel, N. (1984). 'De politieke waarden', in J. Kerkhofs and R. Rezsohazy (eds), *De stille ommekeer*. Tielt: Lannoo, 181–214.

Dewachter, W. (1995). *Besluitvorming in politiek België*. Leuven: Acco.

——and Das, E. (1991). *Politiek in België: geprofileerde machtsverhoudingen*. Leuven: Acco.

Deweerdt, M. (1994*a*). 'Het Belgisch grondgebied', in M. Deweerdt, C. de Ridder, and R. Dillemans (eds), *Wegwijs politiek*. Leuven: Davidsfonds, 45–9.

——(1994*b*). 'De Belgische gezagsorganisatie', in M. Deweerdt, C. de Ridder, and R. Dillemans (eds), *Wegwijs politiek*. Leuven: Davidsfonds, 191–6.

Donkers, B. (1996). 'Interview met oud-premier W. Martens'. *NRC*, 1 July.

Gouvernement Wallon (1998). *La démocratie locale et régionale en Belgique*. Contribution to the COR-project Local and Regional Democracy in Europe. Namur.

Heunks, F. (1996). 'Varieties of Political Participation', in L. Halman and N. Nevitte (eds), *Political Value Change in Western Democracies*. Tilburg: Tilburg University Press, 221–33.

Hofstede, G. (1991). *Allemaal andersdenkenden: omgaan met cultuurverschillen*. Amsterdam: Contact.

Iker, L. (1995). 'La Wallonie et les francophones'. *Res Publica*, 37/3–4: 339–50.

Inglehart, R. (1990). *Culture Shift in Advanced Industrial Society*. Princeton: Princeton University Press.

Istendael, G. van (1993). *Het Belgisch labyrint: wakker worden in een ander land*. Amsterdam: Arbeiderspers.

Kanji, M. and Nevitte, N. (1996). 'Unpacking Environmental Orientations: Deep or Superficial?', in L. Halman and N. Nevitte (eds), *Political Value Change in Western Democracies*. Tilburg: Tilburg University Press, 285–307.

Kerkhofs, J. and Rezsochazy, R. (eds) (1984). *De stille ommekeer*. Tielt: Lannoo.

Kitschelt, H. (1989). *The Logics of Party-Formation, Ecological Politics in Belgium and West-Germany*. Ithaca, NY: Cornell University Press.

Knutsen, O. (1996). 'The Impact of Old Politics and New Politics Value Orientations on Party Choice: A Comparative Study', in L. Halman and N. Nevitte (eds), *Political Value Change in Western Democracies*. Tilburg: Tilburg University Press, 153–89.

Lijphart, A. (1984). *Democracies: Patterns of Majoritarian and Consensus Government in Twenty-one Countries*. New Haven: Yale University Press.

Maes, R. (1997). 'Het profiel van de lokale politiek'. *Res Publica*, 39/1: 3–26.

Ministerie van de Vlaamse Gemeenschap (1991). *Vlaanderen informatiebrochure: van staatsverband naar staatsverbond*. Brussels.

——(1993). *Verder met Vlaanderen: informatie van en over de Vlaamse overheid*. Brussels.

Peeters, L. (1997). 'Tussen buurt en stadsregio. Anderhalf jaar stedelijk beleid in Vlaanderen'. *Res Publica*, 39/1: 125–38.

Ridder, C. de (1994). 'Portret van de Belgische staat', in M. Deweerdt, C. de Ridder, and R. Dillemans (eds), *Wegwijs politiek*. Leuven: Davidsfonds, 27–33.

Rynck, F. de (1992). *De toekomst van de provinciebesturen in België*. Leuven: Katholieke Universiteit Leuven.

RYNCK, F. DE (1994). *Streekontwikkeling in Vlaanderen*. Leuven: Acco.

SUYKENS, M. (1997a). *ACW-Vormingsinitiatief 'In de greep van bestuurlijke vernieuwing'*. Transcript of lecture, Kortrijk.

——(1997b). *De aanpak van de externe communicatie in lokale besturen*. Brussels: Verenigung van Vlaamse Steden en Gemeenten.

VELDKAMP, C. C. J. (1993). 'Schuivende bestuurlijke verhoudingen in België en de relatie met Nederland'. *Openbaar bestuur*, 4/3: 2–9.

WALGRAVE, S. (1994). *Nieuwe sociale bewegingen in Vlaanderen*. Leuven: Katholieke Universiteit Leuven.

——(1995). *Tussen loyaliteit en selectiviteit*. Leuven: Katholieke Universiteit Leuven.

WINTER, L. DE (1994). 'Politiek dienstbetoon', in M. Deweerdt, C. de Ridder, and R. Dillemans (eds), *Wegwijs politiek*. Leuven: Davidsfonds, 425–31.

Part 4

THE SCANDINAVIAN TRADITION

14

Sweden: The End of the 'Swedish Model'?

Anders Lidström

1. History and Concept of Democracy

1.1 Historical Background

The economic, social, and political development of Sweden was slow at the end of the nineteenth century compared with the rest of Europe. Sweden was still a poor country with a population overly dependent on subsistence farming. Industrialization and urbanization lagged behind and political rights were restricted. However, the first decades of the twentieth century witnessed the beginning of a complete transformation of Swedish society. Industries developed rapidly based on the natural resources of timber and ore, rural poverty was eliminated by emigration and urbanization, social problems were gradually reduced, and the Swedes gained new political rights. Democracy emerged via a number of successive steps, but universal suffrage was finally established in 1921.

As Rokkan (1970) has observed, this gradual political transformation is, in itself, a major feature of Swedish society. Contrary to the pattern in several other European countries, democratic control over political institutions was established without explosive conflicts between those in privileged positions and the powerless majority.

During the rest of the twentieth century, Swedish democracy has followed this path of conflict management through cooperation and consensus. Indeed, several writers have identified a Swedish model, which at times has been seen as an alternative to both pure capitalism and communism. Four features of this model seem to have been particularly relevant for the way democracy has been conceptualized in Sweden.

First, Sweden encompasses a large public sector, strongly committed to welfare. Starting in the 1930s, but particularly after the Second World War, a comprehensive and generous public welfare system was developed in order to increase the well-being of Swedish citizens and to even out differences between the wealthy and the less privileged. This was financed by the highest tax rates in the western world. The welfare system has been governed by elected decision-makers at different levels, and, therefore, democratic institutions have played a crucial role in the everyday life of the Swedish citizen.

Second, Swedish democracy has been to a significant extent a corporatist democracy. A precondition was the existence of dominant, centralized organizations, aiming at protecting the interests of their members in various situations. The key area, of course, was the labour market. Membership rates of trade unions were very high, especially among blue-collar workers in industrial trades (Korpi 1981). Organizational strength was obtained not only by this monopoly position, but also by a conscious effort to influence political decision-making.

A third feature of the Swedish model of democracy has been the prominent role played by political parties. A five-party system, in essence established at the beginning of the twentieth century, and linked to a left–right cleavage, has dominated the political scene. Indeed, Sweden has been the most homogeneous of the Western European countries in terms of religion, ethnicity, and language (Lane and Ersson 1994), which elsewhere provided bases for the emergence of specific parties. The role of the political parties has been enhanced by a strong membership base, considerable financial resources from central and local government, and a well-developed local organization.

Among the political parties, the *Socialdemokraterna* (Social Democrats) has had a dominant role. It has been in government for sixty of the seventy-seven years since the introduction of universal suffrage. It has, thereby, been able to make a lasting impact on the development of the Swedish welfare state (Milner 1989). Indeed, some foreign observers have described the situation as a social democratic hegemony (Kesselman *et al.* 1987).

A fourth characteristic of Swedish democracy is the position held by local government. Historically, self-government in rural areas, and to some extent also in cities, has been important. Even if there have been periods of stricter central control, considerable scope for independent, local, collective decision-making has been available (Petersson 1994*a*). A large proportion of self-reliant farmers together with the absence of feudal structures have been favourable for the development and maintenance of this relative autonomy. In the modern era, the growth of public welfare has taken place mainly through local government. Even if this has provided local authorities with new tasks and powers, some of these have been restricted by the aim of central government to set national standards within, for example, education and social services. Nevertheless, the Swedish model of welfare and democracy is to a large extent a local-government model.

Sweden is often lumped together with the other Nordic countries into a general Nordic model of state building. However, as Knudsen and Rothstein (1994) argue, there are distinctive features of the Swedish state-building process. Contrary to, for example, Finland and Norway, the Swedish state was constructed by the Swedes themselves, without foreign coercion or occupation. This is not to say that external influences have been unimportant. During the eighteenth century, French impact on Swedish politics and culture was extensive, and later, the influences of Germany and England were significant.

Nevertheless, endogenous factors in the state-building process were very important. In particular, the combination of free peasants, weak landlords, and weak towns created a certain scope for lower class interests in state building. For example, Sweden was for several centuries the only unified European state in which peasants were represented in parliament. This created a need for broad consensus agreements between different social strata. Indeed, Knudsen and Rothstein (1994) argue that corporatism was well established in the Swedish society before the rise of social democracy, and that state formation became a corporate project. This may have paved the way for the Swedish form of democracy, with strong interest organizations, a dominant social democracy, egalitarianism, and a strong reliance on the public sector.

The four characteristics mentioned above were, until recently, key features of Swedish democracy. However, during the past two decades, a number of changes have taken place that are about to at least modify this picture. The public sector is no longer growing. Instead, reductions in welfare services have taken place in order to adjust costs to available means. To some extent, this has been obtained through rationalization and more efficient provision of services, but it has also included decreased service quality and the abandonment of previous commitments. Hence, the classical question of the desired size of the public sector has been the focus for renewed attention. The state has sold off publicly owned companies and previous state monopolies have been put under pressure by increasing competition from private alternatives. However, despite these changes, the Swedish public welfare system is still the largest in the European Union. It is also highly valued by its citizens (Svallfors 1996).

As a result of the debate about the proper role of interest organizations, a process of 'decorporatization' has taken place (Micheletti 1995). Even if Swedish trade unions still have the highest membership rates in the world (Goul Andersen 1996), the interest organizations are not, in the same way as before, directly involved in decision-making or implementation. This coincides with a general tendency to decentralize agreements in the labour market. Also, new, more *ad hoc* forms of organizing have emerged, providing new channels outside the established organizations.

Major changes have occurred with regard to the political parties. The traditional five-party system has been challenged from several directions. Internally, the parties are suffering from declining membership and difficulties in recruiting candidates for elections. According to some observers, Swedish parties are becoming like elite parties, with fewer members and with their activities concentrated on the election campaigns. Financially, they have tended to become less dependent on membership contributions and more on funds from the public purse. In 1994, the parties received direct financial support from central and local government, to an amount corresponding to Skr1,000 per party member (Bäck and Möller 1995). In addition, previously coherent parties, such as the Social Democrats, are showing signs of inner tensions. Not least, the question of Swedish membership in the EU has divided the party. Externally, the traditional parties are challenged by the emergence of new parties, such as the Christian Democrats, the Environmental Party, and (for a period of time) the populist New Democracy. At the same time, voter volatility has increased, and fewer citizens regard themselves as supporters of a particular party (Gilljam and Holmberg 1995). The previous strength of the Social Democrats can no longer be taken for granted. Since its traditional electoral base—the working class—is declining, the party is attempting to broaden its support among middle class voters. It is still unclear whether this will be successful.

The final cornerstone, a strong local government, seems to have retained and perhaps even strengthened its position. A number of decentralization measures have been undertaken. Local-government discretion to use centrally allocated resources has increased considerably. The transfer of functions, replacement of detailed regulation with governing by objectives, and framework laws have all provided a greater scope for independent local decision-making. Major changes have also taken place within specific policy areas. The Swedish education system, which used to be the most centralized in the western world (Heidenheimer 1983), is now under significant local-government control (Hudson and Lidström forthcoming).

However, there have also been changes pointing in the other direction (Montin and Elander 1995). The financial strain on local government has increased, due to cuts in central-government grants and reduced tax income because of higher unemployment. The regulation of how local authorities should perform various tasks has been replaced by a more thorough evaluation of policy outputs. In addition, there is now a tendency for central government, once more, to set national standards when it feels that local government is not making the right priorities. For example, new legislation has been introduced that contains a guarantee that local authorities will provide sufficient care for the disabled, a place in a day nursery for those who require one, and charge-free local libraries.

All these changes make it reasonable to conclude that the traditional Swedish conceptualization of democracy has been significantly altered and is less distinctive as a political alternative. In several ways, Sweden has become more dependent on international currents and developments, and in terms of policies, Sweden has become similar to other European countries, even if there are still some differences.

1.2 Democracy at the Subnational Level

Is democracy understood differently at central, regional, and local levels? On the whole, the Swedish way of organizing democracy is basically similar at all levels. Differences are to a large extent a matter of scale. The contacts between elected and electors are closer at local level, and it is probably easier for a group of individuals to achieve changes locally than nationally. However, in terms of the major features of the Swedish model, other differences are noticeable. Welfare provision at the local level has been reduced, even if outright privatization of services is unusual so far. Corporatism has also been present locally, and today new forms of cooperation between local government and business interests have been developing for the purpose of promoting local economic growth. In the main, the party system at the local level corresponds to the national structure, but specific local parties, not connected to national parties and focusing on local issues, have become increasingly common since the 1970s.

Swedish local government is not just limited to a mere administrative implementation of central directives at the local level, but exerts considerable self-government. It has a general competence and a right to levy taxes which provides scope for local authorities to take on non-regulated tasks, such as cultural and recreational activities and economic development policies. Through systems of building permissions, municipalities can also decide over land use in its territory. Hence, there are good reasons for people to get involved in local politics in order to influence the shaping of the locality.

2. The Institutional Expression of Democracy

2.1 The National Level

The formal base for Swedish democracy is a constitutional monarchy. The constitution, which dates from 1974, defines democracy as 'rule by the people', based on freedom of speech and general suffrage. It explicitly states that Swedish democracy is realized through a representative and parliamentary system and local self-government. The national parliament is a one-chamber assembly, elected through a proportional list system. However, parties must receive at least 4 per cent of the votes in order to be represented in the parliament. The period between elections, which was three years between 1970 and 1994, is now four years. Since 1970, the election day is the same for national and local-government elections. During the same period, turnout has varied between 86 and 92 per cent, with slightly lower rates at the local-government elections. Public referendums at national level are unusual and have only been held on five occasions since their introduction in 1922.

The relationship between the government and parliament is consistent with the principles of parliamentarism. The government and each minister must not be actively rejected by the majority of the parliament. In Sweden, the government departments are comparatively small, as administrative tasks have been allocated to semi-independent administrative bodies. Swedish public administration is also characterized by its long tradition of open government, based on a constitutional rule already introduced in the late eighteenth century. In principle, everyone has the right to access documents produced by a public authority. There are exceptions relating to, for example, foreign policy, defence, and the protection of commercial relations and private life. However, the openness is still considerable, which has been regarded as enhancing Swedish democracy.

2.2 The Local Level

The Swedish system of local government is regarded as an archetype of a Nordic category of local-government systems, to be found in Sweden, Finland, Norway, and Denmark (Bennet 1993; Norton 1994; Lidström 1996). The system is characterized not only by the extensive scale of local government activities, but also by its relative autonomy *vis-à-vis* the state.[1]

Local government in Sweden consists of two tiers: a *kommuner* (municipal) and a *landsting* (county) level. There are 289 municipalities, ranging in size from Bjurholm's 2,800 to the 727,000 inhabitants of Stockholm. The average population is 30,200 inhabitants, which make Swedish municipalities fairly large, compared to other European local-government systems. However, as the median size is 16,000, there is still a considerable number of small municipalities. Two major amalgamation reforms, during the 1950s and the 1970s, reduced the number of municipalities from 2,500 and increased the population sizes considerably. These reorganizations were undertaken in order to provide local authorities with sufficiently large populations to enable them to carry out the new welfare tasks. However, in many places, amalgamations were contested, and since 1976 there is a slight tendency to divide previously merged authorities, particularly in the case of medium-sized municipalities.

The number of counties is being reduced from twenty-three to twenty as a result of amalgamation processes in western and southern Sweden. The average size after amalgamations will be 442,000 inhabitants, but three of the counties will be exceptionally large, as they together will comprise half the Swedish population. County councils were established in 1862 with the

---

[1] For an overview of the Swedish system of local government, see Häggroth *et al.* (1996).

functions of providing services that required a larger population base than the municipalities could offer and to elect members to the upper chamber of parliament (until 1969). Today, their major task is responsibility for health care. Counties have no authority in relation to the municipalities. Citizens tend to be more aware of and have greater knowledge about municipal than county policies and politicians. At the regional level, there is also a state administrative board, which performs various control and support functions and has regional-planning tasks.

The main decision-making body in the municipalities as well as the counties is the council. This consists of members, elected for four-year periods. The council appoints committees, which are responsible for the running of different local-government services. The committees are composed proportionally to mirror the strength of the different parties in the council, but their members do not need to be councillors. The most important committee is the executive, which is obligatory. It has an overarching responsibility for all local-government activities and prepares all matters to be dealt with by the council. The chairman of this committee is usually the leading representative of the political majority and normally has a full-time remuneration from the local authority. In addition, one or several other politicians, including representatives from the opposition, may be salaried on similar terms. Other committees are also established, with responsibilities for various areas of local-government activity.

The functions of local authorities are basically of two kinds. Some are optional, falling under a general competence. Most commonly, these consist of recreational and cultural tasks, but also include general measures to stimulate economic growth in the locality. The other functions are mandatory, as they are formally performed on behalf of central government. These include education, social services, planning, building permissions, and environmental protection. The county councils, as already mentioned, are mainly responsible for health care, but also fulfil tasks related to public dental care and care for the disabled. In addition, they are in charge of regional cultural institutions and certain regional-development measures. County council involvement in regional-development activities has increased in recent years.

2.3 The Role of Parties

The political parties have a strong position in the local councils, even if party lines tend to be stricter in the larger local authorities. In addition to the local branches of the major national parties, a number of specific local parties have emerged since the 1970s. While there are at the moment seven parties in parliament, 24 per cent of the municipal councils consist of eight or more parties (Pierre 1995). These specific local parties often pursue topical issues that cut

TABLE 14.1   Party strength in the municipalities (percentages), 1988–98

Party	Election			
	1988	1991	1994	1998
Non-socialist parties				
Conservative Party	18.1	22.2	20.2	22.3
Centre Party	12.5	11.2	10.1	8.2
Liberal Party	11.3	9.6	6.9	6.0
Christian Democratic Party	2.8	5.8	3.2	8.0
Socialist parties				
Social Democratic Party	41.6	36.6	43.3	35.1
Left Party	5.5	4.8	6.0	10.2
Other parties				
Environmental Party	5.6	3.6	5.2	4.8
Others and specific local parties	2.6	6.3	4.9	5.4
Electoral turnout	84.0	84.0	84.4	78.6

Source: Gustafsson (1996); SCB (1998).

across traditional party lines, or they may have been created around strong community leaders outside the traditional parties. In several municipalities and counties, such parties had landslide victories in the 1994 and 1998 elections, even though their overall share of the electorate was small. Apart from making majority coalitions less stable and the political majority more unclear, these new parties have also contributed to new patterns of cooperation between parties traditionally split by the left–right divide. The results of the last four municipal elections are summarized in Table 14.1.

Generally, the strength of the parties at municipal level corresponds fairly well to their position at national as well as county level. However, a number of exceptions are noteworthy: specific local parties are more common at municipal than county level. The Centre Party is stronger at local than national level whereas the Social Democratic and the Christian Democratic Parties are performing worse locally than nationally.

The members of the municipal and county councils are elected in local elections held on the same day as the parliamentary elections. In 1976, the right to participate in local-government elections was granted to non-Swedish citizens who have lived in the country for at least three years. From the 1998 elections, the EU standard practice was adopted, giving all EU citizens living in Sweden local voting rights without a three-year delay. This right is also extended to Norwegian and Icelandic citizens.

Turnout in the last election fell to 79 per cent, but in the previous four elections was between 84 and 88 per cent. In areas where unemployment is high,

Table 14.2   Citizen–politician ratio in the municipalities, 1951–95

Year	No. of municipalities	Politicians per municipality	Total	Citizens per politician
1951	2,500	80	200,000	35
1962	1,000	125	125,000	61
1974	278	180	50,000	164
1980	279	250	70,000	119
1993	286	175	50,000	175
1995	288	166	48,000	184

Note: The table is calculated on the basis of data from Gustafsson (1996: 126) and official population statistics. The concept of a politician refers to elected members of the municipal councils and appointed members of municipal committees.

health problems are above average, and where there is a large proportion of foreign citizens, turnout is below average (Petersson *et al.* 1997). Participation in local elections among non-Swedish citizens is decreasing. It was 60 per cent in 1976, but only 40 per cent voted in the last elections. Immigrants from Chile are the most keen to participate, whereas the lowest rates have been reported for immigrants originating from Greece and former Yugoslavia (SCB 1995).

Those who are eligible to vote can also stand as candidates. Female representation in the local councils has increased in recent decades and is now, on average, 42 per cent in the municipalities and 48 per cent at county levels (SCB 1998). This makes women's representation in the Swedish local councils the highest in the world. However, the proportion of non-Swedish councillors is still only 0.9 per cent in the municipalities and 0.5 per cent in the county councils (Bäck and Soininen 1996).

During the past fifty years, the number of elected and appointed politicians has gradually decreased. As Table 14.2 illustrates, it is now more than five times less likely than in 1951 that a citizen is a local politician. The development shown in Table 14.2 reflects a number of changes that together have reduced the number of local politicians: two amalgamation reforms, a reduction in the number of municipal committees, and a reduction in the size of the municipal councils (SOU 1996: 169). Despite a temporary increase in the number of committees during the 1970s, the net effect has still been that elected and appointed positions have become more exclusive; and it is now less likely that citizens will know a local politician personally, or be politicians themselves.

The system of proportional representation has, hitherto, provided very limited scope for the electorate to select particular persons. The parties provide lists of candidates, and, in practice, the choice is between these different lists. Candidates are elected in the order they appear on the list, and the number of those elected depends on the number of votes the list attracts.

Greater possibilities for the electorate to influence the actual choice of candidates by making a mark next to the one they prefer was tested in seven municipalities in the 1994 elections and in the elections to the European Parliament in 1995. The system was introduced in the whole country in 1998, at the local and regional as well as the parliamentary elections. In local and regional elections, 5 per cent of the voters have to choose a specific candidate in order to alter the sequence of names on the list, as suggested by the party. The experience from 1998 indicates that the personal vote only had a marginal impact in the local elections.

The traditionally strong role of political parties is also challenged by means of direct democracy. Since 1977, local authorities have been entitled to arrange advisory referendums. Most of those held so far have concerned suggestions to divide previously amalgamated municipalities, but issues have also included the placing of major roads and the disposal of nuclear waste. In practice, many of them have been binding, since the council majority already before the referendum declared that it would comply with the result. Decisions to hold a local referendum have to be taken by the council and can be suggested by any councillor. In addition, since 1994, referendums are also considered if suggested by at least 5 per cent of the electorate. However, the first forty initiatives of this kind were all rejected by the councils (*KommunAktuellt*, 26, 1996).

Citizens may also attempt to influence political decision-making by other means. Generally, public participation seems to be comparatively high in Sweden. In an investigation of participation rates in Western European countries Sweden is, together with Britain, at the top regarding the proportion of the population engaged in some form of political participation beyond voting (Topf 1995). An extensive survey in 1992–3 by the Swedish Bureau of Statistics indicated that 51 per cent of the Swedish adult population claimed to have, at least on some occasions, tried to do something about shortcomings or incorrect decisions in their own municipality. The most common activities are to sign a petition (38 per cent), to make direct contact with officials or with elected or appointed politicians (21 per cent), and to take part in a demonstration (16 per cent). Activity rates tend to be highest among white-collar workers, the well-educated, and the native Swedes (SCB 1996*b*).

3. The Practice of Local Democracy

3.1 The Role of Policy Networks and Pressure Groups in Local Government

Two local government associations perform important intermediate functions between local and central government. The Swedish Association of Local Authorities organizes the municipalities, whereas the county councils are members of the Federation of County Councils. They both represent local government interests in national policy-making. On the whole, the relationship between central and local government is characterized by a mutual trust and understanding. In an extensive local government system of the Swedish type, parliament and government rely on local government to implement national welfare policies without excessive control, and local authorities expect to be involved at early stages in the decision-making process when changes affecting local authorities are considered.

There are also important informal relations between central and local government. For example, previously established personal contacts with key decision-makers may facilitate access to governmental power, as local-government political leaders try to influence government decisions (Lidström 1995).

Local authorities are also themselves members of other networks, which promote their common interests in various contexts. For example, local authorities cooperate in issues such as education, tourism, and transport (Petersson 1994*a*), and increasingly also in international support and development. In addition, professional and sectoral organizations are important for exchanges of ideas between local authorities. Increasingly, networks including private actors are also established. In particular, such public–private partnerships are used as a means for economic development of the local area.

The new forms of cooperation with local private interests have opened up local authorities because of pressure from private business. It is increasingly seen as important that local policies are adjusted to the needs of private enterprises. Corporatism has traditionally been stronger at the central rather than local level, for example through national labour market agreements. However, at the local level, there are close links between local authorities and organizations. Demands on local decision-makers is put forward by organizations representing the mentally and physically handicapped, pensioners, and patients, and also by sports clubs and various other leisure interests. On the whole, these tend to be strong and well organized. Local authorities are trying to integrate these interests by giving them seats in joint advisory bodies, consisting of representatives from organizations as well as politicians.

3.2 Critiques of Local Democracy

In the public debate on local democracy, the present state of Swedish local democracy has been criticized from several different angles. Indeed, it is unusual to find defenders of the present situation. The official position of all governments since the early 1970s, in fact, is that there are several problems with local democracy. Since the amalgamation reform in the late 1960s and early 1970s, government commissions, with the task of suggesting new means for improving local democracy, have replaced each other. Criticism from the commissions has mainly focused on ways of improving traditional representative democracy. It has been observed that the position of the political parties has been weakened and that the number of elected and appointed representatives has decreased. It has also been pointed out that the focus during recent years on managerialism and efficiency has made democracy a secondary concern in many local councils.

Other critics have suggested means which effectively challenge the representative system itself. The environmental party is a major proponent for more direct forms of democracy (e.g., binding referendums). On the other hand, the political right, but also the broad middle class, criticizes local representative democracy for its limited scope for individual choice. Finally, there is a general concern with declining political participation (e.g., turnout at elections), and that some groups in society, in particular immigrants, have a lower rate of participation than other citizens. The different suggestions will be discussed more in detail in other parts of the chapter.

3.3 Citizens' Attitudes

Swedish citizens generally take a great interest in local politics. A recent survey from the SNS Democracy Advice Board (Petersson *et al.* 1997) indicates that 65 per cent of the citizens are interested or very interested in politics of their own municipality. The corresponding figure for national politics is 75 per cent. Hence, national matters attract more interest, but not much more. However, popular interest in politics at the county level is clearly lower. Only 50 per cent express interest in such matters, which supports the picture of the relative anonymity of Swedish county councils. Also in the minds of people, Sweden is characterized by a combination of strong localities, a strong central level, and weak regions (Petersson 1994*b*).

Behind the formal structure of local democracy, there are a number of informal tendencies that somewhat alter the picture (Bidsted 1997). For example, there is a strong tendency for local government to become professionalized with regard to both officers and politicians. The leading officers tend to be professional specialists or managers, and in the case of the politicians, those who have full-time remuneration clearly have a much stronger position than the ordinary spare-time representatives. This also coincides with a general weakening of the status of the council. As power over details has been delegated to other bodies, remaining decisions are more overarching. These concern setting of goals and objectives and allocation of resources for broad purposes.

Finally, there is also a tendency for public mistrust towards political decision-makers to increase (Gilljam and Holmberg 1995). Generally, the Swedes used to be fairly confident in their municipal elected representatives, but this is clearly decreasing. Table 14.3 provides results from extensive

TABLE 14.3 Citizens' confidence in their municipal elected representatives (percentages), 1978–93

'How do you think your municipal elected representatives carry out their tasks?'	Year		
	1978	1984	1992–3
Very/fairly good	63.4	62.2	48.3
Not so good/not good at all	24.0	20.5	29.8
No opinion/do not know	12.6	17.3	21.9

Note: The table is calculated from data presented in SCB (1996*b*).

population surveys on living conditions and political resources, undertaken by the Swedish Bureau of Statistics.

Nevertheless, there are still more citizens with confidence in their representatives than citizens who are displeased with their performance, but the gap is shrinking. Also from the 1992–3 survey, it has been shown that older citizens have more confidence in local politicians than younger citizens. However, there are considerable variations between different local authorities. Obviously, specific local factors are important for citizens' assessments (SCB 1996*b*). A more recent investigation has reported that public confidence in municipal executive committees is very low; and indeed, in comparison with fourteen other societal institutions that were listed in the questionnaire (banks, large companies, the monarchy, health care, government, etc.), the municipal executive committees gained least support (Holmberg and Weibull 1997).

At local level, mistrust has been reinforced by the occurrence of local political fraud scandals during the early 1990s. A few leading politicians, in different local authorities, used taxpayers' money to pay for leisure travel, visits to dubious nightclubs, or luxury consumption. These events have not helped to enhance trust between the electors and the elected.

4. Challenges and Opportunities for Regional and Local Democracy

4.1 The European Challenge

A major recent challenge for Swedish local authorities is the process of European integration. However, their orientation towards the European Union and local government in other European countries started long before the Swedish membership of the EU in 1995. One early, but still the most common, way of linking the local area with communities outside the national border has been to establish twin-city relationships. Most of those relationships are with local authorities in other Nordic countries, but increasingly they are on a European-wide scale and links are even being developed with local authorities on other continents. Indeed, Swedish municipalities are involved in more than a thousand twin-city contacts, and their number has increased during recent years (Andersson and Lundell 1991; Svenska Kommunförbundet 1996). During the first years, honorary visits, cultural exchanges, and school class meetings were features of these links. However, they have increasingly come to aim at exchanging services and knowledge and to stimulate commerce and local development. Swedish local authorities are also involved in international organizations, for example in different forms of transborder cooperation (Östhol 1996).

Even if the international contacts of local authorities were considerable in the 1980s, they have, nevertheless, increased significantly due to the greater importance of the EU and its subsequent Swedish membership. This international activity has led to some changes in the internal structure and workings of the local authorities. These include, in particular, the provision of EU training courses, but also the employment of international officers and the establishment of an international unit within the local authority. Other changes are externally oriented, for example the undertaking of study visits and cooperation with other municipalities (von Bergmann-Winberg 1997).

The general tendency is that such activities are growing and that the level of involvement is now even higher than in Denmark, which has been an EU member since 1973 (Gidlund 2000). However, there are considerable differences between local authorities. The most active municipalities tend to be densely populated with a concentration of employment in the service sector, whereas low involvement correlates with sparse population and a large percentage of the population employed in agriculture. Interestingly, the referendum on Swedish EU membership in 1994 followed the same pattern. Hence, municipalities with a large share of yes-votes tend to have developed higher activity rates today (Ström 2000). However, on the whole and in terms of local democracy, local internationalization strategies tend to be an elitist project. They create enthusiasm primarily among a few politicians and administrators in the local authorities.

4.2 Financial Strains

In economic terms, the expenditures of Swedish local government represent 28 per cent of the gross domestic product (GDP), and their share of total public expenditure is 38 per cent (1994, Council of Europe 1997). The municipalities are in charge of most of these resources, as the counties only represent one-quarter of the local-government sector. Swedish local government is mainly financed by taxes and central-government grants. The main source of income is a proportional income tax, which provides 63 per cent of municipal (1995 figures) and 75 per cent of county resources (1993 figures). Indeed, Swedish local authorities are dependent on local taxation to a greater extent than local government in any other EU country (Council of Europe 1997).

In principle, local authorities themselves can decide the level of their taxes, a right that has been frequently used. Between 1970 and 1996, the average local tax rate increased from 21 per cent to 32 per cent of taxable income (SCB 1996*a*). However, this right has been restricted by agreements between the local-government associations and the government, and there was a period between 1990 and 1993 when tax increases were explicitly forbidden by law. Between 1997 and 1999, local authorities who increased their tax were punished by a withdrawal of central-government grants corresponding to half the expected gain in new tax income. However, from 2000, no such restrictions remain. Central-government grants, including resources from the social-insurance system, represent 16 per cent of municipal and 20 per cent of county income. Previously, grants were provided for specific purposes, but most of these have now been merged into one all-embracing block grant.

Swedish local government became accustomed to a constant growth in its resources during most of the post-war period. Particularly during the period from 1950 to the beginning of the 1980s, municipal and county consumption, as shares of GDP, increased steadily. Expansion was succeeded by a period of stagnation, and in the beginning of the 1990s, outright reductions in local-government financial resources took place. This was linked to slower growth in the Swedish economy, increased unemployment implying lower tax income, and cuts in grants to local government in order to reduce the state budget deficit. However, neo-liberal influences from Britain and the United States also put pressure on a reduction of the public commitment.

The option of raising local taxes has been used only selectively. Of course, one reason is that this was legally prohibited during 1991 and 1992, but at other times there has been a common concern among different parties not to increase citizens' tax burden further. During the stagnation period, social problems put additional pressure on local-government services. Municipalities have, for example, a responsibility to assist financially those who exhaust their unemployment benefit.

This has resulted in an entirely changed situation for local government. Several commitments, previously taken for granted, have been abandoned. Attempts have been made to increase efficiency, and sometimes the quality of the services has been reduced. New forms of managing local-government services have been introduced, emphasizing the efficient achievement of results. These include purchaser–provider models, governing by objectives, and the establishment of market-like relationships. User charges have increased or been introduced for previously free services.

The number of local-government employees has decreased by 10 per cent during the first five years of the 1990s. The expectation for the coming years is that the financial problems will continue and put further stress on the local authorities (Wetterberg 1997). These changes are profound for local government, but it is still not clear how they will affect local democracy. However, unpopular decisions have created strains between local political decision-makers and the citizens. The emphasis on management and efficiency has also been criticized for not taking concerns for democracy into account.

One effect of the economic problems has been a reduction in the local-government welfare commitment, even if this is still considerable compared with other countries. However, the size of school classes and nursery groups has increased, and the caring element in health care has been reduced, even if medical standards have been retained, on the whole. Corresponding reductions have been made in the national welfare programmes, for example by lowering the child- and unemployment-benefit levels. At the same time, central government has become less willing to intervene and provide additional support to local authorities with suddenly emerging problems, such as the closure of a key industry. The net result is a new situation in which local authorities have to rely on their own ability to develop the local economy. Swedish local authorities are particularly vulnerable, since they rely, to a large extent, on their revenue from local taxes and thus on a flourishing local economy. Hence, a major contemporary change is the shift of focus in local-government policies. Even if welfare provision still retains a dominant position, the promotion of local economic growth has become increasingly important. This may also affect local democracy, since these policies create a dependence between local government and business (Pierre 1994) and do not, as is the case with welfare policies, concern the immediate relationship between the local authority and its citizens.

4.3 Organizational Changes

The ongoing reorganization of local government has been one way by which local authorities have attempted to adjust themselves to changing conditions. As has already been mentioned, this has included shifts in power relations between central and local government. However, the internal structures of local authorities have also been affected (Montin 1993). The establishment of submunicipal committees is one example of an attempt to decentralize powers inside local authorities. From 1979 onwards, it has been possible to organize such committees with responsibility for services within a part of a local-authority area. These are elected by and have the same political composition as the council. The committees were expected to enhance democracy through closer contacts between citizens and political decision-makers. In smaller local authorities, they can be regarded as a way of recreating the local-government system before amalgamations, but within the framework of the new authority. At the moment, about twenty-five municipalities have adopted the system, and during recent years they have been introduced mainly in larger cities. Gothenburg has had submunicipal committees since 1989, and Malmö and Stockholm introduced theirs in 1997. On the whole, the original expectations in terms of improving citizen involvement in local politics were not met. The reform changes the political structure but only marginally facilitates citizen–politician links (Montin and Elander 1995; Jönsson, Rubenowitz, and Westerståhl 1995).

Additional changes concerning the inner organization of local authorities include the establishment of a new concept of management, largely copied from leadership practice in private business. Semi-independent 'results units' have been established, with decentralized responsibility for a school or an old people's home, for example. Purchaser–provider models have been tested in both municipalities and counties. Some of these tendencies have been regarded as components in a movement leading to more depoliticization (Montin and Elander 1995). Political judgement has been replaced by professional decisions, seemingly with a neutral and technical-managerial perspective.

A policy shift with a different emphasis on democracy came during 1991–4 when the non-socialist government introduced new ideas about privatization and choice. Democracy, it was argued, should be enhanced by giving clients greater opportunities to choose between different services and providers. Attempts were made to stimulate the establishment of private alternatives within fields previously totally dominated by the public sector, such as day nurseries and schools. Many local authorities with a non-socialist majority supported this by local means, such as the introduction of voucher systems. Interestingly, choice policies as well as privatization have continued, although less enthusiastically, even after the Social Democratic victory in the 1994 elections. The number of independent schools, private day nurseries, and private old people's homes have continued to increase, particularly in Greater Stockholm, but these still represent only a small part of the local services within these areas. There are signs indicating that these issues are becoming less politicized and can be rather seen as an adjustment to specific demands placed by a growing, well-educated middle class (Hudson and Lidström forthcoming).

The most recent, centrally initiated reform within this field is the introduction of user boards in schools, modelled on experiences from Denmark. The municipalities decide themselves whether they want to establish such boards. Their members are appointed by the municipality, but should contain a majority of parents. The parents' organizations are responsible for selecting the parents to serve on these boards. Representatives of school employees should also be included, and pupils have a right to be present during meetings. The years from 1996 to 2001 are designated as an experimental period, and the experiences will be decisive for whether and how the system will continue to develop. However, despite submunicipal committees and user boards, the net effect of the internal restructuring has been a reduction in the number of municipal committees. This has consequences for democracy as there are now fewer persons holding politically appointed posts.

One consequence of the last few years of organizational changes and decentralization is a more fragmented municipal organization. Standardized approaches are more unusual, and there is also a tendency to establish co-operative devices with other local authorities or non-public bodies. The result is an organization in which it is increasingly difficult for citizens to find their way to the right officer or decision-maker (Montin and Elander 1995; Bogason 1996). The establishment, in some municipalities, of information offices, where citizens can meet just one officer with responsibility for several municipal functions, may be regarded as a way of counteracting these tendencies (Bostedt 1993; SOU 1995: 61).

4.4 The Regional Level

During recent years, there has been an ongoing debate about the appropriate role of the popularly elected county council. Everything, from outright abolition to a strengthening of the county councils by transforming them into regional parliaments and giving them additional tasks, has been suggested. A milder version of the latter position is government policy. Not least the Swedish membership of the EU has emphasized the role of the regions, and the county councils themselves have been successful in arguing that they should have more responsibility for regional development. The number of counties was reduced to twenty in 1999, when the new counties of West Götaland and Skåne were created. As a result, the three largest counties will comprise half the Swedish population and are expected to be major actors in the European arena. This situation is also likely to affect the balance between the different county councils within the framework of the Federation of County Councils and may also challenge the structure of the federation itself.

Contrary to previous territorial reorganization in Sweden, the present regional transformation does not take shape according to one general, and centrally directed, format. Instead, regions are encouraged to develop their own models for democratic decision-making, adjusted to specific regional priorities. However, at the same time, an official experimental programme concerning the regional level has been launched. In four counties, different models of responsibilities for regional development, with varying emphasis on county councils, municipalities, or regional state administrative boards are being tested. Hitherto, these three sets of actors have competed for the decisive influence over regional development, but in the new arrangements, these issues are transferred to directly or indirectly elected bodies at regional level. West Götaland and Skåne, with directly elected councils and an extensive range of regional functions, will be particularly powerful. The experiments will be evaluated and are expected to result in a decision by parliament on how the responsibility for regional matters should be organized in the future. However, it is important to underline that, despite the present focus on the regional level, there are no suggestions to introduce a federal structure. The unitary character of the Swedish state remains intact.

5. Innovative Approaches to Improving Regional and Local Democracy

Among recent innovations affecting local and regional democracy in Sweden, the free-commune experiment, which started in 1984, is perhaps the most famous internationally, and also the one which has been most emulated in other countries (Baldersheim and Ståhlberg 1994). A number of municipalities and county councils were selected and permitted to deviate from certain specified rules, which they themselves suggested. The result was a number of experiments aimed at increasing democracy and efficiency. These included new ways of organizing the committee system, involvement of parents in decision-making at schools and day nurseries, and a less restricted use of resources. Compared to other free-commune experiments, the Swedish one was more focused on democracy and participation. A lasting result from the experiments was changes in the new Local Government Act, which, from 1992 onwards, gave all local authorities greater freedom to organize their own system of committees. This permitted the creation of committee systems adjusted to local needs, but also systems that separated the responsibility for providing services from the role of purchasing them.

A number of additional experiments, with the purpose of enhancing democracy, have also been tried by local authorities or are under way. In order to improve the position of the council, which has been criticized for being powerless and having too few contacts with citizens, changes have been initiated by a large number of local authorities. Initiatives include holding council meetings in places other than the town hall and arranging open question sessions with municipal or county councillors. However, these sessions have generally generated very little public interest (Bidsted 1997).

There are also examples of experiments that challenge principles, previously regarded as fundamental in Swedish local democracy. In the community of Svågadalen, non-party elections to a submunicipal committee took place in 1996 (Olsson and Forsberg 1997). With a participation rate of 70 per cent, seven members were elected. The committee has powers in municipal matters dealing with the local school, child care, care for the elderly, leisure, and culture. This was the first occasion in modern times that local elections were held on a non-party basis. Formally, direct elections of submunicipal committees are not legal, but this was bypassed by giving them the form of an advisory referendum. The results were later formally confirmed when the municipal council appointed the members as suggested by the referendum. Interestingly, the political parties in the municipality accepted, and even used a form of municipal disobedience, to promote a change that challenges the very position of the parties themselves.

The experimental period has been extended to 2002, and new elections were held in November 1998. However, only 62 per cent participated in these, compared to 78 per cent in the general municipal elections in September that year. The same tendency, with lower turnout in the non-political elections than in the local party-contested elections corresponds to observations also from other countries, for example the United States (Norton 1994).

Another example of new forms outside the party structure is the citizens' panel initiated in the Stockholm suburb of Upplands Väsby. Of 1,000 randomly selected citizens, 10 per cent turned up for one day of discussions on municipal matters. The panel had no decision-making powers, but provided opportunities to suggest changes to the elected politicians. Other local authorities focus more explicitly on involving young people in local politics. For example, Haninge, another Stockholm suburb, organizes a 'youth council' with elected representatives of the sixteen-year-olds in the municipality. The youth council meets before the municipal council meeting, to discuss the matters on its agenda and make recommendations concerning decisions. Youth councils have also been set up at county level. In several local authorities, information technology and the internet are increasingly used for providing information to citizens on local-government matters and to offer a point of contact between citizens and municipal and county-council decision-makers.

An interesting example of an innovative approach is the municipality of Örebro's initiative to develop a 'local-democracy balance sheet'. In the same way as with the municipal finances, the state of local democracy is evaluated on an annual basis, beginning in 1998. By using a set of indicators (e.g., public participation in local elections, activity in local voluntary associations, the members' activity in the municipal council, and municipal transparency), changes in the state of local democracy is detected. This pro-vides a basis for political action in order to counteract emerging problems concerning democracy. Örebro is also hoping to involve other municipalities in the experiment, thereby establishing a basis for comparisons (*Kommun-Aktuellt*, 6, 1998).

A recent overview of local democratic experiments in Sweden (Olsson and Montin 1999) comes to the conclusion that the ongoing reform movement encompasses different paths, which are sometimes conflicting. Some changes go in the direction of a more market-based model, others focus on enhanc-ing direct participation. Some experiments aim at strengthening the position of political parties, others try to establish local consensus by attempting to unite parties around local issues, which in fact could weaken parties. In sum, contemporary changes contain elements of continuity, as well as fragmenta-tion and renewal.

The willingness to try non-traditional means is not without limits. A recent parliamentary commission suggested a number of measures that aimed at developing new ideas on how democracy can be improved (SOU 1996:162). Suggestions concerning local democracy included directly elected submuni-cipal committees, the right for a council minority to call a referendum, and the right for citizens to initiate issues on the council agenda. The Social Demo-cratic Government has rejected these suggestions, with one exception. The minister in charge has declared that citizens' initiatives will be permitted. However, as the other ideas are supported by several of the opposition parties in parliament, they may still appear as policies under a different government. Non-socialist parties are also in favour of separating the national and local elections and holding them on different days. They are also more willing to accept separations of previously amalgamated municipalities. The environ-mental party is the strongest supporter of direct democratic means (e.g., binding referendums). It is also in favour of direct elections to submunicipal committees (Wrede 1999).

6. *Conclusions*

Despite changes in recent years, local democracy still retains a strong position in the Swedish system of government. Local government has considerable autonomy, issues are debated in the local media, and there are extensive experiments with new forms of local democracy. Public participation in elec-tions and other activities aiming at influencing local political decision-making continues to be high. There is considerable popular interest in municipal matters. However, a range of problems are emerging: fewer citizens are holding local political positions, an increasing number is indifferent to local political matters and refrain from voting. Traditional political parties are becoming less attractive to those interested in politics. Instead, new forms of individual contacts and *ad hoc* activism are developing.

These problems have inspired responses and initiatives, at national as well as local level. In the midst of the transformation, it seems that at least three major, more long-term, changes are affecting Swedish local democracy. First, the previously strong position of the political parties is likely to be further weakened. Non-party-based committees and a stronger position for voters to choose candidates may only be the beginning of new forms of influence that do not require party membership. Second, there is an ongoing debate about extending citizens' direct involvement in local decision-making, for example by permitting elections to submunicipal committees, to increase involvement through citizens' panels, or by making it possible for citizens to initiate issues on the council agenda. All these suggestions have not become practice yet, but may do so in the future. These changes correspond to a more general European trend, emphasizing direct democratic measures and elections to previously appointed posts (e.g., mayors) (Lidström 1996).

Third, Sweden is undergoing a regional transformation. It is difficult to envisage what the end result of this process might be, as it has only just started. However, under all conditions, it will lead to a new setting, with possibly more powerful actors at the regional level. These may take the form of regional councils or be cooperative bodies comprising representatives from municipalities and/or county councils within the region; but whatever form they take, they are likely to enhance the position of the regional level in Swedish democracy.

References

ANDERSSON, J. and LUNDELL, B. (1991). *Kommunernas kontakter i utlandet.* Stockholm: Föreningen Norden & Svenska Kommunförbundet.

BÄCK, H. and SOININEN, M. (1996). 'Invandrarna, demokratin och samhället'. SOU (Statens Offentliga Utredningar), 162. *På medborgarnas villkor—en demokratisk infrastruktur,* bilagedelen. Stockholm.

——and MÖLLER, T. (1995). *Partier och organisationer,* 3rd edn. Stockholm: Fritzes.

BALDERSHEIM, H. and STÅHLBERG, K. (eds) (1994). *Towards the Self-Regulating Municipality.* Aldershot: Dartmouth.

BENNET, R. J. (1993). 'European Local Government Systems', in R. J. Bennet (eds), *Local Government in the New Europe.* London: Belhaven.

BERGMANN-WINBERG, M.-L. VON (1997). 'The Impact of European Integration on Regional and Local Government in Finland, Norway and Sweden', in M. J. F. Goldsmith and K. K. Klausen (eds), *European Integration and Local Government.* Cheltenham: Edward Elgar.

BIDSTED, C. (ed.) (1997). *Forskelle og ligheder i kommunerne i Danmark, Norge og Sverige*. København: AKF.

BOGASON, P. (1996). 'The Fragmentation of Local Government in Scandinavia'. *European Journal of Political Research*, 30: 65–86.

BOSTEDT, G. (1993). *Samservice. Medborgarkontor i vardande*. Sundsvall: Samhällsvetenskapliga institutionen, Mitthögskolan.

COUNCIL OF EUROPE (1997). *Local Finance in Europe. Local and Regional Authorities in Europe 61*. Strasbourg.

GIDLUND, J. (2000). 'Nordic Bifurcation in Post-Wall Governance Europe', in J. Gidlund and M. Jerneck (eds), *Local and Regional Governance in Europe: Evidence from Nordic Regions*. Aldershot: Edward Elgar.

GILLJAM, M. and HOLMBERG, S. (1995). *Väljarnas val*. Stockholm: Fritzes.

GOUL ANDERSEN, J. (1996). *Membership and Participation in Voluntary Associations in Scandinavia, in a Comparative Perspective*. Aalborg University: Department of Economics, Politics and Public Administration.

GUSTAFSSON, A. (1996). *Kommunal självstyrelse*, 6th edn. Stockholm: SNS.

HÄGGROTH, S. *et al*. (1996). *Swedish Local Government*, 2nd edn. Stockholm: The Swedish Institute.

HEIDENHEIMER, A. J. *et al*. (1983). *Comparative Public Policy*, 2nd edn. London: Macmillan.

HOLMBERG, S. and WEIBULL, L. (1997). 'Förtroendets fall', in S. Holmberg and L. Weibull (eds), *Ett missnöjt folk?*. SOM-rapport 18. Göteborg: University of Göteborg.

HUDSON, C. and LIDSTRÖM, A. (eds) (forthcoming). *Local Education Policy*. Basingstoke: Macmillan.

JÖNSSON, S., RUBENOWITZ, S., and WESTERSTÅHL, J. (1995). *Decentraliserad kommun*. Stockholm: SNS.

KESSELMAN, M. *et al*. (1987). *European Politics in Transition*. Lexington: D.C. Heath.

KNUDSEN, T. and ROTHSTEIN, B. (1994). 'State Building in Scandinavia'. *Comparative Politics*, 26/2: 203–220.

KORPI, W. (1981). *Den demokratiska klasskampen*. Stockholm: Tiden.

LANE, J.-E. and ERSSON, S. O. (1994). *Politics and Society in Western Europe*, 3rd edn. London: Sage.

LIDSTRÖM, A. (1995). 'Actors and Acting in a Central–Local Government Context', in A. Khakee, I. Elander, and S. Sunesson (eds), *Remaking the Welfare State*. Aldershot: Avebury.

—— (1996). *Kommunsystem i Europa*. Stockholm: Publica.

MICHELETTI, M. (1995). *Civil Society and State Relations in Sweden*. Aldershot: Avebury.

MILNER, H. (1989). *Sweden: Social Democracy in Practice*. Oxford: Oxford University Press.

MONTIN, S. (1993). *Swedish Local Government in Transition*. Örebro: University of Örebro.

—— and ELANDER, I. (1995). 'Citizenship, Consumerism and Local Government in Sweden'. *Scandinavian Political Studies*, 18/1: 25–51.

NORTON, A. (1994). *International Handbook of Local and Regional Democracy*. Aldershot: Edward Elgar.

OLSSON, J. and FORSBERG, A. (1997). *Byapolitiken*. Örebro: Högskolan i Örebro.

——and MONTIN, S. (eds) (1999). *Demokrati som experiment. Försöksverksamhet och förnyelse i svenska kommuner*. Örebro: University of Örebro.

ÖSTHOL, A. (1996). *Politisk integration och gränsöverskridande regionbildning i Europa*. Umeå: University of Umeå.

PETERSSON, O. (1994a). *Kommunalpolitik*, 2nd edn. Stockholm: Publica.

——(1994b). *Swedish Government and Politics*. Stockholm: Publica.

——, HERMANSSON, J., MICHELETTI, M., and WESTHOLM, A. (1997). *Demokrati över gränser*. Demokratirådets rapport 1997. Stockholm: SNS.

PIERRE, J. (1994). *Den lokala staten*. Stockholm: Almqvist & Wiksell.

——(1995). 'Den kommunala politiken: Problem eller lösning?', in L. J. Lundqvist and J. Pierre (eds), *Kommunal förvaltningspolitik*. Lund: Studentlitteratur.

ROKKAN, S. (1970). *Citizens, Elections, Parties*. Oslo: Oslo University Press.

SCB (Statistika Centralbyrån) (1995). *Allmänna valen 1994. Del 3, specialundersökningar*. Stockholm.

——(1996a). *Årsbok för Sveriges kommuner 1996*. Stockholm.

——(1996b). *Politiska resurser och aktiviteter 1978–1994*. Levnadsförhållanden, 90. Stockholm.

——(1998). *Allmänna valen 1998. Huvudresultat*. Statistiska meddelanden. Stockholm.

SOU (Statens Offentliga Utredningar) (1995: 61). *Myndighetsutövning vid medborgarkontor*. Stockholm: Fritzes.

——(1996: 162). *På medborgarnas villkor—en demokratisk infrastruktur*. Stockholm: Fritzes.

——(1996: 169). *Förnyelse av kommuner och landsting*. Stockholm: Fritzes.

STRÖM, L.-I. (2000). 'Swedish Municipalities and the European Union', in J. Gidlund and M. Jerneck (eds), *Local and Regional Governance in Europe: Evidence from Nordic Regions*. Aldershot: Edward Elgar.

SVALLFORS, S. (1996). *Välfärdsstatens moraliska ekonomi*. Umeå: Boréa.

SVENSKA KOMMUNFÖRBUNDET (1996). *Utländska*. Stockholm: Kommentus.

TOPF, R. (1995). 'Beyond Electoral Participation', in H.-D. Klingemann and D. Fuchs (eds), *Citizens and the State*. Oxford: Oxford University Press.

WETTERBERG, G. (1997). *Kommunerna*. Stockholm: SNS.

WREDE, M. (ed.) (1999). *Uppdrag demokrati. Handbok för lokala politiker*. Stockholm: Kommunaktuellt.

15

Denmark: Between Scandinavian Democracy and Neo-liberalism

Anders Lidström

1. History and Concept of Democracy

1.1 Historical Background

In the mid nineteenth century, the Danish system of government went through dramatic changes. A two-hundred-year period of royal autocracy was replaced by a system of government based on one of the most modern constitutions of the time. Already in the 1830s, the assembly of estates was reintroduced, which opened up for debate and stimulated liberal attitudes and popular demands for a new form of government. Compared to Sweden, liberal tendencies have been much stronger in Denmark (Knudsen 1995). In addition, Danish farmers, sympathetic to liberalism and individualism, joined forces with the urban bourgeoisie. These pressures were reinforced by the revolutionary tensions in contemporary Europe (Knudsen and Rothstein 1994). As a result, the king agreed in 1849 to share his powers with a new two-chamber assembly. Voting rights were granted to approximately 75 per cent of adult men. Amongst those excluded were those in receipt of poor relief. A setback to the development of democracy came in the wake of the war of 1864, when Denmark lost Schleswig and Holstein to Prussia. The Conservatives managed to achieve a constitutional revision, whereby voting rights to the upper chamber were restricted. This reduced the influence of the popular vote and delayed the introduction of parliamentarism until the first years of the twentieth century. However, the final establishment of universal suffrage took place in 1915 (Petersson 1994; Hastrup 1994).

The constitutional changes of the mid nineteenth century have been viewed as an indication of the precipitate transition to democracy in Denmark (Rokkan 1970). However, even if important steps were taken in 1849, the process towards complete democracy was gradual and took place over a period of almost a century (Svensson 1996). Once the conflicts over democracy were resolved, a certain amount of consensus developed in the Danish polity. As in other Nordic countries, economic growth and the creation of a comprehensive welfare system, together with corporatism and cooperation across political lines, contributed to this sense of agreement. However, by the 1970's, symptoms of an economic and political crisis emerged. Economic problems, including increasing unemployment, developed at the same time as the established political parties experienced problems. New parties emerged, and it became even more difficult to create stable governments.

Denmark shares the main characteristics of the Nordic model of politics and society, but it is, at the same time, clearly its southernmost outpost. The size of the public sector, the extensive welfare commitments, the strong trade union movement, the corporatist arrangements, and the relative social and ethnic homogeneity are features that Denmark has in common with Sweden, Norway, and Finland. On the other hand, Danish society is also a deviant case (Petersson 1994). Industrialization came earlier, but farming still retains a strong position. Population density is considerably higher and Denmark lacks the vast, thinly populated areas of the other Nordic countries. Its welfare system has been more influenced by continental liberalism than Nordic social democracy. It contains fewer standardized approaches and offers a greater scope for choice in education, child care, and care for the elderly. Private provision of, for example, pensions and social care is also more common. The transformation of the welfare system started early in Denmark, as it was already hit by economic problems in the early 1970s. The Danish membership of the European Community since 1973 has further reoriented Denmark towards the continent. However, at the same time, the Danes have been hesitant towards a too rapid European integration.

In the Danish system of democracy, a number of features stand out as being particularly characteristic. Denmark has a distinct tradition of public involvement in political decision-making in at least two respects. First, at national level, there has been a considerable use of public referendums. Since 1915, when the Danish constitution made provisions for this form of direct democracy, seventeen referendums have been held. During recent years, the successive transfers of decision-making powers to the European Union are subject to binding (as opposed to advisory) referendums. The constitution requires such referendums in other situations, for example to change the constitution or to alter the voting age. In addition, referendums may be called upon by a minority in parliament as a way of stopping bills outside the fields of finance, taxation, and international law. If 30 per cent of the electorate votes against a bill, it will not come into force. This was used in 1963 by the non-socialist opposition, which managed to stop new land use laws. Advisory public referendums may be held on any matter. Generally, direct-democracy methods are only regarded as legitimate on certain kinds of issue, such as the relationship with the EU, whereas representative democratic forms are favoured in overarching national decisions (Madsen, Nielsen, and Sjöblom 1995).

The second form of public involvement is through the extensive practice of user influence. This is particularly developed and, in fact, is compulsory in relation to schools and day nurseries. Each institution is run by a board, through which parents, who represent the users, have influence on the decision-making process. The present system was introduced in 1990, but is based on a long tradition of parental involvement in the Danish school system (Lindbom 1995). Today, there are 1,700 boards in primary schools and 4,300 in day nurseries, and the model of user influence is also being developed in old people's homes. The development has been gradual, but it can now be regarded as a comprehensive reform movement (Floris and Bidsted 1996). The increasing presence of user influence is seen, by some observers, as a way of developing an alternative to the traditional forms of representative democracy (Sørensen 1995).

1.2 Democracy at the Regional and Local Levels

The Danish system of local government has its roots in the Middle Ages, but a feudal system and the period of royal autocracy put effective limits on local self-government in both towns and the rural areas until the early nineteenth century. However, at that time a process started that gradually increased local autonomy, provided new tasks for local institutions, and reduced state control over local matters. After the constitutional reform of 1849, voting rights were also extended at the local level, even if the wealthiest citizens still had a greater influence on local decision-making. In 1908, all citizens over the age of twenty-five were given the right to vote (Bogason 1991).

To what extent is democracy understood differently at central level than at local or regional levels in Denmark? Generally, it seems that the major features of Danish democracy also permeate the local level. For example, there is a multitude of political parties at both levels. However, there are also differences. The strong position of the mayor, who may be something of a local 'king', has no equivalent at the central level. At the same time, the extensive practice of referendums at central level has no equivalent at local level. Even if local referendums are permitted, they are still very unusual. It is reported that local politicians generally have a negative attitude towards local direct democracy of this kind. Instead, user influence is preferred (Villadsen 1993).

2. The Institutional Expression of Democracy

2.1 The National Level

Denmark is a constitutional monarchy. Since 1953 it has had a one-chamber parliament, which is elected every four years. A system of proportional representation, based on party lists, is used, but a party must obtain at least 2 per cent of the votes in order to be represented in parliament. The electoral system has facilitated the emergence of a large number of political parties. Ten parties have seats after the 1998 elections, but the number has varied between five and eleven during the post-war period. In addition, the semi-independent areas of the Faroe Islands and Greenland are represented by two seats each. The low electoral threshold has facilitated splits in established parties and encouraged the creation of new parties. The elections of 1973 were particularly dramatic, with the electoral successes of the two protest movements of the Progress Party and the *Centrum-Democraterne* (CD, Centre Democrats), together collecting almost one-quarter of the votes. In the main these parties were against high taxation and an extensive public welfare system. Protest parties appeared earlier and have generally been more successful in Denmark than in the other Nordic countries.

A consequence of the multitude of political parties, and itself a characteristic of Danish democracy, is parliamentary instability. Most governments have been minority governments, and changes of government are frequent. During the 1980s, a new pattern of Danish parliamentarism was established. Despite losing a high number of votes in parliament, the government still remained in power. Indeed, it has been suggested that this opens up a new parliamentary practice, whereby government can lose crucial votes, the opposition shape policy, and patterns of majority can vary from one policy area to another (Petersson 1994).

Participation in parliamentary elections has been fairly stable during the post-war period at around 85 per cent of those eligible to vote. The Danish electoral system provides some scope for choice of individual candidates as well as parties. The parties themselves decide how they want to present their candidates to the voters on the ballot: whether they prioritize certain candidates, or leave the decision to the voters. In practice, about 50 per cent of the voters use the right to express a choice of candidate, the others vote for the party of their choice. The share of female members of parliament is 33 per cent.

2.2 The Local Level

The system of local and regional government consists of two tiers: munici-palities and counties. On the Danish mainland there are today 275 *kommuner* (municipalities). The present structure was established after an amalgama-tion reform in 1970, when the number of municipalities were reduced from 1,390 to the present number. The average population size of the municipalities is 19,200 inhabitants (1997), varying from 2,400 to 484,000. However, as the median size is 10,200 inhabitants, most Danish municipal-ities are fairly small. The upper tier consists of fourteen *amtskommuner* (county councils) with an average size of 336,000 inhabitants (1997). The number of counties was also reduced during the amalgamations in 1970. The City of Copenhagen and the municipality of Frederiksberg, situated within the capital, represent one-third of the Danish population. They have a special organization and are both municipalities and county councils. The powers of self-government of Danish local authorities are protected by the constitution.

Outside the Danish mainland lie the territories of the Faroe Islands and Greenland. They are part of Denmark, but enjoy an autonomous status; the Faroes since 1948 and Greenland since 1979. They each have a directly elected assembly, a government, and considerable freedom to enact their own laws and handle their own affairs. However, defence and foreign policy matters are the responsibility of the Danish government. The two territories are exempted from EU membership, but Greenland was included for a few years. Each has its own representation in the Danish parliament. At the local level, the Faroe Islands have fifty rather small municipalities and Greenland has eighteen slightly larger ones (Benoit and Martens 1992).

In the Faroes there is a powerful movement for independence. The May 1998 elections were a success for the parties who support the establishment of an independent Faroes state. Therefore, the three major parties have decided to initiate negotiations with the Danish government regarding sover-eignty. If an agreement is reached, the final decision will be left to the Faroe Islanders via a referendum. However, independence is not on the immediate agenda.

Each Danish municipality and county has a council, which makes the major decisions. On average, municipal councils have seventeen members; however, numbers can range from seven to thirty-one. In the City of Copenhagen the council consists of fifty-five members. Councillors are elected for four-year periods. The key political figure in Danish local government is the mayor, who is appointed by the council from among its members. The mayor is chair-person of the council and is in charge of the preparation and implementation of council decisions. He or she is also responsible for the day-to-day functioning of the local authority, even if there is also a chief executive officer. The mayor is usually the only local politician who is salaried on a full-time basis. The important position of the mayor distinguishes Danish local government from the systems in the other Nordic countries, where, at least formally, political and administrative leadership are separated and political decision-making tends to be more collective. The combination of being both chairman of the council and political head of the local administration is unusual, also in a broader international context. A number of committees are appointed with responsibility for different local government tasks. Since 1993, local authorities are free to shape their committee structure (Bidsted 1997).

Danish local authorities perform a broad set of functions (Norton 1994). They have a general competence, within the law, to provide services in the interests of their citizens. However, most of their functions are mandatory. Major municipal tasks include social services and primary and adult education. They also provide culture and leisure services, and they are responsible for environmental protection and public utilities, such as water supply and sewage systems. Also, and contrary to local government in most other countries, Danish municipalities administer individual social security assistance. This is largely financed by central government and concerns, for example, retirement pensions, child benefits, and sickness benefits.

The county councils are in charge of hospitals and primary health care, upper secondary education, and regional planning. Their functions were more limited before reorganization in 1970, when they received several tasks that were previously the responsibility of national government. There is also, at county level, a state county prefect, who is appointed by central government. Several of the prefect's tasks were transferred to the county councils as a part of the local-government reorganization reform. Today, the functions of the county councils are more restricted than those of corresponding units in the other Nordic countries.

Generally, county councils are not superior to municipalities. Functions have been divided between them, creating fairly distinctive areas of responsibility. However, in some specified areas, the counties have a supervising or controlling function. For example, they provide advice in complicated social matters and act as a deciding authority when municipal school decisions are being challenged. Also, four county councillors, together with the state county prefect, constitute a county supervisory committee; it investigates municipal decisions that have been formally challenged, and it has the power to declare them invalid.

TABLE 15.1 Municipal election results (percentages), 1989–97

Party	Election		
	1989	1993	1997
Socialdemokratiet (Social Democratic Party)	35.7	35.1	33.1
Det radikale Venstre (Social-Liberal Party)	2.7	2.9	4.6
Konservative Folkeparti (Conservative People's Party)	14.6	13.0	12.1
Centrum-Demokraterne (Centre Democrats)	1.5	0.6	1.0
Socialistisk Folkeparti (Socialist People's Party)	10.0	8.1	7.9
Dansk Folkeparti (Danish People's Party)	0	0	6.8
Kristeligt Folkeparti (Christian People's Party)	1.4	1.2	1.7
Liberal Democratic Party	18.0	24.7	25.0
Fremskridtpartiet (Progress Party)	5.6	4.3	1.8
Enhedslisten–de rød-grønne Unity List–The Red Greens	0.0	1.1	2.7
Other parties, incl. local lists	10.5	8.0	3.3

Source: Danmarks statistik (1998).

2.3 The Role of Political Parties

The number of political parties varies considerably between local authorities, but in many local authorities there is a multitude of parties. The three largest parties tend to be stronger at local than national level. One reason is that small parties abstain from running in some local areas. In addition, the struggle for the mayoral position is, in practice, limited to the larger parties, which is assumed to enhance their attractiveness. However, this effect is limited to the first election after a new mayor has been appointed (Frandsen 1997). Table 15.1 summarizes the results from the most recent municipal elections.

The three largest parties, the Social Democrats, the Conservatives, and the Liberal Democrats, together receive between 60 per cent and 75 per cent of the votes. The rest of the votes are distributed among a large number of small parties and specific local lists. Such lists were more common before reorganization; nevertheless, they attracted 17 per cent of the votes in the 1970 elections (Sundberg 1989). Subsequently, they stabilized at around 8 per cent (Bidsted 1997), but lost further ground in the 1997 elections.

Elections to the local councils are held in November every four years, most recently in 1997. EU citizens living in Denmark may vote in local elections, and other foreign citizens have the same right if they have been residing in Denmark for at least three years. All electors are also eligible as councillors. A system of proportional representation is used. The choice is between parties and specific candidates. Voting for specific candidates is more common at the local level, particularly in small municipalities and in rural areas.

Participation in local elections is about 70 per cent, which is between 10 and 15 percentage points below the figures for parliamentary elections. As local-election turnout has decreased during the post-war period, this gap has steadily become wider. Interestingly, local participation decreased dramatically in the first elections after the reorganization of local government in 1970. However, some of the lost ground was regained in the subsequent elections (Albæk 1996).

In the same way as in national elections, the parties decide on fixed and closed party lists or whether to leave the choice of candidates entirely to their voters. Ranking has become less common and in the 1993 elections; it only characterized a third of the lists (Elklit and Jensen 1995). On average, each elected municipal councillor represents 1,100 inhabitants, which is a large number in a European context (Council of Europe 1995). Twenty-eight per cent of the municipal councillors (1997) and 31 per cent of the county councillors (1993) are women. However, there is considerable variation behind these figures. For example, six of the municipal councils now have a female majority. Male dominance is generally stronger in key positions, for example, only 10 per cent of the municipal mayors are women.

The role of the political parties is challenged by new means of participation. Local authorities may arrange local, advisory referendums, but these are not particularly common. Instead, it is more usual for local authorities to investigate their citizens' opinions on municipal services through surveys. In 1995, 32 per cent of the municipalities made use of such surveys. In addition, 71 per cent investigated how a particular service was perceived by its users. Only a quarter of the municipalities made no use of surveys to map citizen or user opinions (Andersen, Berg, and Buch Jensen 1997).

Public participation is undergoing a change in Denmark. This has been detected particularly since the 1980s (Goul Andersen 1993). There is a general decline in participation: fewer citizens are active in organizations or are members of parties. There has been a gradual decline in party membership since the 1950s, and the fall is greater in Denmark than in other Western European countries (Bille 1995). However, participation in grass-roots activities increased during the 1980s and is now more evenly distributed between social groups than at the end of the 1970s. (Goul Andersen and Hoff 1995). Indeed, the whole pattern of involvement is changing: individual rather than collective contacts are becoming more common, there is a focus on influencing outputs and implementation instead of inputs, and there is an interest in narrow and local issues rather than broad and general issues.

3. The Practice of Local Democracy

3.1 The Role of Policy Networks and Pressure Groups in Local Government

Before the 1970 Local Government Reform, intermunicipal cooperation was very common. The relatively small size of the municipalities forced them to share costs for services, in order to be able to provide them efficiently. After the amalgamations, this cooperation became less essential and rather unusual. During recent years, there is again a new tendency for increasing cooperation between municipalities (Albæck 1996).

The local authorities are represented by two national organizations: the National Association of Local Authorities and The Association of County Councils. These are both major actors, as initiators and coordinators *vis-à-vis* the local authorities, and as groups exerting pressure on central government. The relationship between central and local government in Denmark is characterized by a mixture of control, negotiation, and autonomy. Central government has increasingly shifted its regulation of local government into broader and more general forms, thus avoiding detailed involvement. An important component in the relationship is the annual economic agreement between central government and the local government associations. This agreement is not legally binding for the individual local authority, but it has, nevertheless, contributed to reducing the speed of expansion. In addition, the associations are involved in the policy-making process at national level at an early stage, for example through representation in committees, which make policy suggestions.

Beneath the formal structure of Danish politics, lie informal relationships which are important for policy-making. There are professional networks that link actors who share common interests in different settings. Voluntary associations play a key role in Danish society. Together with Sweden, Denmark has the highest rate of unionization in the world (Goul Andersen 1996). Interest organizations are active in lobbying for their particular interests and, in the name of consensus-seeking, their views are often invited by the formal decision-makers. However, during recent years, these arrangements have changed shape. The decentralization policies have contributed to a move from centralist corporatist arrangements, which were common also at local level, to a more network-based pattern. Today, policies are shaped by an interaction between those in charge of a service, public decision-makers, and organized interests. The result of the process is contracts and agreements, rather than fixed decisions (Sørensen 1999).

3.2 Critiques of Local Democracy

Criticism of local democracy in Denmark has generally concerned the decreasing rate of participation. Turnout in local elections has declined, whereas voting in national elections has been fairly stable. People are also less likely to engage in other means of shaping local policies. This is a major reason for the extensive use of user boards. Critics have also observed that there is an ongoing reduction of the number of elected and appointed politicians. However, criticism tends to focus on ways of improving the representative system. Suggestions about turning towards more direct democracy are not very common.

A particular criticism in Denmark concerns the ambitions by the Faroes and Greenland to gain greater autonomy and even independence. Danish rule has been seen to be too limiting for the people in these regions.

3.3 Citizens' Attitudes to Local Government

On the whole, the Danes are pleased with the state of their local democracy. In a survey by the *Eurobarometer* in 1995, Denmark appeared as the EU member state in which the citizens were most satisfied with democracy at the local level. Eighty-two per cent were very or fairly satisfied with democracy in their own town, compared with an average of 57 per cent for the EU as a whole. Denmark, Ireland, and Austria emerged at the top, with Italy, Greece, and Spain at the bottom of the table (*Eurobarometer*, 43, 1995).

However, despite the high level of satisfaction, other figures indicate decreasing confidence in local decision-makers. Table 15.2 reports the results from two citizen surveys, one undertaken at the end of the 1970s, the other, fifteen years later. It remains to be seen whether this decline in confidence in local politicians will continue. A recent population survey, undertaken by the *Institut for Konjunktur-Analyse*, reports increasing confidence in Danish politicians during the 1990s (IFKA 1998).

TABLE 15.2   Citizen confidence in local politicians
(percentages), 1978 and 1993

'Municipal politicians generally keep their promises to their electorate'	Year	
	1978	1993
Agree	48	30
Neither agree nor disagree, do not know	18	28
Disagree	34	42
No. of respondents	1,836	1,002
'You can generally trust the municipal politicians to make the right decisions for the municipality'		
Agree	50	39
Neither agree nor disagree, do not know	12	25
Disagree	38	36
No. of respondents	1,836	1,002

Source: Berg and Kjaer (1997).

4. Challenges and Opportunities for Regional and Local Democracy

4.1 The European Challenge

Denmark has been a member of the EC/EU since 1973. Danish local government has, therefore, a longer experience of involvement in EU matters than the Swedish and Finnish newcomers. However, local authorities were only marginally affected during the early years of membership, and it was not until the establishment of the 1992 Single European Market project, that Danish local authorities faced the consequences of membership (Klausen 1997). The Single European Market meant a set of new demands on local government, including adjustments to EU regulations, technical standards, and purchase requirements. The establishment of the Structural Funds also provided new opportunities to finance local and regional development projects (Klausen 1994). Hence, from the end of the 1980's, Europe became important for Danish local government.

However, local responses to this new situation vary considerably. Commentators have identified four different ways in which the Danish local and regional authorities have responded to Europeanization. Some authorities are *counteractive*: as they are sceptical about the EU project and/or see no benefits from involvement in activities directed towards the EU. Most local authorities are *passive*: they only make incremental changes and tend to adopt a wait-and-see approach. Others are *reactive*: increasing their international activities, participating in international networks, but generally at a low level of commitment. Finally, there is a small group of *proactive* local authorities, which have developed more extensive strategies towards the EU. These tend to consist of the largest local authorities and those located in the areas of western Denmark that are eligible for EU funding. They have adjusted their external strategies as well as their internal organization to the new setting. The external means may include: establishing an information office in Brussels, either by themselves or with others; participating in international conferences; and developing networks aiming at creating advantages for their local area. Internal changes include: employing officers responsible for EU contacts, creating an office for international affairs, and providing personnel training in EU matters (Klausen 1997, 2000).

Danish local government seems to have adopted a different strategy towards the EU than has local government in Finland and Sweden. The European orientation of the Finnish and Swedish local authorities has increased considerably since the early 1990s and is now more intense than in Danish local authorities. In terms of regional restructuring, Denmark has a policy of wait and see, whereas both Finland and Sweden are, or were recently, changing their regional structures. It has been argued that a split between the Scandinavian countries is emerging, which is linked to different experiences with regard to economic problems (Gidlund 2000). The redistributive capacity of the Swedish and Finnish welfare states has weakened and local and regional authorities are increasingly compelled to take their fate in their own hands. It is hoped that EU-oriented activities and other international links and networks will create competitive advantages for them. Local authorities in Denmark have not faced the same problems and have, therefore, not had the same incentives to develop external/internal strategies.

Nevertheless, it seems safe to predict that the economic incentives to be gained from more internationally oriented strategies will stimulate more local authorities to become reactive and that cooperation across national borders will increase. However, it is unlikely that the number of proactive authorities will increase greatly.

4.2 Financial Strains

Danish local-government expenditures represent 27 per cent of gross domestic product (GDP) (1994 figures), and their share of total public expenditures is 42 per cent (Council of Europe 1997). Taxes are the main source of finance, providing 54 per cent of municipal and 65 per cent of county council income (Committee of the Regions 1996). Tax income derives largely from a proportional, local income tax, but there is also a small property tax. Local authorities have a formal right to decide the level of the taxes themselves, even if the system of annual agreements with the government has restricted tax increases. In 1994, municipal taxes varied between 13.5 per cent and 22.3 per cent and county council taxes between 8.9 per cent and 10.4 per cent.

The dependency on local sources of finance, and hence the state of the local economy, is further emphasized by the amount of local government resources that come from user fees and service charges. This represents 22 per cent of municipal and 16 per cent of county council income, which means that around 80 per cent of local-government resources are locally generated. Danish local authorities rely on local sources of income to a greater extent than local governments in any other European country (Council of Europe 1997). Of the remaining income, central government provides the largest part through block grants, but also makes use of some specific grants. Local authority borrowing is restricted, as each local authority has a borrowing limit set by central government. A system of transfers between local authorities compensates for differences in preconditions between local areas.

As mentioned previously, economic problems hit Denmark earlier than the other Nordic countries. Because of the economic recession in the early 1970s, local authorities were compelled to restrict their use of resources. A policy of several governments during the 1970s and 1980s, both Social Democratic and non-Socialist, was to curb local government expenditure in order to provide scope for private sector activities. However, due to the transfer of functions from central government, there was still a considerable expansion of local government during the 1970s, in particular at county level. In 1977, the budgetary system of local government was changed to increase central government control over local expenditures, which made it easier for central authorities to assess and compare the state of the economy in different local areas (Bogason 1991). During the 1980s, when local government in Finland, Norway, and Sweden continued to expand, Danish local government stagnated (Oulasvirta 1992). This was mainly achieved by massive reductions in central government grants and later also by imposing penalties on local authorities that refused to comply with central directives (Nissen 1991). However, as a consequence, the economic problems of the early 1990s did not hit Danish local authorities to the same extent as its neighbours in Sweden and Finland.

4.3 Organizational Changes

In recent years, Danish local government has also undergone profound organizational and managerial changes. Decentralization measures have increased local autonomy. These measures include transfers of responsibilities from central to local government, replacement of special grants with a block grant, and the setting of frames instead of detailed regulations (Albæk 1995).

It is common to distinguish between three waves of decentralization in Denmark. The first, in the 1970s, consisted of transfers of powers from central to local government as local authorities were merged into larger units. The second, which took place in the 1980s, concerned a strengthening of local units, such as schools and homes for the elderly, including the establishment of user boards. The third wave, starting in the late 1980s, focused on voluntary organizations, and provided them a role in the implementation of services, even if these still were financed by public authorities (Sørensen 1999).

In the wake of the decentralization process, the distribution of functions between municipal, county, and state levels has been subject to debate. A parliamentary committee, which also includes representatives of the local government associations, has recently delivered its conclusions and suggests a number of general principles in order to clarify the division of tasks. These include the principle of subsidiarity and that tasks should be handled by elected rather than appointed bodies. However, a number of minor transfers of functions have also been suggested (Opgavekommissionen 1998).

The internal structures of local government have been altered. However, the solutions selected locally vary considerably, as a common feature is that most changes have been initiated by the local authorities themselves. Nevertheless, almost all local authorities have decentralized powers further, to institutions such as schools and day nurseries (Bidsted 1997). Also, new ways of steering and governing public activities have been introduced with the aim of increasing efficiency. In the same way as in other countries, the emphasis is on leadership and management. Management by Objectives (MBO) and results is very common in Danish local authorities. Privatization of local government responsibilities has been rare, whereas contracting out of public services has been more common. However, this is still limited to technical services and does not so much concern the key welfare functions of local government. In Denmark there is a tradition of parental choice between different public and private service alternatives, in particular with regard to schools. However, this is not unrestricted, as local authorities decide themselves within which areas choice should be permitted. In 1993, 80 per cent of the municipalities provided opportunities to choose within education, childcare, and care of the elderly (Bidsted 1997).

A consequence of these organizational changes is an increasing fragmentation of Danish local government. In essence, in the wake of decentralization, a unifying structural principle is now lacking. It has been argued that it is now more difficult for citizens to find the responsible authority or the relevant officer. It may make representative democracy less relevant, as many decisions are moved from the local council to other bodies. Differences between citizens may also increase. Those who are well organized, perhaps as users, as well as being articulate, would benefit. Others may experience greater difficulty in finding their way in an increasingly complicated landscape of local politics (Bogason 1996*a,b*).

One way of counteracting this has been to establish information offices where citizens' contacts can be limited to just one officer. These offices are present in several municipalities and the government has suggested that their tasks should be extended to include functions performed by other public authorities. Through a recent amendment of the Local Government Act, local authorities are compelled to provide detailed information about their services to their citizens (Indenrigsministeriet 1997).

There are other ongoing changes in the local government structure that may cause problems in terms of local democracy. As previously mentioned, local authorities have been given increased freedom to decide how to organize their committee system, and a general tendency is that the number of committees has been reduced, from an average of 4.5 in 1970 to 3.6 in 1992 (Andersen, Berg, and Buch Jensen 1997). In addition, several local authorities have decided to reduce the size of their local council. This occurs at a time when the number of candidates in local elections is also falling. During the past decade, the number of candidates in municipal elections has decreased by a quarter; in the 1997 elections, there were, on average, four candidates per seat in the municipal councils. As participation in local elections has also been falling and differences in turnout between rural and urban local authorities have been increasing, there is concern about the state of Danish local democracy (Albæk 1996; Indenrigsministeriet 1997).

However, not only the responsible minister is troubled. Among local politicians, there is also a debate about how democracy may be improved, not least against the background of the emphasis during recent years on economic efficiency. This is one reason why The National Association of Local Authorities initiated a broad debate on local democracy in Denmark in 1999. The purpose is to stimulate each local authority to develop locally adjusted solutions to its own problems of democracy.

4.4 The Regional Level

The position of the county councils has been under pressure on several occasions during the past few decades. In 1970, the number of counties was reduced to the present fourteen, while at the same time their functions were extended. During most of this period, there has been a debate about a suggested abolition of the county councils. In particular, both the Conservative Party and the leadership of the National Association of Local Authorities in Denmark, which organizes the municipalities, have claimed that Denmark is sufficiently small and homogeneous to merit only one level of local government. However, the Liberals and the Social Democrats have opposed the suggestions. The debate, which was at its most intensive in 1988, never resulted in any comprehensive changes (Nissen 1991).

As the regional level has gained increased importance in the EU context, the suggestions to abolish the county councils have become less common. Thus, it seems unlikely that this tier of local government will disappear for the moment.

During the last decades, there has been a need for a special government for the Copenhagen area. In 1974, an indirectly elected metropolitan council was established, with decision-makers selected by the three county councils in the area, the City of Copenhagen and the municipality of Frederiksberg. Its tasks included regional planning, public transport, and hospital planning; it was effectively a third tier of local government. Following criticism, this was abolished in 1990 and most of its functions were transferred to the local authorities. However, in 1999, it was again felt that broader cooperation in the Copenhagen area was necessary and in January 2000, a Capital City Development Council was be established. It has overarching responsibility for regional and traffic planning, public transport, culture, economic development, and tourism. In addition, it is in change of cross-border cooperation with Swedish counterparts in the Öresund region. Also, the Council is indirectly elected, but the mayors and leaders of the member authorities are guaranteed seats.

5. Innovative Approaches to Improving Regional and Local Democracy

A number of innovative reforms have been carried out with explicit emphasis on the need to strengthen local democracy. The major and most comprehensive attempts have followed the path of user influence (Bidsted 1997). In 1989, parliament made governing boards for user influence compulsory in relation to municipal schools. These consist of five to seven members, with parents' representatives in the majority. In addition, the employees of the school and the pupils are represented. Later, the practice of obligatory user boards was extended to county council upper secondary schools and municipal day nurseries. The boards have decision-making powers of their own within frameworks set by central government and financial discretion as specified by the municipality. Additional user boards may be established at the discretion of the local authority. These may have decision-making powers or may only make recommendations. They are particularly common in retirement homes, nursing homes, and in connection with libraries and sports facilities.

An evaluation of the user-board system (see Floris and Bidsted 1996) indicates that the user influence is limited to more peripheral matters in the activities of the school or the nursery. These may include decisions about specific activities or excursions but rarely touch upon the more key matters of pedagogy or care. Further, it is difficult for the users to influence the agenda of the board. Generally, there is a strong tendency to reach consensus decisions, but there are also conflicts between the different interests represented in the board. Another effect is that the users' involvement in the day-to-day activities of the school or nursery has increased and this has made such boards more visible in the local community.

An important question is whether user influence is undermining the position of the elected councillor. The Danish experience suggests that user boards generally decide on matters that normally would not have been tasks for the council or a committee. Also, user boards have only to a limited extent been able to influence overall decision-making in the municipality. Hence, it seems possible to combine them with traditional forms of representative democracy. A conclusion is that the user boards are here to stay, particularly as they are not generally called into question in the public debate (Floris and Bidsted 1996). Also, user participation in Denmark appears to be fairly evenly distributed between different social strata, even if there is a slight middle class dominance with regard to parental participation in school and nursery matters (Goul Andersen and Hoff 1995).

Another major reform is the experiment in Copenhagen with directly elected submunicipal committees in four of the fifteen city districts. This started in 1996 and will continue until the end of 2001. Each of the four districts has a population of around 130,000 inhabitants. The committees are responsible for municipal activities with regard to children and the elderly, culture and leisure, streets and roads. However, they have no taxation rights and are dependent on Copenhagen City Council for their resources. Apart from in Copenhagen, submunicipal committees have been tried in a few municipalities in Denmark, mainly within the free-commune experiment (Hansen, Torill, and Aarsæther 1996).

In the same way as in the rest of Scandinavia, Denmark has had a free-commune trial. Indeed, the Danish programme started in 1985, just one year after Sweden and clearly inspired by the Swedish example (Albæk 1994), and it was completed in 1993. In total, thirty-six local authorities participated and these were given certain freedom with respect to specified regulations. However, there seems to have been less enthusiasm about the Danish programme, perhaps because a tradition of local-policy experiments already existed in Denmark (Baldersheim and Ståhlberg 1994).

Initiatives aiming at improving local democracy may also be introduced locally, without reliance on central suggestions or regulation. One example is the establishment of a citizens' panel in the municipality of Sundeved (*Nyhedsmagasinet Danske Kommuner*, 16, 1997). Eighteen people were selected to sit on the panel and asked questions about how they want local government services to be shaped in the future. The purpose was to find new ideas and it was expected that views would appear that were not normally represented in the public debate. However, the panel has no decision-making powers.

Another innovative approach has been developed by the municipality of Fredericia. In 1998, a new type of citizens' meetings was introduced as a part of the budget process. The purpose was to involve the general public in over-arching decisions about municipal priorities. Two meetings were arranged, both with several hundred citizens present. During the first meeting, which was held immediately after the economic preconditions for the coming year were clear, the discussion focused on what to prioritize among municipal activities. Much of the discussion was held in small groups. Later, the munic-ipal council calculated its budget proposal, and this was discussed during a second citizen's meeting. Consequences of different cost reductions were debated and alternatives suggested. In the final decision by the council, several of the suggestions were taken into account. Generally, both politicians and cit-izens have felt positive about this process. Citizens were involved in the general priorities, and not just with a narrow focus on specific topics. But the munic-ipality has been criticized for withholding information about certain priori-ties. However, the process is repeated during future years, and then complemented with a discussion forum at municipal level (Kommunernes Landsforening 1999).

6. Conclusions

To some extent Denmark has followed a different path to many other Euro-pean Union countries in its development of new forms of local democracy. Some have made greater use of local referendums and other means of direct democracy, others have implemented systems of submunicipal committees. However, the Danish contribution to the set of approaches is highly focused on user influence. Through the creation of a large number of school boards and other institutions, users have been extensively involved in decision-making at the micro level. The experiences from these initiatives are suffi-ciently positive for the user boards to continue, and their use has been extended to other areas. Further, as these innovations seem to be compatible with traditional forms of representative democracy, the Danish way forward is likely to continue along the path of user influence.

However, at the same time, local democracy in Denmark is facing similar problems to those in most other western countries: fewer politicians; the decline of traditional forms of influencing political decision-making, such as voting and party activism; and an increasing distrust of local politicians. These developments may be part of a more general restructuring of the way democracy functions, which challenges traditional patterns, not only in Denmark, but also elsewhere. Nevertheless, in Denmark there is an ongoing debate about the state of local democracy and how it may be improved, which is one requirement for the development of future solutions.

References

ALBÆK, E. (1994). 'The Danish Case: Rational or Political Change?', in H. Baldersheim and K. Ståhlberg (eds), *Towards the Self-regulating Municipality*. Aldershot: Dartmouth.

——(1995). 'Reforming the Nordic Welfare Communes'. *International Review of Administrative Science*, 61: 241–64.

——(1996). 'Denmark', in E. Albæk *et al.* (eds), *Nordic Local Government*. Helsinki: The Association of Finnish Local Authorities.

ANDERSEN, V. N., BERG, R., and BUCH JENSEN, R. (1997). *Omstillningsbølger i det kommunale demokrati*. Kommunalpolitiske studier 16/1997. Odense: University of Odense.

BALDERSHEIM, H. and STÅHLBERG, K. (eds) (1994). *Towards the Self-regulating Municipality*. Aldershot: Dartmouth.

BENOIT, F. and MARTENS, G. (1992). 'Municipal Government in Greenland'. *Polar Record*, 28: 93–104.

BERG, R. and KJAER, U. (1997). 'Afspejler kommunalpolitikerne vaelgerne?', in J. Elkit and R. B. Jensen (eds), *Kommunalvalg*. Odense: Odenser University Press.

BIDSTED, C. (ed.) (1997). *Forskelle og ligheder i kommunerne i Danmark, Norge og Sverige*. København: AKF.

BILLE, L. (1995). 'Medlemsudviklingen i otte danske partier 1953–1993: Ett demokratisk problem?', in M. Madsen, H. J. Nielsen, and G. Sjöblom (eds), *Demokratiets mangfoldighed: Tendenser i dansk politik*. København: Forlaget Politiske Studier.

BOGASON, P. (1991). 'Danish Local Government: Towards an Effective and Efficient Welfare State', in J. J. Hesse (ed.), *Local Government and Urban Affairs in International Perspective*. Baden-Baden: Nomos.

——(1996a). 'The Fragmented Locality', in P. Bogason (ed.), *New Modes of Local Organizing: Local Government Fragmentation in Scandinavia*. Commack: Nova Sciences Publishers.

——(1996b). 'The Fragmentation of Local Government in Scandinavia'. *European Journal of Political Research*, 30: 65–86.

COMMITTEE OF THE REGIONS (1996). 'Regional and Local Government in the European Union'. Mimeo.

COUNCIL OF EUROPE (1995). _The Size of Municipalities, Efficiency and Citizen Participation._ Local and Regional Authorities in Europe 56. Strasbourg.

——(1997). _Local Finance in Europe._ Local and Regional Authorities in Europe 61. Strasbourg.

DANMARKS STATISTIK (1998). _Statistisk årsbog 1998._ København.

ELKLIT, J. and JENSEN, R. B. (1995). 'De politiske partier og det lokale demokrati'. _Politica,_ 27/4: 418–35.

FLORIS, T. S. and BIDSTED, C. (1996). _Brugerbestyrelser på tværs—erfaringer fra kommuner og amter._ København: AKF.

FRANDSEN, A. G. (1997). 'Borgmesterpostens inflydelse på valgresultatet', in J. Elklit and R. B. Jensen (eds), _Kommunalvalg._ Odense: Odense University Press.

GIDLUND, J. (2000). 'Nordic Bifurcation in Post-Wall Europe', in J. Gidlund and M. Jerneck (eds), _Local and Regional Governance in Europe: Evidence from Nordic Regions._ Aldershot: Edward Elgar.

GOUL ANDERSEN, J. (1993). 'Politisk deltagelse i 1990 sammenlignet med 1979', in J. Andersen _et al._ (eds), _Medborgerskab. Demokrati och politisk deltagelse._ Herning: Systime.

——(1996). _Membership and Participation in Voluntary Associations in Scandinavia, in a comparative perspective._ Aalborg University: Department of Economics, Politics and Public Administration.

——and HOFF, J. (1995). 'Lighed i den politiske deltagelse', in M. Madsen, H. J. Nielsen, and G. Sjöblom (eds), _Demokratiets mangfoldighed: Tendenser i dansk politik._ København: Forlaget Politiske Studier.

HANSEN, A. D., NYSETH, T., and AARSÆTHER, N. (1996). 'Community Councils—Improved Local Democracy?', in P. Bogason (ed.), _New Modes of Local Organizing: Local Government Fragmentation in Scandinavia._ Commack: Nova Sciences Publishers.

HASTRUP, B. (1994). _Vores Danmark._ København: Akademisk.

IFKA (Institut for Konjunktur-Analyse) (1998). _Danskerne '98._ København: IFKA.

INDENRIGSMINISTERIET (1997). _Kommunal redegørelse._ Indenrigsministerens redegørelse til Folketinget.

KLAUSEN, K. K. (1994). 'EG-konsekvenser för danska kommuner', bilaga 7 till SOU (Statens Offentliga Utredningar), 2. _Kommunerna, landstingen och Europa._ Stockholm.

——(1997). 'Danish Local Government: Integrating into the EU?', in M. J. F. Goldsmith and K. K. Klausen (eds), _European Integration and Local Government._ Cheltenham: Edward Elgar.

——(2000). 'Conflict and Harmony in the Internationalisation of Danish Local Governments', in J. Gidlund and M. Jerneck (eds), _Local and Regional Governance in Europe: Evidence from Nordic Regions._ Aldershot: Edward Elgar.

KNUDSEN, T. (1995) _Dansk statsbygning._ København: Jurist- og økonomforbundets Forlag.

——and ROTHSTEIN, B. (1994). 'State Building in Scandinavia'. _Comparative Politics,_ 26/2: 203–20.

KOMMUNERNES LANDSFORENING (1999). *Kommunerne for fremtiden. Inspirationskatalog.* København.

LINDBOM, A. (1995). *Medborgarskapet i välfärdsstaten.* Uppsala: University of Uppsala.

MADSEN, M., NIELSEN, H. J., and SJÖBLOM, G. (1995). *Demokratiets mangfoldighed: Tendenser i dansk politik.* København: Forlaget Politiske Studier.

NISSEN, O. (1991). 'Key Issues in the Local Government Debate in Denmark', in R. Batley and G. Stoker (eds), *Local Government in Europe. Trends and Developments.* Basingstoke: Macmillan.

NORTON, A. (1994). *International Handbook of Local and Regional Government.* Aldershot: Edward Elgar.

OPGAVEKOMMISSIONEN (1998). *Fordelningen av opgaver i den offentlige sektor.* Betenkning, 1366.

OULASVIRTA, L. (1992). 'Municipal Public Finance in the Nordic Countries'. *Local Government Studies,* 18/4: 106–35.

PETERSSON, O. (1994). *The Government and Politics of the Nordic Countries.* Stockholm: Publica.

ROKKAN, S. (1970). *Citizens, Elections, Parties.* Oslo: Oslo University Press.

SØRENSEN, E. (1995). 'Brugerindflydelse og demokrati: Brukerindflydelsens rolle i udviklingen af det danske demokrati'. *Politica,* 27/1: 24–37.

——(1999). 'Medborgermagt i offentlig virksomhed—det danske exempel', in *Demokratin i den offentliga sektorns förändring.* SOU (Statens Offentliga Utredningar), 40. Stockholm.

SUNDBERG, J. (1989). 'Politiseringen av kommunalvalen i Norden'. *Statsvetenskaplig tidskrift,* 92/1: 25–40.

SVENSSON, P. (1996). *Demokratiets krise?* Århus: Politica.

VILLADSEN, S. (1993). 'Another Century for Local Democracy? Decentralisation, Deregulation and Participation in Scandinavia in Times of European Integration'. *International Journal of Urban and Regional Research,* 17/1: 42–55.

16

Finland: Geo-political Changes and Europeanization

Anders Lidström

1. History and Concept of Democracy

1.1 Historical Background

Finland became an independent state in 1917 after more than seven centuries as an integrated part of Sweden and one century as a semi-autonomous grand duchy within the Russian Empire. During most of the Russian period, the Tsars respected a certain amount of Finnish self-government. However, by the turn of the century, a Russification process was imposed, aiming at increasing Russian dominance and reducing the power of the Finnish institutions. This grip was relaxed in the wake of the turbulence in Russia during 1905, which paved the way for the reform of the system of representation in Finland. In 1906 a one-chamber assembly, elected through proportional representation, was introduced. In practice, the power of the assembly was still restricted, but, nevertheless, Finland now had one of the most modern forms of representation in Europe. Contrary to what happened in Sweden and Denmark, universal suffrage came at the same time as the system of representation was reformed. However, full independence was gained only in the aftermath of the Russian revolution.

Despite these reforms, Finland had retained its originally Swedish constitution of 1772 also during the period of Russian domination. A new modern and democratic Finnish constitution was adopted in 1919. This combines a monistic principle, according to which all power emanates from the people, with the idea of a division of powers between parliament and president. This dualism has several roots. Intellectually, it is based on European parliamentarism as well as on Montesquieuean 'checks and balances' theory. It was also clearly inspired by the French and American political experiences.

However, the modern constitution has also been influenced by Finland's experiences under Swedish as well as Russian rule. Interestingly, the dualism of the new constitution was inspired by the system of rule under the Russian grand duchy, which contained a division of powers between the four estates and the Russian ruler. During the writing of the constitution, the Social Democrats favoured a pure parliamentarian system, but the other parties— the majority—wanted to keep the dualistic principle and in essence replace the Russian governor-general with an elected president. Indeed, several of the powers of the president correspond to the functions of the previous ruler. The Finnish form of dualism was seen as a way of creating a balance between different sources of power, in accordance with national traditions (Nousiainen 1966). Swedish influences, finally, have mainly affected local self-government and forms of central government administration.

The last years of the Russian period and the first decades after independence were characterized by bitter conflicts. The language tensions between the Finnish-speaking majority and the Swedish-speaking minority remained from the days of Swedish dominance. The question of whether to adjust to the Russification process or to resist it also divided the Finns. But above all, a bitter and bloody civil war between socialist and non-socialist forces in 1918 created deep scars in Finnish society. Against this background, it is somewhat surprising that contemporary Finnish politics and society are so stable and balanced and that the wounds from the past seem to have healed. However, this has been achieved through a strong emphasis on consensus, which itself is a major characteristic of contemporary Finnish democracy.

Finland's democracy and the search for consensus have to be understood also in relation to the country's geo-political position between East and West (Lindström and Karvonen 1986), which has put severe constraints on Finland's foreign policy. Particularly after the Second World War and the signing of the Treaty of Friendship, Security and Mutual Assistance with the Soviet Union in 1948, domestic politics became a 'balancing act'. The situation changed gradually from the early 1980s, and the collapse of the Soviet Union in 1991 was particularly significant. This enabled Finland to reorient itself in a westward direction and subsequently become a member of the European Union.

Despite the desire for consensus, political cleavages remain. These are represented by a multiparty system that, previously, was constituted along two dimensions: linguistic and socio-economic. The first parties emerged along the language division, with separate parties for the Swedish-speaking minority and for the Finnish-speaking majority. However, this also corresponded to a socio-economic division, since the aristocracy and state administration were, for historical reasons, Swedish-speaking. As the Finnish majority increased, the language division became gradually less significant, even if the identity and common interests of the Swedish-speakers remain important. For example, a Swedish Assembly, which is a cooperative arrangement between political parties in the Swedish-speaking areas, meets once every year to discuss questions particularly affecting Swedish-speakers. However, they have no self-governing capacity. Today, the traditional left–right scale is the dominant cleavage in society (Berglund 1990).

Ten parties were represented in parliament after the 1995 elections. In comparison with the other Nordic countries, Finland has a weak *Sosialidemokraattinen Puolue* (SDP, Social Democratic Party). Extremist parties have also been stronger. Particularly the *Suomen Kommunistinen Puole* (SKP, Finnish Communist Party) has had an exceptional position. During the two decades after 1945, it received more than 20 per cent of the votes, even if it is weaker today. From 1966 onwards the party was accepted as a coalition partner in several governments. At the other extreme, a right-wing movement was significant during the interwar period. Despite weak overall election results, it had regional strongholds, particularly in the area of Pohjanmaa (Finnish Ostrobothnia) (Lindström and Karvonen 1987).

In several respects, the characteristics of the public sector in Finland resemble the welfare models of the other Nordic countries. These include a highly developed public responsibility for the well-being of the citizens and strong local authorities. However, there are also differences. Even if the public sector is today of the same size as in Sweden, the development of the welfare system happened later in Finland, which was the last of the Nordic countries to be industrialized. This opened up opportunities for adopting impressions and ideas from other systems, and, indeed, there are strong indications of policy diffusion from Sweden to Finland (Karvonen 1981), not least with regard to local government and administration.

1.2 Democracy at Subnational Level

Finnish and Swedish local authorities have common roots in the parish council tradition of the Lutheran church. However, as Aronsson (1997) argues, in Finland Russian domination during the nineteenth century gave local authorities a special importance since the creation of associations at regional and local levels was restricted. In the same way as at the national level, political parties play an important role in Finnish local democracy. However, the dualism of president and assembly that exists at the national level has no equivalent at the local level. Finnish local authorities have considerable powers of their own and thus, are units of local government, rather than just implementers of national policies.

2. The Institutional Expression of Democracy

2.1 The National Level

A significant feature of the Finnish system of democracy is the role of the president. Finland has been labelled a 'semi-presidential' system, containing a mixture of presidentialism and parliamentarism (Arter 1987). The president has an independent sphere of power, in particular within the field of foreign policy, while the government is also dependent on support by a parliamentary majority. However, the strength of the position of the president has varied. During the decades immediately following the Second World War, a combination of outer pressures and weak, short-lived governments gave the president a key role.

From 1980, the balance has tipped in favour of parliament. Changes of government are now less frequent, and from 1966 onwards there have been mainly majority coalitions. Indeed, from 1987, the Social Democratic Party and the Conservative Party, who previously were antagonists, have frequently cooperated in the same coalition governments. In addition, during the Koivisto presidency (1982–94), some of the formal powers of the president were transferred to parliament and to the government. The changing foreign-policy situation has also contributed to a weaker presidency. On the other hand, the legitimacy of the president is stronger, as he is now directly elected since 1994, whereas before, presidential elections were indirect, by an electoral college. Nevertheless, Finnish democracy is increasingly becoming a parliamentary democracy (Petersson 1994).

The Finnish proportional electoral system, based on party lists, provides opportunities for the voters to choose not only between parties, but also between individual candidates. Each candidate has a number, and the voter puts the number of the candidate of his or her choice on the ballot paper. For the electorate, the selection of a party is more important than choosing a candidate, even if the reverse is the case among younger voters (Pesonen 1995). Turnout in parliamentary elections reached a peak in 1962, when 83 per cent of the electorate voted, but it has since steadily decreased to 69 per cent in 1995 (Tilastokeskus 1995). However, 82 per cent of the electorate voted in the second round of the 1994 presidential elections. Electoral participation is now considerably lower than in the other Nordic countries (Petersson 1994). Popular referendums are unusual and have only been used twice, in 1931 on abolition of prohibition and in 1994 on membership of the European Union.

2.2 The Local Level

Local and regional governments in Finland share the general Nordic tradition of local self-government. Finnish local authorities are regarded as having considerable autonomy, today formally protected through the constitution, but have a tradition that goes back long before the time of state independence. The oldest forms of local self-government were already created within the framework of parish administration in the late Middle Ages.

A Municipality Act in 1965 created the municipality as an independent administrative and political unit. In contrast to Sweden, Denmark, and Norway, Finland has only a municipal level of local government. There are 452 municipalities (*kommuner* in Swedish, *kunta* in Finnish) with an average population size of 11,000 inhabitants, ranging from 130 to 520,000; the median population size is 5,000 inhabitants. Some amalgamations have taken place since the 1950s, but a planned comprehensive reform was never carried out. In the mid 1960s, a parliamentary commission suggested that the number of local authorities should be halved. The reform actually reached a preparatory stage but was never implemented, due to the political conflicts it created and opposition from affected municipalities (Ståhlberg and Oulasvirta 1996).

In order to increase efficiency and improve the financial situation for local authorities, central government is now again encouraging mergers. Amalgamated local authorities are offered a stimulation grant during a three-year period. So far, the interest from the municipalities has been limited.

The archipelago of Åland, located between the Finnish and Swedish mainlands, is a special case. After a ruling of the League of Nations in 1921, the islands gained an autonomous position within Finland. Already in 1856, it was demilitarized. Åland has a distinctive history and has Swedish as its official language. It has several emblems, traditionally associated with the nation-state, such as its own flag and stamps. Åland also has a system of regional citizenship (*hembygdsrätt*). Those who are born on Åland are automatically citizens, but other Finnish citizens who have lived in Åland for at least five years, can also apply for such status. Only Åland citizens can vote in local and regional elections and may purchase land on Åland (Loughlin and Daftary 1999). The area is ruled by a directly elected parliament, which has the right to enact its own laws within certain areas. Self-government is particularly salient within health care, education, and culture. All international agreements that affect Åland must be ratified by the parliament in order to be valid for Åland. This also included Finnish membership of the EU. Until 1998, the executive was composed in proportion to party representation in the parliament, but is now ruled according to a parliamentary system. In addition to its regional government, Åland has sixteen municipalities, of which most have fewer than 1,000 inhabitants.

Apart from Åland, Finland lacks directly elected meso level government. Regional influence is instead, to a large extent, channelled through the municipalities by a system of joint municipal authorities and regional councils. The decision-makers of these are appointed by the municipalities. The units have no right to taxation, but are financed through the municipalities which compose them, who also receive central-government grants for these activities. Indeed, as Niemi-Iilahti (1995) argues, this makes the position of the municipalities even stronger than in a two-tier system.

There are two kinds of intermunicipal cooperative arrangements (Niemi-Iilahti 1995). First, 262 special-purpose joint municipal authorities have been established for specific services, which require a larger population base than provided by each member municipality on its own. Some of these are mandatory by law, whereas others are optional. There are compulsory authorities with responsibility for larger hospitals and care of the disabled. In the Helsinki area, there is a separate cooperation authority between the four municipalities in and around the capital, which deals with regional planning, traffic, environmental issues, and waste-disposal matters. Optional joint authorities have been set up for smaller hospitals and vocational education.

Second, in 1994, regional councils were established in the nineteen regions, in which the municipalities of the region are compulsory members. Their main task is to promote regional development. They allocate grants from central government to development projects and are in charge of regional planning. In addition, they oversee the interests of the region and can also perform some voluntary tasks. The regional councils are regional actors in programmes financed by EU structural funds. There is also a central-government level of administration at subnational level. In 1997 this was reorganized, and the number of units was reduced from twelve to five.

In the municipality, the council, elected for a four-year period, is the major decision-making body. Executive matters are in the hands of an executive committee and a number of other committees. After the latest revision of the Local Government Act, local authorities exert considerable autonomy in terms of how to shape their committee system. However, in addition to the executive committee, there are still a number of committees that are mandatory, for example those with responsibility for the fire brigade and building inspection (Niemi-Iilahti 1995). On average, each municipality now establishes twenty committees, which is fewer than before (Ståhlberg and Oulasvirta 1996). According to new regulations from 1995, there must be a more equal representation of women and men. Each sex must have a minimum of 40 per cent of the seats in municipal committees. For example, since the 1996 elections, 45 per cent of the executive-committee members are women. However, this does not extend to the chairs of these committees; only 15 per cent of these are women.

Local authorities have both general and special competences. The general competence concerns all matters that the local authority can perform within its self-government powers. In practice, the most important of these tasks are facilities for culture and recreation and the stimulation of local economic growth. The special competence, which is the most important in economic terms, concerns activities that have been delegated from central government, and these are regulated by separate laws. Health care, education, and day care for children are among the most important of these tasks.

In Finland, a distinction is made between the Swedish-speaking (21), the bilingual (43), and the Finnish-speaking municipalities (391). In principle, a local authority is bilingual if more than 8 per cent of the population speaks the minority language. These municipalities are obliged to have two education committees, one for each language group, or one committee with two subcommittees. Previously, there were separate local-government associations for the Swedish- and the Finnish-speaking municipalities, as well as an association for urban authorities. However, since 1994 these have been merged into the Association of Finnish Local and Regional Authorities (Ståhlberg and Oulasvirta 1996).

2.3 The Role of Political Parties

The major political parties at local level are the same as at the national level. The results from the most recent municipal elections are summarized in Table 16.1. In the same way as in national elections, the three largest parties gain between 65 and 70 per cent of the votes. However, at local level, specific local parties and *ad hoc* parties are more common, even if their share of the votes is decreasing. The large number of parties makes the Finnish local political systems fragmented. However, this is somewhat counteracted by the dominance of non-socialist parties. About 90 per cent of the councils have a non-socialist majority.

Party strength follows an urban–rural and a regional division. The conservative *Kansallinen Kokoomus* (National Coalition) is much stronger in urban areas, and the *Suomen Keskusta* (Centre Party) has its major support in rural areas. In the south, the Social Democrats and the National Coalition are strong, whereas the Centre Party and the *Vasemmistoliitto* (Left-Wing Alliance) are major parties in the north. A long-term trend is a reduced support for the socialist parties in the councils, which mainly is a result of the weakening of the Left-Wing Alliance (Ståhlberg and Oulasvirta 1996).

The political parties have a strong position in the internal affairs of the municipalities. This is not just restricted to setting of goals and making major priorities. Party politics also has a role in the appointment of municipal officers. Ståhlberg and Oulasvirta (1996) report that a considerable share of key appointments is made on the basis of party merits, rather than professional skills. In several such cases, appeals to administrative courts have been made, but the appointments have not been declared illegal.

TABLE 16.1   Municipal election results (percentages), 1988–96

Party	Election		
	1988	1992	1996
Socialidemokraattinen Puole (Social Democratic Party)	25.2	27.1	24.5
Suomen Kekusta (Centre Party)	21.1	19.1	21.8
Kansallinen Kokoomus (National Coalition)	22.9	19.1	21.6
Vasemmistoliitto (Left-Wing Alliance)	12.7	11.7	10.4
Vihreä Liitto (Green League)	2.3	6.9	6.3
Svenska Folkpartiet (Swedish People's Party)	5.3	5.0	5.4
Kristillinen Liitto (Christian League)	2.7	3.2	3.2
Other parties/*ad hoc* groups	7.8	7.8	6.8

Note: The Left-Wing Alliance was formed in 1990. The figure for this party in 1988 represents the total votes of its forming parties. These were the Finnish Communist Party, also known as the Democratic League of the People of Finland (*Soumen Kansom Demokraattinen Liitto*), which gained 10.3% of the votes, and Democratic Alternative (*Demokraattinen Vaihtoehto*), with 2.4% of the votes.

Source: Tilastokeskus (1990, 1995, 1998).

Municipal councillors are elected every four years by a system of proportional representation. The voter makes two choices: a choice between the parties (or other lists); and, within a party list, a choice of an individual candidate. The lists of candidates are established by parties or other organizations. This right is automatically granted to registered political parties, but *ad hoc* interest groups require signatures from citizens. In local elections they need ten names per candidate, so if they want a list with twenty candidates, they must collect 200 signatures. Apart from Finnish citizens, residents from other EU member states or from Iceland or Norway are entitled to vote in local elections. Other non-Finnish citizens can vote if they have lived in Finland for two years. Each elected councillor represents 400 inhabitants (Council of Europe 1995). Among those elected in the 1996 local elections, 32 per cent are women. However, the variation between municipalities is considerable, ranging from 5 per cent to 56 per cent.

Turnout varies between 70 per cent and 80 per cent and has been much the same as in parliamentary elections. However, in the 1996 local elections, which were held at the same time as elections to the European Parliament, only 61 per cent participated. Not only was this much lower than in national elections, but it was also in line with the general, decreasing trend in electoral participation since the 1960s. A citizen survey was undertaken by the Association of Local and Regional Authorities shortly after the elections. The survey indicated that the main reason for abstaining, given by 30 per cent of the non-voters, was the lack of appropriate candidates, while 22 per cent answered that they were not interested in voting or politics. Another study indicated that migration may have contributed to the decrease in turnout. Citizens who have lived longer in their local communities are more likely to vote in local elections. Hence, participation rates are particularly low in growth areas (Mäki-Iohiluoma 1999).

Other forms of public participation, such as contacts with municipal politicians and officers, signing petitions, or active membership of political parties or other politically oriented voluntary organizations, follow the same pattern in Finland as in the other Nordic countries. Party activism is decreasing whereas other forms of participation are stagnating or increasing.

A recent investigation from a municipal research programme in Finland indicates that there are considerable differences in participation rates among the citizens. Those who are well-educated, middle-aged, and employed in the public sector are more active than other citizens. The Swedish-speaking population is more prone to contact local politicians and officers and to participate in protests and boycotts. Attempts to influence local decision-makers through direct contacts are more common in small municipalities whereas protests and demonstrations are more common in larger municipalities (Sjöblom 1999).

The Local Government Act of 1995 has a provision for referendums, but these can only be advisory and only concern matters within the general competence of local authorities. Five per cent of the electorate can suggest that a referendum is arranged on a specific issue, but the final decision to hold one is made by the local council.

3. The Practice of Local Democracy

3.1 The Role of Policy Networks and Pressure Groups in Local Government

The Association of Finnish Local and Regional Authorities is the major interest organization representing Finnish local government. To some extent, it exerts pressure on central government, but it is also involved as a partner in the decision-making process. The relationship between central and local government has changed as central regulation has been relaxed. An important channel bringing the two levels together is the annual negotiations, which involve representatives of government ministries and the Association of Local and Regional Authorities. These have taken place since 1975 and focused mainly on the economic preconditions for local authorities, including prospects for local tax increases, but have also concerned central-government initiatives that may affect local government. The agreements reached in these negotiations are seen as strong recommendations for the different parties, but they are not compulsory. Nevertheless, they are considered to have hampered excessive tax increases as well as creating a forum for confidential dialogue between representatives of the two levels.

Another example of the influence of the association and the municipalities on national decision-making concerns their representation in government advisory commissions. These groups, which are temporary, prepare policy proposals for the government. Next to representatives of central government, municipal representatives are most frequent in these commissions. Municipalities were represented in 40 per cent of the commissions acting during the period 1975–87. This is more than the representation of all other interest organizations, including those of the labour market taken together (Ståhlberg and Oulasvirta 1996).

Local authorities are also involved in policy networks of various kinds. These may be networks of politicians, professions within specific sectors, or just informal forms of cooperation. The importance of networks has been emphasized in a recent study of municipal strategies for the future. Using the delphi-method, based on experts' assessments, it concluded that the most important precondition for municipal success is not what it is in itself, but how it is able to weave well-functioning webs of cooperation. Regional cooperation, international contacts, and close links with the third sector and business are regarded as particularly important (Kivelä and Mannermaa 1999).

However, local authorities themselves are also subject to influence by local pressure groups. Interest organizations are common within the sectors of welfare and local public services. Local labour market organizations are usually well organized, even if membership rates are lower than in Sweden and Denmark (Goul Andersen 1996). Public sector trade unions are represented in cooperative councils, which make recommendations with regard to personnel matters. Local business interests are increasingly brought into local decision-making by means of partnership arrangements (Ståhlberg and Oulasvirta 1996).

3.2 Critiques of Local Democracy

During recent years, criticism of Finnish local democracy has mainly concerned the dramatic drop in electoral turnout, in particular at the 1996 elections. As other traditional forms of participation within a representative democracy have also experienced problems, there is a concern with how channels between people and their elected representatives may be improved. The local authorities have been criticized for their way of using new decentralized powers. They can now more freely decide over their internal organization and the general tendency is that the number of elected and appointed members is being reduced.

A special feature in Finland is the indirectly elected regional level. Even if it has many proponents, and it has recently been reorganized, it still attracts criticism because of its lack of democratic legitimacy.

3.3 Citizens' Attitudes to Local Government

Finnish local democracy has been affected by growing political discontent (Ståhlberg and Oulasvirta 1996). Opinion polls indicate that more Finns regard local as well as national politicians as losing touch with their voters. Some observers have interpreted the signs of political discontent as the beginning of a legitimation crisis, whereas others have seen it as an adjustment to a more normal state of affairs, as the knowledge and education levels of the voters have increased.

Signs of discontent are also a feature of a recent comprehensive investigation on Finnish citizens. Indeed, only 40 per cent agree that local politicians carry out their tasks successfully, and 44 per cent claim that citizens' views play no role in municipal decision-making (Kivinen *et al.* 1997). Two-thirds of the citizens claim that much could be improved in the handling of municipal affairs, more than half think that the real power in the municipality is in the hands of officers, not politicians. Young people, the unemployed, the less-educated and those with left-wing political views tend to be more critical. Also, the Finnish-speaking population is more critical of municipal matters than the Swedish-speakers (Pekola-Sjöblom 1999). However, at the same time, the Finns wish to be more involved in politics. According to the same investigation, 83 per cent want citizens to be offered new means of participation (Kivinen *et al.* 1997).

A surprising result from recent studies is that Finnish citizens identify themselves with their local municipality to a lesser extent than those in the other Nordic countries. Also, in the latter, this tends to be associated with the size of the local authority: the smaller the local authority, the more people identify with it. However, in Finland, the opposite pattern has been observed: local identity is weaker in the smaller municipalities. The larger, more urbanized, and more affluent the municipality is, the more people identify with it (Ståhlberg 1998).

4. Challenges and Opportunities for Regional and Local Democracy

4.1 The European Challenge

Finnish membership of the EU (in 1995) has offered new challenges and opportunities for local government. The recent nature of its entry would initially suggest that it would be unlikely for any direct impact on Finnish local government to be visible yet. However, in practice, the adjustment to the Europeanization process had already started at the beginning of the 1990s. A survey in 1992 indicated surprisingly high levels of orientation towards the EU among Finnish municipalities (von Bergmann-Winberg 1997). For example, 47 per cent were undertaking EU training courses, 24 per cent subscribed to national EU information, and 30 per cent were cooperating with the regional level in EU matters. These figures are particularly high, as at the same time, 61 per cent of the municipalities claimed that EU matters were of no interest to them. Despite Finland not being a member at that time, a large number of local authorities made provisions for a future membership status.

Generally, adjustments have been made mainly by the larger cities and the municipalities with traditional industrial bases, but there are also examples of rural municipalities with well-developed EU strategies. Previous international links, for example, due to the presence of large export industries or tourism, have played a role. However, structural conditions cannot explain everything. A significant factor is also the attitude of the political leadership of the municipality towards the EU. Interestingly, research indicates that Finnish local authorities with the status of free communes tend not to be in favour of developing activities in relation to the EU. It seems as if local authorities that are occupied with internal changes and relationships with central government are not necessarily more oriented towards the European level.

The results from a follow-up questionnaire in 1994, still prior to Finnish membership, indicated that the activity rate among the local authorities had increased (von Bergmann-Winberg 2000). However, the main expansion concerned external strategies. Local authorities in Finland are more actively seeking information about the EU and are, to a larger extent, cooperating with other local authorities and the regional councils.

This picture of an extensive Finnish activism is supported in another study, also undertaken in the mid 1990s. In a comparative study of Norwegian and Finnish municipal internationalization activities, Baldersheim and Ståhlberg (1999) conclude that Finnish local authorities are more active than their Norwegian counterparts, and that these differences have mainly been created during the early 1990s. A major explanation is the new opportunities which emerged in the wake of the collapse of the Soviet Union. Cross-border cooperation suddenly became much more important and Finland found a new role as a gateway to Russia. In a decentralized polity, this was not only a concern for central government. The local authorities also quickly grasped the opportunities this created.

It should be emphasized that even before EU membership was on the agenda, Finnish municipalities had developed transnational links. The Nordic Council, on which Åland has a seat, has acted as a framework for cooperation. Transfrontier cooperation with municipalities and county councils in other Nordic countries had already begun in the 1960s. Later, Russia and the Baltic states were also included. At least initially, cooperation concerned environmental issues, culture, medical care, tourism, and transport. However, European integration has contributed to reinforcing this tendency further, in Finland as well as in other countries (Östhol 1996).

The analyses undertaken so far detect an increasing adjustment to the EU by Finnish local authorities, even if this is limited to a relatively small number of municipalities. It is likely that this development has continued after membership status was obtained in 1995 and that a larger number of local authorities are now active *vis-à-vis* the EU. The consequences for local democracy of these activities are not yet clear. However, it is unlikely that they are a response to strong popular demands, but rather are initiated by political and administrative elites.

4.2 Financial Strain

Municipal expenditures represented 18 per cent of the gross domestic product (GDP) and their share of total public expenditures was 30 per cent (1994 figures) (Council of Europe 1997). The most important sources of income are taxes (40 per cent), central government grants (29 per cent), and user fees (15 per cent) (1994 figures). The main local-government tax is a proportional income tax, which currently is 18 per cent (on average) of taxable income. However, it ranges from between 15 per cent and 20 per cent in different municipalities. Local authorities set the tax rate, but from 1975 onwards agreements have been made about a recommended level of taxation between central government and the different associations of local authorities. The transfer system from national to local government was, until the late 1980s, dominated by specific grants. However, following a reform in 1993, it now mainly consists of block grants. The grants system includes a number of measures aiming at compensating disadvantaged local authorities, but the equalizing factor has become weaker since the 1993 reform (Ståhlberg and Oulasvirta 1996).

A major change with consequences for Finnish local democracy is the strain related to decreasing resources. As in other western countries, local authorities have been forced to reconsider previous commitments, but the Finnish background is somewhat different. For most of the post-war period, the size of the public sector as well as its local-government share was smaller in Finland than in the other Nordic countries. However, during the 1970s and 1980s, the Finnish economy and the public sector experienced a phase of 'catching up' with its neighbours, which also had an effect on the relative size of local government (Mouritzen and Nielsen 1992; Naschold 1995). New major functions were transferred from central to local government (e.g., the maintenance of larger hospitals) (Oulasvirta 1992). Thus, by the early 1990s, Finnish local government was as large as the corresponding sectors in Sweden, Denmark, and Norway.

However, a severe recession which hit Finland at that time, also marked the start of a period of contraction. To some extent, this was triggered by a breakdown of eastern trade, following the collapse of the Soviet Union. Economic decline, with a massive fall in GDP, a depreciation of the Finnish *markka*, and increasing unemployment, forced central government to reduce the size of the public sector. For example, in 1994 the national-government grants to local government were cut by 10 per cent. Even if an increase in municipal taxes managed to compensate for some of the losses, local authorities were still faced with demands to enhance efficiency, prioritize, and abandon services. It is expected that these problems will continue in the future (Niemi-Iilahti 1995), even if the economy shows signs of improvement in the coming years. Nevertheless, popular expectations about what local authorities can provide have to be reduced.

4.3 Organizational Changes

A further change with implications for local democracy is the ongoing reorganization of local government. Amalgamations of local authorities have been rare, but other changes have been more common. The growth of the municipal welfare system in the 1980s was, to a large extent, undertaken on behalf of the central government. In order to control the performance of the municipalities, detailed regulation and monitoring devices set effective limits to local self-government. In particular, the grants system was highly detailed with task-specific grants for various services. However, through a number of decentralization policies, power has been relocated to the local level and a more general form of regulation has been introduced. In terms of local democracy, several reorganizations have provided greater scope for local influence over local matters. However, at the same time, the greater freedom for local authorities has resulted in mergers of committees and a reduction in the number of municipal politicians (Ståhlberg 1994).

The changes with regard to the grants system have been particularly significant as decentralization measures (Oulasvirta 1992). As late as 1987, 99 per cent of the state grants were targeted to specific purposes. In 1993, these were replaced by a few general grants, including two broad sector grants for social services/health care and for education/recreation. Local government exerts considerable discretion in the use of these resources. Somewhat surprisingly, the municipalities were the main opponent to introducing the new system, as they expected it to make grants more susceptible to cuts. Indeed, not long after the reform this actually happened.

Private provision of services for which municipalities are responsible is most common in urban settings and, somewhat surprisingly, in local authorities of different sizes dominated by left-wing parties. The reason is that private provision is seen as a pragmatic, rather than ideological, solution (Granqvist 1997). However, on the whole, reorganizational measures have only to a very limited extent included privatization of public services even if managerial ideas have been borrowed from the private sector. The adaptation of new steering systems, such as Management by Objectives (MBO) and management by results, came comparatively late in Finland. The economic problems in the early 1990s marked a halt in this reform movement. Now, both central and local government combine new and old means of steering (Naschold 1995). However, there are strong indications that Finnish local authorities, during the latter part of the 1990s, are continuing to develop methods in line with New Public Management ideas, emphasizing marketization, private provision, and a focus on outputs and results (Ståhlberg 1998).

4.4 The Regional Level

A major innovation in Finnish local government is the transformation of the regional level. The 1919 Constitution made provisions for a level of elected county councils in Finland, but for several reasons this never came into effect. The necessary political support for the decision to implement the reform was never gathered as, in essence, it was believed that Finland was too small for an intermediate level of elected government. Instead, various forms of cooperative arrangements between municipalities emerged, and have been reformed, over the years. The latest and so far the most important of these reforms concerns the establishment in 1994 of indirectly elected regional councils in each of the nineteen regions. Even if these councils, to a large extent, consist of members of municipal councils, they nevertheless lack the democratic legitimacy of directly elected bodies. However, they still perform tasks which are similar to the meso-level in many other European states (Sharpe 1993). They fulfil a regional government role *vis-à-vis* the EU. Indeed, the adaptation to the requirements of the EU structural funds was an important driving force behind the creation of these councils and has also been important for the set of tasks they have been given (Lindström, Hedegaard, and Veggeland 1996).

The councils are responsible for regional development, which was a task for regional state administration before 1994. They may also perform other functions that the member municipalities regard as feasible. The new bodies are clearly important from a democratic point of view, even if popular influence is indirect.

5. Innovative Approaches to Improving Regional and Local Democracy

In the same way as in the other Nordic countries, a free-commune experimental programme was initiated in 1989. This was inspired by the Swedish (1984) and Danish (1985) experiments. A total of fifty-six 'free communes' were selected and given the opportunity to be exempted from specific legislation. The Finnish experiment was mainly focused on administrative matters and has been regarded as more of a reform than an experiment (Ståhlberg 1994). An important reason was to increase the efficiency of local service production (Ståhlberg & Oulasvirta 1996).

However, the experiment has had a significant impact on the formulation of a new Local Government Act. Certain parts of this Act came into force in 1995 and the rest in 1997. A number of changes were introduced in the new legislation. Municipal responsibility for sustainable development was emphasized as a specific task of local government. The position of the chief administrative officer was clarified. Local authorities were provided with greater freedom to decide the structure of their committee system. Also, a committee that lost the support of the council could from now on be dismissed during its term of office.

The role of the council was also affected by changes in this Act. The minimum required size of the local council was reduced, which has led to fewer elected representatives. Majority constellations in the local councils may be less stable, as previous two-third majority requirements have been abolished. The new Act may also affect local democracy in other ways. Provisions for new forms of user influence have been included as local authorities now are permitted to delegate decision-making powers to, for example, groups of parents on boards of day nurseries or schools (*Finlands kommuntidning*, 10, 1994).

A special feature of Finnish local democracy is the citizens' written motion. If anyone suggests a measure that he or she thinks the local authority should undertake, the municipality is obliged to respond with a decision. If the measure is supported by 2 per cent of the electorate, this decision becomes a matter for the full council and not just a committee.

During the last few years, there are signs of decreasing support for representative democracy in Finland. One manifestation is the exceptionally low turnout in the recent local elections. Therefore, the Ministry of the Interior has initiated a 'participation project', aiming at supporting local projects for improving public participation. The project started in 1997 and continued throughout 1999. On the basis of experiences from the project, suggestions for changes will be presented during 2000. Central government has financially assisted sixty-two projects in fifty-three municipalities. Different approaches are represented among them, for example, support and cooperation between the Swedish and Finnish culture (*Grankulla*), new forums for local participation (*Jyväskylä*), and involvement of youth (*Kuopio, Raumo, Riihimäki*).

A further innovation, tested by several municipalities, are youth councils. These aim at improving young people's influence over municipal matters. In Esbo, thirteen- to twenty-year-olds elect thirty representatives to the youth council. Its role will be to make suggestions whenever the municipality is considering matters affecting young people. Similar councils have been set up in the municipalities of Malax, Lappo, Alahärmä, and Vichtis, for example (*Finlands kommuntidning*, 11, 1997).

6. Conclusions

The preconditions for Finnish local democracy have changed dramatically during the 1990s. Internal changes, such as decentralization policies and experiments with new forms of local governance, have changed the scope for local democracy. External transformations, in particular the collapse of the Soviet Union, have created an opportunity for a Finnish reorientation towards the west, mainly manifested in the Finnish EU membership. These changes have put Finnish local authorities in a gateway position, between West and East. Today, local authorities are trying to reap the benefits from this position by an active involvement in transnational cooperation.

A number of specific features characterize Finnish local democracy compared to other countries. The absence of a directly elected intermediate level of local government is one such feature, and the relatively low level of participation in local elections is another. Nevertheless, local government enjoys a strong position in Finnish society. Further, as there is considerable popular interest in political participation and as new ways of improving local democracy are constantly tested, a great deal can be expected from Finnish local democracy in the future.

Local authorities in Finland have similar problems of democracy as most other local government systems in Europe. Participation rates are declining, at least in traditional forms of electoral participation and membership in political parties. However, at the same time, people turn to other ways of influencing decisions, for example by taking part in protests and *ad hoc* action groups. Government initiatives have been taken which aim at improving public participation. However, it remains to be seen whether national policies can have an impact on these changes or whether they represent a more profound transition in the Finnish, and other western European, polities.

The question of the position of the regional level is likely to cause further debate. In 1997, the Finnish prime minister indicated that the number of regional councils should be reduced, and he is also prepared to consider direct elections to the new, amalgamated, councils. In this way, they are expected to be better able to carry out the extended tasks that are associated with their role in a European context. Regional democracy clearly continues to be a topical question in Finland.

References

ARONSSON, P. (1997). 'Local Politics—the Invisible Political Culture', in Ø. Sørensen and B. Stråth (eds), *The Cultural Construction of Norden*. Oslo: Scandinavian University Press.

ARTER, D. (1987). *Politics and Policy-Making in Finland*. Brighton: Wheatsheaf.

BALDERSHEIM, H. and STÅHLBERG, K. (1999). 'The Internationalisation of Finnish and Norwegian Local Government', in H. Baldersheim and K. Ståhlberg (eds), *Nordic Region-building in a European Perspective*. Aldershot: Ashgate.

BERGLUND, S. (1990). 'Finland in a Comparative Perspective', in J. Sundberg and S. Berglund (eds), *Finnish Democracy*. Helsinki: The Finnish Political Science Association.

BERGMANN-WINBERG, M.-L. VON (1997). 'The Impact of European Integration on Regional and Local Government in Finland, Norway and Sweden', in M. J. F. Goldsmith and K. K. Klausen (eds), *European Integration and Local Government*. Cheltenham: Edward Elgar.

——(2000). 'Finnish Regions and Municipalities in a Nordic Setting. Processes of Restructuring, Internationalisation and Integration', in J. Gidlund and M. Jerneck (eds), *Local and Regional Governance in Europe: Evidence from Nordic Regions.* Aldershot: Edward Elgar.

COUNCIL OF EUROPE (1995). *The Size of Municipalities, Efficiency and Citizen Participation.* Local and Regional Authorities in Europe 56. Strasbourg.

——(1997). *Local Finance in Europe.* Local and Regional Authorities in Europe 61. Strasbourg.

GOUL ANDERSEN, J. (1996). *Membership and Participation in Voluntary Associations in Scandinavia, in a Comparative Perspective.* Aalborg University: Department of Economics, Politics and Public Administration.

GRANQVIST, N. (1997). *Privatisering i princip och praktik. En studie av privata inslag i finska kommuners verksamhet.* Åbo: Åbo Akademis.

KARVONEN, L. (1981). *Med vårt västra grannland som förebild.* Åbo: Stiftelsen för Åbo Akademi.

KIVELÄ, S. and MANNERMAA, M. (1999). *Kuntien tulevaisuus. Kunta-alan tulevaisuusbarometri 1999.* Helsinki: Suomen kuntaliitto.

KIVINEN, T., KINNUNEN, J., NIIRANEN, V., and HYVÄRINEN, S. (eds) (1997). *Kuntalaisten arviot ja osallisuus sosiaali- ja terveyspalveluihin.* Kuopio: University of Kupio.

LINDSTRÖM, U. and KARVONEN, L. (eds) (1987). *Finland. En politisk loggbok.* Stockholm: Almqvist & Wiksell.

——, HEDEGAARD, L., and VEGGELAND, N. (1996). *Regional Policy and Territorial Supremacy.* Stockholm: NordREFO.

LOUGHLIN, J. and DAFTARY, F. (1999). *Insular Regions and European Integration: Corsica and the Åland Islands compared.* Flensburg: European Centre for Minority Issues. Report no. 5, 60 pp., October.

MOURITZEN, P. E. and NIELSEN, K. H. (1992). 'Was There a Fiscal Crisis?', in P. E. Mouritzen (ed.), *Managing Cities in Austerity.* London: Sage.

MÄKI-IOHILUOMA, K.-P. (1999). 'Vaalikäyttäytyminen kunnallis- ja eurovaaleissa', in K.-P. Mäki-Iohiluoma, M. Pekola-Sjöblom, and K. Ståhlberg (eds), *Kuntalaisten valta ja valinnat.* Helsinki: Suomen kuntaliitto.

NASCHOLD, F. (1995). *The Modernisation of the Public Sector in Europe.* Helsinki: Ministry of Labour.

NIEMI-IILAHTI, A. (1995). 'The Structure and Finance of Finnish Local Government in a European Perspective'. *Kunnallistieteellinen aikakauskirja,* 4.

NOUSIAINEN, J. (1966). *Finlands politiska system.* Stockholm: Svenska Bokförlaget.

ÖSTHOL, A. (1996). *Politisk integration och gränsöverskridande regionbildning i Europa.* Umeå: University of Umeå.

OULASVIRTA, L. (1992). 'Municipal Public Finance in the Nordic Countries'. *Local Government Studies,* 18/4: 106–35.

PEKOLA-SJÖBLOM, M. (1999). 'Har kommuninvånarna förtroende för det kommunala beslutsfattandet?' *Finlands Kommuntidning,* 2.

PESONEN, P. (1995). 'The Voters' Choice of Candidate', in S. Borg and R. Sänkiaho (eds), *The Finnish Voter.* Helsinki: The Finnish Political Science Association.

PETERSSON, O. (1994). *The Government and Politics of the Nordic Countries.* Stockholm: Publica.

SHARPE, L. J. (ed.) (1993). *The Rise of Meso Government in Europe.* London: Sage.

SJÖBLOM, S. (1999). 'Deltagande och delaktighet: Oroväckande utvecklingsdrag'. *Finlands Kommuntidning,* 1.

STÅHLBERG, K. (1994). 'The Finnish Case: a Reform Rather Than an Experiment', in H. Baldersheim and K. Ståhlberg (eds), *Towards the Self-regulating Municipality. Free Communes and Administrative Modernization in Scandinavia*. Aldershot: Dartmouth.

——(1998). 'Utvecklingspolitiken i finländska kommuner. Vad, var och vem?', in K. K. Klausen and K. Ståhlberg (eds), *New Public Management i Norden*. Odense: Odense University Press.

——and L. OULASVIRTA (1996). 'Finland', in E. Albæk, E. *et al.* (eds), *Nordic Local Government*. Helsinki: The Association of Finnish Local Authorities.

TILASTOKESKUS (1990). *Soumen tilastollinen vousikirja 1990* [Statistical Yearbook of Finland 1990]. Helsinki: Tilastokeskus.

——(1995). *Soumen tilastollinen vousikirja 1995* [Statistical Yearbook of Finland 1995]. Helsinki: Tilastokeskus.

——(1998). *Soumen tilastollinen vousikirja 1998* [Statistical Yearbook of Finland 1990]. Helsinki: Tilastokeskus.

Part 5

CONCLUSIONS

17

Conclusions: The Transformation of Regional and Local Democracy in Western Europe

John Loughlin

1. Consequences for Regional and Local Democracy

This book reveals the rich and complex tapestry of democratic theory and practice in the countries of the European Union. Two aspects of this complexity stand out. First, countries remain basically faithful to their state and national state traditions of political and administrative culture. But, second, these traditions undergo continual change and adaptation as a result of factors such as globalization, Europeanization, societal, and technological change. Indeed, the capacity to manage change successfully is one of the main features of many European states. On the other hand, the successful management of change is not spread evenly throughout Europe. Some countries, regions, and localities have been quite successful whereas others have had difficulty in coping with the changes. To some extent this is a result of a competitive regionalism which is producing new disparities within the European Union. This is neither a north–south nor a centre–periphery cleavage. Some countries of southern Europe contain highly successful regions such as Catalonia, Lombardy, and Tuscany. Countries that were previously peripheral, such as the Republic of Ireland, Spain, and Portugal have now become centres of dynamic economic growth. Ireland has been called the 'Celtic Tiger' by analogy with the Asian 'Tiger' economies. Some countries that were previously powerful economic 'centres' now contain regions and cities in decline such as the old industrialized regions of coal mining and steel production in Britain, Belgium, France, and Spain which have experienced great difficulties of adaptation.

What is clear from the studies presented in this book is that the old frameworks for responding to these challenges have shifted. Previously, the nation-state was the framework within which solutions were sought and national governments the principal actors that would supply these solutions. This was the old centre–periphery framework analysed by authors such as Rokkan and Urwin (1983) and Mény and Wright (1985). This framework was relevant and applicable up to about the early 1980s. Since then, both the framework and the role of national actors have changed. First, the framework within which solutions need to be found is no longer the nation-state alone but the European Union, at least as this might be conceived as a policy or public space. Second, there was the wave of privatizations and deregulation which spread across Europe in the 1980s, enhanced by the Single Market project of 1992 and the Maastricht criteria for entry into the single currency. These developments changed the role of the state, or at least of national governments, and its relationship with the private sector. National regional policies, archetypal examples of Keynesian-type state intervention, were either abolished, as in the United Kingdom, or significantly reduced in scale. The emerging regional policy of the European Union, limited in budgetary terms and in its scope, could not hope to compensate for the decline of national regional policies. The most important consequences of these shifts for regional and local democracy is that regions and cities could henceforth no longer rely on national governments for the same amounts of aid that had existed previously. In a real sense, they were on their own. This meant the development of a competitive regionalism on a European and, indeed, world scale. Regions and cities found themselves competing within and across countries both for scarce EU funds and for foreign investors. This meant, at least if they were to be successful, a profound restructuring of their political and policy-making systems, of their social and economic circumstances, and of their physical environments.

What is striking about the studies presented in this book is that all the member states of the European Union have been affected by these changes. This is clearly true of the United Kingdom which was the 'pioneer' in the adoption of the 'neo-liberal' model under Mrs Thatcher in the 1980s. It is true that we need to relativize the Thatcherite reforms by pointing out public spending actually continued to increase during this period (Pierson 1994). Nevertheless, the Thatcher period did change in a fundamental way many aspects of British public life and relations between the private and public sectors including at the regional and local levels. This was a cultural revolution more than a successful reduction of public expenditure. It was so radical that the new Labour government elected in 1997 was obliged to adopt many of the neo-liberal reforms such as privatization, internal markets in public administration, and the principle of competition in public tendering which it recognized were now irreversible. But many other countries were affected both by intensifying European integration and by the neo-liberal wave, which, with the single currency project tended to blend into each other. This was true even of the Scandinavian countries, which had been bastions of rooted social democracy and strong social policies. Denmark's conversion to neo-liberalism began even before the arrival to power of Mrs Thatcher. But Sweden, whose social democracy dated back to the 1930s and which had become a 'model' of a certain kind of welfare state, was obliged to do so in the 1980s. France elected a socialist president and a left-wing coalition government in 1981 on a classical social-democratic programme of nationalization and expansion. By 1983, they were forced (by the international environment and their European Community partners) to make a radical shift towards austerity policies. Some countries, such as Ireland, adopted the new approaches willingly and, in conjunction with generous EU structural funds and other factors, have successfully transformed themselves into economic powerhouses. Other countries such as Italy (or at least its southern regions) and Greece, plagued by problems of inefficient and rambling bureaucracies and serious regional problems, have found it more difficult to reform. It was the necessity of meeting the Maastricht single currency criteria that has coerced them into radical restructuring. Italy managed, at the price of far-reaching austerity measures, to be among the first wave of entrants into the single currency zone. Greece failed to meet the criteria but, at the time of writing (2000), has now done so and has applied for membership. What is interesting is that many of these reforms have been carried out by socialist or social-democratic governments who now form a majority of governments in the EU member states, thus signalling a radical transformation in the ideology of such movements. Even Germany, one of the last bastions of the social state and the most resistant to neo-liberalism, has been forced by the financial consequences of unification to seriously examine some of the principles of this state. It is interesting that it is a Social Democrat Chancellor, Gerhard Schröder, who is attempting (with some difficulty) to bring about these reforms. Another significant event was the re-election (in March 2000) of Mr Aznar in Spain on a centre-right programme which is not that far removed from the centre-left programmes of Tony Blair and Gerhard Schröder. The old left–right cleavage is becoming increasingly redundant in this new political environment.

Another striking finding of the present work is the way in which the neo-liberal paradigm has worked itself into the operating systems of regional and local governments. First, it provides a framework within which policy-making now occurs at the subnational level. Second, neo-liberal approaches have been introduced directly into regional and local political and administrative systems. Again, there is a wide variation here across Europe but we might remark that the general statement holds true at least to some extent in all countries. Again, it is the United Kingdom which set the pace, mainly by means of a central government hostile to local authorities imposing unwelcome measures such as rate-capping and compulsory competitive tendering on local authorities fundamentally opposed to these measures. The weak constitutional position of British local government meant that it had little choice but to swallow what central government was forcing down its throat (Scarbrough 2000). It is significant that the Blair government has also been forced to accept these developments as irreversible. It is trying to mitigate some of the more savage features of neo-liberalism through programmes such as 'best value'. This does not fundamentally question the neo-liberal principle of competition at their heart but modifies this by allowing the public sector to compete on the same basis as the private sector to run local public services. One finds similar developments across Europe. The Scandinavian 'free commune' experiments can be interpreted in this light as a form of 'liberalization'. French decentralization, which was initially about enhancing local democracy and improving public administration, after 1983 became increasingly a way of applying the principles of neo-liberalism. Southern European local governments, traditionally marked by clientelistic traditions and high degrees of dependence on the central state followed suit in the 1980s and 1990s. In some cases, it was the European Commission which encouraged these trends through the criteria necessary to receive programme funding (although some of these criteria such as the principle of partnership might be said to go against the neo-liberal approach).

We need to qualify these general remarks with another. What is clear from the studies presented here is that, although significant changes have taken place at the European, national, and subnational levels in all European Union states, this has been somewhat uneven. First, some countries have gone much further than others. The United Kingdom has been the most radical and Germany has been perhaps the least. Furthermore, although all countries have applied the neo-liberal approach, they did so from different starting points and in ways that were closely related to their distinct state traditions. Swedish welfare state provisions were so generous that, even after the austerity measures, they still outstrip what is on offer in countries (such as the United Kingdom or Ireland) which were much less generous. The Netherlands already has a kind of deregulated approach and so its privatization measures were less radical than might have been expected. Furthermore, the Dutch system of strong social compensation was not fundamentally altered. In France, the state still remains the most important actor and many of its Jacobin features have been left untouched even if decentralization has radically altered the position of regions, departments, and communes. The French tradition of Colbertism remains strong. When we examine the subnational level, we can also see variations within and across states. Strong federal systems, such as are found in Germany, Austria, or Belgium, may allow quite distinct approaches to be adopted within the different regions ranging from neo-liberalism to neo-corporatism, depending on the coalition of forces present in that region. The same is true of autonomic Spain and, increasingly, of 'devolutionalized' Britain. Regional and local authorities have also responded in quite different ways to the external challenges of globalization and Europeanization. As the chapters on Scandinavia make clear, this ranges from proactive enthusiasm to a kind of indifferent *attentisme*. This phenomenon seems to be general across Europe.

It is clear that these developments have important consequences for the expression and practice of democracy as the individual chapters of this book have illustrated. Is it possible to draw some general conclusions at this stage? What can be said, in relation to the previous paragraphs, is that the neo-liberal approach, in its original Anglo-Saxon formulation, was not simply about economics but was also a way of understanding politics and, in particular, implied a particular way of understanding democracy. This approach is dominated by the notion of 'methodological individualism', that is, the idea found in rational choice theory that the individual (whether a person or organization) is the basic unit of political analysis and activity. The implications for democracy are clearest from the British experiments in reforming local government. The attempt was made here to redefine the nature of citizenship. The traditional notion was that the individual was primarily a member of a community (whether this was defined nationally or locally) and that citizenship meant participating in some way (either directly or through a representative) in running the affairs of this community. The new approach defines the citizen as a 'consumer', making choices about the kinds of services he or she wishes to avail of. Again, this notion of the citizen as consumer found an echo in some other countries—notably in Denmark and some Dutch cities—but seems to have been treated with caution in most EU member states. In countries such as Germany, Austria, and those of southern Europe, regional and local traditions remain strong as do religious traditions such as Catholicism which stress the notion of the common good. Even within the United Kingdom, Scotland and Wales and parts of the north of England never fully accepted the Thatcherite programme of democracy as consumerism and this was one of the primary reasons why the British Conservative Party was almost eliminated in these nations and regions at the 1997 General Election. Nevertheless, despite this important qualification the neo-liberal concept of citizen as consumer became an important reference point even for these states and some of its features entered into their systems.

2. Critiques of Subnational Democracy and Responses

An important feature of this book has been to outline the critiques of regional and local democracy in the EU member states. In all of these states, democratic practice, especially at the regional and local levels, is only an approximation of an elusive ideal which, as we have seen, may be defined in several distinct ways. In all of the member states, there have been critiques of this practice and suggestions for its improvement. Critiques may be made, of course, from several different perspectives, depending on which democratic model the critic espouses. Critiques might even be mutually exclusive. For example, someone who espouses an elitist Schumpeterian model of democracy will criticize the excessive participation of citizens in decision-making on the grounds that this interferes with the smooth running of the system. A believer in participatory democracy, such as a member of the Green movement, will adopt exactly the opposite point of view. A Marshallian advocate of social citizenship and democracy will criticize local government reforms that attempt to apply neo-liberal principles, while a Thatcherite will criticize anything that seems to lead to greater bureaucracy. What does seem clear from what has been said above is that European political elites, of both right and left, have now chosen to move beyond the welfare state model that characterized the period from the Second World War until the 1980s. However, the most recent period has seen a majority of centre-left governments come to power who are now trying to mitigate some of the aspects of neo-liberalism through combining them with stronger social measures.

All of the EU states have embarked on major reform efforts that have had an impact on the practice of democracy at the national, regional, and local levels. The kinds of reform may be categorized as follows:

- restructuring central–regional/local relationships;
- reform of the internal mechanisms of regional and local government;
- improving relations between the political system at the regional and local levels and the general public;
- responding to and exploiting the European factor.

It is important to remember that these reforms have occurred over several decades since the Second World War and may have different meanings depending on the period in which they took place. In the period of the '*Trente Glorieuses*', the economies of most European states were in full expansion. There was a strong growth of welfare states marked by centralization; redistributive functions, high taxation, and a role for regional and/or local government based on this system of redistribution of collective and individual goods. Restructuring central–local relations during this period was often based on the necessities of indicative national planning and of creating local governments that were of a sufficient scale to deliver the services that were increasingly demanded by citizens. This meant reducing the large numbers of small local authorities to a smaller number of larger authorities. This happened in many countries but there were exceptions such as France. During this period, the European Community had little relevance for subnational government. Internal reforms were mainly about improving the capacity to manage large-scale welfare programmes through the application of rational utility managerialist approaches such as management by objectives or cost-benefit analysis. Relations with the general public were primarily in relation to how efficiently and effectively local authorities provided services. During the neo-liberal period, on the other hand, reformers will understand central–local relations rather differently. Now, the emphasis is on withdrawal of the central state from funding programmes generally whether regional policies or welfare state programmes. 'Decentralization' in this period might mean little more than central governments shedding the burden (and blame) for the cutting back of these programmes onto subnational governments. However, the European factor does become important during this phase as EU regional policy and structural action policy become more important. Internal reforms are now often about a new understanding of managerialism—how to manage cutbacks rather than expansion—with the emphasis on efficiency rather than on effectiveness.

2.1 Restructuring Central–Regional/Local Relationships

Almost all of the EU member states have embarked on this kind of reform in the last twenty years. In some cases it has meant in fact strengthening the centre at the expense of the regional and local. This was the case in traditional centralized unitary states such the United Kingdom and Ireland. In Britain there has been a tendency towards centralization and the reduction of the role and powers of local government, which goes back over fifty years. The post-war welfare state intensified centralization but so too did the attempts by Conservative Governments between 1979 and 1997 to dismantle the welfare state. Ironically, it was Ireland's status as an Objective One priority region in EU Structural Fund terms that strengthened the national government through the key position of the Department of Finance in controlling these funds. Within federal states such as Germany and Austria there has also been a tendency towards the centralization of power, particularly in the financial domain, at the federal level.

However, such centralization is not the only tendency in operation. More often, there has been political decentralization, regionalization, and even federalization. The Scandinavian countries, Denmark, Finland, and Sweden have always been decentralized unitary states with a strong welfare state model (the 'Swedish model') in which local government played an important role. However, although the 'Swedish model' has come under pressure and is being reformed, this has not lessened the importance of local government. On the contrary, the latter seems to have increased in importance. One notable example is the 'free commune' experiment in the Scandinavian countries, which reduces central government controls over local authorities. Belgium is a state that has passed through all of the stages from a classical unitary state to becoming a federation, and the process of decentralization and state reform is still continuing. Italy is a regionalized unitary state with special regions, but is currently introducing reforms that strengthen the regions and give the state some federalist characteristics. Spain made its transition to democracy by creating the autonomic state, which draws on elements of the Italian system as well the German system of cooperative federalism. The tendency here is for the autonomous communities to gain more powers (e.g., fiscal) at the expense of the central government. The United Kingdom has recently embarked on a remarkable programme of devolution that is transforming the relations among its regions and nations as well as with the Republic of Ireland. Even centralized unitary states, such as Ireland and Greece, have begun to introduce some elements of regionalization at least in their systems of public administration. There seems to be a general trend in operation here, but the Portuguese public went against this by voting in a referendum against the setting up of regions in that country, although this may have happened because of party-political struggles rather than any deep-seated opposition to regionalization on the part of the Portuguese people.

These institutional reforms have been carried out for different reasons. Sometimes, they were part of the neo-liberal agenda of the 1980s, which involved shedding responsibilities and tasks from central governments to other levels of administration. Sometimes, they were attempts at modernizing systems of public administration that had become overcentralized, inefficient, and removed from ordinary citizens. However, often they were also genuine attempts at enhancing regional and local democracy by making it easier for citizens to participate in decision-making. It has proved impossible in this book to ascertain fully how successful this has been. This would demand a much larger research project over a longer period of time than was available to the team of experts. Nevertheless, we do feel that these reforms have been worthwhile, and the different experiences across different countries should be studied with care with a view to policy learning across states.

2.2 The European Factor

The European Union has been an important factor in the reconfiguration of central–local relations in its member states. This has happened in a number of ways. First, the EU has meant that, with the passing of sovereignty in certain areas from national governments to the European institutions, the nature, role, and functions of the state itself have changed. This has not meant the disappearance of the nation-state, but it does mean that national governments

operate alongside both European institutions and regions and local authorities. Thus, regions and local authorities have a more important role in the
European policy-making system than hitherto. This higher profile of regions and local authorities has been given expression in the creation of the
Committee of the Regions. The European Commission has also, through its
funding programmes and initiatives such as INTERREG, encouraged the
involvement of subnational authorities in European decision-making and
policy areas. This has stimulated individual regions and cities to develop a
European interest, even if this is sometimes little more than creating a single
desk or the appointment of a European office. Finally, both for reasons of
exploiting these opportunities for European funding, and also for promoting
the regional interest more generally, regions and local authorities have mobilized their forces by forming trans-European interregional associations. The
interests of regions are also represented through the Council of Europe and
the European Parliament.

The country chapters in this book show that regions and local authorities
have responded to these challenges and opportunities of the new Europe in
different ways. Some regions have reacted in a proactive manner; others are
more *attentiste*; and many, perhaps the majority, are quite passive. Nor is it
very clear how Europeanization has affected the quality of democratic practice in the regions and localities of Europe. Very often, 'Europe' is far distant
from the average citizen as the results of the *Eurobarometer* surveys show.
European activities often seem to be the preserve of a small cosmopolitan elite
and to bypass the average citizen. Indeed, there may be resentment at the
amount of money being spent on European activities such as conferences and
trips abroad. Nor is it very clear how the Committee of the Regions enhances
regional and local democracy, despite Jacques Delors' speech to its inaugural
meeting which stressed this aspect of the body. The Committee is often perceived as a distant body with little relevance to the lives of ordinary citizens.
It is probably not too exaggerated to say that, in fact, it is practically unknown
to the vast majority of European citizens. To be sure, this is not totally its own
fault as all European institutions, even the big ones such as the Commission,
the Council of Ministers, and the Parliament have similar problems. Much
work still needs to be done in this regard if the Committee is truly to become
a force for improving the democratic deficit that exists in the EU.

Nevertheless, there exist real opportunities in this area for strengthening
regional and local democracy. Europeanization and regionalization should be
seen as two sides of the same process, but what needs to be inserted now is
the element of democratic participation and accountability. First, more
regions and local authorities need to become active in the European arena,
whether through setting up offices in Brussels or through participation in
activities of the Committee of the Regions, the European Parliament, or the

interregional associations. But, second, these European activities need to be brought to the attention of, and involve more closely, the average citizen. Furthermore, the horizontal learning process across regions and local authorities needs to be strengthened.

2.3 Reform of the Internal Mechanisms of Regional and Local Government

There have also been attempts to reform the institutional forms and working procedures within regional and local government itself. The following trends may be noted.

2.3.1 Structural Reorganization

In some countries there is a tendency today to strengthen the executives of regional and local governments rather than the representative assemblies with a view to providing strong, visible, and effective leadership. This has been tried in different ways in different countries. For example, by changing the position of the mayor (Italy, UK, Germany), the prefect (who has ceded executive power to the presidents of the region or the *conseil général* in France; while he or she is now elected in Greece), or the internal committee system of the local authority (UK, Scandinavian countries). Some of the Austrian *Länder* have attempted to reform some of their parliamentary procedures and even their electoral system so as to make the political system more flexible and open. There is also a debate in Austria on encouraging a more clear-cut distinction between government and opposition rather than the traditional proportional government system, as well as of extending direct elections for the post of mayor. However, this does raise questions about the role of parties and of the representative assemblies and whether regional and local government should be simply a replica of national government or have a specifically subnational expression. In the United Kingdom, the new Welsh National Assembly has deliberately chosen not to adopt the Westminster or traditional local government models in its institutional design (although this has so far not had much success in establishing a viable functioning assembly). There have also been some attempts to decentralize *within* local government, as in the creation of submunicipal committees or the greater financial authority of local authorities in Denmark. Finland, too, has experimented with decentralizing policies within local authorities. However, one problem that has resulted from such decentralization is the difficulty that citizens have to find their way around the system where it is no longer clear who has responsibility for what service. There is thus a delicate balance to be struck between fragmentation and excessive internal centralization around a mayor-type figure.

2.3.2 'Marketization'

This could be seen as another way of reducing the bureaucratic features of local government and was part of the neo-liberal agenda of the 1980s, as discussed above. It involved attempts to introduce 'market' principles into subnational government and also handing over some services, such as street cleansing, to outside agencies. This approach was applied most fully in the United Kingdom where it was known as compulsory competitive tendering (CCT), but one finds similar attempts in other European countries such as Finland. CCT has been replaced in Britain by the new Labour Government by the concept of 'best value', which retains some of the elements of competition from CCT but does not automatically assume that privately provided services are superior to those of the public sector.

2.4 Relations between the Political System at the Regional and Local Levels and the General Public

In a sense, this is the most crucial indicator of the 'health' of regional and local democracy. The chapters in this book show that in many European countries there is a worrying disaffection from politics, in general, and from regional and local politics, in particular, on the part of European citizens. There are some exceptions to this. In the Scandinavian countries and in the Netherlands there is still a quite healthy interest in local politics, as recent surveys have shown. This is perhaps because many important social and welfare services are still delivered at this level. There is also a long tradition of participation in politics in these countries. However, elsewhere the attitude surveys show a widespread disillusionment and apathy and even in the Scandinavian countries and the Netherlands these sentiments are growing. In some countries there is a domination of local politics by the national political parties. While partisanship is not necessarily a bad thing, there is a tendency for regional and local (as well as European) elections to be simply fora for the playing out of national rather than regional, local, or European issues. Politics at the subnational levels might be simply seen in this perspective as a stepping stone to national politics. Citizens, therefore, will not be inclined to take them so seriously. Another indicator of the general switch-off of citizens from local politics is the general trend toward declining turnout in regional and local elections, except, of course, in those countries where voting is compulsory. Once again, this varies across states with some states quite healthy in this regard although they too manifest this tendency. It is possible to put a positive and optimistic gloss on this by speaking of a new kind of 'post-modern' politics and by pointing to the activities of road protestors or the demonstrators who took part in the anti-World Trade Organization meeting in Seattle in 1999. It remains that all the indicators suggest that most citizens, especially the younger generations, are turned off politics both in terms of direct interest and with regard to their own possible participation.

One of the primary challenges for enhancing regional and local democracy, therefore, is to examine how citizens might be brought more fully into the political system at these levels. The following methods have been tried in different countries:

- the use of local referendums (the Austrian *Länder*, some German *Länder*, Finland, Luxembourg, the Netherlands, Portugal, Sweden);
- petitions (most of the Austrian *Länder*, some of the German *Länder*, Portugal, Sweden);
- involving individuals or interest groups in decision-making through user boards (Denmark, Sweden);
- the citizens' written motion, which, if supported by 2 per cent of the population, must obtain a response from the local authority (Finland);
- prior appraisal of legislation by the public (some of the Austrian *Länder*);
- giving representation to specific categories of citizens through various forms of consultative forums (e.g., the disabled, women, low-income, foreigners, etc.) (UK, Luxembourg, the Netherlands, Spain);
- 'future' and 'scenario' workshops—to enable citizens to participate in planning processes (Germany, the Netherlands);
- multistage dialogue—involving three stages following the schema 'look, appraise, act', which allow citizens to work out solutions to particular problems (e.g., xenophobic violence in Buxtehude in Lower Saxony);
- 'partnership' boards and attempts at 'social integration' (Ireland, Spain);
- citizens' juries or panels (UK, Denmark, Spain, Sweden);
- youth councils (Finland);
- the search for openness and transparency (France);
- opinion polls and consumer surveys (UK, the Netherlands, France, Spain);
- local democracy 'balance sheet' (Sweden);
- electronic democracy and use of the internet (UK, Spain).

It is difficult to assess these experiments. The general picture that emerges from the country chapters in this book is that the use of these techniques has had limited success. Much will depend on the particular culture and levels of socio-economic and political development of the region or locality. Some authors, such as Putnam and the 'social capital' school of thought, argue that this elusive feature is necessary if democracy is to work. Whatever difficulties there are in operationalizing the elusive concept of social capital, it seems to be the case that some societies are better able to use such techniques than others. In some cases, there is a long-standing tradition of associationalism and active involvement in local affairs. In others, the regional or local society might be more marked by clientelistic forms of relationship or may have been devastated by serious industrial decline or economic collapse. There seems to be no general theory that is applicable to all cases. On the other hand, lessons may be drawn from particular experiences, which then need to be translated into different contexts. This in itself demands a distinct method-ology which is not always present in many cases of attempted cross-national learning.

A major problem, which occurs in most of the countries covered in this book, is how to reconcile the traditional mechanisms of liberal democratic representation with the election of councillors (through secret ballots) and the representation of specific categories of the population. Reservations on the part of the elected representatives have arisen in countries such as Ireland and Sweden. Councillors have political legitimacy won through the ballot box, while groups might be representing just themselves. Despite these difficulties, such experiments do point the way forward to a new kind of democratic prac-tice. Much thought needs to go into the kind of institutionalization necessary to make it work and to avoid conflict between the two kinds of representa-tion. The Irish government, for example, has introduced legislation, which attempts to reconcile the kinds of representation. Most other countries are struggling with the same problem.

As a final comment, it might be remarked that our political systems derive from the institutions of the liberal-democratic nation-state that emerged in the nineteenth century after the French Revolution, on the basis of the prin-ciples of the Enlightenment of the eighteenth century. These institutions have served us well and are immensely preferable to political systems based on authoritarianism and dictatorship. Nevertheless, the conditions in which they were born have changed beyond recognition. The challenge facing Europeans and others is to reinvent their own institutions in ways that take into account these new realities for the twenty-first century. These should preserve the gains that derive from the nation-state system such as citizens' rights and freedoms, solidarity through social welfare and public policy programmes, the general rise in educational, health, and well-being of our societies. Nevertheless, there have also been many problems associated with industrialization and mass society, which make it difficult to realize fully the potential that these advances have provided (such as environmental degradation, societal fragmentation and anomie, and a sense of meaninglessness and alienation). Regions and local authorities have in today's Europe a newfound freedom to engage in democratic experimentation and to devise new democratic forms that can provide some solutions to these problems. It is easier to reform a political system at this level than at the level of the nation-state. The European Union provides them with a new framework in which to carry out such reforms. We hope that this book will be a useful contribution to a reflection on how they may do so.

References

MÉNY, Y. and WRIGHT, V. (eds) (1985). *Centre–Periphery Relations in Western Europe*. London: Allen & Unwin.

PIERSON, P. (1994). *Dismantling the Welfare State: Reagan, Thatcher and the Politics of Retrenchment*. Cambridge: Cambridge University Press.

ROKKAN, S. and URWIN, D. (1983). *Economy, Territory, Identity: Politics in West European Peripheries*. London: Sage.

SCARBROUGH, E. (2000). 'Les deux faces de la démocratie urbaine en Grande-Bretagne', in O. Gabriel and V. Hoffmann-Martinot (eds), *Démocraties urbaines: L'État de la démocratie dans les grandes villes de 12 pays industrialisés*. Paris: L'Harmattan.

INDEX